# Research-Based
# Counseling Skills

## The Art and Science of Therapeutic Empathy

Ron Hawkins

Anita Kuhnley

Gary Sibcy

Justin Silvey

Steve Warren

Contributing Authors

John Kuhnley

Elias Moitinho

Alex Gantt

*Liberty University*

**Disclaimer**

This book is not intended as a substitute for the medical advice of physicians or other clinicians. The reader should regularly consult a physician or clinician in matters relating to his/her health or the health of another; and particularly with respect to any symptoms that may require diagnosis or medical/clinical attention.

# CONTENTS

# Acknowledgements

*"One can never pay in gratitude. One can only pay in 'kind' somewhere else in life."*

—Anne Morrow Lindbergh (Lindbergh, 2001, p. 41)

There are many people who contributed to the completion of this manuscript, and we owe them a debt of gratitude that we cannot repay!

First, we are thankful to God, our Heavenly Father, who has given us "who has given us life, breath, and the educational and work opportunities…" and afforded us the educational and work opportunities to gather these educational materials and seek to share them with our students. Moreover, we are thankful to his beautiful creation that provided a beautiful backdrop for the writing of this manuscript.

We thank our students and clients who have taught us so much over the years and have allowed us the great privilege and honor of being a part of their journey.

We would like to thank the Department of Counselor Education and Family Studies Research Team that has demonstrated supererogation and a commitment to excellence in serving clients with best practices.

We are thankful to Curtis Ross, our publisher, who provided countless resources and encouragement, without whom this project would not be possible.

We are very thankful to Katie Wortendyke, our research assistant, who has helped with countless details.

We would like to thank our colleagues who have made generous contributions to this text and have collaborated with us on research and other projects.

*If you have the opportunity to do amazing things in your life, I strongly encourage you to invite someone to join you.*

—Simon Sinek (2009a)

*Read more at: https://www.brainyquote.com/quotes/simon_sinek_568161*

We would like to especially thank:

- Justin Silvey, for many cups of green tea and countless hours brainstorming, conceptualizing, finding sources, and writing.

- Elias Moitinho, for his contributions and excitement about the impact of culture in counseling.

- John Kuhnley, for his cheerful contributions from the psychiatry literature, and the beautiful flowers that inspired the writing of many of these pages.

- J. Kim Penberthy, who shared content from her forthcoming work as well as other key sources and whose previous work on the treatment of PDD among other things has been an inspiration.

- Randy Miller, our Research Librarian, who has consistently gone the extra mile to obtain difficult manuscripts, even scanning and emailing them to us with a very short turnaround time.

- Dorel Captari, whose dedication to counseling skills and personal development has been a source of great inspiration.

- Alex Gantt, whose thoughtful feedback and review and willingness to roleplay have contributed much to these educational materials. Moreover, her contributions to the empathy chapter are much appreciated.

- We would like to give special thanks to Amanda Smith and the Kendall Hunt editing team for their commitment to excellence and making this book aesthetically appealing.

- Kristin Huaswirth, thank you for your careful assistance in reviewing copy edits and finding sources.

- Charles Mike Molina, thank you for sharing your editing insights and your feedback and input to help shape the book into the final product!

# PART ONE

# Foundations

*Kindness is the language that the deaf can hear and the blind can see.*

—Mark Twain (Holms & Baji, 1998, p. 16)

In this section, we discuss foundational concepts and a framework for learning counseling skills. Dr. Hawkins, founder of our counseling program, sets the stage for how B counselors can honor and retain their own worldview while interacting with clients in a way that is ethical. For example, Christians who operate as clinical mental health counselors may find themselves in a variety of clinical contexts. Some may work in overt Christian settings such as church counseling centers, whereas others may work in agencies or hospital settings. It is important for counselors not only to understand how to retain their values without imposing them on their clients but also to provide a safe atmosphere for clients to unpack those values and explore what it means to live a life that allows for a congruent and coherent expression of their personhood. **Context** is a key word to remember, and Dr. Hawkins emphasizes its importance. Context refers to the setting in which a counselor practices; different contexts call for different practices, and integration in a church counseling center may look different from integration in a hospital setting.

Context is also important in terms of the theoretical lens we look through and how theory can inform what we listen for when we exercise counseling skills. In Chapter 1, Dr. Sibcy and Dr. Kuhnley discuss theoretical foundations including how attachment theory may shed light on our case conceptualizations and help us to explore meaning and purpose with our clients. These foundational themes related to integration of faith and contextualizing theory will re-emerge throughout the text. We then transition into considerations for the journey of becoming and the importance of empathic presence and being intentional about demonstrating empathy. Let us progress to the introduction and discover the foundational knowledge, including our worldview and theoretical framework, needed to build a foundational integrative framework for future skills. Please view this video on the page below to hear Dr. Hawkins discuss the importance of context.

**Video**

## Context

# Inspiration: Integration of Faith in Counseling

## Ron Hawkins, Anita Kuhnley, Justin Silvey, Gary Sibcy, and Steve Warren

*Priority is a function of context.*

—Stephen R. Covey

Early in the morning, with the aroma of coffee in the air, we, a small group of counselor educators, gathered in an academic conference room surrounded by shelves filled with a variety of books. A discussion emerged, and Dr. Hawkins began sharing the importance of the key word *context* (Hawkins, personal communication, 2017). Hawkins discussed how context influences integration. For example, if a counselor is practicing in the context of a church counseling center, the way he or she integrates will be different from the counselor who is practicing in the context of a state-run hospital facility. This sparked ideas in Dr. Sibcy, who began chiming in on what ethical integration looks like. A synergy developed out of this like-minded discussion, and it was out of this conversation that this textbook was birthed.

Dr. Hawkins's personal story and philosophy on integration inspired us to seek to craft a text that would allow for current research on counseling skills, an ethical model of spiritual integration, and insights from the attachment literature. One primary purpose of this text is to consolidate these constructs into a text that students from different institutions could access to learn the strategies included to enhance their ministry and counseling practice. After hearing about Hawkins's experiences including the impact of seminary and the difference a school counselor (Ms. Webb) can make, we were inspired to craft this text. As we discussed integration, we also found that we were in agreement on both the science and the art of counseling, meaning that the empathic warmth and establishment of rapport and a strong therapeutic alliance combined with research-based approaches are critical to effective practice. Below, this concept is referred to as the *sweet spot* of counseling in Figure 1.1. You may consider applying the model below to each chapter. For example, the discussion of empathy, warmth, and other empathic skills may fill up the left circle entitled the "Art of Counseling." The research, including but not limited to the discussion of Gottman's work applied to the therapeutic relationship, Mayer, Salovey, and Caruso (2002, 2008) research on emotional intelligence, and attachment research supporting the why behind meaning making from the work of Bowlby, Ainsworth, Main and others may comprise the right circle entitled the "Science of Counseling."

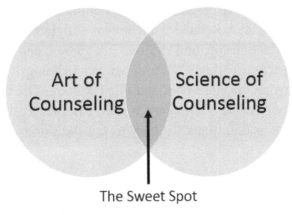

The Sweet Spot

**Figure 1.1.**

The purpose of this text is to offer a journey of training for counselors that provides the skill set needed to create a safe atmosphere for clients to dig deep and feel supported to take courage to address deep concerns and struggles with the support of the empathic other, the skilled counselor. In addition to creating safety and rapport, we also explore the insights the attachment literature offers to make sense of the journey of becoming (see Chapter 2). One of the ways these essential interviewing and counseling skills integrate with the attachment research is in training the storyteller. Our lives can be described as a series of stories. The key to moving toward a secure autonomous attachment or a secure relationship style is developing a coherent and fluid story about your relationship history.

*The key to moving toward a secure autonomous attachment or secure relationship style is developing a coherent and fluid story about your relationship history.*

We invite you to seek to make sense of your narrative and tell your story in a compelling way. When you experientially navigate your own journey, it can help illuminate the path as you seek to walk alongside others. We encourage you to make the most of the exercises in the text and the attachment illumination sections as you contemplate your own journey of becoming. Taking the time to share your narrative via journaling, sitting in the other chair as a client, or even disclosing your story to a close friend can allow for greater mindful presence (which leads to less preoccupation with your own story) as you sit with others. Beginning counselors often struggle with too much self-disclosure or making the session about them, as opposed to having a client-centered session. The Concept to Contemplate sections (in each chapter), *The Journey of Becoming* chapter, and the Attachment Illumination sections (within each chapter) create outlets to focus on the personhood of the counselor along the journey of becoming a healing person.

In each chapter, you will find components such as a chapter overview, to help you prepare for your reading. You will also find a section entitled "Attachment Illumination," in which we will explore implications for connecting the counseling skills' literature with attachment as a paradigm for counselor education. We appreciate the ideas of authors such as Greggo and Becker (2010) who propose using attachment theory as a framework for counselor education, including the supervisory relationship as a safe haven.

*As you experientially navigate your own journey, it can help illuminate the path as you seek to walk alongside others.*

We embrace this conceptualization of counselor education and their focus on the Council of Accreditation for Counseling and Related Educational Programs (CACREP) standards, self-reflection, the supervisory relationship, and spiritual integration, and we have sought to integrate it within this book. The section entitled "Recommended Readings" includes literature to help continue your learning beyond the classroom and this textbook. The bolded key terms will help you build a repertoire of counseling vocabulary words, and the "To-Do Lists" at the end of the skills' chapters will provide action items for how to put the skills into practice. May the Lord bless your journey as you seek to develop as a counselor!

## Recommended Reading

We recommend reading beyond your course textbook and course materials in order to make the most of your learning experience. Ethical integration is an important concept, and we suggest some of the following readings to further your knowledge in this area:

© Shutterstock.com

- Bohecker, L., Schellenberg, R., & Silvey, J. (2017). Spirituality and religion: The ninth CACREP common core curricula area. *Counseling and Values, 62(2)*, 128–143.

- Clinton, T. & Hawkins, R. (Eds.), *Popular encyclopedia of Christian Counseling.* Eugene, OR: Harvest House.

- Entwistle, D. N. (2015). *Integrative approaches to psychology and Christianity: An introduction to worldview issues, philosophical foundations, and models of integration* (3rd ed.). Eugene, OR: Cascade Books.

- Hawkins, R., & Clinton, T. (2015). *The new Christian counselor: A fresh Biblical & transformational approach.* Eugene, OR: Harvest House.

- McMinn, M. R. (2011). *Psychology, theology, and spirituality in Christian counseling* (2nd ed.) Wheaton, IL: Tyndale.

- *Modern psychotherapies: A comprehensive Christian appraisal.* Batavia, IL: Christian Association of Psychological Studies.

## Chapter One

# Theoretical Foundations

## Gary A. Sibcy and Anita M. Kuhnley

*He who loves practice without theory is like the sailor who boards
ship without a rudder and compass and never knows where he may
cast.*

—Leonardo da Vinci

### Chapter Learning Objectives

1. To explore various theories and models of counseling, such as attachment theory (CACREP II.F.5.a, 2016, p. 11)
2. To develop an understanding of a model of expertise development (i.e., the emergent model of clinical expertise)

## Chapter Overview

As you begin this journey of becoming, an implied goal is to become an expert and to develop expertise as a skilled clinician. The process for the development of expertise is discussed. In this chapter, we introduce a model called *the emergent model of clinical expertise* (Sibcy, 2017). Furthermore, in this chapter we explore some of the theoretical factors that influence the counseling process, including relationship rules that inform much of how people operate interpersonally. Attachment theory and how it provides implications for counseling is explored, including the four primary attachment styles.

We want to measure mentalization in our clients. We would describe measuring mentalization in clients as "fantastically fun." For example, we had a client who was an executive and presented to work through challenges with her children cutting her off. The therapist probed her to think about what her son would say about her, and she noted that he would probably say that she was angry. When the client was Inquired (repetition) regarding the triggers that lead to her anger, she immediately shifted the focus of the dialogue back to the reasons she had to be angry. The therapist then worked hard to redirect her back to "seeking to understand" (see more about the process of "seeking to understand" in Part 2 of the text) her child's thoughts toward her. For some clients, understanding another person's state of mind is difficult. In order for us to facilitate this kind of understanding in our clients, we need to first facilitate it in ourselves. In this chapter, we will explore the value of self-awareness, mentalization, and meta cognitive monitoring. These characteristics are important to cultivate in the therapist; these are the characteristics that make the counseling skill development process and rapport building process easier.

Welcome to the developmental journey of becoming. As we begin, we first want to look at an important goal associated with the process of becoming a skilled clinical mental health counselor, which means the goal of becoming an expert or developing expertise. Who is an **expert counselor**? An expert is someone who is highly competent and effective at what he or she does.

© Shutterstock.com

*A Concept to Contemplate*

How is expertise developed?

Dreyfus and Dreyfus (1986) shared a model for the development of expertise. Their model is in keeping with a growth mindset, which postulates that skills can be acquired overtime through various strategies. Research on cognitive psychology and growth mindset emphasizes the idea that expertise is not an innate characteristic but rather a set of skills that are learned overtime. Researchers believe expertise is developed through practice that progresses and quality practice (Kuhlmann & Ardichvili, 2015, p. 263). Their grounded theory study addressed the research question, "How does expertise develop in an applied profession?" They found that as time in a profession unfolds, professionals progress from novice to proficient. However, they distinguished between proficiency and expertise and indicated that movement from proficient to expert takes more than the unfolding of time practicing a profession. They found that the groups that were not experts focused on finding solutions to frequently occurring problems and developing routines instead of searching out new challenges (2015; see Figure 1.2).

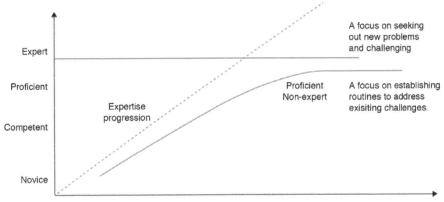

**Figure 1.2.** Development of expertise versus proficiency.
© Kendall Hunt Publishing Company

When it comes to defining expertise in counseling, there are a number of different models and heuristic road maps available. Some focus on the core tasks (Meichenbaum, 2017) or core competencies (Rodolfa et al., 2005; Sperry, 2010) of expert therapists, which help us to make sense of what experts do differently from their novice or mediocre counterparts. Others, such as Bennett-Levy (2006), discuss the progressive process involved in how counselors acquire the knowledge, skills, tactics, and strategies involved in expertise. Out of this knowledge base, (Sibcy & Knight, 2017a) constructed a heuristic for understanding the knowledge and skills needed to become an expert counselor, someone who is both highly competent and effective in the helping professions. You might ask, "What does it mean to be an expert counselor?" An expert counselor is someone who is highly competent and effective,[1] and becoming an expert requires many thousands of hours of intentional, focused learning and practice (Sibcy & Knight, 2017a; see Figure 1.2).

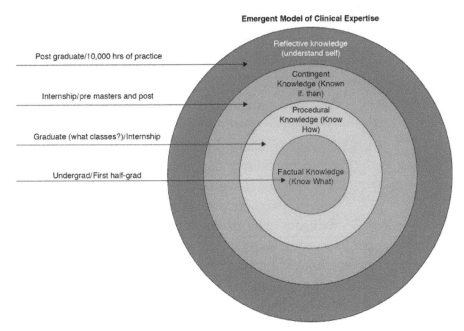

**Figure 1.3.** Emergent model of clinical expertise.
© Kendall Hunt Publishing Company

# The Emergent Model of Clinical Expertise in Counseling and Psychotherapy

**The emergent model of clinical expertise in counseling and psychotherapy** views the acquisition of knowledge, skills, tactics, strategies, and techniques as an emerging model, where more complex skill sets and capacities emerge out of more basic ones (Figure 1.3). As we will see, the higher-order abilities grow out of the lower-order ones, and as they do, higher-order skills can actually expand and strengthen the lower-order knowledge base and skill sets.

## Factual or Declarative Knowledge

As we embark on the journey of developing strong counseling skills, it is important to discuss the theoretical framework that gives context to these skills. The **factual or declarative knowledge** represents the conceptual and factual foundation needed to practice as a counselor. "This text will discuss the skills, such as active listening, that will allow you to help clients feel heard and tell their story in a more coherent way." of helping clients feel heard and helping them to tell their story in a more coherent way through the use of active listening and other counseling skills. Conceptually, you will need to be able to draw from several theoretical perspectives to help you translate your clients' raw clinical narratives into workable case formulations. From these formulations, you will construct an effective treatment plan. Although many counselors learn to rely on one or two theoretical perspectives as their core, they develop more ways of conceptualizing cases from a variety of different theoretical perspectives over time.

It has been said, "There is nothing more practical than a good theory" (Lewin, 1952, p. 169). As a counselor, you will learn to listen to your clients and help them feel heard and understood. Beginning counselors will find that using the active listening skills and core skills that are central to counseling may become smoother when their skills are informed by **good guiding theory**, which helps with the process of making sense of what the client is saying.

## Attachment Illumination

© Shutterstock.com

You may have noticed a **lighthouse** on the cover of the text and noticed several images of lighthouses throughout the book as you have flipped through. These are reminders and representations of the **secure base** and **safe haven** principles that are central to attachment theory. When a ship is out at sea and the captain sees the light breaking through the darkness in the distance, this is a reminder that the safe haven of the shore is nearby. However, ships are not made to stay at shore. So, another part of the attachment system is the exploration system. Once a child (like a ship) is safe and secure, he or she is often able to go out and explore his or her environment. During times of danger, the child needs to go back to the secure base or safe haven to get charged, so to speak, to go back out to explore. "Making sense of what the client is saying, discussed in the previous paragraph, can be facilitated by the use of attachment theory." In our text (Knight & Sibcy, 2018) entitled *Redeeming Attachment: A Counselor's Guide to*

*Facilitating Attachment to God and Earned Security*, we discuss how this process of being able to acknowledge, describe, and "make sense" of our attachment histories can help foster movement toward a secure attachment style and how, according to the compensation hypothesis, some may experience healing from early attachment wounds via positive spiritual experiences with God and developing a sense of a secure attachment with him (a caveat is to ensure that a person has a congruent God image and God concept before embarking on this work). Our colleague, Dr. Dan Siegel, has also completed the Adult Attachment Interview training (which has shaped much of our thinking on attachment). Siegel (2010a) discusses the importance of "making sense" of experiences with relationship to move toward a secure attachment style. The gold standard assessment for measuring the adult attachment is called the "Adult Attachment Interview" or the AAI for short (Main, Goldwyn, & Heese, 2002). This thorough assessment reveals that the most important predictor of a secure autonomous attachment style is coherence. Coherence could be described as how well a person's story is characterized by the following: cohesiveness, smoothness of expression, flow, consistency, and collaboration. These are well represented by Grice's maxims of collaborative communication, which include the following: quality, quantity, relevance, and manner. These will be discussed further in Chapter 8. So, by hearing and understanding a client's story and helping him or her to make sense of his or her own experience (which is also facilitated by the counselor being able to make sense), a client can be helped to develop a coherent narrative and to move toward attachment security. Thus, attachment theory may be one of the most helpful guiding theories as we walk alongside our clients and help them to make sense of their experiences (see Chapter 8 for a comprehensive discussion on this).

You can also use good theory to help you ask good questions and acquire more meaningful information about your client. This will provide an avenue for helping clients not only to feel heard and understood but also to extend their understanding of themselves. Although this book is not designed to be about theories of counseling per se, we do want to provide a conceptual framework for understanding the value and power of the therapeutic relationship and the clinical skill of listening. These clinical skills will be developed in more detail and precision throughout your training and especially in your practicum and internship experiences.

## Procedural Knowledge

Procedural Knowledge is the "how-to" knowledge that is needed to function as a professional counselor. It involves specific types of tasks such as doing an intake evaluation, which includes identifying the chief complaint (also referred to as the "presenting problem"), obtaining the history of present illness and a psychosocial history, conducting a mental status exam, and rendering a clinical diagnosis with an initial treatment plan. This can also involve many other procedural tasks such as conducting a risk assessment

© Shutterstock.com

for suicide and other directed aggressive behaviors and a substance abuse assessment (you will read more details about conducting a risk assessment for suicide in Chapter 7). Counselors need to know how to administer certain kinds of treatment procedures, each involving a different set of steps, tactics, strategies, and techniques. For example, counselors may be interested in learning how to treat trauma symptoms using Edna Foa's **prolonged exposure** therapy protocol (see Figure 1.4; Foa, Chrestman, & Gilboa-Schechtman, 2008), which involves teaching clients about the nature of traumatic stress and posttraumatic stress disorder, identifying targets for in vivo (real-life) exposures versus imaginal exposures, setting up an exposure hierarchy, and helping clients engage in exposures both in session and after session. These types of knowledge sets are derived from a conceptual foundation but involve more than just knowing *what* but knowing *how.*

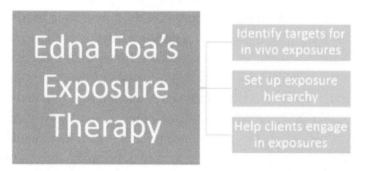

**Figure 1.4.** Edna Foa's prolonged exposure therapy protocol.

In some ways, the difference between declarative and procedural knowledge is like the difference between passing the written part of a driver's license exam and the actual driving task. The written test helps to ensure that you understand important information, laws, traffic signs, and safety information. The driving test itself involves your procedural skills in handling the car effectively in different kinds of situations.

## Contingency-Based Knowledge

**Contingency-based knowledge** emerges out of both factual and procedural knowledge, where the counselor learns how to make contingency-based decisions or if–then decisions. For example, a counselor may be talking to a client about her recent argument with her spouse. She says, "I don't think I can handle this anymore. I'm sick of it. What's the point if no one would care if I was gone?" Obviously, the client is feeling overwhelmed and distressed about her relationship, and the therapist would need to empathize with that while exploring her emotional reactions more deeply. However, if a client makes a statement indicating that no one would care if he or she was no longer around, should the counselor inquire about suicidal thinking? If so, what happens if she does indicate having suicidal thoughts? What if she has suicidal thoughts and has thought about different plans she might use, such as overdosing on the medication prescribed to her by her doctor or driving her car off the road? If this happens, then what does the counselor do? These are important questions, many of which are not invented in clinical cookbooks but are learned through multiple clinical situations where the counselor makes these kinds of decisions based on ever-changing circumstances. For example, if this client had suicidal thoughts with some achievable plans but no intention on acting on these plans and no history of self-destructive behavior, a no-suicide contract and a safety plan might be the best course of action. However, if she has a history of self-destructive behavior and has failed to follow through with previous safety contracts, this may not be the best course of action. You can read more about the various types of scenarios you could encounter with clients such as this in Chapter 5. The point is that this type of contingency-based knowledge is part of what distinguishes an expert counselor from a novice or a less-experienced one. In addition to clinical experience, another contributor to this capacity has been identified as the presence of self-awareness (Young, 2016), the capacity to be aware of one's own thoughts, emotions, and actions and the impact he or she may have on the self and others. This **self-awareness** may be developed when counselors take time to "sit in the other chair," the client chair, and do their own clinical work, journal about feelings, or participate in group therapy, and begin to become more aware of multiple perspectives and have a broader perspective in how to cope with such circumstances.

There are other kinds of contingency-based decisions counselors need to make. For example, if someone is depressed, what is the best course of treatment? When do I use cognitive behavioral therapy versus interpersonal therapy? What happens if I start with cognitive behavioral therapy and then discover that many of the clients' concerns center on interpersonal conflicts? Do I switch to interpersonal therapy? Or should I just stay with cognitive behavioral therapy and try to make it work no matter what? What if someone reports having a history of trauma but presents with feelings of depression with low motivation, energy, and pleasure but no trauma-related symptoms, such as intrusive memories, avoidance behaviors, or hypervigilance? Should I treat the depression symptoms and ignore the trauma? If so, when should I treat the trauma symptoms? These are all tricky questions (sorting through these questions involve an integrative model and case conceptualization process, which will be covered in Chapter 4 and Chapter 13 respectively) and require a higher degree of clinical expertise than seen in the previous two levels of knowledge. Notice, the counselor may be very skilled at treating both depression and trauma, but knowing if and when to use the skills and under what conditions is based on contingency-based knowledge and not on factual or procedural knowledge.

## Reflexive Knowledge System

After many thousands of hours performing different counseling procedures and making different contingency-based decisions, these activities become encoded into the brain and become a part of who you are. When I (Gary Sibcy) was being supervised in my family therapy training by Steve Greenstein, Salvador Munuchin's protégé, we were using the classic text, *Structural Family Therapy* (Umbarger, 1983). Many of us, the young trainees, kept referring back to the text about different situations we encountered in our therapy sessions. Greenstein would often admonish us, saying, "You need to get to a point where that book goes on the shelf and you work from your gut." At first, I had a difficult time understanding what he was saying. However, there was wisdom in his words. That is, you need to get to a point in therapy where you have practiced so much you no longer need to refer back to the manual. This is a growth process, and we will eventually get there. Knowing what to do and how to do it becomes secondhand. It is just like driving a car, riding a bike, swinging a tennis racket or a golf club: after you have done it for so long, you no longer have to refer to the manual to figure out what you are supposed to do or how you are supposed to do it. This is what Greenstein was referring to when he said to go with your gut. This kind of gut-based knowledge is also referred to as **reflexive knowledge** (reflexive, meaning knowledge that is so automatic it works like a reflex). Recall getting a physical where a medical doctor may have used a reflex hammer to check your knee's reflexes, and you likely had an immediate response that did not require thought, but your body knew what to do. Likewise, as we develop expertise and practice, we want to move toward reflexive knowledge. Irvin Yalom (1980, 1999, 2017), a prolific writer and veteran therapist, has written many books that describe his therapeutic experiences (Yalom, 1980, 1999). He discussed the topic of personal disclosure and shared that early on in his career as a therapist, he was less likely to self-disclose, but as he has practiced more and more, he mentioned that he has come to the point of being able to trust his subconscious mind to be therapeutic.

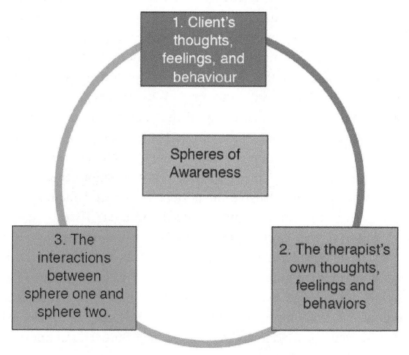

**Figure 1.5.** Spheres of awareness.
© Kendall Hunt Publishing Company

## Reflexive Knowledge

Reflexive knowledge is the highest level of learning and signals the beginning of expertise. It assumes that the declarative, procedural, and contingency-based knowledge systems are in place. The counselor's reflexes are already established, and she is able to do things automatically with a smooth and natural flow. The counselor's gut-based intuitions are uncannily accurate and insightful. However, with the reflexive level of expertise, the therapist is able to do all these things without thinking explicitly about them while maintaining a continuous moment-by-moment

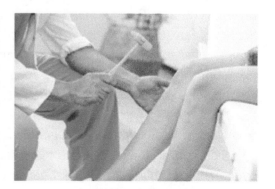

© sebra/Shutterstock.com

awareness of what is happening in the session. The expert therapist is tracking awareness of three spheres of experience simultaneously: (a) the client's thoughts, feelings, and behaviors, (b) the therapist's own thoughts, feelings, and behaviors, and (c) the interaction between spheres (a) and (b) (see Figure 1.5). This interaction refers to the reality that the way client is thinking, feeling, and behaving influences the way a therapist is thinking, feeling, and behaving. At the same time, the therapist is also aware of how his or her own thoughts, feelings, and behaviors are influencing the client.

This ability to be aware of your own thoughts, feelings, and behaviors (insight) while also having an awareness and appreciation of your client's thoughts, feelings, and behaviors (empathy) and the interaction between the two is referred to as mentalization (Allen, Fonagy, & Bateman, 2008). This moment-by-moment awareness helps the therapist become more flexible and responsive to changing and often unpredictable circumstances.

For example, an experienced therapist in our practice had successfully treated a number of people with panic disorder using an evidence-based cognitive behavioral protocol. This treatment has a number of different treatment steps, but one of the early interventions is to help clients see that when their chest feels somewhat tight, it is difficult to take in a deep breath; in contrast, the natural tendency is to overbreathe. This actually backfires because it leads to hyperventilation, which then exacerbates the panic cycle. So, an important intervention is to teach the client how to slow down his or her breathing using a breathing retraining exercise. The therapist envisioned the client looking calm and relaxed as in the image below. He did a very nice job explaining this breathing retraining to his client and demonstrated how to effectively use the technique. He then asked her to close her eyes and began to focus her attention on her breath. At that very point, she began feeling anxious and tense and could not focus her attention and kept opening her eyes. The therapist could not make sense of why she was having such a difficult time, and he could feel a sense of frustration and anxiety building. Part of him thought that she was just being distractible and resistant to the intervention. He wanted to impress her so much with his knowledge and skill that he was unable to make sense of her negative responses to what he considered relatively straightforward and simple intervention. They aborted the exercise, and when the client opened her eyes, she could see the annoyance and frustration on his face. They tried to process what had happened; the client only told him that she was not feeling well and that she would try harder to relax in the next session.

The therapist sought some consultation about this incident. As we discussed the case, it was clear that he had thought that the client only suffered from panic disorder because she was referred by her psychiatrist with this diagnosis. What became apparent was that he had not taken into consideration the possibility that this person had suffered some type of relational trauma. It is not uncommon for people who have experienced outright rape or incest in childhood to underreport these experiences to medical professionals. In his next session, he was able to use some advanced forms of

© Olena Zaskochenki/Shutterstock.com

empathy to help repair the therapeutic relationship. The insights from consultation allowed him to respond with greater intentionality. It is noted that consultation is similar to the process of supervision.

© Marzolino/Shutterstock.com

*When Drs. John and Julie Gottman refer to the four horsemen of the apocalypse, they refer to the four behaviors found in partners that are predictive of the deterioration of a relationship. They include (a) defensiveness, (b) stonewalling, (c) contempt, and (d) criticism.*

Many times when our supervisees are struggling in session or feeling frustrated with clients, we help them to move toward break through using empathy-building exercises. I (Anita Kuhnley) was once working with a supervisee who had stellar counseling skills. This supervisee had a client during his residency who was making accusatory comments toward him during group counseling when he would use advanced skills such as immediacy ("What are you feeling right now as we discuss this feeling?"), and the client responded with some harsh words such as, "You just don't know how to let things go, do you?" A natural response may be to become defensive at a moment like this. However, it is important to remember why defensiveness is not a helpful route and to remember the work of Dr. John Gottman, a renowned marriage and family therapist. He found that defensiveness was one of what he called, "the four horsemen of the apocalypse" (Gottman, 2007, p. 72; see the call out box entitled "The Four Horsemen."). He called them so because they are indicative that "the end is near." So, thankfully, my supervisee (familiar with these horsemen) had gone above and beyond to practice his skills, and he knew that a defensive response would not be helpful to his client, so he brought this up in supervision. We did an empathy-building exercise to explore how his client may be feeling. As we unpacked his client's situation, we came to realize this client was facing a malpractice case and on the verge of losing his medical licenses. He had investigators at his practice, and when his counselor probed and asked him questions, he seemed to be triggered and to feel as if yet another person was interrogating him. When the supervisee was imagining being in the client's shoes, he had this insight and had increased empathy. In the next session, he was able to connect with his client and build the rapport, and his client was able to open up and be more vulnerable. If he had insisted on using probing or immediacy rather than being willing to "flex with intentional competence" (Ivey, Ivey, & Zalaquett, 2018) and shift to using empathy, he may not have been effective, and it may have disrupted the counseling rapport. We will talk more about flexing with intentional competence in Chapter 4.

Later in this text, we will discuss some of the strategies for handling relationship disruptions in counseling that can occur as a result of the four horsemen or lack of insight into client experiences. Returning to the discussion of the client with presenting symptoms of panic disorder, the insights the counselor gleaned from consultation opened the door for the client to acknowledge that she had been taken advantage of sexually by two of her uncles when she was in her early teens. She had always adored and trusted them when she was in early and middle childhood. However, as she progressed into early adolescence, she began to

*It is important to consider a client's interpersonal history and how it may impact the client's response to an intervention in session.*

feel uncomfortable in their presence: she noticed their eyes focusing on her developing body and they touched her inappropriately. Although they never actually forced her into any kind of sexual activity, she always felt like she had to be on guard while in their presence. To make matters worse, she learned that one of her same-aged female cousins was sexually abused by both of these uncles. The cousin never told her parents or anyone else except this client. This only increased her sense of vulnerability to men.

This information helped the therapist better understand her reaction to the breathing exercise. The idea that he was asking her to sit back in her chair and close her eyes while he sat in front of her giving instructions in a soft, charming tone of voice activated her sense of vulnerability. The therapist felt badly that he had not considered this possibility in the session itself and just assumed that his client trusted him unconditionally. At the time, he thought of himself as trustworthy and reliable. Of course, he was safe and he had

© SpeedKingz/Shutterstock.com

her best intentions in mind. He also thought that she trusted him based on the quality of their interactions up to this point. What he had not considered was how the situation demands had changed that sense of trust in her. He had not considered her interpersonal history and how it might be activated by such an intervention.

Now this counselor is better able to understand the differences people have in their responses to this and other kinds of interventions. He more thoroughly explores a person's interpersonal history before initiating these kinds of interventions. He also knows that just because relational trauma is not reported does not mean it has not occurred. In some instances, clients do not even remember these kinds of experiences. So, he is very much aware of and sensitive to negative responses, carefully attuning to his clients' verbal and nonverbal responses and then, as necessary, making adjustments. For example, he now informs clients before they start that if they prefer they can keep their eyes open and focus on a spot on the wall or somewhere on the bookshelf while practicing the breathing and relaxation exercise. This helps to give them a greater sense of control.

This level of awareness only develops once you have mastered the other aspects of the counseling situation. Considering this, there are various other important areas of declarative and procedural knowledge you will need to learn, which are related to the counseling setting you work in. For example, if you work in a community counseling center, there are all the policies and procedures you must learn:

*Just because relational trauma is not reported does not mean it has not occurred.*

client scheduling (for parallelism) intake forms, informed consents, release of information, and the charting system. Many practices now have their own electronic medical records that require considerable comfort with digital technology.

*It is important to be compassionate and empathic to yourself when learning*

As the counselor, in the scenario above was frustrated and annoyed by the client's lack of response and cooperation, he thought of himself, at the time, as trustworthy. Further, every indication up to this point suggested that she did in fact trust him so the counselor assumed that her negative reaction must have indicated that *and remember that the learning process is a journey. Even this licensed, experienced therapist sought consultation with a more experienced colleague. Thankfully, the process of becoming a licensed professional counselor (LPC) or clinical mental health counselor (LCMHC) includes supervision, which is similar to the consultation process.*

she just did not want to feel this way. He could feel his own anxiety building, actually contributing to the panic. The client is able to engage in What's "this"?; however, By whom? that one needs to be aware of his or her feelings and internal experiences while considering his or her client's thoughts, feelings, and actions. However, just like anything else, reflexive knowledge has flaws: The gut can become contaminated. Even the most seasoned expert therapists can have incorrect gut instincts. For the most part, under normal traffic conditions, you can drive without really thinking about it. That is the automatic mode. However, if conditions become more complex, you can switch out of automaticity and into an intentional, focused state. This is why we like to use the BASIC ID framework as a way of helping therapist to see the various lenses through which to view different clinical presentations. In some ways, we argue that schoolism is dead in the sense that the idea of thinking that there is just one theoretical lens through which to formulate all types of clinical cases is completely inadequate. It is akin to physicians saying something like this: "Yes, I'm a cardiologist because the only organ in the body that really matters is the heart. It is, after all, the heart of the matter," or a gastroenterologist saying something like this: "I study the gut and intestines because these are at the core of who we are—unlike those dermatologists who only go skin deep." Obviously, these statements are absurd because we all, even those not involved directly with the medical profession, recognize that the body operates as a whole system. Although we can in fact separate each organ system and specialize in it, it does not mean that all the other organ systems are unimportant. They all work interactively. Likewise, we will see that there are many different theoretical perspectives in counseling, and each captures a very important area of human functioning, from behavior to cognition to emotion to relationships to development, and so on.

## Attachment Theory

This section explains attachment theory and the theoretical framework behind the "Attachment Illumination" sections you encounter throughout this text. As a developing counselor, you will study several counseling theories: psychoanalysis, cognitive therapy, behavior therapy, emotion-focused theories, family systems, and many others. In Chapter 3, we attempt to give you a basic overview of these theories in a way that you can conceptually organize them in a coherent manner and decide which theoretical lens may best

© TetyanaRusanova/Shutterstock.com

apply to your clients presenting clinical concerns. Just as wearing a pair of glasses (such as those pictured to the right) with a blue tint or a rose-colored tint may color how we view our external surroundings, a theoretical lens will color the way we perceive client behavior and motivation.

For those of you who have completed an undergraduate degree in counseling or psychology, this overview will make more sense, as you should have already been exposed to theories of personality and theories of learning. For those of you who do not have this background, we hope this overview serves as a helpful introduction to these theories. Either way, whether you have or have not had any previous training in counseling theories, we believe these two chapters will provide a basic understanding of these concepts so that you can learn how to "make sense" of what you are listening to when clients tell their stories about what motivated them to seek counseling.

## The Basics of Attachment Theory

*This attachment relationship also sets the foundation for us to experience a sense of confidence needed to explore the world and feel life has meaning and purpose and to have the capacity to experience both empathy and intimacy with others without losing our sense of self-identity.*

Cognitive psychology has shown that the mind best understands facts when they are woven into a conceptual fabric, such as a narrative, mental map, or intuitive theory. Disconnected facts in the mind are like unlinked pages on the Web: They might as well not exist.

—Steven Pinker (as cited in Wood, 2014, p. 275)

**Attachment theory** is based on God's design that human beings come into the world completely helpless to take care of their own needs and that to develop as a person, they must rely on others who are stronger, wiser, and loving. This relationship begins at birth with the parent(s) or caregivers and then extends to others (teachers, friends, spouse, and ultimately God). Attachment is a powerful relationship that not only can affect

© Martin Novak/Shutterstock.com

how a child learns to think and feel about himself and others but also can literally shape the brain's capacities to regulate emotions, read and understand other people's feelings and intentions, and engage in enduring intimate relationships. This attachment relationship also sets the foundation for us to experience a sense of confidence needed to explore the world and feel that life has meaning and purpose and to have the capacity to experience both empathy and intimacy with others without losing our sense of self-identity.

## Attachment Theory and the Secure Base System

Just like a lighthouse is a beacon of safety and direction in a storm, a secure base serves as a launching pad from which to go out and explore the world and a safe haven to return to during times of distress. It is a key component of the attachment system.

**A behavioral system** is an organized set of behaviors designed to accomplish an important survival goal. The systems are biologically preprogrammed into our genetic code and are activated by specific kinds of environmental stimuli. **The secure base system** is governed by three different, but dynamically interactive, behavioral systems: the caregiving system, the exploration system, and the attachment system. **The caregiving system** is contained within the parent or caregiver, and it involves two functions: (a) providing a secure base from which the child explores the world with zest and curiosity and (b) providing a safe haven from which a child seeks safety and comfort when under duress. The child utilizes two behavioral systems: (a) the exploration system and (b) the attachment system proper.

Castle Hill lighthouse at sunset with setting sun.

© Stuart Monk/Shutterstock.com

The basics of attachment may be best understood by conceptualizing what I call the secure base system, which involves the dynamic interaction of all three behavioral systems (see Figure 1.6). In the cycle, notice the secure base. In early childhood, children use their parent as a source of felt security. When a child feels secure (experiences a neurobiologically balanced autonomic nervous system), the exploration system is activated, and the child experiences a sense of confidence and curiosity to zestfully explore the world around her. In the background, she needs her parent to watch over her,

© Andrea Danti/Shutterstock.com

delight in and encourage her exploration (Marvin & Seagroves, personal communication, April 25, 2017), set limits on her behavior if needed, and be available to her if she feels threatened or in trouble. On the far right side of the circle, she feels threatened from some internal or external source, the exploration system is immediately deactivated, and the attachment system proper is turned on. Notice that these two systems are incompatible: when one is on, and other is off. When the attachment system is turned on, it generates anxiety and the child *signals* to the parent when there is a problem and she needs help.

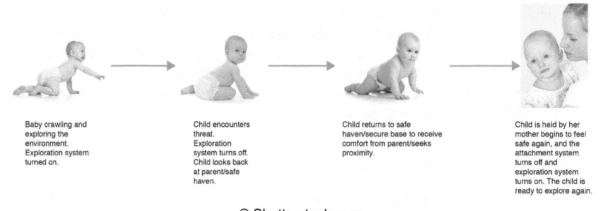

Baby crawling and exploring the environment. Exploration system turned on.

Child encounters threat. Exploration system turns off. Child looks back at parent/safe haven.

Child returns to safe haven/secure base to receive comfort from parent/seeks proximity.

Child is held by her mother begins to feel safe again, and the attachment system turns off and exploration system turns on. The child is ready to explore again.

© Shutterstock.com

Bob Marvin's circle of security portrays the top side of the cycle, including the exploration process, and the bottom side of the cycle, where the child returns to the safe haven of the parents.

We often refer to this diagram when using the language "They are on the top side of the circle," meaning that the attachment system is not activated, the exploration system is activated, and the needs as presented in Figure 1.6 are present. When we say, "They are on the bottom side of the circle," we are referring to the idea that the attachment system is activated, and they are seeking proximity to the primary caregiver for comfort during distress or any other of the needs listed below. Given Dr. Marvin's nearly 50-year training with Mary Ainsworth (the research partner of Dr. John Bowlby, the father of attachment theory) with Mary Ainsworth, we believe this circle is an important contribution to the field. We recommend his training on the circle of security and his resources for those that are

*When a child feels threatened from some internal or external source, the exploration system is immediately deactivated and the attachment system proper is turned on.*

interested in learning more (see www.circleofsecruityinternational.com). This is a user-friendly model that Dr. Marvin and Dr. Seagroves presented at Liberty University (2017):

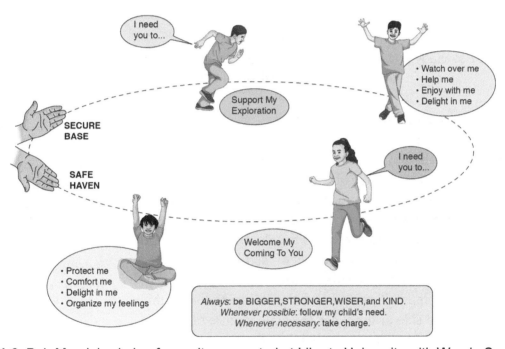

**Figure 1.6.** Bob Marvin's circle of security presented at Liberty University with Wanda Seagroves.
© Kendall Hunt Publishing Company

*Proximity-seeking* behavior is what a child uses to get closer to her mother (crying, walking or running, lifting her arms). She and her mom engage in a *goal-directed partnership* to help the child experience a safe haven (for young children, melting into their parent's embrace). Once felt security is achieved (which may only take a few seconds), the child launches back to the top of the cycle and returns to explore the world. presented his "Circle of Security" in our department recently. One of our colleagues asked, "If you could only share one thing about attachment with future counselors, what would you want them to know?" Dr. Marvin paused for a moment and pondered the question. He then went on to say that he would like counselors to see a comic (Rose is Rose, 2002; see below; Marvin & Seagroves, 2017). This comic illustrates the process where the exploration system shuts down due to a threat encountered by the child. This threat

Shouldn't this be turns on the attachment system? When exploration turns off, attachment turns on? shuts off the attachment system, causing the child to seek out the safe haven of the parents' arms for comfort. Once the comfort is received, the attachment system turns off, and the exploration system turns on, as evidenced by the "fully charged indicator wiggle."

**Rose is Rose** by Don Wimmer and Pat Brady

ROSE IS ROSE

In the early years of life, children progress around this circle thousands of times. Young children experience safe haven and secure base through physical proximity to their caregivers. However, over time, they may be able to experience secure base in a more symbolic way over greater distances, for example, talking, a telephone call, or a text message. It is through this secure base system that a person develops the capacities described above. On the top of the cycle, the child's sense of self-confidence and identity form. This is where a child learns autonomy and self-direction while learning self-control and the ability to live within limits. On the bottom side of the cycle, the child's sense of other is molded. Here he learns how to appropriately manage emotions and to work collaboratively with others to solve problems and manage stress, anxiety, sadness, and anger. The bottom is where children learn that others are trustworthy, reliable, and accessible in times of need. In Chapter 9, we will discuss the theoretical framework behind the regulation of emotions and how attachment theory and proximity seeking may inform that regulatory process.

*When the exploration system is activated, this is where a child learns autonomy and self-direction while learning self-control and the ability to live within limits.*

This secure base system is internalized by the child into what is referred to as an **internal working model (IWM)** and forms a set of beliefs about themselves (Am I worthy of love and capable of experiencing intimacy?) and others (Can I trust others to be there for me in times of trouble and can they help me?) (Clinton & Sibcy, 2002). It also wires the brain for experiencing intimacy, coping with stress, and regulating emotions (Clinton & Sibcy, 2002; see Recommended Reading for resources that discuss the development of IWMs in more detail).

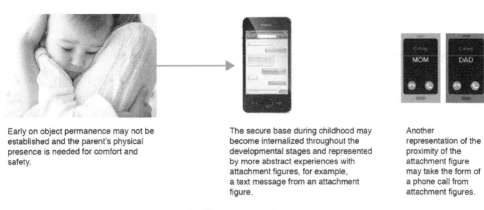

Early on object permanence may not be established and the parent's physical presence is needed for comfort and safety.

The secure base during childhood may become internalized throughout the developmental stages and represented by more abstract experiences with attachment figures, for example, a text message from an attachment figure.

Another representation of the proximity of the attachment figure may take the form of a phone call from attachment figures.

© Shutterstock.com

## Styles of Attachment

Based on the child's experiences in the secure base system, these IWMs are organized into different patterns or styles of attachment. Four main patterns have identified: secure, avoidant, preoccupied, and fearful avoidance. In addition to these four primary patterns or classifications, some assessments such as the AAI (Main et al., 2002) are also often cited in research as including multiple subtypes.

## Secure Attachment

Those with secure attachment were able to effectively use their parent as a secure base for exploring the world, and when they were emotionally distressed, they could effectively use their parents to help regain a sense of calm. From these experiences, positive relationship rules (Clinton & Sibcy, 2006) including a positive sense of self (I am worthy of love and I can explore the world and make a contribution to society in a meaningful way) and a positive sense of others (I can count on my attachment figures to be reliable, accessible, and trustworthy, capable of meeting my needs and helping me in times of distress), may be developed. One's sense of self and sense of others synergistically interact with each other in a way that promotes a balance between experiencing a sense of self-definition and identity and experiencing a sense of enduring closeness and intimacy. The securely attached individual can move fluidly and flexibly between the exploration system and the attachment system, based on what is happening in his (or her) life. Recall that attachment serves a regulatory function. In other words, when a child learns that he or she can seek out his or her secure base during times of distress and receive a sense of comfort and safety and receive help organizing their feelings, this process becomes internalized and one is able to more easily regulate negative emotions.

*Those with secure attachment are able to experience their emotions, both positive and negative, without becoming overwhelmed and resorting to defensive and sometimes destructive behaviors to compensate for their inability to effectively cope with their feelings.*

## Avoidant Attachment

Avoidant attachment develops when children's parents overemphasize the top of the cycle, often pushing their children to become independent and autonomous even when the child does not feel a sense of security. These parents are often overly concerned that if they do not push their child to behave independently early on, the child will become too clingy and dependent. Moreover, when the child is on the bottom side of the cycle and signaling attachment anxiety, the parents often ignore these signals and can be quite rejecting, cold, and harsh. The result is a person who avoids experiencing his or her attachment-related emotion. In other words, his or her attachment system is underactivated, and his or her exploration system is overactive. The result is that the avoidantly attached person tends to depend on his or her environment (things, money, fame, achievement, addictions) rather than relationships to regulate his or her emotions. Consequently, they have difficulty experiencing empathy and durable intimacy with others. It is important to note that these individuals can be very friendly and outgoing; the difficulty comes in feeling close to others, especially in times of need.

Infants who develop an avoidant attachment system have a history of rejection (Cassidy, 1994), and this impacts their capacity to regulate emotion. They tend to "minimize negative affect in order to avoid risk of further rejection" (Cassidy, 1994, p. 228).

## Preoccupied Attachment

Preoccupied attachment occurs when the caregiver discourages the child from exploring the world. The parent is often threatened by the child's autonomy and so unwittingly and unknowingly sabotages her efforts to launch from the secure base. Also, parents may feel quite anxious and overwhelmed, and so the child actually finds herself in a role-reversed position of attempting to take care of the parents' emotional needs. When on the bottom of the cycle, the child experiences the parent as unreliable and unpredictable. At times, the parent, if she or he is feeling good, can be supportive and caring. However, on other occasions, the parent can get overwhelmed and angry with the child for being needy. The child learns that in order to get her parent to respond to her needs, her emotions must be intense and even dramatic. The result is a child with a negative sense of self (The child may have the following relationship rules: I am not worthy of love and I am uncomfortable with autonomy and exploration) and an often idealized sense of other (I desperately need others to take care of me, but I must be in great need in order for them to respond to my emotions). Unlike the avoidant individual, the preoccupied person's exploration system is underactivated, and their attachment system is hyper-activated. Even when their caregivers are responding to their needs, preoccupied individuals may have difficulty feeling relief or feeling loved. And because they do not feel others respond with enough affection and concern, they may use defensive measures (over-submissiveness, anger, clinging, demanding) and destructive behaviors, such as threats, self-injury, and promiscuity in order to soothe their emotions. Cassidy (1994) reported that infants who have an ambivalent or preoccupied style and likely have a history of an inconsistently available primary attachment figures may be more likely to intensify negative emotions (unlike the avoidant attachment style that may be associated with minimizing negative emotions). The strategy that is used to cope with negative emotion and to interact with the attachment system is to maximize negative emotion in order to obtain the care of an attachment figure that is often unavailable.

## Fearful-Avoidant (Disorganized) Attachment

Fearful avoidance, sometimes referred to as a disorganized attachment style, occurs when the person has experienced difficulties on both sides of the circle. This often occurs in abusive environments, where caregivers place the child in a biological paradox in which the parent, the child's secure base, becomes his or her source of threat. The result is that, biologically, the child is motivated to (a) "run away" from the threat and (b) to seek comfort from his or her secure base. The child does not know if she or he is coming or going and so the solution is to disconnect from his or her experience. This is believed to be the genesis of dissociation (Van Dijke, Hopman, & Ford, 2018). Another result is that the child has a negative view of himself or herself (she or he may have relationship rules that indicate "I am unworthy of love and I am uncomfortable with autonomy") and others (I cannot count on you to help me in times of stress). He or she can rapidly vacillate between both strategies of avoidance and preoccupation: "I don't need you; go away; I do need you; go away." Finally, he or she with fearful avoidance struggles with both autonomy and intimacy and may find himself or herself strangely attracted to people who are likely to re-enact abusive behavior.

## Measuring Attachment

Unlike the AAI, where attachment style is determined by the quality of a person's narrative about their childhood attachment experiences, adult attachment self-report instruments, like the Experiences of Close Relationship scale, measure attachment beliefs that fall along two dimensions: anxiety and avoidance. High scores on the anxiety dimension indicate fears about rejection and abandonment. The attachment system is stuck in high gear, so even when attachment figures are present and engaged, those with high scores on the anxiety dimension still feel a sense of being unloved. The fear of abandonment always gnaws at the edge of their mind. Low scores on anxiety indicate that a person feels close to others and is generally satisfied with the amount of time and attention they receive from their attachment figures. High scores on the avoidance dimension refer to a discomfort with close relationships. There is a fear of opening up about feelings and a reluctance to rely on others for support and nurturance. The attachment system is underactive, so the person does not register a need to seek others in times of trouble. Low scores on avoidance suggest a willingness to be close to and vulnerable with others, openly sharing feelings and accepting comfort and reassurance. In short, secure attachment is defined by low scores on both dimensions: Secure people are comfortable with intimacy and feel satisfied with the amount of time and attention they receive from their close relationships. Avoidant people score high on avoidance and low on anxiety. They are afraid of intimacy. Preoccupied folks score high on anxiety and low on avoidance. They are afraid of abandonment. Fearful-avoidant individuals desperately long for closeness, but because of their intense fear of abandonment, they avoid intimacy. Both the fear of abandonment and the fear of intimacy are simultaneously active. Let us examine the case of Gabby for an example of fearful-avoidant or disorganized attachment:

## The Case of Gabby

Gabby was referred to counseling by her psychiatrist, who had been treating her for depression and anxiety for the last five years. She first sought psychiatric care when she was an 18-year-old college freshman. After graduating high school, she desperately wanted to move far away from home, so she left the West Coast and entered college in Virginia. Within a month, she started having panic attacks, holed herself in her room, and sunk into a deep depression that landed her in the hospital for a week. In addition to taking a combination of medications, Gabby entered therapy but soon felt annoyed and frustrated with the counselor. "We would just talk about nothing. There would be long pauses where he wouldn't say anything to me but just sat there, staring at me. It felt creepy to me. So I just quit." Her psychiatrist tried to refer her to another therapist, but Gabby refused. She just wanted medication treatment and felt that it was helping enough to get her through.

Gabby eventually graduated a semester later than expected and began working as an account manager at a local distribution company. Her symptoms soon worsened to the point that her psychiatrist insisted that she see a therapist. This time, the therapist, a well-seasoned counselor with over 20 years of experience, was much more engaged and would work with Gabby's passive personality style. Although he was engaged and active, he encouraged Gabby to participate in the process of therapy. They made a problem list and began focusing on one or two problems at a time. At the top of Gabby's problem list was her loneliness. She felt isolated and alone. She did not feel like she had any close friends, other than Amanda, a workmate, who was five years older and married and thus had little time to spend with Gabby. Gabby's daily routine was drab and boring. She went to work in the morning and came home in the evening. She very rarely did anything outside of her home besides necessary tasks like going to the grocery and going to dinner with a few college friends who lived in the area. She had very few activities she enjoyed other than binge watching Netflix and HBO series like *"House of Cards" and "Game of Thrones"*. She also spent several hours a day surfing Facebook, which only intensified her feelings of loneliness and worthlessness as she saw all her friends living the life she so desperately wanted.

Her therapist saw this was the port of entry, as it were, into Gabby's core attachment beliefs: She longed for intimacy but was too afraid of rejection and abandonment to seek it out. Although she was about 30 pounds overweight, Gabby was quite attractive, with long, dark locks of hair, emerald green eyes, and delicate facial features. When she was comfortable, her personality blossomed, and she could hold a delightful conversation. The therapist was able to work with Gabby on expanding her social network and helping her make some deeper connections with friends. She began taking an interest in herself: joining a fitness club, exercising, and losing weight.

She wanted to start dating, but this frightened her deeply. The fear of abandonment always lurking just beneath the surface. When guys showed an interest in her, Gabby would become somewhat cold and aloof. This produced exactly what she expected: rejection. She wanted guys to really pursue her. "If they really wanted to have a relationship with me, they'd accept me just the way I am." The counselor was able to help Gabby see that her "real self" was not cold and aloof. "What kind of guy wants to be with someone who acts like they'd rather be at home doing laundry than being out on a date with him? If you want guys to want to be with you, you've got to show them some signs of wanting to be with them. It is a two-way street." Again, this was one of the core conflicts of the fearful-avoidant style of attachment. However, the counselor knew that the real attachment conflict would flare up once Gabby was actually in a close relationship.

A few months later, it happened. Gabby came to therapy miraculously cured of all psychiatric illness. She was in love. She found a soulmate, Adam. The relationship went from 0 to 100 in a matter of two dates, and Gabby was sure she had found "the one." Although Happy that Gabby was finally able to open up to someone, the therapist knew that darkness would soon fall upon this bright day, bringing bitter nights of abandonment, anger, and anxiety. A few months later, it started to happen. Gabby came to therapy, furious that Adam was not as committed to the relationship as she was. He planned to spend a precious Saturday afternoon with a buddy to go fishing on the river. Leaving his phone safely in the car for fear of dropping it in the water, he was unresponsive to Gabby's incessant texts and phone calls. He returned to find his phone blasted with dozens of texts and several long, angry, desperate voice messages of Gabby railing him out for not responding to her. Fearing her anger, Adam did not respond to any of her messages. Eventually, Gabby went to his apartment and began pounding on his door. He eventually let her in, and they began arguing. Adam lost his temper and insisted that Gabby leave. The relationship was all but over, and Gabby was suddenly back in throes of a deep, suicidal depression.

## Unresolved (or Disorganized) Loss

It can be very difficult to come to terms with the loss of an attachment figure. Bowlby (1980) described loss as "inherently disorganizing" (p. 138). As we are often oriented to our attachment figures, experiencing the external loss of an attachment figure through death requires a person to make some internal shifts to come to terms with the idea that the attachment figure is no longer available. Let us now take a look at the case of Lizzy, for an example of an attachment style characterized as unresolved loss.

## Unresolved Loss: The Case of Lizzy

Lizzy came to counseling because she had become profoundly depressed and suicidal following the tragic death of her boyfriend, Allan, who was killed in a motorcycle accident only minutes after leaving Lizzy's apartment. In a flat, matter-of-fact tone of voice, she unpacked the details of that horrific day. She had just kissed Allan and said goodbye and watched him as he revved the engine and popped a wheelie on his red and black Ducati Street Fighter 1098. She went back inside to get her bookbag, hopped in her Honda Civic, and headed off to class. When she got to the end of her road, her heart leaped with terror when she saw a commotion of cars and people rushing to a person lying motionless in the middle of the road. Twenty yards up the away from the lifeless body was her boyfriend's mangled bike—she knew he was dead.

Lizzy became severely depressed over the next six months. She was flooded with guilt, anger, hopelessness, and an intense desire to die. She could not imagine herself ever being happy again. Her roommate found her collapsed, unconscious on the bathroom floor, and Lizzy was rushed to the hospital. After five days in the ICU, Lizzy was transferred to the psychiatric inpatient unit. After a week, her depression began to subside enough that she no longer was suicidal, and she was referred to outpatient counseling. The counselor, Steve, read Lizzy's discharge report and learned that she had a previous major depressive episode when she was a teenager, following the tragic death of her grandmother, who drowned in a swimming pool, while taking a morning swim. After nearly a half a dozen therapy sessions, Lizzy's depression was still significant but less intense. The counselor decided it was time to administer the Adult Attachment Interview (AAI).

Lizzy listed her grandmother as an important caregiver in her life, as her parents worked until 6 in the evening during the week. Her grandmother would pick her up from school and bring her home, feed her a snack, talk with her about her day, help her with homework, and then stay for dinner with her and her parents. When Lizzy was a teenager, her grandmother continued to play an important part in her life, and she talked fondly of her as warm, caring, and fun. She was able to recall specific examples of how her relationship with her grandmother exhibited each of these characteristics. Steve and his supervisor listened to the recording of this interview together, and Steve was convinced that Lizzy was secure in her attachment style. Lizzy exhibited a number of secure qualities in her AAI: She was clear and concise and was able to provide specific, relevant memories to support her descriptions of her caregivers, including her grandmother. However, Steve was missing a glaring problem: Lizzy described her grandmother in present tense—as if she was still alive. "She's such a loving and caring person. She wants me to blossom and to be someone who makes a difference in this world. That's the story of her life. . .she always looks out for others more than she does herself."

Lizzy was unresolved with respect to the loss of her grandmother. Lizzy had not come to terms with the reality of her grandmother's death. She lived as if her grandmother was still alive and well. In the following therapy session, Steve gently challenged Lizzy about this in a supportive way (see Chapter 12 for more on challenging skills). She was surprised and completely unaware that she was talking in present tense about her grandmother. As they explored this more deeply, Lizzy stated, "I guess that's the way I had to cope with the situation. I pretended it wasn't her who died. They must have found somebody else in the pool." She remembered feeling completely numb and hollow at her grandmother's funeral, and she refused to view her body. "I felt the same way at Allan's funeral. And his family had a closed casket so I never saw him. I have to tell myself he's not really dead. It wasn't him lying in the road dead. It must have been somebody else. I know it sounds crazy. . .but it's the only way I can cope."

Lizzy was so overwhelmed by the prospect of feeling the emotion of grief. So, as a defense against these feelings, she tried to convince herself that her grandmother and boyfriend had not really died. Unresolved grief is not viewed so much as a person who gets very sad and overcome with emotion when they talk about the deceased, but as someone who has not been able to "effectively process these emotions"? Depression does not arise from intense feelings of sadness and grief; instead, it is rooted in one's inability to experience and process feelings of grief. When one blocks grief, it prevents the mind from registering the reality that the deceased person is actually dead and not coming back (at least not in this life). Grief is the body's way of registering the value of the lost object. Failure to accept the feeling of grief results in the failure to cognitively and emotionally accept the reality of death.

## Redeeming Attachment

The instillation of hope even in situations of disorganization is not impossible (see Yalom, 1975, a group psychotherapy textbook, where he discussed that the instillation of hope is one of the therapeutic factors). Bob Marvin and other authors who specialize in attachment (Clinton & Sibcy, 2002; Knight & Sibcy, 2018) indicate that one is not stuck with the attachment style he or she developed during childhood, but that there can be movement toward a secure autonomous style and a secure narrative on the AAI through the course of intentional empathic therapy and/or relationship with present and sensitive attachment figures.

## Attachment in Scripture

Scriptures for how parents should shape children's behaviors:

Deuteronomy 6:20–25 New International Version (NIV)

20 In the future, when your son asks you, "What is the meaning of the stipulations, decrees and laws the LORD our God has commanded you?"

21 tell him: "We were slaves of Pharaoh in Egypt, but the LORD brought us out of Egypt with a mighty hand.

22 Before our eyes the LORD sent signs and wonders—great and terrible—on Egypt and Pharaoh and his whole household.

23 But he brought us out from there to bring us in and give us the land he promised on oath to our ancestors.

24 The LORD commanded us to obey all these decrees and to fear the LORD our God, so that we might always prosper and be kept alive, as is the case today.

25 And if we are careful to obey all this law before the LORD our God, as he has commanded us, that will be our righteousness."

Many principles behind attachment theory are illustrated through stories found in the scriptures that reflect how parents shape the child's behavior (see Deuteronomy 6:20–25; 1 Kings 14:12–13). In other cases, such as in the lives of King Saul and King David, the scriptures illustrate various themes of attachment.

In the Old Testament, we see that when confronted by the prophet Samuel (1 Samuel 15), King Saul excused his behavior using a reasoning that closely

© Joseph Thomas Photography

follows the logic of a person with an ambivalent attachment style (Holmes, 1993)—Saul was afraid of being rejected because he already thought himself flawed. In contrast, King David took responsibility for his sin when the prophet Nathan called him out for his adulterous behavior (2 Samuel 12). King David's secure attachment style gave him confidence to admit the truth because his relationship with God was based on trust; he was confident in God's willingness to forgive his sins and restore his relationship with him.

1 Kings 14:12–13 Holman Christian Standard Bible (HCSB)

12 "As for you, get up and go to your house. When your feet enter the city, the boy will die.

13 All Israel will mourn for him and bury him. He alone out of Jeroboam's house will be put in the family tomb, because out of the house of Jeroboam the LORD God of Israel found something good only in him.

The New Testament is filled with attachment themes that illustrate both sides of the secure base system. For example, as noted in the What epithet? Do you mean epigraph?, Jesus portrays himself as a haven of safety for those on the bottom side of the cycle, encouraging those who are weary and in need of comfort to come to him to find rest. Note that this requires believers to acknowledge their pain and needs, a task that is difficult for those who are more avoidant. Similarly, Jesus states that those who are at the bottom of the cycle and vulnerable enough to acknowledge their thirst (emotionally and spiritually) should "Come to me to drink. . .[and for those who do] out of his heart will flow rivers of living water" (John 7:38, ESV). Note that after one drinks from his water, a river of living water flows, implying the person launches to the top of the cycle and takes this peace, joy, and security with him and offers it to others. The act of launching to the top of the cycle with the heartfelt knowledge of Jesus as one's secure base and source of confidence is poignantly illustrated in Matthew 28:18–20 when Jesus tells his disciples "go" into the world and carry out God's purposes with the knowledge of His eternal presence: "And behold, I am with you always, to the end of the age." The interplay of the call to come to Him when weary and then to go out into the world aligns with the attachment system's function to help one move to a place of security and then to shift the to exploration system based on a feeling of being energized to go out and explore the world.

This dynamic is poetically and articulately described in a song entitled "King of My Heart" by Bethel music artist Steffany and J. Riddle: Gretzinger and J. Riddle: "Let the King of My Heart be the shadow where I hide, the ransom for my life. . .be the wind inside my sails and the anchor in the waves, Omit He is my song." The wind inside a sail fuels the ship's exploration, and the anchor helps provide stability and safety. This is a vivid metaphor that illustrates the dual function of the attachment system to provide stability during the storms or waves of life and confidence or fuel for exploration.

Finally, in Philippians 4:4–7, Paul describes key aspects of the secure base system. Bring flush with previous line begins stating that we should **rejoice** because we know that "The Lord is at hand." Thus, He is our ever-present secure base from which we launch onto the top of the cycle, experiencing positive emotions and reasonableness. However, notice that when we get on the bottom of the

© VectorPot/Shutterstock.com

cycle and our attachment system is activated, instead of getting preoccupied with anxiety, fear, dread, and fretful worrying about all that could go wrong, acknowledge (i.e., signal) your concerns to God and through "**prayer and supplication**" (i.e., proximity-seeking behavior) bring those concerns to Him. The result is the experience of great peace, which is beyond our understanding (i.e., safe haven).

© De Visu/Shutterstock.com

REJOICE
ALWAYS

When tempted to
worry, instead....>>

PRAY

+

=

© Shutterstock.com

## Attachment Styles and Pathology

Attachment styles are fairly stable across the lifespan. Typically, attachment security promotes psychological and emotional health and can act as a source of resilience in times of stress. In some ways, attachment security is equated to emotional and psychological health just like the body's immune system is to our physical health. The immune system does not protect us from exposure to pathogens, but when exposed to them, it helps protect against diseases—sometimes preventing illness altogether, but even when illness does occur, a healthy immune system helps keep the illness process at bay so that one does not get as sick as long as those with compromised immune system. Likewise, attachment security does not protect people from stressful life events, but it helps us to cope more effectively with stress so that it does not result in the onset of psychological and emotional disturbances.

*Attachment security does not protect people from stressful life events, but it helps us cope more effectively with stress so that it does not result in the onset of psychological and emotional disturbances.*

Research does not demonstrate that attachment insecurity directly causes psychopathology and maladjustment. In fact, these insecure styles of attachment appear to be effective ways of managing the anxiety stress that results from insensitive, rejecting, chaotic, and sometimes abusive parenting. The difficulty is that if these patterns of attachment carry forward and are not somehow offset by alternative sources of secure attachment (e.g., family friends, teachers, coaches, and youth pastors), they can increase one's vulnerability to various forms of maladjustment. According to Alan Schore (1994), arguably the John Bowlby of our day, attachment security is tantamount to emotion regulation and healthy self-development. In contrast, attachment insecurity results in emotion dysregulation. Current research suggests that it is emotion dysregulation that is at the heart of most forms of psychopathology, especially anxiety, depression, and emotional disorders.

The current research on all forms of anxiety disorders and depression shows that there is a great deal of overlap of symptoms between these disorders and there is a great deal of comorbidity or overlap among different disorders. For example, someone who has an anxiety disorder is increasingly at risk for developing depression over the course of his or her lifetime. Also, it is very common for people who suffer from a depressive disorder to also experience significant co-occurring anxiety. Interestingly, researchers found that treatments designed to target specific disorders (e.g., panic disorder) help reduce symptoms of other co-occurring disorders (like generalized anxiety disorder symptoms) in addition to helping improve mood symptoms. Moreover, **affective neuroscience** suggests a common underlying brain structure for all anxiety and emotional disorders, characterized by two features: (a) overreactive limbic system circuits and (b) underactive cortical structures such as the prefrontal cortex, resulting in limited inhibitory control of the limbic system.

## Charting the Course Forward

In this chapter, we have discussed the development of clinical expertise, attachment theory, and the multidimensional nature of counseling. Moving forward in the text, you will learn the skills that are needed to develop a strong therapeutic relationship. Building and maintaining relationships are skills required in all forms of the helping profession. This involves several different subsets of skills such as:

- building a therapeutic alliance

- assessing a client's motivation for change

- dealing with resistance

- proactively identifying potential challenges to a strong therapeutic alliance

- repairing therapeutic ruptures

- identifying and understanding client experiences that may contribute to their difficulty in participating in an effective therapeutic relationship, and

- being aware of one's own history of relationships and how it may affect your ability to work effectively as a therapist or counselor.

Many of the skills are discussed in detail in this book. As you continue your journey of becoming and your study of this text, you will encounter the topics listed above.

## Skills and Future Coursework

These essential interviewing and counseling skills are often used in combination with diagnostic interviewing and treatment planning, which is another skill needed by competent counselors. We will touch on these in the latter part of this book in Chapter 13 on Case Conceptualization. This requires a working knowledge of the *Diagnostic and Statistical Manual of Mental Disorders, 5th edition* (*DSM-5*)-based diagnoses and the ability to conduct a streamlined initial assessment that would include identifying relevant clinical diagnoses, and a history of present problems, a mental status exam, a relevant psychosocial history, and basic case formulation strategies. Traditionally students were trained to pick a theoretical orientation and then formulate different cases from within the framework of that theoretical system, whereas more recently, counselors are encouraged to understand different clinical problems (e.g., depression, panic disorder, social anxiety disorder, posttraumatic stress disorder [PTSD], bulimia, and anorexia) and identify evidence-based treatments that apply to these problems. Although typically many of these treatments are within the behavioral and cognitive behavioral traditions, they often involve the integration of treatment components derived from different theoretical traditions. As we will discuss, this requires that counselors have an increasingly broad theoretical framework that allows them to conceptualize problems from multiple perspectives and not get pigeonholed into just one theoretical lens. The counseling skills will facilitate the conversation the client has with the counselor to unpack the symptoms that could inform relevant diagnosis and treatment planning. These skills will be discussed in Part Two of the text, and Part Three of the text will touch on case conceptualization; you will also more about that in future treatment planning courses.

*A Concept to Contemplate*

Let's take a moment to contemplate a concept. You may wonder, why do I need to learn these things if I want to be a counselor? One of the extrinsic motivators or reasons may be that if you become a licensed professional counselor and you want to receive payment from third-party payers (insurance companies) you will need to know what these

© Shutterstock.com

things are. What are some intrinsic reasons that may motivate you to learn this information?

## Recommended Reading

In this chapter, we discussed concepts related to attachment theory. We recommend the text entitled *Why You Do the Things You Do: The Secret to Healthy Relationships*, 2006, by Drs. Clinton and Sibcy. This text provides an overview of attachment theory and compelling stories and breaks down relationship rules

© Shutterstock.com

into layman's terms. We also recommend the text *Redeeming Attachment: A Counselor's Guide to Facilitating Attachment to God and Earned Security* by Drs. Kuhnley and Sibcy. This book focuses on healing early attachment wounds and moving from an insecure attachment style to a secure or, better yet, an earned secure attachment style using research-based strategies. Another text is by Dr. Dan Siegel entitled *Parenting From the Inside Out: How a Deeper Self-Understanding Can Help You Raise Children Who Thrive*, 2003. This text discusses concepts that may help with understanding the confluence of neuroscience and behavioral principles.

We also recommend an article written by James Bennett-Levy, from the University of Sydney. The article is entitled, *Therapist Skills: A Cognitive Model of their Acquisition and Refinement.* This article was published in January of 2006 in the journal entitled, *Behavioural and Cognitive Psychotherapy* and was retrieved from the Research Gate website via the following link: https://www.researchgate.net/publication/228625546_Therapist_Skills_A_Cognitive_Model_of_their_Acquisition_and_Refinement Bennett-Levy discusses information processing theory and how this theory lays the groundwork for a model of skill development. Bennett-Levy also explores the ideas of the systems of declarative (e.g., empathy and warmth are important in counseling), procedural ("how to" implement therapy and warmth in session) and reflective knowledge (a metacognitive skill that involves the observation, evaluation, and awareness of one's own thoughts) and provides an explanatory model for how a variety of skills develop.

## Chapter Summary

One overarching goal of this chapter is to have you begin to think about your journey and the level of competence that you may be striving for and the confidence to know when a level has been reached. The emergent model of clinical expertise is explained and described. In order to frame this journey, we also discussed attachment theory in hopes of you being able to make sense of your story so that you can use this as a tool to help clients make sense of theirs.

---

1. We have colleagues who also use the term *ethical counselor* as part of their definition of expertise. However, it is our contention that a highly competent and effective therapist is by definition ethical. Traditionally, a therapist who violates ethical standards is not considered competent and typically is not very effective. However, it is possible to be ethical but not competent or effective.

## Chapter Two

# The Journey of Becoming

## Justin Silvey and Anita M. Kuhnley with Gary Sibcy

*A professional counselor is an amateur who did not quit.*

—Justin Silvey

### Chapter Learning Objectives

1. To identify strategies for personal and professional self-evaluation and implications for practice (CACREP II.F.1.k, 2016, p. 10)

2. To discuss self-care strategies appropriate to the counselor role (CACREP II.F.1.l, 2016, p. 10)

3. To address the role of counseling supervision in the profession (CACREP II.F.1.m, 2016, p. 10)

4. To develop an understanding of the impact of heritage, attitudes, beliefs, understandings, and acculturative experiences on an individual's views of others (CACREP II.F.2.d, 2016, p. 10)

5. To synthesize the impact of spiritual beliefs on clients' and counselors' worldviews (CACREP II.F.2.g, 2016, p. 10)

6. To classify counselor characteristics and behaviors that influence the counseling process (CACREP II.F.5.f, 2016, p. 12)

7. To identify strategies for understanding and practicing consultation (CACREP II.F.5.c, 2016, p. 11)

# Chapter Overview

We decided to use the metaphor of a journey because of the progressive nature of the road to becoming. This thought originated as we found that counselors in training are asking for specific tasks to do in counseling, but we believe that the correct approach is not a journey of "doing" counseling but more about "being" a counselor. The main goal of becoming is to understand that we want all to be in the process of seeking to develop healthier and more well-adjusted, adaptive, and resilient lives. In this chapter, we will explore the value of self-awareness through self-care and supervision, mentalization, meta cognitive monitoring, and counseling characteristics that influence the counseling process. These are characteristics that are important to cultivate in the therapist that may aid in his personal journey and the process of assisting clients on their journey.

When we are travelling to a new destination or a conference in unfamiliar territory, we often use our GPS for directions. Have you ever noticed how forgiving the GPS is? If you take a wrong turn rather than saying, "What is the matter with you, you missed my clear directions and got off track?!", the GPS simply says, "recalculating," for example, and helps us by identifying the next needed action to get back on track or in other words, to "proceed to the route." Another feature of the GPS that we really appreciate is what happens when you get to your destination! The GPS often

© stockphotofan1/Shutterstock.com

says the exciting phrase, "You have arrived!" We enjoy and relish in this because in life we do not "arrive"; we are on a lifelong journey of becoming and growing into a more therapeutic, whole, and kind person. Since the personhood of the counselor is one of the greatest tools the counselor brings to the session, we believe that this is a very important process. In addition, we have embarked upon a research journey to identify the most effective characteristics or habits of effective counselors (you will hear more about this in Chapter 4). In this chapter we discuss the journey and how embracing the idea of becoming can be facilitative of being better equipped to be present with clients.

*The hardest step in a thousand mile journey is the first one.*

—Chinese Proverb

A journey begins with a starting point. In the developmental process, the starting point may be viewed as birth, or you may think about your beginning as being much earlier. For example, you would not be who you are without your ancestors being who they were. This is a reason why you might visit Ancestry.com or work through a genogram in counseling courses. We think that you must first know where you have come from to determine where you might go. The first step of your journey may have begun with a hope, a dream, or a desire. In Scripture, 2

**A Verse to Remember:**
"And the things you have heard me say in the presence of many witnesses entrust to reliable people who will also be qualified to teach others."
2 Timothy 2:2

Timothy 2:2 confirms that we are not only to grow on this developmental journey for self-gain but also for the benefit of others or to teach others. The Apostle Paul in this passage urges us to commit to faithful people who will teach others. Likewise, we do not only grow through trials to experience character development and comfort ourselves but also to help others. Paul, in his second letter to the church at Corinth, states, "Praise be to the God and Father of our Lord Jesus Christ, the Father of compassion, the God of all comfort, who comforts us in all our troubles, so that we can comfort those in any trouble, with the comfort we ourselves have received from God" (2 Corinthians 1:3). The first verse mentioned here, 2 Timothy 2:2, parallels the supervision process; once counselors complete the licensure process and practice for their state's given time requirement, they can in most states (see your state board requirements) be eligible to provide supervision and train or teach others to provide effective, evidence-based counseling and treatment for clients. Likewise, the second scripture referenced (1 Corinthians 1:3) parallels the clinical process. As we go through our own struggles and pains in life and receive comfort and overcome, we are better able to be present with others and share comfort with them. Another aspect of the starting point is to understand why you have decided to embark on this journey. Please watch this video, where Drs. Silvey and Kuhnley explore the concept of the journey. Our desire is that this video provides you with context and an image of the beginning of an unfolding path as you embark on the journey of empathic counseling skill development.

**Video**

**Becoming: Justin Silvey & Anita Kuhnley**

## Understand Your Why

Simon Sinek discusses in his book *Start with Why* and in his Ted Talk (2009a, 2009b) the importance of beginning with why. He developed what he calls "The Golden Circle," which consists of three concentric circles. Figure 2.1 is a visual of "The Golden Circle":

Sinek explains the circles in terms of business, mentioning that all companies know what they make or do, and many employees may know how their product or service is made, but very few may know why they have the product or service. Sinek suggests that organizations start from the outside and work toward the inside of the circle; however, he continues by stating that we need to start with "why" and end with "what." For example, a local restaurant might advertise, "We make the best hamburgers in town. We flame grill our burgers to perfection. We add fresh ingredients to create our delicious burger." Would you be inspired to drive by this burger joint for a burger? This advertising model really works from the outside to the inside of the circle— addressing what the business makes and how it is created. What drives the company? What is

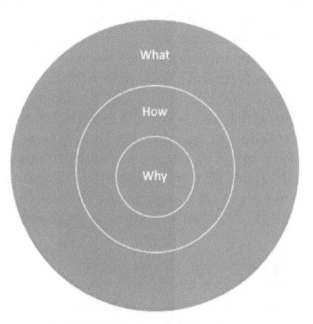

**Figure 2.1.** The Golden Circle

the company's "Why?" Would this marketing work better? "We have a desire to bring foodies together to share in the most inviting experience! We have a desire to use the freshest ingredients to create a cornucopia of flavors that join together to create a culinary experience like never before. We just happen to make hamburgers!" Does this marketing change the dynamic altogether? It sounds different because it starts with "why" and moves outward to "what." What is the "Why?" To join people together, to create community, and to create a shared experience. Food was meant to bring people together. We can look throughout history and see people joined together around food, so why not (no pun intended) start with a purpose like that? So, how does this relate to counselor training? We feel that you need to determine, define, and be driven by your "why," which is the purpose behind why you decided on the counseling field in the first place. Why have a "Why?" It is important to understand your why, not only for personal development purposes but also in order to be able to help clients unpack their why. Becoming a clinical mental health counselor is not just a vocational journey or training for a job, but a calling that involves a deeper purpose and meaning.

We were among the 40 million people who have copies of *The Purpose Driven Life* by Rick Warren. We believe that this book is a prime example of how individuals are looking for purpose, as it sought to provide guidance to answer the question, "What on Earth am I here for?" We found that the first sentence in the book was telling about where our purpose should come from when Rick states, "It's not about you." We think that when purpose is found outside of yourself (in God's plan) that true drive, passion, joy, and intentionality can then come into focus. As you begin to process your "why" about counseling, here are a few questions that might help you as you begin this very important leg of your journey.

# Questions to Unpack Your "Why"

## The Equation for Understanding Why

1. In what areas of your life are you finding the most satisfaction?
2. How did you categorize these things as going well?
3. What motivates you to do the things that are going well?

Notice that we did not ask "why" questions above, even though that is what we are searching for. It is important to use "how" and "what" questions in order to move deeper into counseling. Basically, we can have you think about "why" without asking "Why?" We will discuss more in Chapter 10.

By addressing these three questions, you can start to uncover unknown beliefs or motivators (see Chapter 4 for more) and some of the things that might "get you out of bed in the morning," provide you something to strive for throughout the day, and provide you with some peace at the end of the day when you accomplish them. Additional questions to help you unpack your "why" come from a message from Liberty University's founder, Dr. Jerry Falwell,

1. What is it that you really want to accomplish in your life?
2. What would you try to do if you thought you might succeed?
3. What goals would you set if you know you could not fail?
4. What price are you willing to pay?
5. What sacrifice are you willing to make?

Again, these types of questions can help deepen personal insights, motivations, and passions as we begin to self-reflect through the journey.

# Aspects of "Why" and Self-Care

We believe that developing your "why" will provide you with the antithesis to burnout. If you develop your passion for why you entered into counseling, then that can be used as the thing that keeps you in the field should you begin feeling burned out in practice. Here are a few strategies to consider when addressing self-care or burnout (these are not in any particular order):

1. Start with and understand your "Why".
2. Make a sleep schedule and stick to it.
3. Develop good eating habits.
4. Monitor stress.
5. Make time for family and friends.

6. Be intentional about self-care—if you have to take a day off of work, be sure to do something intentional to increase your level of care.

7. Create an exercise plan and stick to it.

8. Engage in daily reading, writing, and/or other types of academic or intellectual activities.

9. Laugh.

10. Give yourself and extend grace.

11. Ask yourself questions like these

   a. What or who motivates you to be better?

   b. What helps you recharge when you are feeling depleted or needing renewal?

   c. What would help you connect to your "Why?"

   d. Let us tie some additional thoughts into this aspect of understanding your "Why?"

## Attachment Illumination

© Shutterstock.com

One goal of this chapter is to help future counselors make sense of why they want to be therapists. We feel that understanding our personal history of relationships can help us realize who we are, which may help uncover the reason for the decision to come into this field. One of the ways that we work on that with our more advanced graduate students in a doctoral course on advanced psychopathology and attachment theory, taught by Dr. Kuhnley, is by having students complete a modified version of the Adult Attachment Interview (George, Kaplan, & Main, 1985). During this activity, students work through a series of questions with one another and describe their earliest experiences with their caregivers, usually their parents, and attempt to deduce a coherent understanding of those experiences, in attempt to try and make sense of them. Particularly, students are asked to develop very concrete, specific memories about the kinds of interactions they had with their parents and how those experiences affect who they are today in terms of how they feel about themselves, how they relate to others, their ability to experience intimacy, and their ability to be cared for and care for others. It is a very powerful experience. Next, they write a paper reflecting on their interview, as the interview has been taped. Last, they reflect on how these experiences may affect them as a therapist and how they may affect their ability to listen to and respond sensitively to clients. The goal is to help future counselors determine how they handle conflict, how they handle closeness in intimacy, how they experience their own emotions, and how they regulate their feelings when they are activated. Understanding onself in this kind of way begins to lay down a nice foundation for better understanding Of oneself? Of clients? and becoming a better therapist as you realize that you are affected by your own history. Every client will interact with the history and experiences that you have had, which will create a very specific kind of reaction. In many cases, those reactions can be good, but it is not uncommon for them to also be potentially dangerous or negative if they are not properly understood.

It is important to note that later parts of this book may focus more on how the skills that are needed are used as a road map to help clients move toward their why—knowing your why is part of the motivation. For example, as Dr. Silvey and I write this chapter, we are also discussing our "whys." We both believe in the scientist practitioner model, which involves using research to inform practice and practice to inform your research. Notice the term "practice" is also embedded here, and Justin strongly believes part of his why is to make these concepts practical and applicable to counselors so they can use them in their everyday work.

## Ethical and Spiritual Implications of Self-Care

Of course, ethically speaking, counselors have a responsibility to monitor their health so they can operate at the optimal level. Since counseling is a helping profession, we feel that it is best to think about ourselves as a vessel that needs to be filled. We should avoid giving out of our vessel directly, but we should be overflowing into the lives of others out of the excess. The vessel may be filled with some of the specific strategies listed above or tools that you might have in place to be poured into. This reminds us of 1 Corinthians 3:5–8, where the Apostle Paul is warning about the church focusing on religiosity as opposed to their new position in Christ. He begins Chapter 3 addressing how believers need to shift in their spiritual diet, moving from milk to solid food. He then acknowledges Apollos and his work to the readers by saying, "Who then is Paul, and who is Apollos, but ministers through whom you believed, as the Lord gave to each one? I planted, Apollos watered, but God gave the increase. So then neither he who plants is anything, nor he who waters, but God who gives the increase. Now he who plants and he who waters are one, and each one will receive his own reward according to his own labor" (NKJV). We see several truths that emerge from this passage. First, we can understand our place in the work we do. We are responsible to plant and water in the lives of others, but we are not responsible for the outcome—that is God's role. Second, the work that each counselor does separately is still seen as one, so this shows equality and a shared responsibility in the work that we provide. Considering this, the ground is level at the foot of the cross and at the empty tomb, so we should view ourselves in the context of a much larger picture of colaborers. Just as Paul also uses the picture of the body of Christ in 1 Corinthians 12:12–31, we see a unity in diversity—where each member of the body plays a specific role but is still part of the whole body. Furthermore, we are reminded that Christ is the head of the body. This truth should bring us peace, knowing that Christ is the lead, but we have the opportunity to play a role in the work of the body. Finally, we see that we will receive a reward for our labor, so we should know that we do not labor in vain (1 Corinthians 15:58). In summary, we need to know our ethical responsibilities and what the Bible says about our role and work in Christ. A final application of these aspects is to also look at multiculturalism. From this perspective, we see that each individual (both counselor and client) is unique in his or her perspective and approach, so we should attempt to meet individuals where they are while providing insights into where they could be. Within a counseling setting, Dr. Silvey is a believer in the idea of "differentiated counseling." He likes to think about this in the analogy of a toolbox, where counselors in training are "packing their toolbox" with a variety of evidence-based practices that may be used with a wide variety of clients' needs at the appropriate time. If we think about this in terms of construction, a carpenter would pack his toolbox with a variety of tools and he would never use a hammer to drive a screw or a screwdriver to drive a nail. He would use the appropriate tool at the appropriate time to address the presenting need. Likewise, counselors need to begin to think of counseling skills as a variety of tools and be comfortable enough to use a specific tool to address a specific need. The concept here is that the counselor aligns his or her practice to the needs of the client, just as a teacher uses different strategies to meet the wide variety of students' needs and a doctor uses different instruments, keeping the client in the center of the counseling session to address the clients' specific needs. Furthermore, we feel that it is the counselor's responsibility, through activities like continued professional development and additional training, to "pack their toolbox" while keeping their tools in good working order through self-care. Another way of looking at this is how Ivey et al. (2018) discussed a concept called "flexing with intentional competence" that involves predicting how a skill will impact a client's response, and if that prediction is not accurate, then remaining flexible and willing to use a different skill as needed. In summary of this section, counselors have an ethical responsibility to train well and remain sharp, which can take place through reflection, self-awareness, and self-care to meet clients' needs.

## Belief and Hope

Next, let us explore the idea of instilling belief and hope in clients. A prerequisite or a starting point for this journey is belief or hope. We believe there are at least a few "musts" in counseling (this is not a comprehensive list):

1. We must have hope that we can become an expert counselor or a counselor who can make a difference and contribute something of value.

2. We must seek first to understand our clients.

3. We must be aware of our beliefs of clients.

4. We must create an environment where clients can believe in themselves and in the process of counseling.

5. We must believe in the counseling process.

**Figure 2.2.** The Four-Way Street
© Kendall Hunt Publishing Company

To provide a visual for this, let us think of it this way:

We see belief as being a "four-way street—belief from the client to the counselor that the counselor is trustworthy and the skills can work in session, belief from the counselor to the client that the client has the ability and desire to change, belief from the client that the counseling process can work for him or her, and belief from the counselor that the counseling process can work for the client. We will attempt to delve deeper into each of these areas more. The first street that we want to highlight in Figure 2.2 is the client buy-in to the counseling process. One key sign of buy-in could be if a client reached out for counseling services, as opposed to being required to attend counseling (i.e., court ordered). Another aspect of buy-in would be based on the early change that might take place to encourage more buy-in. A solution-focused approach to counseling would call this "pre-therapy change," or, in other words, change that has taken place even since making the call to attend counseling. This early change might encourage a client to remain in counseling, or they could not see the need for counseling based on short-term progress that might have

© DanBun/Shutterstock.com

taken place (see section "Conceptualizing Change Based on Theory" in Chapter 13); however, the support of counseling might prolong the sustainability of change. A second, yet very related, street of buy-in is the client's trust that the counselor will be able to promote or provide an environment for change during counseling. This book is really about the counselor being able to recognize and practice what they can to promote the relationship and, in turn, buy-in from the client, so consider what you will have control over in the counseling journey as you embark further into this text.

It has almost become an axiom in the field of mental health, but, as Carl Rogers emphasized, the counselor or client relationship is the most important Of what?. Clients may not engage in the process without first having a feeling of a trusting, safe, or secure relationship. A third street is based on the counselor trusting the counseling process. We know through empirical research that the counseling process, in both individual and group settings, has been found to be effective. Of course, we may not see change; sometimes we may just be planting or watering a seed in the process, but we must trust the research on various theoretical approaches and/or evidence-based treatments. We feel that through modeling trust, the client will have a greater likelihood of trusting the process and, in turn, the counselor. The fourth, and final, street that we see is the counselor's trust in the client. To explore the concept of counselors' beliefs in clients, Rosenthal and Jacobson (1992) conducted a research study where public elementary teachers were told that certain students were expected to perform well in class based on their results on a fictional standardized assessment. Of course, the teachers did not know that the students were selected at random and had not completed the assessment. The results of the study found that when teachers expected that certain students would perform better and exhibit greater intellectual development, students did, in fact, perform better and exhibit greater intellectual development. Using this as a case in point, the beliefs that we have about clients' ability to change may impact the progress that could be made in counseling. We should ask ourselves at least a few questions in light of this:

1. What do you believe about individuals? It is important to understand what basic tenets you have about individuals. What do you base these basic tenets on? We will discuss this in more detail in the section "How We Perceive Ourselves and Others" later in this chapter.

2. What role does nature and nurture play in the life of a client? It is important to understand whether you look at individuals as more of a product of an environment or more influenced

by genetics. Do you view clients having the ability to overcome their environment and/or genetics or do clients need to just accept who they are more?

3. What role does spirituality play in your beliefs about clients? What does the Bible say about individuals? Are individuals created in the image of God? What role does sin play in the lives of individuals? How does God's son, Jesus, impact the lives of clients? What role does the Holy Spirit play in the lives of client or in the counseling session itself?

4. What role does a growth and/or fixed mindset play in your beliefs about clients? Would you say that we should counsel the ways that we have always counseled because that it has worked, or are there new, undiscovered ways to counsel better?

5. Do all clients have the ability to change? If we do not believe this, perhaps we should think about the "why" of counseling.

6. Are you always the best counselor for every client? If we believe that we are the best counselor for every client, perhaps we should self-reflect on how this might be exhibited in counseling, especially if the client is not making progress.

7. Would you say that there are "right" and "wrong" answers to the questions above? If so, are you doing anything to determine the "right" answers?

For a further detailed discussion on the theory behind change, see Chapter 13's, section entitled "Conceptualizing Change Based on Theory."

Another aspect of belief is also belief in ourselves and our skills as a counselor. Bandura (1997) addressed self-efficacy, which is an individual's belief that he or she is able to perform a specific task (Bandura, 1977, 1986). Bandura also pinpointed four distinct sources of increased confidence in skills. The first is mastery experiences, the idea that having success in an area increases the likelihood of future success in that area. For example, have you ever noticed in sports how success tends to bring more success? This is shown prevalently when a specific team wins consistently and a dynasty begins to form. How does that happen? If we think of a team winning a national championship, it is able to recruit better for the next year. If they continue to build a team that has the best talent and is cohesive, then they may be able to continue to win, which, in turn, allows the team to recruit better. Therefore, we begin to notice the upward trend that continues to add to the success of the team. As we relate this to counseling, Dr. Silvey likes to say it this way: "If you feel more competent in a task then your confidence in performing that task should be higher." Therefore, competence leads to confidence. It is important not only to gauge your strengths and counsel from them but also to recognize your weaknesses and strengthen them through "mastery experiences." Second, Bandura mentions vicarious experiences as a source of building self-efficacy. Using this approach, we should watch others that exhibit a behavior that we would like to model. Dr. Falwell, would often say, "You should always surround yourself with people that are better [at skills] than you are." More specifically, we should approach counseling with a teachable spirit and find others that perform specific counseling skills at the highest level and learn vicariously through them. Third, Bandura mentions verbal persuasion as a way to grow in our self-efficacy. Can you think of a comment (either positive or negative) that a parent or guardian, teacher, site supervisor, or another influential person gave you that made you believe that you could (or could not) do something? Our words have power to build up or tear down self-efficacy! Finally, we need to be mindful of our emotional and physiological states. If you are experiencing acute (or chronic) depression, have not eaten or slept well, are experiencing stress, or going through other situations that can impact your emotional and physiological state, be sure to remain mindful of how those might be influencing your self-efficacy. In summary, we need to know what our beliefs about our clients and ourselves are. Our beliefs should be focused on instilling hope (Yalom & Leszcz, 2005) and seeking to understand, for without that, we have no purpose.

## How We Perceive Ourselves and Others

Along the journey, we need to ensure that we have an appropriate perspective of ourselves, clients, and the journey. First, as Genesis 1:27 (NKJV) states, "So God created man in His own image; in the image of God He created him; male and female He created them." This provides us with a starting point for how we should view ourselves and clients. So, what does it mean to be created in the image of God? We believe that it starts with understanding interrelated parts that work in relationship. Just as God is triune, three in one, it stands to reason that individuals, including ourselves, have three parts—a physical body; an intellectual, emotional, cognitive aspect; and a spiritual component. Those three parts interact. We know that if our physical bodies are neglected, then our intellectual, emotional, cognitive, and spiritual parts can suffer. Likewise, if another area is out of balance, then the other two could be impacted. So, we begin to see ourselves and our clients from a perspective of an intrapersonal relationship. Second, we can begin to see ourselves and clients engaged in horizontal relationships with each other and, most importantly, the vertical relationship with God. Let us unpack the horizontal relationship with each other first. We notice that in counseling relationships that many of the concerns that clients bring to counseling have a social aspect. Either something has been done to the client (this will usually be the way that it will be presented in session), or they have done something to someone else that has caused some conflict. By viewing clients as social beings, then we can begin to help them work through personal aspects that may have an impact on their social settings.

Let us discuss the vertical relationship with God now. First, God, as our creator, already knows the most intimate details of our lives and the lives of our clients. We feel that if He knows what clients need, then we can rest assured in His sovereignty; however, they may not be able to see the work that He is doing or is able to do in their lives. One personal goal may be for clients to see this view clearly; however, ethically, we may be limited in the approach or depth that we will be able to go with helping them see this. Tying this back into the "why," we need to ensure that our "why" is not to proselytize in a counseling setting (unless the setting calls for an evangelical aspect, like lay or pastoral counseling). We believe that counselors can view their clients from a specific perspective (i.e., created in the image of God) but not feel like they must convert their clients to a specific religion. We believe quite the opposite. To practice ethically, we must not impose our own values on a client; however, we do have an ethical responsibility to be able to address spiritual and religious needs of clients. In regard to a client's relationship with God, we should allow God to give the increase while we work in an ethical, legal, multiculturally sensitive manner.

A verse to remember, Matthew 22:37–39: "Love the Lord your God with all your heart and with all your soul and with all your mind. This is the first and greatest commandment. And the second is like it: 'Love your neighbor as yourself.'"

In summary, it seems that the best way to conceptualize ourselves and clients is to view individuals in the context of relationships. More specifically, we are in relationship with ourselves intrapersonally and in relationship with others interpersonally, and God desires to be involved in our intra- and interpersonal relationships. We see God's outline for this in Matthew 22:37–39, when Jesus outlined the two greatest commandments, "Love the Lord your God with all your heart and with all your soul and with all your mind. This is the first and greatest commandment. And the second is like it: 'Love your neighbor as yourself'" (NIV). We see in this passage how God desires us to be in right relationship with Him, in right relationship with others, and in right relationship with ourselves.

As you meditate on how we should view ourselves, you may enjoy reading an excerpt from the poem "To a Louse" from the Plowman poet known as (Robert) "Bobby" Burns:

> "O would some Power the gift to give us
>
> To see ourselves as others see us!
>
> It would from many a blunder free us,
>
> And foolish notion:
>
> What airs in dress and gait would leave us,
>
> And even devotion!"

The poem discusses how it would be a gift to see ourselves as others do, but Dr. Kuhnley's clinical supervisor, Dr. George Jefferson, used to say in response to this poem, "Burns says it would be a gift, but it would not because we would never believe it" (Jefferson, personal communication, 2005). As counselors, we need to have the confidence and teachable spirit to be molded into an effective counselor on our journey through the feedback from site supervisors, interactions with clients, and self-reflection. We also need to challenge our core beliefs about clients in order support them through their journey. When both the counselor and the client are at work, then the process can work to its greatest potential and the trajectory of the journey will be upward.

With these thoughts in mind, let us now look at a case where a counselor started well on the journey and was sidetracked in the process but had a supervisor in place to help the counselor course correct.

## Case Study: Bull in a China Shop (A Case From Gary Sibcy, personal communication, 2018)

A counselor named Bullwinkle walks into his private practice located above the China Shop. Bullwinkle has had much training in influence-based stress reduction mindfulness training (for more on this see the work of Jon Kabat-Zinn, who is a notable expert in the field of mindfulness training). He had attended several of trainings and went to a prestigious Ivy League school to learn how to apply this sequence of mindfulness skills training to a wide variety of problems. He felt that this was an enormously beneficial approach—one that he himself actually benefited from. When he started internship, he decided that teaching his clients how to do mindfulness would be a fabulous way of helping them. The idea, in his mind, rather rigidly applied, was that if this worked for him and for all of these very smart individuals at prestigious university settings, then certainly it would apply to the next person. The problem was that whenever he began to see clients, very quickly he moved past their concerns or why they came to therapy and began trying to entice them into learning how to do mindfulness. Very quickly, he would get them in the office and have them start to work on these skills. The problem he was running into was that a lot of his clients just stopped coming. They would call and cancel or they would just not show up. One particular client came out even more dysregulated than she was when she began therapy. The problem was that she did not feel comfortable practicing mindfulness techniques (e.g., closing eyes, breathing). She became flustered and overwhelmed, and he had no real understanding as to why she could not do these simple tasks. Bullwinkle then became quite frustrated and annoyed with the client, suggesting that she was just being resistant to the treatment. However, the difficulty is that he had no real understanding of this person's history of trauma, especially of her personal trauma by people that she was in the care of. In this case, helping Bullwinkle see what was happening was a crucial piece. Bullwinkle began to question his fit for the counseling profession. Bullwinkle sought consultation with a supervisor to learn from these experiences and realized that he cannot just apply one technique to all clients, assuming that everyone is the same. Through this experience, Bullwinkle learned more about how to listen to clients, understand their stories, understand their reasons for why they are coming to therapy, and have some understanding of their history of relationship experiences.

This is an example of how Bullwinkle began to learn how to conceptualize a case and pay particular attention to one's history of relationships. Bullwinkle became increasingly aware of interpersonal trauma and abuse that may negatively influence his client's ability to build a therapeutic alliance with the therapist, paying particularly careful attention to shared goals and agreed-upon methods for treatment. We also need to realize that clients may simply acquiesce and do or say whatever we ask them to do. As Abraham Maslow once said, "I suppose it is tempting, if the only tool you have is a hammer, to treat everything as if it were a Citation?"

## Self-Evaluation

The final leg of the ongoing journey leads us to personal and professional self-evaluation. This part of the journey should be intertwined throughout the process; however, ensuring that we have a mile marker in place to address this important aspect is vitally important. One part of self-evaluation is to consider that "Now yells louder, but later lasts longer" (Lusko, 2017 p. 18). The "now" that is yelling right now might be for you to rethink why you went into counseling. We are certainly not attempting to talk people out of embarking on the journey, actually quite the opposite; however, we do want counselors in training to understand what their journey might look like in order to self-reflect and self-evaluate the tenacity that it might take to make it through this journey as unscathed as possible.

> **A Verse to Remember:**
> *1 Corinthians 1: 3-5, Praise be to the God and Father of our Lord Jesus Christ, the Father of Compassion, the God of all Comfort, who comforts us in all our troubles, so that we can comfort those in any trouble, with the comfort we ourselves have received from God.*

The "now" that is yelling might be that you feel like you need to be further on the journey than you are. To this "now" we would say, the journey is not about a destination, it is about enjoyment along the way. Also, we must rest assured that God is a patient teacher and may have you where He does to teach. It is important to know where you are so that you can remain humble knowing where you might want to be. It is also important to keep the "imposter syndrome" in mind. The imposter syndrome might cause you to look around in your training and have thoughts like "I am not as good as that counselor," "I am not as smart as that counselor," and/or "I do not belong here. I am an imposter." We must combat these types of thoughts along the journey as we look at the "now" versus the "later." The "now" could also creep into the session with a client. The client might have some of the same thoughts that we combat, but they might be applied to their progress. The "later" is the potential that we see in ourselves and in our clients.

As we think of the journey of becoming, we need to consider the journey that has brought us to the point of counseling. We find that individuals go into the helping profession for several reasons, but the spectrum can range from "I want to help all people" to "I need help myself." We hope that there would be a balance between these two extremes. On one hand, we think we need to believe that all individuals can be helped, but we may not be the best counselor to provide help to all individuals. On the other hand, we think that all counselors have experienced some level of personal trauma and may need some level of personal help in order to be an effective counselor. As Henri Nouwen outlines in his book *The Wounded Healer* we find that counselors practice out of and through their own hurt. Counselors need to understand that we may be able to provide a deeper level of empathy based on our experiences; however, we need to ensure that counseling a client not turn into a personal counseling session. One way to guard against that is to ensure that the skill of self-disclosure is used appropriately—with correct intent or motive.

## Questions to Consider

Do you feel called on this journey of becoming or is this just an opportunity for employment? Write and reflect what inspired this calling.

## QTIP or Openness to Feedback and Direction (Opportunities for Growth in Your Journey)

One important aspect in the journey of becoming is cultivating a teachable spirit. It can be painful to receive negative feedback, but it is necessary for growth. If we take the feedback personally and become defensive, then it can have a negative domino effect. As discussed in Chapter 1, defensiveness is one of the four horsemen of the apocalypse. Chapter 6 provides a full discussion on this topic, where we will discuss more about indicators of defensiveness and how it is not associated with therapeutic adherence. However, it is important to note that taking growth-oriented feedback personally can be detrimental. This is where we are reminded of the "QTIP" principle, which is an acronym for Quit Taking It Personally. Dr. Kuhnley sometimes passes out Q-Tips to her counseling skills students as a reminder of this important truth. Dr. Silvey takes this one step further by recognizing how many relational conflicts that take place are usually based on one (or more) party(s) holding onto an offended (rather than teachable) spirit. Based on this, can you think of a time that you (or another person) might need a whole box of Q-Tips? As we think about job readiness, we often encourage students to indicate their strengths, weaknesses, opportunities, and threats on resumes, and we attempt to help students to prepare for the infamous, "What are your strengths?" and "What are your weaknesses?" questions in an interview. We should go into any counseling relationship, whether it be a counselor/client or counselor/supervisor, with a teachable spirit. We feel that we can learn from all.

## The Role of Supervision and Consultation on the Journey

As we think of our training as blazing the trail and laying the pavement for our journey, we need to also understand that we do not have to forge this path alone. Hopefully, you are able to identify a support team or structure around you, which may consist of family, friends, faculty members, classmates, and one especially important group, supervisors. Later, once you are licensed and confer with another licensed professional, we call it **consultation** rather than supervision. Supervision affords you the opportunity to practice under the tutelage of a seasoned counselor. At face value, this may seem a bit overwhelming because you may be thinking, "They are going to critique me really hard" or "I am not as good as them" or "What if I do not live up to their expectations?" On this note, imagine you are asked to provide supervision for an intern. What qualities would you be looking for in an intern? What do you think you could learn from your intern? Do you feel that you model or exhibit these qualities? If not, in the words of reality or choice theory, what needs to change? Now, recall what is required to become a supervisor of an LPC (licensed professional counselor). For us, this requires completing a master's degree, a comprehensive exam, two years of residency with 4,000 hours of practice, and a minimum of one hour a week of supervision (note: supervision at one hour a week for 50 weeks at a rate of $100.00 per session is a cost of $5,000 per year. For two years, the length of residency, this is a $10,000 value). So, consider the investment of time of three years for a master's degree, two years for a residency and education and supervision. Then, a student asks you to supervise him (or her) under your license that you have worked very hard to obtain and take full responsibility for all of their clinical actions. What would make you most likely to say yes?

What are specific characteristics or habits you would be looking for in a supervisee that would help you to say yes?

How might an intern's teachable spirit or openness to your feedback make it easier to supervise him (or her)?

This reflective process can help serve you to become a better clinician; taking the time to think about what you may be looking for as a supervisor can help you to develop empathy toward your supervisor and can help fuel the process of becoming. If you have not already, please go back and take some time to thoughtfully consider the answers to the above questions and to jot down your thoughts.

## Spiritual Implications for the Journey of Becoming

As we conceptualize the journey, let us also think about spiritual journey. We know the journey, including the spiritual walk, takes time. We heard a joke about this matter. A gentleman was talking with God outside the pearly gates and asked, "God is it true that what is a thousand years to me is only a second to you? God said, "Yes, son." Then the man responded, "Is it also true that you own the cattle on a thousand hills and what is thousands of dollars to me is only a penny to you?" God said, "Yes, son, that is true." The gentleman worked up his courage and asked, "Okay, since a thousand dollars to me is only a penny to you, God, can I have a penny?" God responded, "Just a second." Through this joke, I think we can see that God might have a different perspective than us. We think in terms of time and space, but God may view time and space differently than us, as He is not bound by time or space. May we be able to operate from a Godly viewpoint and enjoy the process or journey more—instead of thinking about the journey as limiting, may we find the journey as freedom and an opportunity to learn and grow more. We think that many students focus on the end result (e.g., a grade, a degree), instead of focusing on the process, the journey. The comfort of the journey is that we can know that God both guards and guides us. Psalm 139:5 (NIV) reminds us, "You hem me in behind and before and you lay your hand upon me." Another translation, the New Living Translation (NLT), says, "You go before me and follow me. You place your hand of blessing on my head."

## *A Concept to Contemplate*

© Shutterstock.com

In light of the journey of becoming, let us contemplate this poem:

## Thinking

By Walter D. Wintle

If you think you are beaten, you are;
If you think you dare not, you don't.
If you'd like to win, but think you can't
It's almost a cinch you won't.
If you think you'll lose, you've lost,
For out in the world we find
Success being with a fellow's will;
It's all in the state of mind.

If you think you're outclassed, you are;
You've got to think high to rise.
You've got to be sure of yourself before
You can ever win a prize.
Life's battles don't always go
To the stronger or faster man,
But soon or late the man who wins
Is the one who thinks he can.

Does this poem summarize how you might feel? Does it help you change the way you might view adversity? As you start reading through this book, may you believe that you can!

## Recommended Reading

In order to further develop your expertise in the areas discussed in this chapter, we recommend the following resources:

© Shutterstock.com

- Gladding, S. T. (2009). *Becoming a counselor: The light, the bright, and the serious* (2nd ed.). Alexandria, VA: American Counseling Association.

- Lusko, L. (2017). *Swipe right: The life-and-death power of sex and romance*. Nashville, TN: W Publishing, an imprint of Thomas Nelson.

- Sinek, S. (2009). *Simon Sinek: How great leaders inspire action* [Video file]. Retrieved from https://www.ted.com/talks/simon_sinek_how_great_leaders_inspire_action.

- Wintle, W. (1927). Thinking In. J. G. Lawson (Ed.), *The world's best-loved poems.* New York, NY: Harper & Brothers.

## Chapter Summary

During this chapter, we have discussed the importance of starting with "why" to provide us with direction on this journey to become the most effective counselor. Through methods such as past self-reflection, as shown in the attachment illumination, one can begin to find the answer to his or her why. We also discussed the importance of self-care during your journey as we know that we can grow weary and tire on the journey. We then focused on challenging our beliefs about clients and the counseling process and client's beliefs about the counselor and the counseling process. When these important factors work in unison, counseling can work as it was intended and not feel like a struggle. Next, we discussed the importance of evaluation, more specifically self-evaluation, and the role of the supervisor in evaluation. These aspects can serve as a type of compass on the journey, providing clear, objective direction to our training if we are open to feedback. Finally, we discussed briefly, different spiritual implications of the journey. We need to rest in the fact that God has a specific, distinct calling for us and a journey that He has prepared for us and prepared us for. Dr. Kuhnley mentioned this idea during the journey of writing this chapter: "'What feels like the end of the world, is often only the beginning,' said the butterfly to the caterpillar." May this chapter serve as a new beginning as you embark on your journey!

## Chapter Three

# Intentional and Advanced Empathy

*Real empathy is sometimes not insisting that it will be okay, but acknowledging that it is not.*

—Sheryl Sandberg (as cited in Lee, 2015)

**"**

BEFORE YOU CRITICIZE A MAN, WALK A MILE IN HIS SHOES.

© Orange Vectors/Shutterstock.com

## Chapter Learning Objectives

1. To explore counselor characteristics and behaviors that influence the counseling process, such as empathy and advanced empathy (CACREP II.F.5.f, 2016, p. 12)
2. To identify skills and strategies for empathic communication (CACREP II.F.5.g, 2016, p. 12)
3. To explore research related to development of becoming an empathic counselor (CACREP II.F.8.a, 2016, p. 13)
4. To learn essential interviewing, counseling, and case conceptualization skills (CACREP II.F.5.e, 2016, p. 11)

# Chapter Overview

Sometimes, one helpful way to understand a skill is to first understand what it is not. Do not be deceived; empathy is not just reflecting feelings, and it is distinctly different from sympathy. Empathy is a foundational skill that can be understood as the base of the skills pyramid. It is important for counselor trainees to begin learning about and applying empathy in their day-to-day interactions. In this chapter, we take a look at some sample reflections of feeling that may be infused with empathy and juxtapose those with dialogues that do not demonstrate empathy well and unpack the differences. Here we will explore the different types of empathy, both cognitive and affective. We will also unpack current research on strategies for increasing empathy.

## Defining Empathy

Let us start by looking at what empathy is not. What is the opposite of empathy? Empathy is not sympathy, and it is also not schadenfreude, a noun that means the derivation of pleasure from another person's experience of pain. One popular example is when you are cheering for your team, and the other team's star player is injured and taken out of the game I don't see this comic. As many of our clients may be encountering schadenfreude, it is important to ensure that when they come to therapy, they experience the empathic presence of the counselor. Let us look at some of the definitions of empathy encountered in the literature.

Empathy can be understood as a process, not just an outcome. Carl Rogers described empathy as experiencing the client rather than just identifying with him or her (Teich, 1992). Decety and Moriguchi (2007) explained empathy as "the capacity to share and understand emotional states of others in reference to oneself" (p. 22). Zahavi (2008) defined the concept as "a basic, irreducible, form of intentionality that is directed toward the experiences of others" (p. 517).

As you can see, although a significant amount of literature exists on empathy in the realm of counseling, understanding the concept may be confusing because of the lack of consensus regarding a definition (Cuff, Brown, Taylor, & Howat, 2014). Berkhout and Malouff (2016) attributed this disagreement to questions regarding empathy as a cognitive or affective process.

Cognitive empathy has been defined as the ability of an individual to understand the mental state or emotions of another. Cognitive empathy may also be understood as what researchers call

**theory of mind**, which is the ability to express the mental constructs of another, such as thoughts, desires, and beliefs, leading also to the prediction of behavior.

**Affective empathy** is more than just understanding or identifying the emotions of others, but actually experiencing what those emotions are like for, in this case, the client (Blair, 2005; Premack & Woodruff, 1978; Singer & Lamm, 2009).

However, despite the definitional disagreement mentioned earlier, research points to many widely recognized benefits of empathy in the counseling room, which make empathy extensively regarded as integral to psychotherapy (Feller & Cottone, 2003). These benefits include, but are not limited to, the following:

- Increased trust,

- likelihood of positive treatment outcomes, and

- compliance and client involvement in the treatment process (Barrett-Lennard, 2003; Bohart, Elliot, Greenberg, & Watson, 2002; Moyers & Miller, 2013).

Dr. James Coan and Dr. John Gottman co-authored a chapter in the *Handbook of Emotion Elicitation and Assessment* called **"The Specific Affect Coding System" (SPAFF)**, and they discussed the SPAFF, a coding system for affect that Gottman has used in his research, which has predicted marital success and failure. Empathy is one aspect of affect they measure as a latent variable. Here is what they say about empathy:

*"Empathy.* Empathizing individuals mirror the affect of their partners. Such mirroring need not be verbal, but, however, it is expressed, and it should be obvious that the intent of the mirroring is to express an understanding of the partner's feelings. Importantly, empathy does more than simply validate the partner's thoughts and feelings—by mirroring the affect of the partner simultaneously, it conveys a level of care that surpasses validation, per se." (Coan & Gottman, 2007, p. 272)

© Shutterstock.com

## A Concept to Contemplate

We are conducting research on empathy-building exercises and the effectiveness of short-term empathy building workshops. One of the questions that has come up in our discussions is, "Would you say empathy is a characteristic or a set of skills?" If empathy is defined as a characteristic, can a person still be considered an "empathic person" if they do not exhibit behaviors, or in the case of counseling, counseling skills that manifest their empathy to others?

For the purposes of this text we define empathy not only as a capacity to exhibit care for another person via the effort to seek to understand his or her experience and feelings about an experience, but we go one step further and believe that clinical empathy is also characterized by being helpful to the client in a manner that facilitates the development of agreed-upon goals and agreed-upon means of accomplishing those goals. A key concept is the idea that: *As the title of this text suggests, there is both science and art to empathic connection with clients, and clinical empathy is effective when a caring concerted effort to seek to understand the client and confirmation from the client that they feel understood is combined with the collaborative establishment of goals and agreed-upon helpful methods for accomplishing those goals.*

## A Special Set of Communication Ingredients

In Chapter 13, we will talk about the metaphor of the good chef. The good chef considers many factors about what makes for a good recipe, and here we will talk about some that mix well together to form empathy and other communication skills that are needed when dealing with clients who are angry (or what some therapists may conceptualize as resistant) and struggling with progressing in therapy for different reasons. What we find is that therapists can be great at empathizing with people's concerns, anger, frustration, sadness, depression, or anxiety when they work with people in other situations. However, when their

© fiydragon/Shutterstock.com

concerns are directed toward the therapist, then sometimes our ability to effectively use empathy may decrease a good deal. We all have probably experienced some of that. These are the three skills that we try to use in combination, referred to by the acronym EAR.

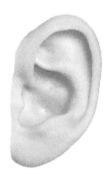

# EAR

Empathy    Assertiveness    Respect

**Figure 3.1.** Three components of EAR recipe.

© schankz/Shutterstock.com

Figure 3.1 shows three components of the EAR recipe: empathy, assertivenss, and respect. We will explore each one individually.

The first skill is **empathy**, which is technically designed within the model primarily developed by Dr. David Burns. Dr. Burns is a cognitive therapist who also developed the cognitive interpersonal therapy model. Burns, in his research on the treatment of depression, introduces his work by emphasizing the literature on the importance of the therapeutic relationship and the importance of empathy; he says, "Orlinsky and Howard (1986) reported that in approximately half of 86 findings drawn from 40 studies, therapeutic empathy was significantly correlated with therapeutic outcome (see also Luborsky et al., 1986)." This is good evidence to support the importance of empathy in therapeutic outcomes! Burns also concluded in his study that depressed patients at his clinic who were treated by therapists who were the warmest and most empathic (empathy was measured by the Empathy Scale developed by Persons and Burns [1985]) improved more (had a greater reduction in Beck Depression Inventory [BDI] scores) than those who were treated by therapists who had lower ratings of empathy (Burns & Nolen-Hoeksema, 1992).

The E in EAR, empathy, is defined in this model is *expressing or acknowledging the other person's feelings and why he or she feels that way.* You notice the emphasis here is to actually acknowledge the emotions and faults or the reasons behind those emotions. Sometimes this is an iterative process during which the therapist is trying to help clients label what it is that they feel (reflect feelings, see Chapter 9 for more on this) and identify what they think by paraphrasing or reflecting content (see Chapter 7 for more on this). You may be wrong, but the client will let you know if you are and then you may work to ensure you are in alignment with them. We will look more closely at those skills in a moment.

The second set of skills, which are more advanced have to do with being assertive. With **therapist assertiveness**, a therapist needs to be able to *acknowledge various dynamics, most of the time acknowledging his or her own feelings or his or her own concerns regarding the client or client–therapist interaction. In some cases, this includes being able to identify limitations themselves—what things you can do and things you cannot do (sometimes this may mean making a referral where appropriate).* We will take a closer look at how assertiveness needs to be applied in a very disciplined way. What might be appropriate assertiveness with your spouse may not be the same kind of assertiveness that you would use in a therapy relationship. As we see, assertiveness can also reflect feelings that you have about yourself. For example, if you feel like you messed up—you let a client down—for you to be able to express, "Gosh, I feel really badly that I've done this," is crucial to the service. However, note that any self-disclosure should always be in the best interest of the client. Although this is an important part of the EAR equation, we typically do not encourage a lot of self-disclosure early in counseling because beginning therapists tend to be used to social conversation that is reciprocal and includes both parties disclosing, while therapeutic dialogue does not, and thus sometimes the beginning therapist is likely to move into oversharing when practicing self-disclosure. The application of EAR demonstrates how applied empathy can be beneficial.

The third set of skills is regulation and respect. The "*dos*" of being respectful, of course, include *being kind, being considerate, and really giving up our tendency to be defensive.* When someone attacks us, one of the things we want to do is to defend ourselves and the reasons behind what we do. Unfortunately, as we will see, those instances almost always backfire, so try not to get defensive or engage in blaming. Learning how to inhibit some of the feelings you experience when people do criticize you is actually very important. These are the skills that you should continue to work on. Importantly, respect also means that you are conveying, not implicitly but explicitly, that you value the relationship that you have with the client. In addition, respect also involves the idea that it is important to you and you want to work on improving that relationship and be able to help them.

Those are the basics of those skills in a 30,000-foot fly-by. We just want to highlight a little more about the skills involved in empathy, so we want to go back to the top. One of the most important skills is inquiry. **Inquiry** is asking a person for more clarification. Sometimes you can tell a person is upset, but you do not really know why. So asking them, "What is happening?

What is your concern? You do not look like you are very happy," or "Something looks like it is bothering you. Help me understand that," is part of inquiry in order to get better understanding.

The next piece is thought empathy vs. emotion empathy. Emotion empathy is having an idea of what a person is feeling and uses feeling words such as *angry, frustrated, annoyed, perturbed, sad, anxious,* or *worried.* Thought empathy is being able to link reasons to those feelings. Therefore, if you are frustrated because I spend too much time talking about why things happen rather than exploring them with you, I would want to naturally put the feelings and the reasons behind them together. This helps people better understand what they are thinking and feeling, but it also validates to them that you understand and can see it from their perspective.

Finally, the most advanced skill that comes with Thought empathy or emotion empathy? Or empathy in general? is disarming a person. This is really tough because it requires the counselor to use humility. This is difficult because when somebody is criticizing you, as we said, you want to defend yourself; which is a trap that will oftentimes get you in trouble. What we teach folks is that even when somebody is criticizing you and they are completely inaccurate and it just does not reflect the way that you feel or what you are actually doing, it is important for you to see whatever grain of truth is in what they are saying and acknowledge that. Instead of looking at what is not true and then focusing on that, it can be very important to be able to acknowledge this grain of truth. Also, acknowledging how at times you can, in fact, give people the wrong impression, may assist you in accomplishing disarming by, for instance, stating: "Gosh, I had no idea I was affecting you this way and it wasn't what I was intending to do but apparently I've been sending those kinds of signals." Notice that you help a person see that you can do things that you do not want to and it can have an effect, so you appreciate the fact that they are drawing attention to it.

Those are the basics, and we are going to take a few seconds to do some roleplays here and see how These what? work together.

## The Case of Grace, an Example of EAR in Action

**Counselor:** One thing I noticed that you noted on your scale of satisfaction is that when it came to me understanding your feelings, you gave me a 4 instead of a 5, but my concern is that means that I missed about 20% of what you were saying.

**Client:** So I gave you a four when you wanted a five and you want to understand what happened?

**Counselor:** Well, it is not so much that you gave me a 4 instead of a 5, but the idea that represents I missed something that may have been important to you. My hope is that after a session, you would think I have a pretty good sense of where you're coming from.

**Client:** Well, I felt like you were rushing toward the end of our sessions to get out so I started to shut down. However, I felt like we were starting to really dive into my story toward the end of our sessions but that is around the same time I felt you starting to check out. I started to feel cut off or rushed. Like I was just another client and not important to you.

**Counselor:** When you start getting to the end of a session, you're kind of really opening up and sort of getting to important material, and then we have to wrap it up and I'm coming across as if I'm ready to wrap it up and move on.

**Client:** Yeah, it seems like you're understanding and you're interested, and then there's a shift and you're ready to go.

**Counselor:** Okay. And that's frustrating for you. **(empathy, expressing/acknowledging feelings)**

**Client:** Yeah. I see you look at your watch or look at the clock that is located over my head. You look uncomfortable and ready to head for the door. I don't want to hold you back. . .but we also just got into something. . .

**Counselor:** This is important. I had no idea I was having that effect on you. One thing that may be useful for us is to talk about what a transition should look like. **(assertiveness)**

**Client:** Yeah, this is a bright spot in my week. I think I'm just upset that it has to come to an end.

**Counselor:** Well, there are some good things about that. It seems therapy is something that you enjoy; you're motivated. Other clients are sometimes ready for therapy to end and not as motivated. You're on the other end of the spectrum, and that's good. **(respect)**

**Client:** You know how I feel. I know it's not you—our time has to come to an end. I just really value our time together.

In this session excerpt, the counselor utilizes the EAR model to aptly address the client's feelings and experience. The counselor empathizes with the client by reflecting feeling ("and that's frustrating for you"), letting the client know she is understood and affirming her feelings. In his next statement, the counselor conveys assertiveness by acknowledging his own thoughts to the client. Respect is maintained throughout the interaction; specifically, at the end of the session, the counselor provides direct encouragement and reassurance (you're motivated). The client disclosed after this session that she felt very understood by the counselor, Dr. Sibcy, and that he had connected with her in a way that no one had in the past; she reported this further increased her tendency to feel safe with him.

In the video link included here Dr. Gary Sibcy is working with his client Kristen. She is feeling a bit misunderstood because they have not explored a recent interaction she had with her brother. Dr. Sibcy introcues the concept of EAR here and utilizes it with his client. To watch this video, please visit the Kendall Hunt companion website to your text, or if you are reading the ePublication, click on the link below.

**Video**

**Dr. Sibcy conducting an EAR session with Kristen**

Go to www.grtep.com to view this video.

Here Dr. Sibcy debriefs some of what happened in the demonstration including secure base/safe haven concepts.

**Understanding empathy.** Empathy is the umbrella skill we have been talking about throughout this chapter. All the skills discussed in this text should be used in a context of empathy. As one of my clinical supervisors, Dr. George Jefferson, taught me many years ago, one of our guiding principles in counseling is "seeking to understand." This is also a principle originally attributed to St. Francis of Assisi. This often requires giving up our right to be understood and seeking to understand what it is like for our clients to journey through the struggles they face. As we walk alongside them and help them narrate their story, we approach an understanding of their experience. However,

© Shutterstock.com

we do not fully arrive at understanding their experience because we can never fully experience their world as they do. In empathy, there is a certain degree of epistemic humility. Our colleague, Dr. Hawkins, who founded the counseling program at our institution, has often emphasized the value of epistemic humility.

Empathy → Connection          Sympathy → Disconnection

Empathy has been a topic that has been popularized by storyteller, social worker, and shame researcher Dr. Brené Brown. She created an animation to illustrate empathy. Dr. Brown distinguishes between empathy and sympathy in her presentation. She starts out by illustrating the concept of empathy in one circle and the concept of sympathy in another. She indicates that empathy "fuels connection," whereas sympathy "drives disconnection" Brown, B. (2010). The power of vulnerability.

*A Concept to Contemplate*

© Shutterstock.com

Consider the above distinction between empathy and sympathy. Breneé Brown associated empathy with connection and sympathy with disconnection. Take a moment to contemplate this concept.

Do you remember the last time someone expressed empathy toward you? Recap the situation.

*Empathy is feeling with people (Brown, 2013).*

Recall the last time someone expressed sympathy toward you (e.g., I am sorry for your loss, I am sorry you feel sick, etc.). How was this different from your experience of empathy?

How did the expression of empathy or sympathy impact your perceived level of connection to the person expressing empathy or sympathy?

Brené Brown goes on to cite nursing scholar Theresa Wiseman, who studies professions where empathy is needed and determined four qualities that are important in empathy: (a) perspective taking, (b) staying out of judgment, (c) recognizing emotion in others, and (d) communicating that recognition of emotion.

She describes a short definition that we like as follows: "Empathy is feeling with people" (Brown,

© UntimelyNinja/Shutterstock.com

2013). She describes empathy as representing someone being in a deep hole that is dark where the individual says things like, "I am stuck; it is dark; I'm overwhelmed."

*Empathy is feeling with people (Brown, 2013).*

Empathizing with someone who is stuck in this dark place is represented by making a bid for connection (as some attachment researchers call it; Clinton & Sibcy, 2006) by climbing down and saying, "Hey, I know what it is like down here and you are not alone."

Sympathy is represented in the cartoon by the character that looks down into the hole and says, "Ew, it is bad, uh huh. . ."

Brown indicates that empathy requires connecting with the feeling in oneself and makes a great point that empathic responses typically do not begin with "at least" However, the highlight of the video illustration is the ending that indicates, "Rarely can a response make something better; it is connection that makes something better."

I was having a discussion with a colleague of mine who served as a counselor and educator for many years, Dr. Amanda Rockinson-Szapkiw. We were asking the question, "What makes a master therapist? What characteristics do the greats have in common?" The theme we kept returning to in this

© abeadev/Shutterstock.com

qualitative discussion was the theme of "presence": the idea of "being with." This could also be described as mindful empathy, or when we are fully present with a client and in a state of empathic connection.

Recall, the skill of advanced empathy involves attunement to another person's emotion such that one may identify and reflect back a client's emotion before the client himself or herself is aware of exactly what he or she is feeling.

## Attachment Illumination: Attachment and Empathy

© Denna Jiang/Shutterstock.com

Recall that at the beginning of this chapter, we discussed empathy as the foundation of the pyramid that all other skills are built upon. Advanced empathy goes one step further and involves a clinician identifying a feeling before a client identifies that feeling in themselves. It requires skills discussed in Chapter 1 related to mentalization, metacognition, and mindsight. Metacognitive monitoring is a practice and characteristic associated with a secure autonomous attachment style.

The feeling wheel provides examples of feeling words and insight into words that can be linked to core feelings. Note that men are socialized not to express sadness, whereas women are socialized not to express anger. So, if we look at the outer circles of the feeling wheel, we hear feelings like tired, exhausted, sleepy, and other similar feelings, which may be associated with sadness (as a core feeling). Sadness could also be associated with (based on the AAI) unresolved loss (or even valuing). In the case of unresolved loss, a client may go back to the person being there, similar to when a person loses their keys. When someone says they lost their keys, what do you say? "Where is the last place you had them? Go back to that place." It is as if the person who lost a loved one is mentally returning to the time when the lost person was still living and preserving that in their mind so that they do not instead go to the feelings of sadness, the perception of loss, and the action potential of having a shutdown in energy, motivation, pleasure, and exploration. Advanced empathy may arise from a conspiracy of factors, being able to place an experience and understanding a client in a way that helps them to feel "held" and helps them gain insight into their experience.

Skills such as mindsight and metacognitive monitoring allow a clinician to be more present and to help a client make sense of his or her story. In order to be present, one must not be preoccupied. Thus, if a clinician is able to engage in metacognitive monitoring, this suggests they have the capacity to be present in moment and monitor his or her own thoughts and feelings in session. This capacity may in turn allow them to free the cognitive space necessary to be mindful of their clients' intellectual and emotional experiences and practice advanced empathy.

## Communicating Empathy via the Skills

Empathy can be communicated via skills, word usage, attitude, and demeanor. Approaching clients with an attitude of what Carol Rogers (1961) would describe as unconditional positive regard or nonpossessive love, is essential. From a Christian perspective, we could describe it as interacting with clients with the belief that they are made in the image of God and should be treated as such. This may seem intangible, but there are behavioral manifestations of this attitude and belief. It may be communicated by different skills such as:

- Tone of voice

- Warm smile

- Handshake or appropriate greeting

- Open-ended questions

- Minimal encouragers

- Validation of thoughts

- Validation of feelings

- Congruent nonverbal presence

In terms of tone of voice, our colleague Dr. Silvey reminds us of the scripture, "A gentle answer turns away wrath, but a harsh word stirs up anger." Proverbs 15:1 NIV So, it is important to remember that it is not always which skill that we use, but how we use it. If we reflect, but our tone of voice communicates harshness, then this could be incongruent. As you read about the skills in Chapter 10, notice the importance of congruence in nonverbal communication and keep in mind that each of the skills we explore in this book should be practiced with an empathic presence.

## Recommended Reading

As the chapter suggests, empathy is an umbrella skill, meaning that all other counseling skills should be practiced with an empathic presence. Therefore, it is important that counselors in training continue to learn about, practice, and implement the skill of empathy. This recommended reading list is a good place to start, and we have included more recommended readings in this chapter than most others due to the critical nature of empathy in counseling:

Barrett-Lennard, G. T. (2003). *Steps on a mindful journey: Person-centered expressions.* Ross-on-Wye, United Kingdom: PCCS Books.

1. Barrett-Lennard (2003) provides mindful reflection, as the title suggests, on lessons learned throughout his experience as a counselor, including information on the therapeutic alliance, theory, and various other areas of counseling. Most in line with the content of this chapter, Barrett-Lennard explores in Chapter 4 the concept of empathy, detailing the importance of not only hearing the words a client speaks but also receiving those words and experiencing what it is the client is feeling. Barrett-Lennard states, "Genuine, communicated empathic understanding is like oxygen to the living self within" (p. 2).

Blair, R. J. R. (2005). Responding to the emotions of others: Dissociating forms of empathy through the study of typical and psychiatric populations. *Consciousness and Cognition, 14*(4), 698–718.

2. In this article, Blair (2005) summarizes the literature, making a case for the importance of understanding various aspects of empathy, including cognitive empathy, as described in this chapter, along with motor and emotional empathy. Moreover, the author also explores autism and psychopathy, two disorders oftentimes associated with decreased levels of empathy, detailing the specific types of empathy typically lacking in individuals with these diagnoses.

Cuff, B. M., Brown, S. J., Taylor, L., & Howat, D. J. (2014). Empathy: A review of the concept. *Emotion Review, 8*(2), 144–153.

3. Recognizing the confusion and lack of consensus regarding the definition of empathy from the onset, Cuff, Brown, Taylor, and Howat (2014) afford the reading a deeper understanding of multiple definitions of the term and identification eight themes surrounding empathy, such as "cognitive or affective," "congruent or incongruent," and "trait or state influence" (p. 144). As such a wealth of literature exists on empathy, this article may assist counseling students in understanding the term from numerous points of view.

Decety, J., & Moriguchi, Y. (2007). The empathic brain and its dysfunction in psychiatric populations: Implications for intervention across different clinical conditions. *Biopsychosocial Medicine, 1*(22). doi:10.1186/1751-0759-1-22

4. Decety and Moriguchi (2007) explore empathy in terms of various psychological disorders. Disorders addressed include antisocial personality disorders, psychopathy, narcissistic personality disorder, borderline personality disorder, and autism spectrum disorders, among others. Helpful charts and graphics assist readers in comprehending the cognitive processes involved in relaying empathy, as well as neurological aspects of the concept.

Feller, C. P., & Cottone, R. R. (2003). The importance of empathy in the therapeutic alliance. *Journal of Humanistic Counseling, Education and Development, 42*, 53–61.

5. In entry-level graduate counseling skills courses, emphasis is oftentimes placed on creating rapport with the client or strengthening the therapeutic alliance. Feller and Cottone (2003) explain empathy as skill necessary for such and synthesize past as well as current literature on this idea. The authors also provide insight on how empathy may be used with specific counseling theories, information that may prove helpful as further insight is gained on the theory you most closely align with.

Moyers, T. B., & Miller, W. R. (2013). Is low therapist empathy toxic? *Psychology of Addictive Behaviors, 27*, 878–884. doi:10.1037/a0030274

6. Moyers and Miller (2013) shed light on the difference in effectiveness between therapists, noting the importance of maintaining a high level of empathy with the client. This article prompts further consideration of the benefits of fostering empathy in therapists, along with the costs of low levels of empathy. Specific skills, as mentioned in this chapter, are also expounded upon, such as reflective listening and accurate empathy.

Teding van Berkhout, E., & Malouff, J. M. (2015). The efficacy of empathy training: A meta-analysis of randomized controlled trials. *Journal of Counseling Psychology, 63*(1), 32.

7. Building upon research that suggests the necessity of empathy in counselors, Teding van Berkhout and Malouff (2015) evaluate the effectiveness of empathy training programs. Authors determined that these training programs are successful overall in increasing empathy levels; training implemented in this study included cognitive and behavioral

interventions. This article may provide counseling trainees with a foundation for improving their own empathy skills.

Teich, N. (1992). Backgrounds: Origins, locations, and multiple definitions of empathy. In N. Teich (Ed.), *Rogerian perspectives: Collaborative rhetoric for oral and written communication* (pp. 241–247). Norwood, NJ: Ablex.

Carl Rogers, the founder of person-centered therapy, first introduced many of the vital counseling skills we still use as groundwork today. Teich (1992) provides an in-depth exploration of Rogers's ideas and writings, forming a comprehensive analysis of Rogers's impact on communication and teaching. Specifically, in Chapter 17, students may find helpful Teich's well-organized chapter on empathy, which encompasses information on the definition, varying models of empathy, and the relationship between empathy and language. Delivering information on empathy from the unique vantage point of rhetoric, this book may provide counselor trainees a broader understanding of true empathic language.

Zahavi, D. (2008). Simulation, projection and empathy. *Consciousness and Cognition, 17*, 514–522. doi:10.1016/j.concog.2008.03.010

After providing background on simulation in utilizing empathy, Zahavi (2008) explains his argument for an understanding of empathy beyond the popularized simulation-plus-projection method. Criticism of several theories of empathy is provided, along with discussion on the importance of viewing empathy as more than "some mysterious form of telepathy" (p. 522). Readers are also urged to contemplate empathy in a broader context, cognizant of social and cultural factors.

## Chapter Summary

Heavily researched, a necessity for building the therapeutic alliance, and imperative for therapeutic success, empathy is a concept central to counseling. Although understanding and displaying empathy may seem confusing or daunting to a counselor in training, through exploring various definitions, aspects, and practical means of implementation, this chapter sought to deepen student understanding of empathy. Chapter 3 explored the basics of empathy, the differences between cognitive and affective empathy, and practical means of employing empathy with clients, such as through the EAR model. Research points to empathy as a construct that may be increased through training; Students may continue to improve their own empathy skills in many ways, such as participation in empathy trainings and further reading on the matter.

PART TWO

Demonstrating Evidence of
Listening with Core Skills:
Seeking to Understand

I n Part Two of this text, we will explore the process of developing habits and skills that can be used to facilitate effective counseling. We introduce one skill or subset of skills at a time, provide practice guidelines, and then add on the next skill. Thankfully, research supports that these skills can be learned over time with practice (Knight, 2009). We have divided the skills into two categories: basic and advanced. Nonverbal, attending skills, paraphrasing, reflection of content, and reflection of feelings fall in category one. Reflection of meaning, challenging while supporting, and goal setting, among others, fall in category two. This is in keeping with other texts and approaches to teaching counseling communication skills such as Egan (1975, 1994) and Smaby and Maddux (2010). We also discuss each individual skill; this is not unlike Allen Ivey and Mary Bradford Ivey's approach to microskills. We also often draw upon tenants of attachment theory to inform conceptualizations.

Following each chapter summary will be a to-do list which contain skills or sample strategies for practicing skills in future pseudo-counseling sessions (or practice counseling sessions). Note, it is important to take time to practice and master each skill and then progress to the subsequent skill. Some research on skills training conducted (Kuntze, van der Molen, & Born, 2009, has revealed that "The microcounseling method is very effective on the level of separate microskills. However, students perform better on the basic skills than on the advanced skills. More training seems to be needed in the latter to achieve the same level of mastery" (p. 175). Thus, it requires much practice to master the basic skills, and we recommend developing them until they become second nature, but it may be helpful to spend even more time developing the advanced counseling skills.

As summarized in the graphic below, we start with a foundation that relates to the counselor's attitude and approach to counseling, including multicultural competencies and ethical practices. This should serve as the basis for everything within the counseling relationship. Next, we must begin to conceptualize and apply skills, which we see in steps two and three. Beginning this stage with identification of counseling terminology and moving toward application is the most important aspect of counselor training. Step four, which is more advanced but adds a layer of depth to the counseling relationship, includes attending to the needs of the client and assisting the client in making sense of his or her story. This is a stage where counselors who have not conceptualized their own background may begin to make the session more counselor centered, as opposed to remaining client centered. Counselors may begin to use self-disclosure incorrectly and need to ensure that the skills are applied correctly. The fifth stage is based on case conceptualization and goal setting (see more in Chapter 13). Many counselors could become "stuck" in the first four steps of this comprehensive model of counseling and fail to conceptualize the case fully or help the client set goals for future sessions or work outside of counseling. The last stage is based on even future counseling training and an even higher level of counseling work. As you think about these stages, we would recommend that you gauge the stage that you might be on in your training, consider the next stage in progression, and consider how to work toward the highest levels while not neglecting stages that you feel competent in or that have proven to work well in sessions.

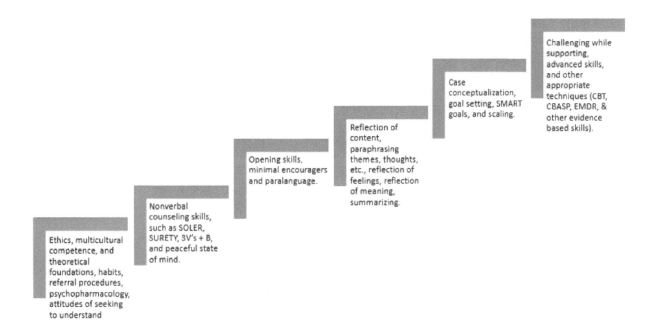

In the peer-reviewed literature on clinical counseling skills, some of the key skills have been identified; let us look at what some of those are. Clinical mental health counselors and other helping professionals are said to use seven basic counseling skills include seven basic counseling skills (Kuntze et al., 2009; Lang, Molen, Van der Molen, Trowere, & Look, 1990). The skills below (the skills below are not in brown text) are the ones focused on in this text.

1. **Minimal encouragers:** Short spoken utterances that encourage the client to continue disclosing and communicate to the client that the counselor has heard them

2. **Questions:** Probes that are designed to facilitate the client articulating their struggles into words, which have been further subdivided into open and closed categories.

3. **Paraphrasing of content** (sometimes referred to as reflection of content): Restating the essence of a client's narrative in the counselor's own words

4. **Reflection of feeling:** Paying attention to feeling words or indicators of feelings and validating these feelings and naming or labeling emotions as they arise

5. **Concreteness:** A skill composed of the other skills mentioned, and all the previously mentioned skills serve the development of this skill and facilitate accuracy in client responses as struggles are articulated

6. **Summarizing:** A skill that the counselor uses in facilitating structure to the sequencing of the client's story

7. **Situation clarification:** The capacity of the counselor to identify and discuss any items in the client's story that are unclear or ambiguous or other items that are unclear or ambiguous within the therapeutic alliance

The subsequent five advanced skills that have been discussed have included:

1. **Advanced accurate empathy:** The counselor provides an interpretation of the client's story that involves a reframing or alternate perspective that is adaptive

2. **Confrontation** (which we prefer to call "**challenging while supporting**"—more on this in Chapter 12): This has been described as the counselor providing a viewpoint on a client's struggle or experience that differs significantly from the client's perspective.

3. **Positive relabeling** (similar to the skill we call **reframing**, or **paraphrasing content**): It involves providing an alternate more adaptive perspective on a client's presenting problem.

4. **"Examples of one's own"** (Kuntze, van der Molen, & Bron, 2009, p. 177): It involves therapists disclosing their own experiences that are relevant to therapy and is similar to the skill we typically refer to as self-disclosure (components of an advanced skill referenced in Cognitive Behavioral Analysis Systems of Psychotherapy (CBASP) disciplined interpersonal involvement—see Chapter 9). Note, due to the tendency of counselor trainees to be tempted to overdisclose, this skills is not emphasized in this text.

5. **Directness:** The advanced skill of directness is described as involving discussion about the experiential events of the present. We often refer to this skill as immediacy (see Chapter 12 for more on **immediacy**).

We draw on the work of previous counselor educators and authors in the field of mental health such as Ivey and Ivey, Egan, Gladding, and Yalom. We also build on the work of counseling researchers that emphasize evidence-based practices and case conceptualization to discuss the following seven basic skills and five advanced skills, which fall in the **sweet spot** of the Venn diagram, capturing both the art and the science of empathic counseling.

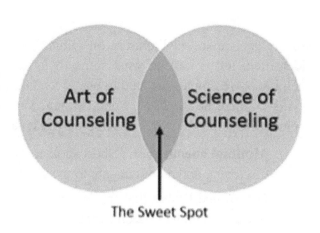

The Sweet Spot

Basic skills that are the focus of this text include:

1. Informed disclosure of limits of confidentiality or informed consent (starting the session with a script for limits of confidentiality)

2. Door opener

3. Minimal encouragers

4. Key word encouragers

5. Paraphrasing

6. Reflection of feeling

7. Summarizing

Advanced skills emphasized in this text include:

1. Questions

2. Reflecting meaning

3. Challenging while supporting

4. Reframing

5. Immediacy

6. Scaling

The advanced skill of scaling is discussed in Chapter 13, where Dr. Hawkins shares the idea that we are engaging other people "in the journey of moving toward greater levels of shalom or peace." We believe in setting these approach goals (moving toward peace), and these foundational and advanced skills covered in the following chapters are aimed at walking alongside our clients, being present, and moving toward greater levels of peace and shalom. Please watch this video to hear Dr. Hawkins expand on the "power of presence" and moving toward shalom.

> *"We are engaged in helping people in the journey of moving toward greater levels of Shalom."*
>
> — Dr. Ron Hawkins

**Video**

**Power of Presence: Ron Hawkins video 2**

In summary, the chapters below will provide more of a framework and explanation of the basic skills by discussing the habits of an effective counselor, ethical considerations for consent, suicide risk, and using technology, and several basic counseling skills, such as nonverbal skills, paralanguage and minimal encouragers, reflection of content, paraphrasing, summarizing, and reflecting and exploring feeling. Furthermore, Part Three will be dedicated to advanced skills, multicultural counseling, termination, and psychopharmacology.

## Chapter Four

# Habits of Effective Counselors

## Justin Silvey and Anita M. Kuhnley

*Sometimes the best pathway to success is to avoid the pathway we know leads to failure.*

—Anita M. Kuhnley

### Chapter Learning Objectives

- To define markers of effectiveness and success in counseling (CACREP II.F.6.d., 2016, p. 12)

- To define practices of successful counselors (CACREP II.F.5.f., 2016, p. 12)

- To discuss the research that has popularized focusing on habits to facilitate success

- To synthesize current literature on practices of effective counselors (CACREP II.F.8.a., 2016, p. 13)

- To apply relevant action items to cultivate as an effective counselor (CACREP II.F.8.j., 2016, p. 13)

## Chapter Overview

What makes an effective counselor? How do you know when you have been effective in counseling? The subjective nature of defining, rating, and executing specific counseling skills creates a challenge in identifying the most important counseling skills and practices. The goal of this chapter is to explore research that may help determine common characteristics of an effective counselor and to begin to funnel down further into the skills that have been identified to make a significant impact in a clinical setting. This chapter explores the science and art of counseling. Both approaches are valued and unpacked for what they offer the helping professions. Moreover, we journey into the question of what makes a counselor an effective counselor. The research literature on successful counseling is examined from the perspective of the past, present, and future. From the research that has been the conducted the in past and present, we begin to crystallize what we see as key characteristics that lead to success in counseling and characteristics that the beginning counselor can seek to develop.

## Defining Effectiveness

How do we define effectiveness in counseling? Two related themes, as we have discussed effectiveness in counseling with colleagues, emerged—presence and mindfulness. Perhaps a term to capture this construct is engagement. How do we measure counselor engagement or connectedness with clients? There are multiple definitions of counseling effectiveness in the literature; rather than advocate for one, let us consider the many. Some markers may include the following:

- Regular attendance to sessions

- Follow-through on homework between sessions (such as journaling, biblio-therapy, and behavioral charts such as situation analysis)

- Compliance with treatment plan and goals both verbally and behaviorally

- Emotional engagement in session

- Increased immediacy in session

- Depth of self-disclosure

- How often the counselor asks for feedback, for example, "On a scale of 1 to 10, 1 being $X$ and 10 being $Y$, how would you rate the helpfulness of this session?"

- How often the counselor then seeks to solicit feedback on repairing any deficits in the connection or helpfulness with follow up questions such as, "What would it take to bring the session from an 8 to a 9?"

- How often the counselor asks for feedback such as, "How much progress toward the agreed upon goals, do you sense you have made this session, on a scale of 1 to 10?"

- How often the counselor gauges the client's sense of connectedness by asking questions such as, "How connected do you feel during this session, on a scale of 1 to 10?"

As we turn to the literature to see what the research has to say about counseling effectiveness, one group of researchers evaluates effectiveness as follows (Lambert & Cattani-Thompson, 1996):

an effort to determine whether counseling helps the client solve problems, re-duce symptoms, and improve interpersonal functioning (beyond the improvements that can be expected to result from naturally existing social supports) and inner homeostatic mechanisms, as well as to determine whether working with a professional person adds anything of significance to client health and adjustment.

This quote addresses the importance of attempting to reach a point of normalcy for the client. Furthermore, a goal of counseling should be to help the client(s) see other approaches to their specific needs to change what "normal" might be to them. It is important to not impose a value of "normalcy", from the perspective of the counselor, onto the client. However, the counselor should operate from a standard of care, valuing the client, and using Kitchener's (1984) guiding principles: (a) encouraging client autonomy, (b) only doing good (beneficence), (c) doing not harm (nonmaleficence), (d) practicing justice, and (e) modeling fidelity. Measuring effectiveness also provides another overlapping point between the art and science of counseling. The art tends to camp in the subjective; however, the science tends to focus on the objective. A counselor needs to find a benefit in the overlap of the subjective and objective.

In summary, effectiveness is certainly a subjective aspect of counseling; however, counselors need to determine how they might measure it. The measurement should be standardized, as much as possible, to begin to normalizing progress. In other words, if you think about a normally distributed bell curve, it is easier to recognize abnormalities when a sense of normalcy has been established. One way to consider looking at effectiveness is to attempt to set a treatment goal, establish a baseline with a client, using some sort of standardized assessment, then using proximal and distal assessment throughout the process, to show progress from the baseline and toward the agreed-upon treatment goal(s).

Let us discuss more about additional, specific aspects of the mindsets of a counselor that can begin to funnel down to habits of an effective counselor. First, let us begin to unpack self-awareness.

## What About Self-Awareness in Relation to Effectiveness?

We often think about self-awareness as a part of counselor effectiveness; however, is it also a part of client effectiveness? We certainly think so. For example, one of our goals in writing this chapter was to be in a state of relaxed focus. We used iced green tea with no sugar in order to achieve this state of effectiveness as writers. Likewise, do clients use self-reflection to be effective in reaching their counseling goals? Let us explore several ideas or models as we begin to conceptualize effectiveness in relation to self-awareness.

© goran cakmazovic/Shutterstock.com

In this discussion on the definition of effectiveness, an important question comes up. We hear much in the literature and professional dialogue related to the importance of self-awareness. However, is self-awareness predictive of an effective counseling relationship? Or, in other words, is a more self-aware counselor more effective?

Let us look at three figures below as we begin to explore the idea the Johari window and how it can relate to self-awareness.

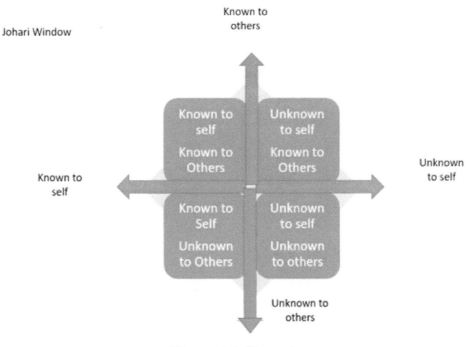

**Figure 4.1.** Phase 1

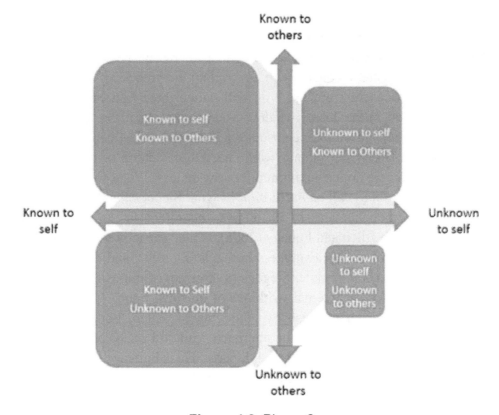

**Figure 4.2.** Phase 2

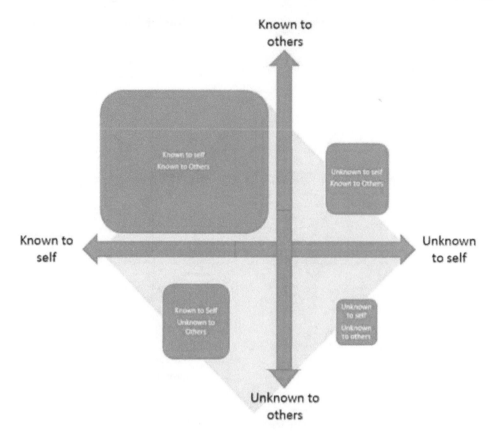

**Figure 4.3.** Phase 3

When the idea of self-awareness is addressed, then the model of the Johari window may come to mind. The window includes four quadrants that represent personal awareness and the awareness of those that we are in contact with. To explain the process of self-awareness and how it might influence the counseling process, you will notice three figures above. We notice two specific entities identified in the Johari window—ourselves and others. It is important to note that "ourselves" would depend on the perspective taken—the model can be applied to both the counselor and the client. Likewise, "others" would need to be determined by the person applying the window. Furthermore, we notice a continuum of awareness. When we consider awareness of others, what Allen et al. (2008) call *mentalization* or what Siegel calls *mindsight*, it is important to focus on our own thoughts and to encourage the client to explore deeper reflection. Mentalization, according to Allen and Fonagy (2006), is the "capacity to be specifically aware of mental states as such and to use this awareness in regulating affect and negotiating interpersonal relationships" (p. xvi). On a similar note, Siegel's (a) concept of mindsight is "a kind of focused attention that allow us to see the internal workings of our own mind" (p. xi). We would like to introduce a combined approach to these two thoughts by Allen, Fonagy, and Siegel, which integrates both definitions. We will call the approach "mindful *presence,*" which addresses the personal mindful and the mindfulness of the other party. This aligns well with the Johari window as a counselor needs to be self-aware and aware of the individual he is engaging with.

In Phase 1, four quadrants are equal, representing a balanced or equal approach to the information or state known personally or externally. In Phase 2, we notice more of a shift from the "unknown" (right) side to the "known" (left) side, but that the "unknown to self or known to others" (top, right-hand corner) is slightly larger than the "unknown to self or unknown to others" (bottom-right-hand corner). As we grow in self-awareness, more information becomes known to all parties, but there could be information that is perceived from the other party involved. The difference in Phase 1 and Phase 2 is that more information becomes known by us and the other party, so more information can be explored. Some ways to consider creating this type of environment of exploration is to create a safe space through good counseling skills, such as empathy, unconditional positive regard, active listening, reflecting thoughts and feelings of the other party(s), self-disclosure, and techniques to draw the party out, to name a few. In Phase 3, we notice even more of a shift to the "known to self or known to others" quadrant (top-left-corner). The other two quadrants where "knowing" is present ("known to self or unknown to others" and "unknown to self or known to others") are more balanced or equal, but the "Unknown to Self or Unknown to Others" quadrant is significantly smaller. As you may imagine, this is the overall point of counseling—for awareness to grow and for blind spots to shrink. As clients become more self-aware, what is unknown decreases and what is known increases. As this phenomenon occurs, people are able to more accurately face the truth of their story. Then, the things that are unknown to others become smaller and the opportunity for connection and intimacy increases. So as things become known to the self and others, things are "brought to light."

Another way to look at this concept is to think of an iceberg (see Figure 4.4). Just like other organic materials, the conditions must be correct for an iceberg to form. Due to the buoyancy, the iceberg floats in the water; however, researchers have found that 90% of the iceberg is actually underwater, exposing just the top portion of the larger object. Now, let us apply this analogy to counseling. First, we need to consider the environment in the counseling office. Interestingly enough, we usually think about buoyancy as an object's ability to float; however, a second definition is "an optimistic and cheerful disposition." Therefore, when the conditions are right in a counseling setting, could it be that the client may be more buoyant—optimistic, cheerful? In this analogy, the goal of counseling is to use empathic skill and engage in "mindful presence" in order to promote the lowering of the waterline. It is important to note that client's underlying feelings, explanations to impulses and automatic thoughts, and strongly held beliefs or motivators should be uncovered.

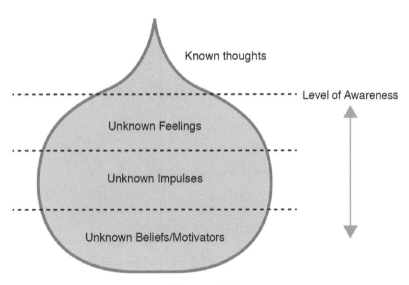

**Figure 4.4.**
© Kendall Hunt Publishing Company

## Case Study

Let us take the above examples and begin to apply it to a counseling session. Johana is an 11th-grade student at Draper High School. She is the middle child, with an older brother and a younger sister. She has struggled in school since fifth grade when her parents divorced. She lives with her biological mother, her siblings, and her stepdad. Her mother, a university professor, is very strict with her children because she "wants them to do as well as she did." Johana is nearly the halfway point in her junior year in school, and report cards have just been sent home. Johana knows that she will have one B, one C, three Ds, and two Fs, which will make her mother very upset. Johana has been called into the school counselor's office, and she knows it is because of her grades. Johana believes that she studies enough at night, she believes that her mother is "just too strict" on her, and she feels that her siblings "have it easier." When going through the session, the school counselor, who operates from a solution-focused, cognitive behavioral approach, explores the interrelationship between Johana's thoughts, feelings, and behaviors. One goal that Johana and the counselor agree on is to explore how Johana's decisions impact the relationship with her mother. Johana states, "My mom just doesn't understand how hard it is living under so much pressure. Her words make me feel defeated, like I can never do enough to make her proud. I think I am just going to give up and drop out because I am just not cut for school." The counselor draws the following circle for Johana to explore or discuss:

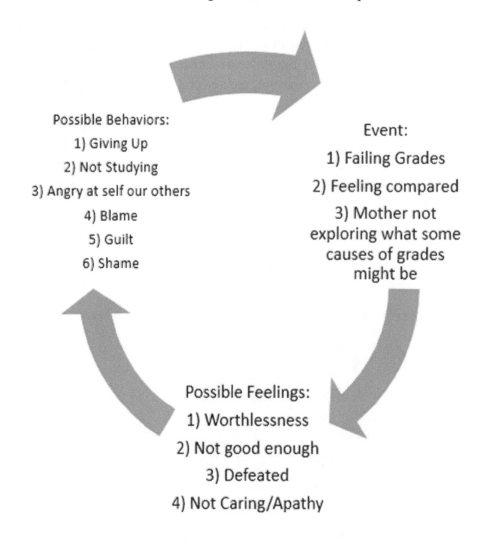

Possible Behaviors:
1) Giving Up
2) Not Studying
3) Angry at self our others
4) Blame
5) Guilt
6) Shame

Event:
1) Failing Grades
2) Feeling compared
3) Mother not exploring what some causes of grades might be

Possible Feelings:
1) Worthlessness
2) Not good enough
3) Defeated
4) Not Caring/Apathy

The counselor seeks first to gain a deeper understanding of Johana's situation. As the counselor works through the cycle with her, Johana begins to feel heard and validated. Johana begins to look at the situation from her mother's point of view as she roleplays through a conversation with her mother with the counselor. Johana begins to see how she might have misinterpreted messages from her mother and added in her own misguided beliefs and she starts to gain a deeper understanding of her own impulses and motivations. She comes to the conclusion that her mother wants what is best for her and cares for her but may not be articulating love, compassion, care, or regard for her. Basically, as the counselor explores with Johana, the "unknown" becomes "known" and can be explored more deeply. Furthermore, the "waterline" of awareness is lowered and deeper meaning is made.

## Spiritual Implications of Developing Habits

Ephesians 4:32 says, "Be kind and compassionate to one another, forgiving one another just as Christ forgave you." When a counselor responds to a client's confession of struggle with compassion and forgiveness, Ephesians 4:32 is manifested. As the client becomes more consciously aware of coping mechanisms that were necessary at one point in time, but now may be keeping him or her stuck, it is important to be able to provide time to explore automatic thoughts and instincts. One way to think about this is to challenge while supporting the client in session. We should challenge a deeper level of self-awareness while also acknowledging the vulnerability the client might be experiencing while becoming aware and reflecting. This level of self-awareness involves both a confession to self and a confession to others in the counseling session. As the client is able to share her or his insights with the counselor and sense the counselor's presence and compassion, the client may be more able to be aware of God's presence or divine compassion. The scriptures discuss the healing properties of confessing struggles and experiencing prayer. For example, James 5:16 (NIV) says, "Therefore confess your sins to each other and pray for each other so that you may be healed. The prayer of a righteous person is powerful and effective." Even though counseling should not be viewed as a "confessional" session, it is still important to recognize that many topics that arise in counseling might be the first and only time a client might have shared or will share their deepest thoughts. A person's thoughts should be viewed as a prized possession and should be handled with great care. We believe that when this care is taken, then healing can begin.

On that note, it is important to note that this increased self-awareness brings things to light. Note, there is an image of a lighthouse on the front of this text, and you also see attachment illumination sections throughout this text. As you consider the concept of self-awareness and self-reflection shedding light this word picture used here is congruent with the messages throughout the book. The themes here are shedding light, illumination, and guiding light. Likewise, when a person experiences this light that just illuminates, what was once in darkness, their words, and actions, and

© S. Borisov/Shutterstock.com

values can move toward congruence (recall Rogers said congruence was therapeutic and one of the primary goals of treatment). This need for light due to the human perpetual struggle with blind spots is highlighted by the Apostle Paul in his letter to the church in Corinth (1 Corinthians 13:12a, NLT). Consider these different translations of the verse, which capture the sentiment with different words:

- For now we can only see a dim and blurry picture of things, as when we stare into polished metal, I realize that everything I know is only part of the big picture (The Voice).

- Now we see things imperfectly, like puzzling reflections in a mirror (New Living Translation).

- For now we see through a glass darkly (King James Version).

- For now [in this time of imperfection], we see in a mirror dimly [a blurred reflection, a riddle, an enigma] (Amplified Bible).

As we consider the previous translations of 1 Corinthians 13:12a, take a moment to contemplate the meaning behind these sentiments. What does it mean to see through a glass darkly? Have you ever seen a blurred reflection in a mirror? As humans we are imperfect, and at best, our perceptions of life's experiences and our personal estimation of truth are also limited by our imperfections. What are the implications of these thoughts?

Reflecting on these verses may be helpful in avoiding the pitfalls of epistemic pride or epistemic arrogance. Recall that epistemology involves knowing what we can know and how we can gather the information that we can know. Maintaining a sense of epistemic humility (as opposed to epistemic pride) can help us avoid making absolutist claims about what we know about clients and/or how to gather information about clients. This also helps shed light on why it is important to avoid advice giving in counseling. Even if the client has shared with us all that he or she knows about a situation, the information is still incomplete, as we are hearing only his or her side of the story and only his or her estimation of the truth that is influenced by the practice of as the scripture says "seeing through a glass darkly"; thus any advice we give would be based on incomplete knowledge.

## Why not to give advice and a good laugh from the top 1%!

You have likely heard of Dr. Gladding (pictured here), since he has been a key contributor to the counseling profession. Dr. Gladding has been honored as a key contributor in the field and listed as in the top 1% of contributors to the *Journal of Counseling and Development*; in addition to this honor, he has produced more than 40 books and published more than 80 articles in peer-reviewed journals among other publications and contributions (Gladding, 2018).

Copyright © 2018 by Samuel Gladding. Reprinted by permission.

Leaving the 2017 American Counseling Association, I was trying to hail a cab to the airport when Dr. Samuel Gladding generously invited me to share his, as he was on his way there too generously invited me to share his taxi to the airport. We discussed our sessions and respective universities. I shared that one of my students told me her favorite joke that I told in class was one I heard from a preacher. An older man went in to see his doctor because he was having trouble with his heart, and the doctor checked him out and sent him on his way. A few days later, the doctor saw him in the park with a beautiful young woman and he said, "You look like you're doing great! What have you been doing?" The gentleman said, "I'm just following your advice."

The doc said, "What advice?" The man said, "You said to find a hot mama and stay cheerful." The doctor said, "No, I didn't! I said you have a heart murmur; be careful!" Dr. Gladding laughed and said, "Well, the advice he heard was probably better than what the doctor originally said." I reflected, "Well, that is a great reason why we should not give advice!" What we say when we give advice may be different from what the other person hears! Dr. Gladding joked, "They can live a long, happy life if they follow what they think they hear." This humor represents something we both agreed upon. We both agreed this was a great example of why not to give advice.

Returning to analogy of the lighthouse, even when we think we have a clear picture, there may be more illumination that we need that we are not aware of. Recall that as the number of counseling sessions increases, the amount of "substantial improvement" also increases (Lambart & Cattani-Thompson, 1996, p. 601).

## A Concept to Contemplate

© Shutterstock.com

As you think about your work with clients, it is important that the work first begins in you. Using the Johari window and the iceberg models, do you have more thoughts, impulses, and beliefs or motivations "known" or "unknown"? How can you move more of these things to the "known" category, or how can you decrease the water level? One major tool to grow in your awareness is to be open to feedback. Feedback is the opportunity for you to open yourself up to insights from other people. One prerequisite of feedback should be that you have surrounded yourself with individuals that are wise, discerning, caring, and trustworthy, to name a few.

## Habits—General Definition and Content

*We are what we repeatedly do. Excellence then is not an act but a habit.*

—Aristotle

Conceptually speaking, a habit could be seen as a repeated behavior based on the perceived positive response that is received. Some research has noted the amount of time needed in order to develop a habit, which may vary. Another aspect of a habit is the subjective nature of determining whether the habit is good or bad, which may be stated in words like "healthy" or "unhealthy." Instead of approaching habits from a subjective view, we will attempt to draw from research to determine the evidence of effect or success of different habits. This section will be the start of a literature review of ideas of different authors about a variety of habits, but we hope to end with a list of common habits that may serve as themes to provide a starting point.

## What We Know About Habits

**Who is Stephen Covey?**
Dr. Stephen Covey is the author of the book, *The Seven Habits of Highly Effective People: Powerful Lessons in Personal Change.* This is likely the text that he has been most known for. He has popularized the idea of using habits to impact personal and professional effectiveness. He has also written a host of other books in the personal development literature, including (but not limited to): *The Speed of Trust: The One Thing that Changes Everything, First Things First, Principle Centered Leadership, The Seven Habits of Highly Effective Families, The 8th Habit, The Third Alternative: Solving Life's Most Difficult Problems, Primary Greatness,* and *Everyday Greatness.* A major idea that he has popularized that is very congruent with counseling skill development is habit number five, "Seek first to understand, then to be understood" (Covey, 2004, p. 235).

The importance of developing habits to influence effectiveness has been popularized by Stephen Covey (2004) in his best seller *The Seven Habits of Highly Effective People: Powerful Lessons in Personal Change.* In this book, he discussed the habits that he believed were associated with success. Covey likened these habits to natural laws and shared that one of the most profound things that he has learned is the idea that "If you want to achieve your highest aspirations and overcome your greatest challenges, identify and apply the natural law that governs the results that you seek" (Covey, 2004, p. 7). He devoted much time to studying the success literature that was available starting from 1776 and summarized this literature as defining success as being associated with the "character ethic" (Covey, 2004, p. 18) and stemming from works such as Ben Franklin's autobiography. He contrasts the personality ethic with the character ethic and emphasizes the importance of developing and attending deeper motivations as well. Covey shared how the importance of the distinction manifested as he and his wife focused on the character ethic in the raising of their son. They saw the fruit of their approach in his success in many areas of life, and Covey discusses reasons for this such as being a function of the feelings that their son had about himself.

We recommend reading Dr. Covey's book to learn more about these seven habits, but here we will summarize the key habits that Covey found from his literature review and personal experience to be associated with success. His book provides one chapter on each habit and summarizes them in more detail (Covey, 2004). The habits include: (a) be proactive: principals of personal vision, (b) begin with the end in mind: principles of personal leadership, (c) put first things first:

principles of personal management, (d) think win–win: principles of interpersonal leadership, (e) seek first to understand or then to be understood, (f) synergize: principles of creative cooperation, and (g) sharpen the saw: principles of balanced self-renewal. Given that Dr. Covey wrote a chapter on each of these habits, there is much more to say about them, but we will provide a brief introduction here and relate each habit to the counseling profession. Of course, we would recommend that you refer to the full text for more information.

Habit number one is "Be Proactive" (Covey, 2004, p. 64). Dr. Covey draws on experiences of key figures such as Viktor Frankl, as he overcame the grave atrocities of the concentration camps in Nazi Germany. There is a focus on responding rather than reacting, taking personal responsibility, and avoiding blame.

Following the first habit, the second habit also includes intentional action and is "Begin with the End in Mind" (Covey, 2004, p. 95). Here readers are encouraged to use the movie theater of the mind to imagine themselves at their own funeral and to envision what their loved ones would say about them and what they would like for them to say in the end. Keeping this in mind is part of what this habit is all about. Counselors need to both practice and model proactivity in their own lives and attempt to foster proactivity in the lives of their clients. Within the counselor's professional life, a proactive approach might be growing in his or her level of competence through professional development activities (e.g., professional conferences, workshops, listening to ebooks or audiobooks about counseling skills, approaches, techniques). To be more specific, counselors need to be more purposeful and proactive with their time. You should attempt to make the most of all working or workable time so that you can feel good about stepping away to establish professional boundaries. By listening to an audiobook while driving between meetings or on the way to church, you have made your car into a "four-wheel university." Being proactive, from this approach, will serve as an opportunity for counselors to "pay it forward" to themselves and their practice, which could make a direct impact on their clients. Within the counselor's personal life, being proactive might include engaging in personal counseling, journaling, bibliotherapy, religious or spiritual activities, self-care activities, or other types of activities that promote personal care that can translate into professional care. In summary, it is important to be an effective leader of your life (Covey, 2004).

*The second habit—Be Proactive–includes intentional action*

In addition to the above two habits, the third habit involves priorities and is called "Put First Things First" (Covey, 2004, p. 145). Counselors who have insecure attachment-related anxiety may be triggered by clients' actions, such as cancelling appointments or not showing up to appointments and this may trigger a fear abandonment. This could be a function of the client not living in what Stephen Covey would call quadrant two. Covey outlines four quadrants to describe how we spend our time. Quadrant one represents tasks that are urgent and important, such as a project that is driven by a deadline or a crisis. Quadrant two represents important but not urgent tasks. Examples of tasks in quadrant two include activities that we may as counselors refer to as self-care or professional development activities. These activities may involve investing in relationships, planning recreation, exercising, and exploring new opportunities. Quadrant three represents urgent tasks that are not important. These tasks include some phone calls, some meetings, and some mail. Quadrant four is the last quadrant, and this one represents tasks that are neither urgent nor important. This could include busy work, time wasters, and some phone calls. Covey indicates that effective people spend more time in quadrant two. This requires much intentionality. Note, one of the tasks that is in quadrant two involves prevention. This may include participating in counseling. If a client is not keeping counseling appointments, this may be a function of many things, such as lack of a therapeutic alliance, the client not living in quadrant two/prioritizing preventative and self-care practices, or other factors. As counselors, we want to be intentional about practicing habits such as operating from quadrant two; however, we want to remember to hang onto our QTIP (our reminder to quit taking it personally), and remember that something else could be going on, and it is very difficult in some situations for people to maintain quadrant two behavior.

The fourth habit is "Think Win–Win" (Covey, 2004, p. 204). We know that the word *win* assumes that there is also another party who has "lost." In a counseling, the counselor may address a presenting issue as a "win" for the client and a "win" for the social setting (e.g., marriage, family, work) that the client is operating in. For example, is it not true that when an individual is healthy, restored, supported, and making positive change that his or her habitat or setting is also not benefited? Likewise, if a client is living in an unhealthy manner and not up to his or her fullest potential, does the environment not also suffer? The counselor can approach counseling from a systems approach, where if the client is successful, then the client's setting can also benefit (of course, there are times where the environment could be playing a large role in the client's overall mental health and by the client changing environments, he or she could experience a positive outcome). It is important to help aim the client toward success and consider how others can also benefit from that success. Furthermore, as mentioned earlier, we need to know how to define effectiveness and success and beware of the thinking that the client success or failure is always tied to the worth of us as the counselor.

According to Covey (2004), the fifth highly effective habit is "seek first to understand, then to be understood" (p. 235). Covey also calls this *empathetic communication* (2004). In counseling, counselors must put their clients' needs first. Ethically speaking, a therapy session must not become therapy for the therapist. This role reversal must be kept in check, and the counselor has a responsibility to monitor herself and practice self-care. Another aspect of this habit for counselors is to develop a litmus test for determining the level of understanding that the client feels from the counselor. There are other chapters that address intentional empathy, active listening, seeking to understand content, and meaning in this book. We think a pitfall of some counselors is to attempt to be a "fixer" as opposed to an empathic listener. Counseling skills that can be used to prompt more understanding include: (a) clarifying and (b) summarizing. On the other hand of this habit, counselors also need to be clear about expectations for counseling.

The sixth habit, synergizing (Covey, 2004), focuses on creating cooperation. Within the counseling relationship, we might call this the therapeutic alliance—the relationship or bond between the counselor and the client. The relationship has been found to be a core piece of counseling, without which the relationship change cannot happen. When was the first or last time that you were able to impact or affect another person that you did not know? Within counseling, we need to see it that way. However, within the relationship, we may hear and attempt to work through deep issues. The deeper into the relationship we are able to go, the lower the "waterline" may go, as discussed with the iceberg analogy previously. We need to be emotionally ready for the information and situations that we are called to help the client sort through (and attempt to make sense of). Another aspect of synergy is to understand how we can use good, empathic counseling skills to create this type of environment. A few of the major skills that we address later in this chapter and book may shed light (going with the theme of illumination again) on how we can have different tools in our toolboxes to create synergy. From the attachment theory approach, we may start with helping clients find a secure base or safe haven. By doing this, the client may feel safe enough with us to work toward synergy or trusting the counselor more in building a stronger therapeutic alliance as well. We need to be cautious to ensure that the client is not reliant on us to where the secure base or safe haven becomes the counselor making termination harder for the client.

Finally, "Sharpening the Saw" (Covey, 2004, p. 287) is the final habit outlined by Covey. This habit focuses on attempting to create a "balanced self-renewal." We think this is a great place for the habits to end because just as a carpenter may sharpen his saw throughout a project, counselors need to do the same. As noted earlier, as we engage more deeply with the client in an empathic, therapeutic relationship, we need to find even more opportunities to stay sharp. Also, the idea of sharpening means that friction must be created—friction between the client and the counselor, perhaps, and/or friction between the counselor's desire to help and the need for self-help. In order to sharpen ourselves as counselors, we need to engage in specific activities that provide reprieve, opportunities to make sense of the situation personally, and/or activities for growth in areas that can have an impact with the client, to be broad. To be more specific, we could do some of the following activities: (a) listening to audiobooks, (b) journaling, (c) intentional relaxation, (d) physical exercise, (e) spiritual renewal, or (f) attending a professional conference, to name a few. The main idea with "sharpening your saw" is to be intentional about self-care.

In addition to Covey's concepts, more focus and attention have been brought to the importance of developing good habits by Brendon Burchard, the author of *High Performance Habits*. He identified two types of habits, personal and social, and six individual or specific habits. The personal habits include: (a) seeking clarity, (b) generating energy, and (c) raising necessity, and the social habits include (d) increasing productivity, (e) developing influence, and (f) demonstrating courage. As a counselor, these habits could all be effective in our practice because we continue to see the theme of being intentional or purposeful in our practice. In a way, we see the opportunity to practice the skill of "modeling" for clients as we practice the personal and social skills outlined by Burchard. As we may model these types of habits, we also need to ensure that we are not leaving clients behind or expecting too much from the work that we might want to see from clients. We also need to ensure that we are behind and going before clients to providing them opportunities to attempt new skills in the counseling office that can translate into their personal lives.

Now, let us look at specific counseling literature that focuses on effective counseling skills that should be practiced to move into habits. According to an APA letter by Bruce Wampold (article can be found at https://www.apa.org/education/ce/effective-therapists.pdf), there have been several similar and different characteristics of a highly effective counselor according to the following sources:

- Anderson, Ogles, Patterson, Lambert, and Vermeersch, 2009;

- Baldwin, Wampold, & Imel, 2007;

- Duncan, Miller, Wampold, & Hubble, 2010;

- Lambert, Harmon, Slade, Whipple, & Hawkins, 2005;

- Norcross & Wampold, 2011;

- Wampold, 2007

Wampold continued in his work by including qualities and actions of effective therapists, including the following:

1. Effective therapists have a sophisticated set of interpersonal skills, including:

   a. Verbal fluency

   b. Interpersonal perception

   c. Affective modulation and expressiveness

   d. Warmth and acceptance

   e. Empathy

   f. Focus on other.

2. Clients have a sense that they are heard, the counselor is seeking to understand them, and the counselor is competent to help them.

3. Effective therapists form a working alliance.

4. The therapist is able to explain the etiology of the psychopathology.

5. The counselor develops a treatment plan and explains the rationale with the client, thereby increasing the likelihood of client compliance, and all of the items within the treatment plan are healthy.

6. The counselor is able to communicate to a client in such a way that he is able to influence and persuade a client. For example, the effective counselor is able to provide an effective explanatory model so that the client understands the purpose of the treatment plan and believes that it will make a difference.

7. Effective counselors assess client progress on a regular basis in an authentic and congruent manner. Detached assessment apart from authentic concern about progress is not effective.

8. The effective counselor is okay with being wrong and is willing to, as Ivey and (Ivey, Ivey, & Zalaquett, 2018) would say, "flex with intentional competence."

9. The effective counselor approaches rather than avoids.

10. Hope and optimism are infused through therapy by the effective counselor. As Yalom 1975 would say, "instillation of hope" is a therapeutic factor.

11. Effective counselors have a sense of the ethnic and/or cultural characteristics that impact the client, such as age, race, ethnicity, socioeconomic status, etc. They also have a sense of the client's developmental level.

12. Effective counselors are reflective and take time to "sit in the other chair" or do their own work.

13. Effective counselors stay up to date on best practices and seek to implement them.

14. The effective counselor has a growth mindset.

In order to summarize these qualities and actions, it seems that effective counselors are intentional or purposeful with their thoughts, feelings, and behaviors in their craft. Intentionality, based on our empathy, seems to serve as the umbrella under which all other skills, approaches, and treatments should be carefully considered under (notice that we did not state "fall" here) in order to model intentionality with our wording.

Furthermore, Pope and Kline (1999) interviewed a panel of experts and invited them to rank the most important personality characteristics for counselors, they were as follows, in order from most important to least important:

| Skill | Definition | Rating |
|---|---|---|
| Empathy | | |
| Acceptance | | |
| Warmth | | |
| Genuineness | | |
| Sensitivity | | |
| Flexibility | | |
| Open mindedness | | |
| Compatibility | | |
| Emotional stability | | |
| Confidence | | |
| Nonthreatening | | |
| Patience | | |
| Awareness of limitations | | |
| Interest in people | | |
| Friendliness | | |
| Cooperative | | |
| Sincerity | | |
| Fairness | | |
| Tolerance for ambiguity | | |
| Resourcefulness | | |
| Sympathy | | |
| Sociability | | |

Pope and Kline (1999) provide us with very useful information as we begin to think about the skills that may be the most effective with a wide variety of practice. It is our opinion that the skills listed above might change in order based on the needs of the client; however, by identifying and practicing or fine-tuning these skills, we feel that you will be on your way to developing habits of effectiveness for counseling. This list may seem daunting, so we would encourage you to engage in the following exercise:

In the above chart, you will see 22 counseling skills. It would be best to look up definitions of each of the skills, which will help in the identification process. Then, rate each skill on a scale of 1 to 10 (1 being weak and 10 being strong) in terms of how well you feel that you perform each (this will help identify self-efficacy).

# The Literature on Factors that May Influence Counselor Efficacy

## Why Study Habits of Effective Counselors?

In this section, we will review some studies from the peer-reviewed literature across various presenting issues or theoretical frameworks and examine themes that emerge across the board. We apply some of the principles of qualitative research to review literature and identify themes. This is a part of an ongoing research project, and we have enlisted three researchers in evaluating and synthesizing themes related to factors associated with counselor effectiveness.

We feel that it is important to study habits of effective counselors because just as a code of ethics provides a standard of care, a theoretical framework provides an approach to conceptualizing the presenting issues that the client might be bringing to counseling, and an evidence-based practice provides research to support a treatment plan, habits can begin to provide effective practices of a counselor in order to increase personal effectiveness.

In summary, here is a compelling quote on the matter from a study by Vocisano et al. (2004):

> The large-scale and influential studies that have given therapist characteristics some attention confirm that therapists vary substantially in their success even when they are working with patients who are all being treated for the same disorder with the same form of carefully monitored, manualized treatment (Blatt, Sanislow, Zuroff, & Pilkonis, 1996; Huppert et al., 2001). P. 256

We think this quote can be interpreted in several different ways, including, but not limited to, the following:

1. it may be relieving because the counseling process is not just dependent on the counselor but also on the level of depth that the client wants to go. Counselors need to understand that even though they provide the environment for therapeutic work, the client has a shared responsibility for the outcome.

2. It may cause anxiety because a counselor may feel like his or her worth as a counselor is dependent on the success of the client. There could not be anything further from the truth! Counselors need to understand that it is not about them but about addressing the needs of the client. If we do not feel that all clients can be helped, why are we in the profession? However, if we think that we can help all clients, we may need to check our pride or our self-awareness for areas that we might be able to grow in.

3. It may make a counselor feel that there is no point in counseling because change may be seen as haphazard, uncontrolled, unmeasurable, or not guaranteed. Even though there may be change that was unexpected or the process might be halted by a variety of variables, it is important to dig deep in evidence-based practices and trust the process!

## What Do We Learn About Counselor Characteristics From the Common Factor Research?

How do theoretical orientation and efficacy of theoretical approach inform adaptive counselor characteristic development? Counselors typically have a theoretical lens through which they view their clients. Some counselors may indicate that they use several different approaches and integrate them into an eclectic approach. Even though we are moving away from theoretical schools of thought toward evidence-based treatment modalities, these evidence-based practices (EBPs) are still informed by theoretical orientation. To summarize earlier statements, we feel it is important for the counselor to use empathic case conceptualization skills at the onset of counseling in order to determine the best approach. However, a counselor must also feel he or she has a high level of self-efficacy in one or, preferably, multiple theoretical orientations in order to apply different ways to conceptualize a case.

## Attachment Illumination

© Shutterstock.com

The habit of self-awareness and the willingness to develop a coherent narrative are habits related to attachment security and affective counseling. In order to effectively help clients process their stories and make sense of them, it is important for the counselor to facilitate self-awareness and to go through the process of making sense of his or her own story. Some of the current research indicates that counselors who have insecure attachment-related anxiety may be triggered by clients' actions to fear abandonment and then may be less empathic. We recommend the Rubino, Barker, Roth, and Fearon et al. (2000) article for reading. It is also important for counselors to process their story. Consider the hallmark question of the Adult Attachment Interview (AAI): What are five adjectives you would use to describe your childhood relationship with your mother (before age 12)? After you have identified five, try to think of a story or autobiographical memory that illustrates this. Record your adjectives and memories below.

Adjective 1: _____

Adjective 2: _____

Adjective 3: _____

Adjective 4: _____

Adjective 5: _____

    Memory that illustrates why my childhood relationship with my mother (or primary caregiver) was _____ (adjective 1)

Memory that illustrates why my childhood relationship with my mother (or primary caregiver) was _____(adjective 2)

Memory that illustrates why my childhood relationship with my mother (or primary caregiver) was _____(adjective 3)

Memory that illustrates why my childhood relationship with my mother (or primary caregiver) was _____(adjective 4)

Memory that illustrates why my childhood relationship with my mother (or primary caregiver) was _____(adjective 5)

*A Concept to Contemplate*

© Shutterstock.com

How can we unpack evidence-based approaches, or in other words, treatment modalities? Remember evidence-based practices are treatments that have demonstrated effectiveness, identify some of the characteristics of those treatment approaches that have made them effective, and then apply these principles to the development of the personhood of the counselor?

## What Do We Learn About the Habits From Theoretical Orientation Literature?

Some literature (Morrow, Lee, Bartoli, & Gillem, 2017) has indicated that specific EBPs are effective across groups of counselors and there is no statistically significant difference between groups. In other words, the approach works because of the quality of the intervention regardless of individual differences in counselors. However, other researchers (Sommers-Flanagan, 2015) have emphasized the relationship and the therapeutic factors more than technique. Recall from your assessment classes that a battery of assessments is typically considered better than an individual assessment because it provides a clearer picture of what is going on with the client. Likewise, we believe that both the literature on EBPs and the nature of the therapeutic alliance can provide valuable insight into habits that are top priorities for effective counselors. In this section, we will explore what theoretical approaches, schools of thoughts, and EBPs teach us about how to be effective as clinicians. Instead of focusing on a particular camp, that is, evidence based, or common factors, we would like to integrate the lessons learned from the literature in both camps. In this chapter, we have adopted a both-and rather than an perspective or a full color rather than black-and-white perspective.

Don't walk in front of me; I may not follow. Don't walk behind me; I may not lead. Just walk beside me and be my friend [counselor]. --Unknown

Let us do a reframe of the above quote. If a counselor walks in front of the client as expert all of the time, then he or she may miss the client's meaning or presenting challenge or make assumptions that are not appropriate. If the counselor has an agenda and asks leading questions seeking to lead a client along a particular path, then the client may not buy into or resonate with the treatment modality (but may not feel comfortable enough to speak up and let the counselor know that he or she dislikes the approach). However, if the counselor walks alongside the client, then he or she can facilitate the dialogue in a way that uses the counselor's expertise in an empathic manner that helps the client engage with collaborative goal setting and agreement on goals of in treatment. As we conceptualize the role of the counselor, some may see the counselor as strictly an expert, some may see the counselor as neutral, and others may see the counselor as walking

© villorejo/Shutterstock.com

alongside the client. We believe it is possible to remain flexible in our stance and let the client drive the session and find balance. The expert approach may be more directive, whereas the approach of walking alongside is less directive. However, it is possible to maintain the flexibility to move between stances, which may be similar to what Ivey, Ivey, and Zalaquett (2018) call flexing with intentional competency, where a clinician seeks to anticipate the outcome of using one particular skill, and if the predicted outcome is not accomplished, the clinician may use a different skill. For example, I may ask my colleague how he is feeling and he says fine, but I notice some tension. Then, later if I ask a closed-ended question, such as, "Does this lack of congruence in decision making on this team lead you to feel anxious," and then he responded, with "Yes, I do feel anxious," this illustrates how we may believe an open-ended question would be most helpful for facilitating the exploration of feelings; however, the counselor may need to remain flexible and try a different skill. Likewise as we discussed, the different attitudes counselors may take in the session on one end of the continuum may be the counselor who sees himself or herself as an expert and leads the client forward toward resolution of a conflict, and on the other end of the continuum may be the counselor who sees himself or herself as one who walks alongside the client moving toward collaborative goals. However, there may be times where the counselor who tends toward more collaborative approaches needs to be more direct. And there may be times where the counselor who had a tendency to be more direct needs to be more collaborative or more open to client influence and feedback.

With this flexible mindset that allows us to see how various theoretical frameworks or approaches may be appropriate and useful at various times in the course of treatment, we can now examine some truths from the theoretical approaches that can inform our investigation of which habits counselors should cultivate.

## Trends in Counseling

We should consider the evolution of the counseling field of the seminal theories of the late 1800s and early 1900s to its current robustness. Smith (1982) provided thoughts on the direction of counseling and how therapists were transitioning from one school of thought to a variety of schools. Even in 1982, when the article was published, therapists were reporting abandoning an eclectic approach and were trending toward more of a systems approach. It seems that this trend has carried us in the more recent past. For example, it seems that the focus of theoretical orientations has progressed from a singular focus on a school of thought to more of a systems approach (Smith, 1982) and integration (Siegel, A). It seems that theoretical orientations could move more toward an ecological approach, where seemingly different aspects of an individual and social environments overlap. In regard to the use of counseling techniques over time, it appears that techniques have been used in more static ways and related to one school of thought in the past. Today, we see more branching out from specific theories to more applied theories. Additional research will need to be completed to find techniques that may be developed or refined to address a growing number of needs with clients. As we think about the integrated approach to counseling, it is important to always match the counseling strategy with the client's presenting need. For example, if we think of theoretical orientations and techniques as tools in a toolbox, then we should always attempt to add more tools so that we will be prepared for a wide variety of presenting needs to might arise. Similarly, when working on a project around your home, you would not pull out a hammer to drive a screw and you would not pull out a screwdriver to drive a nail. We would have to let the presenting issue dictate the approach. In summary, may we always be learning, growing, challenging ourselves, surrounding ourselves with individuals that challenge us, listening to audiobooks on counseling approaches, theories, or ideas, attending professional conferences and workshops, and engaging in supervision and other practical professional activities to add more tools into our toolbox to be prepared for future trends in counseling. Based on our readings, participation at recent conferences, and discussions with other faculty, we began asking ourselves these questions: (a) "What are great counselors of the present doing?" and (b) "What are current trends?" Here are a few answers that we came up with:

1. We are noticing a focus on approaches or models or specific techniques in counseling (e.g., motivational interviewing, DBT (dialectical behavior therapy), EMDR (eye movement desensitization and reprocessing).

2. We are noticing more of a focus on mindfulness.

3. We are noticing a use of technology to bring the distant into proximity (connecting with others at a distance). We feel that we need to maintain the importance of connecting and networking.

4. We think that counselors need to seek to understand research or science that drives new methods of counseling and the connection between counseling and science (e.g., epigenetics).

5. We think that counselors should continue to think of ways of making the complex simpler to help clients make sense of their world, especially as we think about application of evidence-based practices in counseling sessions.

6. We think that counselor should continue to adapt to societal or cultural shifts in hopes of maintaining relevance and effectiveness in diverse settings.

7. We think that counselors should continue to add more tools to their toolboxes (we will discuss this next).

# Example of New Tools in Your Toolbox

## Embracing the Science and Art of Counseling

Being an effective counselor means embracing both the art and the science of counseling; some consider the art of counseling to involve processes such as the therapeutic alliance and development of trust (Lapertosa, 2009). The scientific process may be viewed as the development of effective treatment plans based on evidence. In the field of helping, there may be biases in both directions. Critics on both sides of the equations may seek to deny the presence of the other. Humanistic counseling theories may have been criticized as not being scientific enough although they are based on science (Lapertosa, 2009). Likewise, systematic approaches such as cognitive behavioral therapy (CBT) may be criticized as being less empathic and relational. Many times, it seems that the art of counseling attempts to interpret the science of counseling; likewise, the science of counseling attempts to explain the art of counseling. Within the field of counseling, there is room for both the art and the science.

As there are different philosophies about how people change, different theoretical approaches associated with helping people change (e.g., psychotherapy) have developed over time. Rogerian counselors may believe that people have an internal compass and sense of what they need and the counselor acts as a fellow traveler walking alongside them as they uncover their own answers —the belief that the client is the expert on their own life and experience and an "unconditional positive regard" may be distinguishing features of the approach. On the other hand, other approaches such as CBT may see the counselor as being the expert and the therapy or treatment as the agent of change. One of our purposes in this chapter is to identify the overlap between both the science and the art of counseling and to see the value and common interests in both approaches. The breadth of perspective adds richness and robustness to our work as counselors. The counseling skills discussed in this textbook can be used with a variety of theoretical perspectives.

Remember, Baskin Robbins has 31 flavors of ice cream, not just chocolate, vanilla, and strawberry. Hence, the counseling skills are like toppings, and you can add hot fudge, peanuts, sprinkles, whipped cream, cherries, bananas, and so on to any ice cream flavor. That is, the counseling skills discussed in this text can be used with all flavors of counseling, including Rogerian, CBT, and so on.

There are many different models of cars, yet all cars need a driver to make progress and get to their destination. Likewise, the theoretical approaches come in all different models from Rogerian to CBT, but the counseling skills fuel the progress forward. The counselor and client collaborate to form a treatment plan that is like the car's GPS that helps ensure that they arrive at the destination within a set time frame. If they begin to take a circuitous route, then the GPS will say "recalculating." In counseling, the therapist may need to redirect the session and refocus on the treatment goals or talk with the client about whether or not they need to redirect the goals.

In this metaphor, the science looks at the mechanics of whether the car works and can be a vehicle to support the journey to the desired destination. The art may involve how the driver uses the science. In summary, when people talk about nature or nurture, the answer is yes, it is both. It is science and art you cannot separate the two. In order for the science to work, the trust and rapport must be built. Unlike the physical sciences where we can mix two molecules of hydrogen and one molecule of oxygen and get $H_2O$ or water, when we combine three different experiences with people, For example, some people who have been through trauma experience posttraumatic growth, some experience posttraumatic stress, some experience bitterness and anger, and some develop gratitude and a desire to help others. who have been through trauma, some experience post-traumatic growth, some experience post-traumatic stress, people go through hardship some experience bitterness and anger, some experience gratitude and desire to help others. Therefore, of creating rapport, trust, and understanding is necessary but not sufficient. The science of identifying effective treatment relies on the rapport cultivated by the art of counseling.

The pitfalls of using the scientific components of counseling such as interventions and treatment plans without the artistic components of rapport and therapeutic alliance can lead to premature termination and a sense that the client is not heard, understood, or valued. Likewise, the pitfall of using the art of counseling without the science is that the client may enjoy coming to counseling; he or she may feel a sense of relief from processing his or her thoughts and feelings; however, he or she may not accomplish his or her goals and stagnate. Thus, each individual component is necessary but not sufficient.

The science of counseling may involve a greater focus on the outcomes associated with counseling. Many clinicians do this informally by assessing client progress using scaling. For example, if a client presents indicating they are struggling with anxiety about an important decision, a counselor may invite the client to assess his or her anxiety on a scale from 1 to 10 (see Chapter 13 on scaling for more information). This creates a baseline that indicates where the client is initially. Then, the counselor may ask the client to rate his or her anxiety once again in follow-up sessions in order to monitor progress informally. For a more formal assessment, a counselor may invite the client to complete an assessment such as Beck Anxiety Inventory. Collecting data and assessing efficacy of counseling help us to approach counseling as a scientific study. The following is quote from Rex Stockton (2010), who was a keynote speaker at the Association for Specialist in Group Work. He discusses a strategy for conducting relevant research that is a helpful component for establishing the science of counseling:

> As my colleague, Keith Morran, and I have recommended, those who want to conduct research should plan to develop an ongoing program of study that will evolve and can be modified to provide increasingly relevant data. This is important because an evolving program also offers the advantage that each round of data collection serves as a pilot study for the next. Data collection can be expanded to include promising outcomes and the elimination or reduction of areas that show little promise. Thus, such programmatic studies, as they evolve, can become increasingly focused on the real world concerns of group practitioners. (p. 324)

In summary of the science part of counseling, the question arises, "Are counselors superheroes or brain surgeons?" The answer is a resounding, "Yes!"

## Integrative Framework

One way of looking at epistemology or ways of knowing that allows us to glean the benefits of multiple fields and put them together in order to deepen and broaden understanding is to create an integrative framework. Dr. Dan Siegel (B), the founder of a Norton series of more than 20 books on related topics, emphasizes how the field he promotes Is this the field he promotes? If so, enclose in commas. integrates at least 14 other fields including the following: anthropology, biology (developmental, evolution, genetics, zoology), cognitive science, computer science, developmental psychopathology, linguistics neuroscience (affective, cognitive, developmental, social), mathematics, mental health, physics, psychiatry, psychology (cognitive, developmental, evolutionary, experimental, of religion, social, attachment theory, memory), sociology, systems theory (chaos and complexity theory).

Thus, we believe that in counseling, we can integrate ways of knowing from other fields in order to identify strategies to become effective counselors and create an atmosphere for change within our clients. As we begin to use an integrated model, we feel that we are beginning to practice client advocacy with the client at the center of the model. For example, when singers sing harmony, depth and variety are added because the harmony is complementary to the melody, but when we have a choir singing with an orchestra, then richness and robustness are added. Similarly, by using a theoretical framework and research to help us know what to listen for and how to personally conceptualize while keeping the client in the center, we are advocating for clients and beginning to see an integrated model. An outcome of integration is harmony (the pieces are fitting together in a pleasing way) just like you also have different parts of the choir singing together; in counseling, you have the overlay of differing approaches that actually adds to the ability for the hearer to conceptualize the presenting issue in a way that might make sense to the client and for the counselor to have better clarity in session.

## CBASP and Therapist Characteristics

James McCullough is the developer of the CBASP approach, and he worked with Vocisano and colleagues to conduct a large clinical trial on therapist variables that are associated with changes in symptoms of chronically depressed clients. This is a compelling quote from the article: "The largest and most influential psychotherapy outcome studies have focused primarily on technique efficacy (Richards & Bergin, 1997), despite the fact that therapy out-come is more closely related to therapist characteristics than to type of treatment (Lambert & Okiishi, 1997; Luborsky et al., 1986);" (Vocisano et al., 2004, p. 256). This certainly makes a case for examining therapist characteristics!

Let us look at the counselor characteristics revealed in this study to be associated with positive client outcomes:

- Greater emphasis on therapeutic relationship

- Lower overall psychotherapy caseload

- Therapist psychodymanic theoretical orientation

- Supervisory status (Vocisano et al., 2004, p. 256)

Based on this research, we find four important aspects that might, when integrated, provide an ideal environment for the counselor that, in turn, will provide an ideal environment for the client. In other words, if the counselor is operating out of a place that is based on intentional balance, direction, and support, he or she then provide the highest level of care in counseling.

## Brief Motivational Interviewing

A group of scholars, Gaume et al. (2014), wrote an article that was published in a journal called, *Alcoholism Clinical and Experimental Research* where they investigated counselor behaviors and characteristics that impacted the efficacy of an intervention (**Brief Motivational Interviewing [BMI]**). They used the gold standard to address their research question, a randomized control trial. They address a gap in the literature indicating that "little attention has been given to counselor influence on treatment mechanisms" (Gaume, Magill, et al., 2014, p. 2138).

## Spiritual Implications

Just as different theories have emerged based on philosophical differences about how change and healing take place within counseling, a parallel process is seen within the realm of spirituality. This is not unlike how, within the Christian faith, different denominations have developed within one religion. For example, a Christian may provide a specifier for his or her particular approach to faith such Southern Baptist, Nazarene, Methodist, and Presbyterian. Although the various positions on topics such as baptism may differ, the common belief in Jesus Christ as Lord and savior is a common link that ties them together.

## Attachment Illumination

© Shutterstock.com

Just like we mentioned in the chapter overview, we have looked at research on the habits from the past, present, and future. Here we will look at the counselors' personal attachment story, past, present, and future. Note the Adult Attachment Interview (AAI) starts out discussing the past in terms of adjectives and memories, moves to the present in terms of what your current relationship with attachment figures is like, and then future (e.g., the question that asks what you would like your child to have learned from his or her experiences with you)

One of the characteristics of an effective counselor is being present, and a counselor's attachment history can impact his or her capacity to be present. The challenge to make sense of our own attachment stories so we can move toward these discussions with clients avoid experiencing preoccupation is tiring.

Rubino et al. (2000) indicated that when therapists are anxious, they are less empathic to clients. Using strategies like completing the AAI with an empathic counselor, journaling about one's attachment story, and making sense of one's story all help the client move toward a coherent secure autonomous style. This may make it easier for the counselor to be present and mindful with the client and less likely to be preoccupied.

Consider Sitting squarely; Open posture; Leaning in; Eye contact; Relaxed (SOLER) and peace needing to be in place. In Chapter 6, we will discuss the posture of listening and the nonverbal skills. In the acronym SOLER, the R represents relax. . . and the core feeling is peace, so practicing activities such as making sense of one's story, praying contemplatively and journaling may be facilitative of this state. Just as we may journal about the past, present, and future to make sense of our story, God can see our past, present, and future. He is outside of time, He is I AM, and His presence is not only peace, but the scriptures tell us fullness of joy.

"You make known to me the path of life; in your presence there is fullness of joy; at your right hand are pleasures forevermore." Psalm 16:11, (ESV).

As we consider the use of SOLER and empathic connection, we see that Lucy does not seem to be presenting a posture of listening in her psychiatric booth (see image on previous page). Consider the power of presence as you engage with clients in an empathic manner. Also, new counselors may feel overwhelmed, like Lucy, so be sure to remain present in an empathic way in each session.

Lucy in her psychiatric booth

PEANUTS © Peanuts Worldwide LLC. Dist. By ANDREWS MCMEEL SYNDICATION. Reprinted with permission. All rights reserved.

## Recommended Reading

In order to continue to develop your expertise in the area of habits of effective counseling, we would recommend reading the following texts to expand your knowledge in this area. These are recommended readings as they provide the basis of some of the research used for this chapter. Moreover, these texts add to a counselor's repertoire of resources in the field Suggest alphabetizing these entries.

© Shutterstock.com

- Allen, J. G., Fonagy, P., & Bateman, A. (2008). *Mentalizing in clinical practice.* Washington, DC: American Psychiatric Publishing.

- Covey, S. R. (2004). *The 7 habits of highly effective people: Restoring the character ethic* (Revis. ed.). New York, NY: Free Press.

- Luft, J., & Ingham, H. (1955). *The Johari window: A graphic model of interpersonal awareness.* San Diego, CA: University of California Western Training Lab.

- Szapkiw, A., & Silvey, R. (2010). The use of wikis to aid in communication and collaboration within the helping profession: A pilot study. *Journal for Human Service Education, 30*(1), 71–75.

## Chapter Summary

There are several ways to summarize this chapter, but we think this quote from a veteran therapist is appropriate: "I trusted my subconscious mind to respond in a therapeutic way." The overall goal of discussing and, ultimately, developing habits of an effective counselor is to become the best counselor that you can (we have discussed this more in Chapter 2). As we have researched the habits and scoured the literature and reflected on our clinical and teaching experiences, ideas have emerged that inform the habits that we see as central to effective counseling. We think that the picture of Lucy in the psychiatry booth (as seen and addressed previously) tells us quite a bit about how new counselors might feel overwhelmed, pensive, or concerned: "So, what is it that I will do as a counselor and how do I do it?" Well, we feel a good starting point is personal emotion regulation and attempting to help others regulate well. There is a point where we have to gather information and begin making connection with the material in order to make connection with clients.

## Chapter Five

# Ethical Informed Consent, Suicide Risk Assessment, and Using Technology in Counseling

### E. John Kuhnley, MD

*Whoever walks in integrity walks securely, but whoever takes crooked paths will be found out.*

—Proverbs 10:9

## Chapter Learning Objectives

- To identify essential elements of informed consent
- To identify essential elements of confidentiality and exceptions to confidentiality
- To identify situations that mandate reporting
- To explore suicide prevention models and strategies (e.g., SAFE-T approach; CACREP II.F.5.1, 2016, p. 12)
- To address ethical and culturally relevant strategies for establishing and maintaining in-person and technology-assisted relationships (CACREP II.F.5.d, 2016, p. 11)
- To explore the impact of technology on the counseling process (CACREP II.F.5.e, 2016, p. 11)

# Chapter Overview

C lients have a right to treatment. Clinicians, including counselors, have an obligation to provide all necessary information, materials, and opportunity for clients to learn and understand the recommended interventions including goals, risks, benefits, and alternative options. With this understanding, the client may share with the clinician the decision for treatment and sign informed consent. This produces a collaborative foundation for the treatment process. Failure on the part of the counselor to provide opportunity for informed consent or violation of the treatment agreement may invoke legal ramifications.

Counselors must respect the confidentiality of the client's information and disclosures. Clients may authorize disclosure through specific written consent. There are a few exceptions that override confidentiality. There are situations in which the counselor has a legal obligation to disclose, such as when a client is a danger to self or others. Laws governing informed consent, confidentiality, and mandated reporting or disclosure vary among the states, and

> *Confidentiality is the essence of being trusted.*
> —*Billy Graham*

counselors must be aware of the statutes in the states in which they practice. Local and national counseling organizations provide guidance. This chapter provides a brief overview of the essential elements.

Suicide risk assessment is an essential skill for all clinicians, including counselors. The SAFE-T method is one of many possible tools to guide the counselor.

## Ethical Informed Consent

Informed consent is a process. The counselor must provide certain information about the proposed treatment to the client, ensure that the client understands the information, engage the client in a collaborative development of a treatment plan, and obtain signed consent from the client (or from the parents or guardian of the client if the client is a minor; ACA, 2014, § A.2.d.). Some of the key elements of the consent process include, but are not limited to, the following:

- A disclosure statement regarding the counselor's professional background and qualifications (ACA, 2014, § A.2.b.) and the counseling process

- Detailed disclosure of the proposed treatment, including the possible risks and desired benefits consistent with the goals of the client (ACA, 2014, § A.2.b.)

- Disclosure about the risks and benefits of other options, including not getting treatment (ACA, 2014, § A.2.b.)

- Discussion with the client to ensure that the client understands the information to make a decision that is in the client's best interest (ACA, 2014, § A.2.c).

- Provision of opportunity for the client to deliberate and discuss the proposal with significant others or other providers if the client chooses to do so (ACA, 2014, § A.2.d).

- Securing the signed consent of the client to accept the proposed treatment (Remley & Herlihy, 2016, p.96; ACA, 2014, B.6.g)

- Informing the client of the right and process to withdraw consent (ACA, 2014, § A.2.b.)

- Disclosure of the limits of confidentiality (ACA, 2014, § A.2.b.)

The informed consent process employs the six core tasks of attachment-based therapy: safety, education, containment, understanding, restructuring, and engagement (Clinton & Sibcy, 2012). These skills are necessary to begin to establish a secure, healthy therapeutic relationship with the client by assuring the client and counselor have a clear and consensual understanding of the treatment goals structured to the best interests of the client, addressing negative emotions that may impact the beginning of the therapeutic relationship, and engaging the client in willing consent to proceed with the treatment.

The American Counseling Association (ACA) is an organization that represents and provides valuable guidance for counselors. The ACA Code of Ethics (ACA, 2014, § A.2.b.) addresses the counseling relationship, confidentiality and privacy, and professional responsibility in Sections A, B, and C.

The American Association for Christian Counselors (AACC) is "the world's premier Christian counseling organization" (AACC, 2014a). The AACC website provides a code of ethics "utilizing eight foundational principles" including (a) compassion, (b) competence, (c) consent, (d) confidentiality, (e) cultural regard, (f) case management, (g) collegiality, and (h) community presence.

These organizations provide professional resources to guide counselors in skill development and the practice of professional counseling.

## Clients' Rights to Treatment

Clients have a right to treatment, and they have rights within the treatment process. The list may vary from one organization to another. Client's rights commonly include but are not limited to the following:

© Tashatuvango/Shutterstock.com

- The right to treatment

- The right to refuse treatment

- The right to informed consent

- The right to privacy and confidentiality of health information and disclosures

- The right to establish advanced directives (while in possession of full decision-making capabilities) to direct medical care in the future when this capacity is lost.

The Health Insurance Portability and Accountability Act (HIPAA) of 1996 (Pub.L. 104–191, 110 Stat. 1936; devised and enacted by the U.S. Congress on August 21, 1996 and signed by President Bill Clinton in 1996) is U.S. legislation that provides provisions for the privacy and safeguarding of medical information. It includes delineation of patients' rights, including informed consent and confidentiality. Healthcare providers must maintain the privacy of protected health information. The patient must provide written consent for disclosure of this information to specific individuals or organizations. There are exceptions when disclosure is required by regulation or law. The exceptions include situations of medical emergency, legal action, and the required release of certain limited information for billing purposes. In addition to HIPAA, counselors must be familiar with the laws in the states in

© zimmytws/Shutterstock.com

which they practice and the policies of organizations who may employ them. In "Ethical, Legal, and Professional Issues in Counseling," Remley and Herlihy (2016) discuss the idea that since HIPAA is not a state law, but a federal law, "it applies throughout the United States and overrides state laws that are more lax. However, state laws that are stricter than HIPAA about protecting consumer health care privacy must be adhered to, if they exist" (p. 145).

## Breaching Confidentiality

There are situations in which clinicians are required to breach confidentiality, including, but not limited to, the following:

- Some states permit mental health providers to disclose confidential information to close family members and others involved in the treatment of the client without consent if it is thought to be in the best interest of the client (HHS, 1996).

- Attorneys, police officers, or courts may request information from a counselor, and legal guidance may be necessary for the counselor to handle these requests.

- Utilization review organizations, physician peer reviewers, and third-party payers may have access to hospital charts.

## Mandated Reporting

Clinicians, including counselors, are mandated reporters in situations where they observe or suspect abuse of a vulnerable person. This includes cases of child and elder abuse or neglect. Each state has guidelines and agencies to whom the counselor would make the report. It is not up to the counselor to determine whether abuse or neglect is happening. The counselor must provide an objective report to the agency that will determine if investigation is necessary. The U.S. Department of Health and Human Services (n.d.) provides state guidelines to assist clinicians.

Other cases of mandated reporting include when a client reports being at risk of harming the self or another person and when there is a court order for the notes or reports from sessions (American Counseling Association, 2014).

## Prevention and Intervention

You may be familiar with the proverbs "An ounce of prevention is worth a pound of cure" and "A stitch in time saves nine." These two statements are based on the premise that a prevention may save a necessitated intervention. As we think about this, a connection between prevention and intervention is clear. In the model below, you will see the relationship between prevention and intervention. Ultimately, the goal of prevention is to avoid the need for an intervention; however, the goal of an intervention is to address the issue at hand and prevent the need for a future intervention.

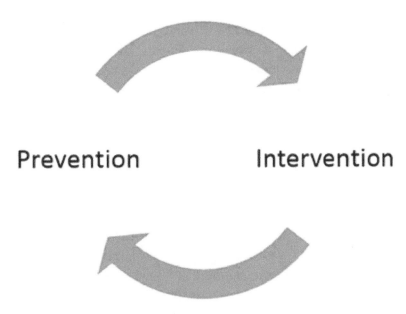

**Prevention**          **Intervention**

**Figure 5.1.** The Relationship Between Prevention and Intervention

Dr. Kuhnley Dr. Silvey, and I think that model provides a visual of how the goal of interventions can be to prevent future occurrences and how the goal of preventions can be to avoid interventions. Counselors can use this to attempt to make sense of the direction and/or purpose of the counseling session, especially when a client seems to encounter an impasse in the session.

*A Concept to Contemplate*

© Shutterstock.com

The idea that an intervention may be a prevention may help the counselor instill hope into the session. As a counselor, how might you use an intervention as a prevention? Take a moment to contemplate Figure 5.1 in your response to this question.

## Threats of Suicide and Homicide

When counselors encounter a client making threats of suicide or homicide, they may breach confidentiality to address the danger to the client or others. In 1976, the Supreme Court of the State of California decided the case of Tarasoff v. Regents of the University of California. The court held that a mental health professional had a legal duty to warn an identifiable victim of the threat of harm by a client. According to the National Behavioral Intervention Team Association (n.d.), many states have a mandatory duty to warn statute, some states have a "may warn" (permission to warn but not mandated) statute, whereas other states do not have a duty to warn statute but may impose duty through case law. It is advisable for a counselor to seek immediate legal and other guidance in such a situation. Threats of suicide by a client invoke the responsibility of the counselor to conduct a suicide risk assessment.

## Suicide Risk Assessment

Suicide is the voluntary and intentional act of killing oneself. It is a leading cause of death in the United States. According to the Centers for Disease Control and Prevention ([CDC], 2017), in 2016, there were 44,965 deaths by suicide, making it the 10th-leading cause of death in the United States. It was the second-leading. Also fourth-leading later in this sentence cause of death in the groups between the ages of 10 and 34 and the fourth leading cause of death in the group from ages 35 to 54. The CDC website (www.cdc.gov) provides information on violence prevention, including suicide prevention, stating that "Suicide is a serious public health problem that can have lasting harmful effects on individuals, families, and communities."

Suicide risk assessment is an attempt to determine the likelihood that a person will engage in suicidal behavior that might result in death. It is crucial that counselors establish and maintain a solid therapeutic relationship with clients to encourage trust and disclosure. Counselors must have a degree of comfort in discussing sensitive issues with clients, including asking about the possibility of suicidal ideation, inclinations, plans, and attempts. An open, caring, nonjudgmental approach is important in creating the secure emotional environment within which the client is more likely to disclose suicidal thoughts, feelings, and behaviors. Carefully, the counselor must explore the nature and extent of the client's potential for suicide. The art and science of therapeutic empathy, a genuine collaborative stance, and an approach to achieve and express understanding of the client's struggle with the desire to die are of the utmost importance in determining risk and moving toward safety. Conducting suicide risk assessment is an important step in suicide prevention.

There are many tools to assist clinicians, including counselors, in suicide risk assessment. The Substance Abuse and Mental Health Services Administration, a branch of the U.S. Department of Health and Human Services (2009), provides the SAFE-T, the Suicide Assessment Five-Step Evaluation and Triage method. Guidelines, a manual, a card, and a mobile app are available.

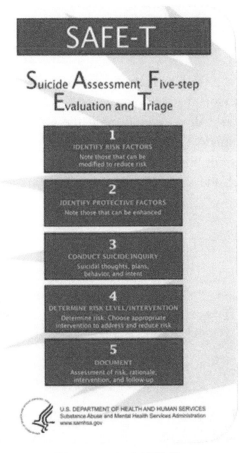

**Figure 5.2.** SAFE-T

The SAFE-T (Education Development Center & Screening for Mental Health, 2009) explores:

- Ideation: frequency, intensity, duration—in last 48 hr, past month, and worst ever

- Plan: timing, location, lethality, availability, preparatory acts

- Behaviors: past attempts, aborted attempts, rehearsals (tying noose, loading gun) vs. nonsuicidal self-injurious actions

- Intent: extent to which the patient (1) expects to carry out the plan and (2) believes the plan/act to be lethal vs. self-injurious; Explore ambivalence: reasons to die vs. reasons to live. (Suicide Inquiry)

The first step is the identification of risk factors. Many factors may contribute to the risk of a person contemplating suicide. They may include personal issues, relationship problems, spiritual concerns, societal problems, mental and physical illness, and stresses of everyday living (National Center for Injury Prevention and Control, 2018). A clinician must take a careful history to elucidate the risk of the client. Personal history, family history, and the person's psychosocial circumstances provide clues as to the intensity of the risk factors.

## Protective Factors

The second step of the SAFE-T is to identify "protective factors." These include strengths, attributes, or assets of the person that may mitigate the risk and promote healthy decisions. Resources available in the world of the person and the community may buffer the individual from acting in furtherance of suicidal ideation or inclinations. The counselor may elicit from the client a focus on the reasons for living and strategies for overcoming the issues that led to suicidal ideation. Please watch the video of Dr. Kuhnley conducting a suicide risk assessment with Alex.

**Video**

**Imminent Risk Assessment: Dr. Kuhnley**

## Protective factors include

- Effective clinical care for mental, physical, and substance abuse disorders

- Easy access to a variety of clinical interventions and support for help seeking

- Family and community support (connectedness)

- Support from ongoing medical and mental healthcare relationships

- Skills in problem solving, conflict resolution, and nonviolent ways of handling disputes

- Cultural and religious beliefs that discourage suicide and support instincts for self-preservation. (U.S. Public Health Service, 1999)

## Attachment Illumination

© Shutterstock.com

In previous chapters, we have discussed the importance of early caregivers in healthy development. In the section directly above on protective factors, you may have noticed that family and community support (connectedness) was listed as a protective factor. For those who have grown up with sensitive and responsive caregivers, their family of origin may indeed provide the sense of support that comes from a secure base and safe haven that is associated with the ability to explore and secure support within their community. However, as it the case with many of our clients, approximately half of the population grows up with inadequate family of origin support and develops an insecure attachment style. For these individuals, relationships may be like storms rather than ports in the storm.

In counseling, it is important to explore the client's interpersonal history (the attachment or relationship patterns) to determine deficits and to assist the client in identifying alternative support systems that may be more protective. For example, some clients may find support with extended family members such as a grandparent or aunt. Others may find support from individuals other than family members including a pastor, a teacher, a coach, or a sponsor in an Alcoholics Anonymous or Narcotics Anonymous group. Counselors may assist clients in revising attachment or relationship rules that govern whether the self is worthy of love and whether others are able to competently love them (Clinton & Sibcy, 2002). This will be important for ensuring their interpersonal future looks different than their interpersonal history, thus helping them to develop community support and connectedness that can serve as a protective buffer. For more on connection and empathy, see Chapter 3.

The third step of a suicide risk assessment is to inquire about the nature of the suicidal thoughts, plans, behaviors, and intents. It is important to determine the nature and extent of the potential for suicide over the preceding 48 hours. **Suicidal ideation** is common and involves thoughts that life is not worth living or the client and/or others may be better off if the client were dead. Most individuals who have suicidal ideation do not go on to attempt or complete suicide. **Suicidal gestures** are acts in furtherance of ideation but without intent. They may be impulsive or well conceived. However, gestures are dangerous because the individual might "accidentally" succeed in dying because of the gesture. **Suicidal plans** represent active thoughts about how to proceed with the act of suicide, and action on the plan represents an **act in furtherance** toward possible completion of suicide. **Suicide intent to die** indicates the person has made a commitment to attempt suicide, and a **suicide attempt** represents an action to cause death.

The fourth step of a suicide risk assessment is to determine the level of risk that the person will make an act in furtherance toward suicide. Despite abundant information on suicide assessment and intervention, and regardless of the level of skill of the clinician, it remains difficult to predict with accuracy whether a person will attempt suicide. Although most clients who consider suicide will not go on to complete suicide, it is devastating to the family, the community and the clinician if the client commits suicide despite all efforts to prevent it.

A thorough assessment of causation, risk factors, protective factors, and the mental status of the client may guide the counselor to an informed decision as to the best intervention. If there is any doubt about safety, seek intervention. This may involve family or community resources to provide observation until the suicidal thoughts or inclinations pass. The client may require admission to an emergency room or a hospital if there is evidence of a high degree of lethality, if the client is psychotic (out of touch with reality), impulsive, or having diminished judgment (the ability to evaluate evidence and make a considered decision), or there is a lack of resources to assure safety. If the risk is low, then the counselor may collaborate with the client to modify risk factors (such as having weapons removed from the home) and mobilize protective factors (such as having a trusted family member or friend accompany the client) to increase likelihood of safety and progress toward improved health and well-being. The counselor may address preventive measures and set up further counseling sessions for development of coping strategies and problem solving. The counselor may refer the client to a specialized psychotherapist, a community program, and/or a psychiatrist or other prescriber who may need to consider psychotropic medication. A plan for follow-up is essential.

> **A Quote to Remember**
> "The presence of a mental disorder is an important risk factor for suicide. It is generally acknowledged that over 90% of those who committed suicide had a psychiatric diagnosis at the time of death." (Bertolote & Fleischmann, 2002, p. 183)

The fifth step of conducting a suicide risk assessment is to document the findings from the first four steps as to the nature and extent of suicidal thoughts, feelings and behaviors, risk and protective factors, treatment plan, and rationale for the chosen interventions and course of action. Documentation serves as a means of communication among care providers. It must provide an accurate accounting of the care provided by the counselor and demonstrate professional credibility.

Documentation must provide clear, objective information without speculative opinions. Comprehensive documentation includes the full evaluation from the client and collateral sources (such as family, friends, teachers, and employers), the client's condition and level of risk, and the recommendations for safety and treatment, including plans for follow-up. The counselor must provide evidence to support impressions and recommendations. When it comes to review, if it is not in the documentation, it didn't happen. At all times, liability and accountability are important considerations, especially in the assessment of danger and risk such as the suicide potential of a client.

The National Suicide Prevention Lifeline is a valuable resource. It is a free and confidential support for individuals in distress. Counselors may provide the client with the number: 1-800-273-TALK (1-800-273-8255)

**Figure 5.3.** Suicide Prevention Lifeline Retrieved from URL:
https://www.cdc.gov/violenceprevention/suicide/definitions.html

## Ethical and Culturally Relevant Strategies for Establishing and Maintaining In-Person and Technology-Assisted Relationships (CACREP II.F.5.d)

Counselors must build trusting, sustainable relationships with clients. This serves as the foundation for goal achievement by clients for improved health and well-being. Understanding, acknowledgment, and awareness of the impact of the cultural identity of the client and potential cultural differences between the counselor and the client are necessary to establish trust and will impact the effectiveness of the counseling.

Cultural aspects include age, gender, maturity, sexual orientation, socioeconomic class, family nationality of origin, geographic location, spirituality, and religion. The counselor must be prepared to acknowledge these aspects openly with the client, verbalize, and demonstrate willingness to learn and respect the beliefs and worldview of the client. Self-awareness by the counselor of the counselor's beliefs and worldview is necessary in identifying cultural differences, the impact of the client's culture on the counselor, and impact that the counselor has upon the client. "A Concept to Contemplate" section in Chapter 6 provides an exercise on counselor worldview and the impact this has on the client or counselor relationship.

Relevant, culturally sensitive strategies and situations abound for counselors and may include the following:

1. Addressing the importance of the role of family with a client.
2. Working with your supervisor to determine appropriate behaviors in the setting in which you are working.
3. Seeking to discern verbal and nonverbal cues from clients that reveal their cultural beliefs and behaviors.
4. Maintaining self-awareness of personal impressions that result from the cues within the expressions of the client.

It is important to note that there may be both spoken and unspoken cues that inform the counselor about the client. Counselors must understand that culture is multifaceted and, therefore, the counselor must be aware that the client may have multiple cultural characteristics.

Often, there are as many differences among individuals within a culture as there are between cultures. Based on this, the counselor must address the individual needs of the client in a diverse manner. This is also an example of "differentiated counseling" as addressed in Chapter 2.

The empathic counselor collaborates with the client to establish goals with the focus on the client. The counselor must be patient, flexible, unbiased, and professional (with clear boundaries) and must follow the code of ethics for counselors while remaining relevant with the use of technology. The counselor must understand how clients are using technology and the impact it might be having in their lives. This applies to both in-person counseling and technology-assisted counseling. For example, the National Center for Biotechnology Information (2015) resource "Using Technology-Based Therapeutic Tools in Behavioral Health Services," notes:

> Digital media and resources, such as email, smartphone/tablet applications (apps), online forums, Web sites, DVDs, CD-ROMs, blogs, computer software, online social networks, telephone and televideo communication, and mobile devices, are becoming universal in our culture. The use of electronic media and information technologies in behavioral health treatment, recovery support, and prevention programs is rapidly gaining acceptance. (p. 3)

These tools can provide an enhancement to the counseling experience. However, they can cause clients experience anxiety, ethical issues, or boundary issues. Integration of technology-based tools into clinical practice provides counselors and other health-care professionals with valuable options to facilitate care. Telehealth allows counselors to reach clients who have limitations in access to services because of resource limitations or geographic locations. There are clients who are fearful of interacting face to face with a provider but may accept the distance aspect of interacting with a counselor on a screen. Telehealth may save time and resources. However, the counselor is responsible to ensure ethical and culturally relevant use of technology. The National Center for Biotechnology Information (2015) resource advises, "Use of advanced technologies also requires consideration of a number of legal and ethical issues, such as confidentiality, scope of practice, state licensure regulations, privacy, data security, consent management, and the potential for misuse" (p. 4).

## Explore the Impact of Technology on the Counseling Process (CACREP II.F.5.e)

In summary, it is necessary to explore technology from at least two angles: (a) how the client may use technology and the impact it might have in the life of the client, and (b) how the counselor may use technology to provide or enhance counseling services. The use of technology in counseling must align with the needs of the client. Second, technology provides a broad array of modalities to add to core counseling techniques with which to deliver care to a broader number of clients that may otherwise have no access to care.

## Recommended Reading

In order to continue to develop your expertise in the area of informed consent and suicide risk assessment, we would recommend looking over the resources found on the following websites to expand your knowledge in this area:

- The CDC website: https://www.cdc.gov

- The NIMH website: https://www.nimh.nih.gov/index.shtml

We also highly recommend the following texts:

Remley, T., & Herlihy, B. (2016). *Ethical, legal, and professional issues in counseling.* New York, NY: Pearson.

Clinton, T., & Sibcy, G. (2002). *Attachments: Why you love, feel, and act the way you do.* Nashville, TN: Integrity.

The latter text was co-authored by one of the primary authors of this textbook, Dr. Gary Sibcy, who unpacks concepts related to attachment style in a compelling, easy-to-understand manner. The text is also available as an audiobook.

## Chapter Summary

Counselors must conduct themselves in an ethical manner in the provision of services to clients. Informed consent and confidentiality are essential and mandated by law. They provide a foundation of trust for the counselor–client relationship. There are circumstances where the counselor may determine need to breach confidentiality, especially when the situation poses a danger by the client toward self or others. The ability to conduct a suicide risk assessment is a crucial skill for all mental health professionals. It is important for counselors to seek guidance from their local and national organizations as well as the laws of the state in which they practice. It is imperative that counselors know ethics and practice ethically, especially when using technology. Counselors need to consider the use of technology, but the technology must align with the needs of the client.

## Chapter Six

# The Posture of Listening: Nonverbal Counseling Skills

Anita Kuhnley and Steve Warren

*Listen with your eyes as well as your ears.*

—Graham Speechley (2016)

### Chapter Learning Objectives

1. To learn counselor characteristics and behaviors that influence the counseling process, such as congruence, nonverbal behaviors, and vocal tone (CACREP II.5.f, 2016, p. 12)

2. To explore essential interviewing, counseling, and case conceptualization skills, gaining an understanding of how nonverbal counseling skills (such as SOLER) are essential counseling skills (CACREP II.5.g, 2016, p. 12)

3. To explore the impact of spiritual beliefs on clients' and counselors' worldviews (CACREP II.F.2.g, 2016, p. 10)

4. To identify a systems approach to conceptualizing clients when using nonverbal behaviors (CACREP II.F.5.b, 2016, p. 11)

# Chapter Overview

This chapter explores nonverbal counseling skills. Both the art and the science of nonverbal communication and how nonverbal skills apply to counseling are unpacked here. We examine the nonverbal dance that takes place as a therapist welcomes the client into the office, perhaps initiates a handshake (if appropriate), begins to use gestures to invite him or her to take a seat, the adopts a posture to communicate a congruent and authentic desire to listen, and uses other nonverbal dimensions of the counseling process. We communicate using different strategies; the beginning counselor may not be aware of how some of these nonverbals communicate to his or her clients. This chapter will unfold enhancing awareness and being intentional and purposeful in our nonverbal communication with our clients.

## Why Are Nonverbal Skills Important?

*We respond to gestures with extreme alertness and one might almost say, in accordance with an elaborate secret code that is written nowhere, known by none, and understood by all.*

—Sapir (1949)

Let us begin unpacking the secret code that underlies the behaviors "understood by all." Before addressing why nonverbal skills are important and how to develop these skills, let us first define what they are. **Nonverbal counseling skills** often refer to vocal tone and quality as well as body postures and movements or gestures and facial expressions (Duncan, Rice, & Butler, 1968; Haase & Tepper, 1972). Nonverbal counseling skills have been prioritized as

*93% of communication occurs through nonverbal behavior & tone; only 7% of communication takes place through the use of words—thus the 93/7 Rule.*

important competencies for counselors for decades (Hermansson, Webster, & MacFarland, 1988). Consider the last time you were in a conversation and you were in the speaker role, and your conversation partner took out his or her phone and began checking text messages and typing. If you said, "Oh, I will wait while you finish that" and the listener responded saying, "Oh no, go ahead; I'm listening. I'm just multitasking" in this situation, would you feel heard? Probably not. Not only was the listener communicating something incongruent, but the nonverbal message may have

—John Stoker,
*Overcoming Fake Talk: How to Hold Real Conversations That Create Respect, Build Relationships, and Get Results* (2013, p. 32)

communicated more strongly so that your motivation to continue sharing diminished due to not feeling heard.

## The Nonverbal Behavior of Counselors

*What you are stands over you the while, and thunders so that I cannot hear what you say.*

Ralph Waldo Emerson (1875, p. 80)

The nonverbal behavior of counselors has also been demonstrated to impact the counseling outcomes of clients. One example is illustrated in the research of Kim, Liang, and Li (2003); they conducted a study to investigate the impact of the variables of ethnicity and counselor nonverbal behaviors on outcomes with Asian clients. Their results revealed that there was a statistically significant positive correlation between frequency of smiles and session positivity as rated by the client.

It has also been suggested that a counselor's nonverbal skills impact the following interpersonal therapeutic processes (Highlen & Hill, 1984):

1. Convey emotions

2. Communicate changes within the therapeutic relationship

3. Serve to regulate the interaction between therapist and client (e.g., the process of turn taking in dialogue is regulated by nonverbal interaction)

4. Help the counselor to investigate emotions that are masked beneath the surface

5. Reveal attitudes toward the self

6. They reinforce or complement one's verbal expression or contradict it

Like their verbal counterparts, the purpose of nonverbal counseling skills is to create a facilitative and safe environment for clients to self-disclose. Although more research has focused on verbal counseling skills that are facilitative, nonverbal counseling skills have also been investigated and found to contribute to the manifestation of process skills such as empathic understanding, a sense of genuineness, and respect (Carkhuff, 1969; Haase & Tepper, 1972; Kelly & True, 1980; Smith-Hanen, 1977; Truax, 1962).

Research also supports the role of nonverbal counseling skills in the expression of empathy. As you now noticed by the title of this textbook and Chapter 3 devoted to empathy, empathy is an umbrella skill that is associated with positive outcomes and one that should cover or be infused into all of the other skills we will use. We believe that just like agenda setting is the heart and soul of CBT, empathy is the heart and soul of effective counseling skills. Early research by Fretz (1966) demonstrates the role of nonverbal behaviors in the expression of counselor empathy as judged by clients.

We communicate all the time, but as counselors it is important to be intentional about what we communicate. Entering into someone's pain and distress is a sort of sacred trust, and in order to facilitate a sense of safety for our clients, it is important to communicate one very clear message that we care. We want to communicate that we are empathic, truly listening, and fully present with them; congruent nonverbal skills are a central tool for these purposes. If our words say that we are interested, but our nonverbal communication reveals otherwise, even perhaps subconsciously, then we are sending mixed messages and can cause obstacles to the therapeutic relationship and the facilitation of personal disclosure. One of the first rules of counseling is to "seek first to understand." The posture of listening opens the counselor to the client's need to be heard. Often, messages are communicated that are beyond words but can interfere with the transmission of the verbal message. For example, if the counselor uses a door opener that invites the client to share by saying, "What would you like to accomplish during our time together today?" but then turns away from the client and writes a note, this may undermine the authenticity of the invitation for the client to share. Consider the last time you visited a coffee shop or restaurant and saw people at a table together texting or on social media rather than interacting with the person that they were with. In the image on the following page, what is being communicated? We may not be aware of these tendencies and patterns where internal preoccupations are manifested in a lack of nonverbal attending behavior. Part of what we want to do is to be intentional about having our nonverbal and verbal communication in agreement, and this is known as congruence.

One way to think of the difference between congruent and incongruent communication may be to look at the difference between music and noise. When we listen to music with a melody and harmony, the sound is congruent. However, when we hear tires screeching, a horn honking, and a dog barking in unison, what we hear is noise. Likewise, in a counseling session, when our verbal and nonverbal communication align, we are conveying a congruent message. But when our nonverbal behavior conflicts with our

© WAYHOME studio/Shutterstock.com

verbal communication, it is like noise that undermines our ability to form a therapeutic alliance. Congruence is an important goal for the intentional counselor. One of the tasks for moving toward congruence is to move from being unaware of or unintentional about our communication to being thoughtful and intentional. This comes out in the idea of presence.

## Therapeutic Presence

*I understand now that I'm not a mess but a deeply feeling person in a messy world. I explain that now, when someone asks me why I cry so often, I say, For the same reason I laugh so often- because I'm paying attention.*

Doyle Melton (2016, p. 226)

**What does it mean to be present with a client?** Although this text is designed for courses in counseling skills and techniques, many of the counseling skills taught and exemplified in this text are designed and implemented for the purposes of establishing rapport and building the therapeutic relationship in intentional and specific ways. Dr. John Gottman and Dr. Robert Levenson conducted a study in 1999, which is published in the journal *Family Process*, investigating the impact of emotional expression in couples who were experiencing conflict over time.

This research has been discussed in other articles and texts; Gottman has used mathematical modeling and has managed to predict with over 90% accuracy whether a couple will experience longevity or dissolution. He and Dr. Levenson identified nine items that served as predictors of divorce during conflict: "disgust, contempt, defensiveness, stonewalling, domineering, and belligerence" (Gottman & Levenson, 1999, p. 143). However, they also discovered a predictor of marital stability—positive affect. Moreover, the positive affect was found to be present in couples with marital stability in a 5:1 ratio. In other words, they had five positive interactions for every one negative interaction. Gottman identified different types of couples, which he described as volatile (those who maintained the ratio with high levels of positive affect and high levels of negative affect), the validator (who had moderate amounts of positive and negative affect), and the avoider (who had minimal amounts of both positive and negative affect). Interestingly, there were no statistically significant differences across these three types of couples, and all had a stable 5:1 ratio (Gottman, 1994, p. 183). Counselor education researchers Andrew Baker and Paul Peluso recently discussed their research in a presentation entitled *Researching Therapeutic Relationship Behaviors Among Expert Therapists* at the 2017 conference in Atlanta, GA (Baker & Peluso, 2018) and extended the work of Dr. John Gottman to the therapeutic relationship. They noted that the mode number of counseling sessions attended by an individual is **one** and coded recorded counseling sessions using a specific affective coding system similar to Gottman's. They were able to identify behaviors that were associated with client's continuing to engage in counseling; some behaviors were described as "high validation" and tended to be associated with longevity (Baker & Peluso, 2018). The verbal and nonverbal skills discussed in this section (with perhaps the exception of the skill "challenging while supporting"—depending on how it is used) are designed to be coded as positive and to contribute to strengthening the therapeutic relationship, building the positive ratio and furthering rapport and therapeutic alliance.

In the text *Therapeutic Presence: A Mindful Approach to Effective Therapy*, Geller and Greenberg (2012) indicated that the creation of their text involved a journey toward mindfulness, and they thanked their clients in part for teaching them to pay attention. This idea also resonates with the quote above from Doyle Melton; that presence involves paying attention. In therapy, it is very important to pay attention to both what the client is saying and what the client is not saying. This requires being fully present.

Sometimes clinicians can struggle with distracting thoughts and feelings. However, if we allow ourselves to be preoccupied with other things, our focus will not be on the client and the present moment (see the attachment illumination that illustrates how preoccupation can distract a person from the awareness of the other in the present moment).

## Spiritual Implications

Those that are practicing counseling from a Christian worldview may notice the emphasis on presence throughout the scriptures. For example, the Lord provides comfort to those who are hurting by his presence. His words to those who are brokenhearted are "The LORD is close to the brokenhearted; he rescues those whose spirits are crushed" (Psalm 34:18, New Living Translation). In a chapter in the *Encyclopedia of Christian Counseling*, grief is discussed as an inevitable part of the human experience, but the reminder of God's presence and the reminder to grieve as those with hope are also discussed (Knight, 2011a). He is I AM and His presence is mentioned. As we are present with our clients, and they have the sense that we are with them through their painful feelings; the sense that they are not alone may help them to become aware of God's presence, as his Holy Spirit dwells within us.

Dr. Robert Neborsky, in his article entitled "Brain, Mind, and Dyadic Change Processes" published in the *Journal of Clinical Psychology: In Session* (2006), writes about the idea of the impact of attachment injuries, which relates to presence and perhaps more so the impact of a *lack of presence*. Neborsky writes about the confluence of three areas of research including adult attachment, developmental neuroscience, and the outcomes of psychodynamic therapy. Neborsky draws on research from these three areas to enhance the delivery of treatment and to state profound truths about the importance of the "empathic other." Consider the following profound statement (Neborsky, 2006, p. 526), What statement? The one in the box? Recall from Chapter 3, we drew upon the language of Brené Brown. Brown emphasizes

*"Attachment failures lead to unprocessed feelings of unregulated grief, which without the empathic other, lead to unbearable states of aloneness that can only be regulated with defenses."*

the idea that it is connection that leads to a sense of relief and makes things better. Here Neborsky indicates it is the unbearable aloneness that leads to unregulated grief; this in part illustrates the powerful role of empathy and empathic connection in healing attachment or relationship injuries. We see that relationship, depending on how it manifests, both holds power to trigger painful unregulated grief on the one hand and therapeutic connection and healing on the other. It may be helpful to review Chapter 1's discussion of attachment theory and Chapter 3's discussion on empathy in order to dive deep into the present discussion. Remember, as our colleague Dr. Silvey likes to say, no relationship is perfect, except the relationship that God has with us, because He made it perfect. However, the human connections lack perfection, but as we seek to understand using empathy as the primary method of connecting, we are striving for a more perfect connection. As His Spirit is within us, we can connect with others, and as they experience the concreteness of another human being, it is easier to sense God's presence and closeness with them. Notice the role of presence; here we may be referring to the attachment figure's unavailability to the child, but later we can consider the implications of the same statement for therapy. (Please review Dr. Hawkins's video entitled, "Presence" on the companion website for more on this topic). In therapy, the "empathic other" here may be thought of as the counselor, and the presence of the counselor can diffuse the impact of the "unbearable aloneness" that can be triggered by facing the attachment failures alone and thus perhaps allow a client the opportunity to choose a new coping mechanism other than the defensiveness that has been the only option given the intensity of pain triggered by the confrontation of intense pain an unregulated grief. The defense mechanism that was appropriate at the time of the pain and served to protect the child may be something to take a second look at in therapy later to see whether it is serving the adult child well. The impact of these interpersonal traumas may be hard to estimate and vary depending on the nature and pervasiveness of the attachment injury. Neborsky (2006) explains the impact as follows: "If the trauma is prolonged, the infant creates an internalized representation of the attachment failure in the form of a punitive superego, that ends the state of unbearable aloneness, but at a price" (p. 527). Let us now look at how therapeutic presence.

The importance of therapeutic presence is hard to quantify. We can see that Psalm 34:18 (New International Version) says "He is close to the brokenhearted and saves those who are crushed in spirit." Neborksy also seems to capture this idea in the discussion of the impact of attachment challenges. The skills that we will discuss in this chapter are designed to help counselors communicate a nonverbal therapeutic presence. From an integration of spirituality perspective, we also believe that as our clients experience our presence, they can also experience the presence of the living God who dwells within us present with them (see the introduction for more on the impact of therapeutic integration).

> **A Verse to Remember:**
> *"He is close to the brokenhearted and saves those who are crushed in Spirit."*
> ***Psalm 34:18 (NIV).***

In the text entitled *Celebration of Discipline* (1988), Richard J. Foster, inspired by the writings of Dallas Willard, wrote about the spiritual disciplines. Chapter 10 of the Foster text is devoted to the discipline of confession. Foster discusses how central to God's heart is the act of forgiveness. Foster helps offer a method for making sense of Jesus prayer on the cross found in Mark 15:34 (New Living Translation), which says, "Then at three o'clock Jesus' called out with a loud voice, "'Eloi, Eloi, lema sabachthani?' which means 'My God, my God, why have you abandoned me?'" Some translations such as the NIV translate the term "forsaken" rather than "abandoned." Foster makes sense of this prayer by indicating that Jesus had identified to such a great degree with sin in his work on the cross that he experienced the abandonment of God that allowed him to redeem sin. He refers to this as his "moment of greatest triumph" (Foster, 1988, p. 143). In another book entitled *Prayer: Finding the Heart's True Home* (1992), he dedicates the second chapter to this prayer; it is entitled "Prayer of the Forsaken" (Foster, 1992, p. 17). Foster indicates that our goal is to consistently stay close to our Heavenly Father; then we will all, at some point, pray this same prayer.

## Universality

*Alone we can do so little. Together we can do so much.*

Helen Keller (Lash, 1980, p. 498)

Foster says, "Times of seeming desertion and absence and abandonment appear to be universal among those who have walked this path of faith before us" (Foster, 1992, p. 17).

This theme of facing abandonment is said to be a universal experience for those seeking after a relationship with Christ. This is not unlike the concept and therapeutic factor of **universality** that Yalom and Leszcz (2005) talked about in group counseling, This is one of 11 factors including other powerful factors such as the instillation of hope, interpersonal learning, and catharsis to name a few. (Yalom & Leszcz, 2005). **Universality** is in some ways the antidote to the fantasy of absolute uniqueness and social isolation. When clients experience trauma and pain and a series of painful and difficult experiences, these experiences may manifest themselves in part by inspiring a feeling of lonely uniqueness and the sense that no one else can relate to the painful, shameful, or uniquely challenging situations one faces. In group therapy, universality is a very powerful therapeutic factor (sometimes we use the term "normalizing" to describe this feeling when a client comes into therapy with a sense of "it is just me," but then leave with a different thought such as, "I thought it was just me, but now I realize that I am not alone!") Yalom considered his predecessor Freud's imprint indicating that part of the reason why we label practices such as incest or even patricide is that these thoughts and impulses are present in (fallen) human nature. Universality reminds us that we are not alone and that there are many problems common to man; in most cases, this is associated with a client's sense of relief. As we return to the discussion of Foster's prayer of the forsaken, this is an example of a struggle that some Christ followers may perceive as unique, but like Yalom and Foster both remind us, that as humans who struggle, we encounter many common struggles and are not alone. Foster also shares that particularly among those who are seeking communion with the Father, this sense of God being hidden is universal (at times). However, there is one very important distinction that Foster makes here. This is not "a true absence, but rather a sense of absence," in other words, a felt absence (Foster, 1992, p. 17–18). We know from the scriptures that God never leaves us or forsakes us. Hebrews 13:5 (NIV) reminds us, "[5] Keep your lives free from the love of money and be content with what you have, because God has said 'Never will I leave you; never will I forsake you.'"

## Nonverbal Behavior and Worldview

In some ways, we may be communicating aspects of our worldview through our nonverbal behaviors. Take a moment to think about what specific gestures and skills may communicate to clients. When you hear the name Rogers, who do you think of? Carl Rogers, or perhaps Fred Rogers? Both Fred Rogers and Carl Rogers revealed aspects of their worldviews through their writings and work. Perhaps what both influential Rogerses of our world have taught—Fred Rogers, the late host of *Mr. Rogers' Neighborhood* (a public television show of yesteryear), and Carl Rogers, the father of person-centered therapy—is the idea of unconditional positive regard. In Carl Rogers's influential journal article "The Necessary and Sufficient Conditions of Personality Change" (Rogers, 1957), published in the *Journal of Counseling Psychology*, Rogers wrote about the conditions he believed were necessary for therapeutic change to occur. Some of these conditions include that

> Deuteronomy 31:6a: "Do not be afraid or terrified because of them, for the Lord your God goes with you; he will never leave you nor forsake you."

the therapist be congruent and that the client be in a state of incongruence. Another is that "The therapist experiences unconditional positive regard for the client" (Rogers, 1957, p. 95). Fred Rogers taught something similar to children closing each show with words such as, "I like you just the way you are". We see similarities between the values that Carl Rogers and Fred Rogers communicated, including acceptance and valuing of other people; this is consistent with a Christian worldview, seeing people as created in the image of God. So, now let us explore your worldview and values and how you may expose some of these beliefs in counseling. Remember, there is a difference between imposing and exposing. Exposing could involve sharing your values, and imposing involves telling another how they should live, think, believe, and so on, based on the counselor's personal beliefs or values. Sire (2009) provides a very readable discussion on worldviews. His text is entitled *The Universe Next Door: A Basic Worldview Catalogue* (note it is beyond the scope of this text to discuss worldviews in full), and we recommend it for further study on the important topic of world view.

## *A Concept to Contemplate*

How would you describe your worldview?

How may your worldview impact the counseling process?

What strategies could you use (nonverbally) to draw out and work within your client's worldview?

© Shutterstock.com

## Key Players in Clinical Research

Dr. James Coan share his research at the International Attachment Conference, as he described the impact of attachment relationships in neural threat responses. He is an associate professor of Psychology at the University of Virginia and is a key player in research that involves attachment and neuroscience.

Dr. Gary Sibcy and I had an opportunity to hear

However, as the heart can be deceitful, there are times when we are less consciously aware of God's presence than other times. Specifically, for this reason, it can be very therapeutic for a client to experience the presence of a counselor. When a counselor uses congruent nonverbal behavior listening with his or her eyes, face, heart, and mind, as well as his or her words, then perhaps a client can feel a sense of God's presence more clearly as he or she becomes acutely aware of the fact that someone is truly present with him or her, and perhaps he or she becomes more attuned to God's presence as well.

**A Verse to Remember:** Hebrews 13: 5 (NIV): *"'Never will I leave you; never will I forsake you.'"*

# Attachment Research on Presence

*Shared joy is double joy. Shared sorrow is half sorrow.*

—Swedish Proverb

Dr. James Coan is an associate professor of psychology at the University of Virginia. Dr. Coan worked with some of his colleagues to investigate how a mutually supportive relationship (**relational mutuality**) influenced neural responses to threat (Coan, Kasle, Jackson, Schaefer, & Davidson, 2013). Coan et al. (2013) defined mutuality as reflecting "the degree to which couple members show mutual interest in the sharing of internal feelings, thoughts, aspirations, and joys —a vital form of responsiveness in attachment relationships" (p. 303). Coan and colleagues specifically investigated the impact on wives who rated themselves highly on their perceptions of mutuality in their relationships with their husbands and who also attended the research study session together with their husbands. These individuals were given mild electric shocks, and their neural threat responses were measured. The researchers hypothesis was supported by the data, and they found that as mutuality of relationship increased, the neural threat response decreased.

## Attachment Illumination

© Shutterstock.com

Sometimes one way to define a concept is to look at what it is not. Presence is not preoccupation. If we are preoccupied with something, we may convey this with an expression such as, "I have a lot on my mind." If we are seeking to be present with a client, then we have to set aside our own concerns and seek to understand and be present with our client; some days this may be more challenging than others.

In the AAI (George et al., 1985), the scoring can lead to a transcript's classification in one of several attachment classifications. One of these classifications is often referred to as the "preoccupied attachment style" (Main, Goldwyn, & Heese, 2002). Some characteristics of the preoccupied style include self-blame for rejection from others, difficulty trusting others, negative view of self, and difficulty regulating emotional affect (Zimmerman, 2018).

However, one common theme in the preoccupied characteristics discussed above involves a lack of collaboration in communication among the self and others; in other words, the absorption in the topic distracts the speaker from attending to the questions and the agreed-upon goals of the interview. This is a good example of why this is on the "don't list" for therapists. The nonverbal skills discussed in this chapter used with the other foundational skills discussed in this text can serve to help a counselor communicate a congruent message of presence. However, this should also be accompanied by a coherent state of mind, where the counselor is collaborative and able to facilitate movement toward a coherent state of mind for the client.

Coherence during an AAI conveys a sense of collaboration and a clear story that makes sense to the interviewer. A coherent state of mind for a therapist may be one of the most important components of communicated congruence to clients. If a therapist is fully present, at peace, and intentionally using verbal and nonverbal skills to walk alongside the client toward clear mutually agreed-upon goals, then the outcome is likely to be positive.

We often encourage our students to prepare their hearts by practicing the presence of God (Lawrence, Delaney, & Nouwan, 1977). One strategy that can be helpful in preparing our hearts or state of mind to be peaceful, coherent, and collaborative may be to practice listening in relationship to God. Some call this listening prayer or contemplative prayer. In a conversation with a colleague who works at the Amen clinics (these clinics have the largest collection of SPECT scans that allow psychiatrists to view the brain) indicated that listening or meditative prayer is more likely to calm the brain than other types of prayer. Moreover, some counselors find it helpful to write down preoccupying thoughts or worries and release them from the mind; this is a helpful alternative to rumination. Prayer journaling and giving these concerns to God can be especially helpful. This allows us to cast our cares on him as directed in 1 Peter 5:7.

## How Do Family Interactions Inform the Importance of Nonverbal Congruence?

Early family systems theorists discussed a dysfunctional pattern of communication known as double bind communication. Double bind communication is a communication where the receiver of a message receives two conflicting messages. For example, one could be receiving the message "come close" while also receiving the message "stay away"; thus, whichever message they respond to, they are in a bind and have violated the other message. Early family systems theorists called this "crazy making behavior." This dynamic is to be avoided in therapy. We want to send a congruent message to clients. We are inviting them to open up and share their story, to unpack their traumas, and to begin to work through things. If we ask them verbally to open up and share, but our nonverbal communication is sending the signal that we are not interested in hearing their story, then we are sending them mixed messages, and this may be considered double bind communication. Clients may not notice the nonverbal per se; however, they may leave the session saying to themselves, "I don't think this is a good fit" or "I may want to find a different counselor" or "Something did not feel right" or even "I did not really like that counselor." As some of the goals of therapy include building rapport, creating a safe environment, and exploring thoughts and feelings, sending mixed messages is not in alignment with these goals. The nonverbal skills we will discuss in this chapter will help counselors who practice them to communicate a consistent and congruent message. In other words, both their words and their bodies will communicate, "I am here to listen to your story, create a safe place, and walk with you toward healing." This theme of congruence will be central throughout the textbook, and it cannot be overemphasized. Carl Rogers, the father of person-centered therapy, believed that congruence was a primary goal of psychotherapy (Bateson, Jackson, Haley, & Weakland, 1956; Rogers, 1961).

Clients may be making attributions of our interactions. Early on in my counseling career, I was working with a client who had been diagnosed by his psychiatrist with paranoid schizophrenia. He was from China, and I was not as familiar with the pronunciation of some of his family member's names, so I jotted down some of the names he mentioned and an abbreviation that indicated to me the relation of the family member to him (such as unc for uncle). He looked at the note with wide eyes and asked, "What are you writing down? What will you do with that information? Will anyone else see it? Where will you keep it?" These questions were spoken like rapid fire. I paused, and assured him of confidentiality, that all of our notes were kept behind lock and key and that I was just making a note for myself to recall the names of his family members, but that I would shred it and throw it away if it would make him feel more comfortable. Another client that I worked with had some histrionic features, and when making a note during her session regarding her children's ages, she asked what I was writing down and assured me, "I have much more interesting things to tell you than that! I will give you something else to write down!" I realized that taking notes was a needless distraction and may communicate that my focus was on writing down information rather than being present and seeking to understand my client. Subsequently, I discussed this with my supervisor and made the decision **not** to take notes in session. Thus, unless a counselor and a client are working collaboratively on an advanced technique such as a situation analysis, I recommend not taking notes in session. This is our recommendation and what we suggest for our students. However, if you talk with ten different clinicians, you may receive ten different opinions on the matter. We encourage students to avoid taking notes in session because the purpose of their practice sessions is to demonstrate the skills discussed in this book, and time spent taking a note is time not spent making eye contact, reflecting content, paraphrasing, reflecting feeling, and so on. An important point to remember here is that we are always communicating, and even our well-intentioned efforts (such as making a note) can communicate that we are distracted or can distract our client. So, it is important to be intentional about demonstrating the skills discussed here including the 3Vs plus B, SOLER, appropriate vocal tone, appropriate use of a handshake, and so on.

## Congruence

It is important for verbal and nonverbal communication to be congruent. Recall, congruence is consistency between internal self-talk and external communication and between internal nonverbal messages (such as feelings) and external nonverbal messages such as SOLER and minimal encouragers. We are asking our clients to open up and share, but perhaps they have grown up with rules that indicate that they should be quiet, not disclose negative emotion, and not question or think (maybe they heard phrases such as "children are to be seen and not heard," "turn that frown upside down" or "don't complain or I will give you something to complain about). Now, we invite them to open up and share their thoughts, feelings, and more by communicating a congruent verbal and nonverbal message by intentionally attending to our nonverbal skills, which can help them to feel safe and take courage to do something that is perhaps very unfamiliar.

Dr. Silvey likes to describe the four dimensions of congruence with the chart below (Figure 6.1). Consider the four dimensions and how you may seek to use the counseling skills to communicate in a congruent manner.

## Dimensions of Congruence

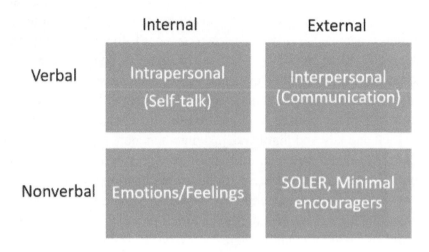

|  | Internal | External |
|---|---|---|
| Verbal | Intrapersonal (Self-talk) | Interpersonal (Communication) |
| Nonverbal | Emotions/Feelings | SOLER, Minimal encouragers |

**Figure 6.1.** Dimensions of congruence.

## Facial Expressions

One important aspect of nonverbal communication is facial expressions. Perhaps you have encountered someone whose facial expression communicated they were unhappy despite verbal messages to the contrary. In session, it is important to communicate an appropriate and generally pleasant facial expression. If a client is communicating an experience involving grief or anger, then the counselor may adjust to a neutral expression or other appropriate expression of concern.

© Shutterstock.com

*A Concept to Contemplate*

Here are some questions to contemplate as you consider nonverbal counseling skills. Have you ever encountered a salesperson or customer service representative who said something pleasant such as "have a great day" or "my pleasure" with a facial expression that communicated pain or discomfort?

If so, how did this incongruent verbal and nonverbal message impact you? Which made the stronger impression?

What does your resting facial expression communicate?

If you took a picture of your thinking face and asked a few friends for feedback, what do you think they would say? On a scale of 1 to 10, what is your comfort level with soliciting this type of feedback?

You may be communicating your internal world to the external world via your facial expressions. Are you communicating what you would like to communicate?

Take some time to ponder and write down the answers to the above questions to facilitate self-awareness and growth.

One important caveat to remember with facial expressions is that sometimes clients feel uncomfortable with a particular feeling (see Chapter 9 for more information on this topic). For example, men born in the United States may be less comfortable expressing sadness because they are socialized not to communicate sadness within the U.S. culture. Likewise, women may be less comfortable communicating anger because U.S. women are socialized not to communicate anger. In order to cope with the discomfort and downregulate it so that the client can press through and self-disclose to a safe counselor, he or she may smile when sharing something painful or something that was associated with anger. It is important for the counselor to be careful not to mirror back this facial expression, lest the counselor portray a message that minimizes the client's pain or suffering.

## Necessary But Not Sufficient

It is important to remember that the core counseling skills, sometimes referred to as the microskills, are necessary (Ivey et al., 2018) but not sufficient. The father of the microskills approach is Dr. Allen Ivey (Ivey et al., 2018). Ivey is the author of more than 40 different books and more than 200 articles and book chapters and is a prolific writer in the area of counseling psychology. Ivey defines the "microskills" as follows:

*They are the specific communication skill units of the counselor/client session that provide specific alternatives for you to use with many types of clients and all theories of counseling and therapy. You master these skills one by one and then learn to integrate them into a well-formed session.*

Ivey and Zalaquett (2018, p. 11)

## Practice Activity

What does your partner perceive you to be communicating—and how do you work on this? One strategy often used during counseling skills training is the practice of taking video footage of the counselor and client during a practice counseling session (Knight, 2009). It is painful, but to be a skilled counselor, we need to be aware of our posture. Try obtaining consent from a friend or a classmate to videotape a conversation. Make sure to ask permission and confirm that the conversation partner is comfortable with being videotaped. Then, take some time to review the video and watch your nonverbal facial expressions. What do they communicate? Is your nonverbal message congruent with your verbal message to your clients?

## An Important Note

Most students are required to videotape their counseling sessions during counseling skills courses, practicum, and internship, so it may be helpful to grow comfortable with this process early. This could be very revealing; for example, we had a counseling skills student whose student client asked "Did I say something wrong?" several times during the session. The counseling student practicing her skills assured the client that she had said nothing wrong. After the practice session while they were debriefing, the counseling student asked her what led her to ask this question. The student who had been in the client role confessed, "Well, you were making this face where you moved both eyes sideways, and looked up and to the left, and you scrunched up your eye brows and frowned a little." At that moment, the counseling student made the same face again, and both client and observer said, "There it is! That is it!" Later the observer took a picture of the student counselor with that expression and showed it to her. She was shocked and said, "I guess that is my thinking face, at that moment I was just thinking about what the client had said and beginning to do a paraphrase, but I did not realize I had that expression!" We encouraged her to be aware of and intentional to maintain a pleasant or neutral facial expression in those moments. She was very thankful for the feedback, because otherwise she would not have known the impact she was having on others through her facial expressions.

## Best Practices in Nonverbal Communication

There are terms used to describe nonverbal communication that may not be a part of the average person's vernacular. Some of the dimensions fall under the umbrella of nonverbal communication (Payrato, 2009): gesticulation, which includes gestures that are similar to their verbal counterparts (this may include pantomimes, which involves dramatic license in acting out content through gestures, often accompanied with music); proxemics, the study and management of space; chronemics the study and perception of the passage of time; haptics, the study of touch; oculesics, which is the study of eye contact behavior, and olfactis, the study of olfactory stimuli. Physical appearance and characteristics of the environment may sometimes be grouped under the umbrella of nonverbal communication (Payrato, 2009, p. 163).

## SOLER

SOLER (also adapted to SOLAR) is an acronym that has been developed to help make remembering the recommended nonverbal counseling skills easier. It was introduced as part of Gerard Egan's skilled helper model (Egan & Reese, 2019). His skilled helper model involves three distinct stages. The first stage involves getting a picture of the current situation, the second stage involves goal setting or determining what the client wants, and the third stage involves identifying next steps.

As we look at each component of SOLER, it is important to remember that you do not want this to be unnatural; this is not a military protocol; it is meant to facilitate connection. Often nonverbal skills are called facilitative skills for that reason. One caveat for cultural considerations: D.W. Sue and D. Sue (2016) discuss how silences can communicate that the client may be holding back, but silence can also create a feeling of uneasiness. Silence can be viewed negatively by Americans. In some Asian cultures silence may communicate respect, For

**Key Players in Counseling**

**Who Is Gerard Egan?**

Dr. Egan is Professor Emeritus at Loyola University of Chicago. Dr. Egan is the author of *The Skilled Helper* and more than 14 other books. He has helped develop management systems that are broadly used. He serves in the role of a consultant and a counselor to those he works with.

instance in Japanese culture silence my in fact be used to indicate the desire to speak often silence is respect for others, and indicates the person does not wish to maintain their conversational turn (Shea, 1998).

In the acronym **SOLER**, the first letter, S, stands for squarely face your client, the O indicates that the counselor should exhibit open posture (no crossed arms or crossed legs, ankles, etc.), L indicates leaning in as appropriate (e.g., with a good movie, you are on the edge of your seat), the E is for eye contact, and the R represents the idea that the counselor should seek to relax. Now, at first this may sound very difficult; remember to squarely face your client, do not cross arms or legs, lean in (but not too much or at the wrong time), make eye contact (or to make SOLER more inclusive for the visually impaired, Egan & Reese (2019) has suggested replacing E with A to represent aiming your body toward the client), and while remembering to do all of these things, we are also telling you to relax! We have consistently found that the more practice a counselor-in-training has at implementing these nonverbal skills, the easier they become. However, implementing these skills may be uncomfortable at first, but we encourage you to lean into the discomfort. Imagine going to give a friend a hug. You would not fold your arms across your chest but would remain with an open posture. If crossing arms has been a comfortable position for you, then not doing so may feel uncomfortable. In high school gym class, there was an award available called the Presidential Physical Fitness Award, and you could earn this award if you met certain criteria on physical fitness measures such as running a mile within a given period and being able to stretch your hands to a certain distance past your toes. The first time I attempted the stretching procedure called "sit and reach" I could not get my fingers to my toes much less past them. However, each time I stretched (although it still felt uncomfortable), I was able to stretch a bit farther. Likewise, it is so with the nonverbal counseling skills. Sitting in the SOLER position may feel uncomfortable at first, but with practice and leaning into the discomfort, you will stretch farther into the R or relaxed state of SOLER.

Now, that we have on overview of SOLER, let us take a closer look at each of the components (Egan, 2010).

## S—Squarely Face Your Client

Squarely facing the client is the first part of the SOLER acronym.

**S**—When meeting someone new, it is often customary to shake hands and say some iteration of "it is very nice to meet you." When someone introduces you to a new person, typically the first thing we do is step toward them and seek to squarely face them. If our body is positioned to face away from the client, the nonverbal message may convey that we are in a rush or not available to attend to the other person. Egan emphasizes that this is not a term to be taken too literally; if direct posture seems too threatening, he advises facing them at an angle.

## O—Open Posture

**O**—O represents open posture. Recall that defensiveness is one of the four horsemen of the apocalypse. On the contrary, openness communicates a willingness to engage and a desire to connect. Congruent communication includes an open posture along with the spoken skills.

Recall from Chapter 1, Dr. John Gottman is the founder of the Family Research Institute, which is affectionately known as the "Love Lab." He and his research team have used several coding systems to analyze video-recorded counseling sessions of couples. One of the coding systems he uses is the specific affect coding system (SPAFF). Gottman has uncovered many interesting and helpful predictors of relationship success, and he has also uncovered pitfalls that can serve to impede relationships. For example, using the coding system, Gottman and colleagues have discovered that negative interaction is more frequent in couples that are unhappily married than in couples who are happily married. Gottman indicates that the SPAFF is able to dismantle the broad variable of negative affect and break it down into five different categories: anger, contempt (which has been referred to as the "sulfuric acid of love,") fear, sadness, and even whining (Gottman & Krokoff, 1989). Gottman is known as an expert on relationships and what leads to their success or failure. Baker and Peluso (2018) extended Gottman's finding to the therapeutic relationship. Consider the following recommendations that emerged from findings from Gottman's research:

> *In terms of recommendations for marriage, our results suggest that wives should confront disagreement and should not be overly compliant, fearful, and sad but should express anger and contempt. Husbands should also engage in conflict but should not be stubborn or withdrawn. Neither spouse should be **defensive**.*
>
> Gottman & Krokoff (1989, p. 51)

Notice, defensiveness is on this list of items that both partners should avoid! It was also referred to as one of the four horsemen or predictors that the end of a relationship is near (Gottman, 2007). Crossed arms are the classic sign of defensiveness. If you think about an incoming attack, if someone goes to hit you or throw something at you, what might be your first response? Many would defend themselves by crossing their arms in a V shape to protect oneself. We want clients to feel safe and open to self-disclose, and so we want to model that by having an open nonverbal posture that is congruent with our message, that we are interested in the client opening up and sharing his or her story. *So open posture typically indicates congruent openness (no crossed arms or crossed legs).*

## L—Lean In

The **L** in SOLER represents the postural shift of leaning forward. If you watched a good action movie recently or a ball game that went into overtime and wanted to convey to a friend the intensity of the movie or last few minutes of the game, you may have used the expression, "it kept me on the edge of my seat." This posture communicates an interest and attention toward the speaker in counseling. Although it is important to be sensitive to cultural differences as well as individual differences, typically a slight lean toward the client communicates nonverbally, "I am interested in what you have to say," or "You have my full attention." On the other end of the continuum is the backward lean, which may communicate to clients that we are disinterested with what they are saying, distracted, or even bored (Egan, 2010). However, it is also important to use discernment with postural shifts; leaning in too much could be overarousing to a client, and it is considered unethical to use techniques that would be overly physiologically arousing.

Postural shifts can change proximity of counselor to client and can communicate interest. There have been some conflicting findings in the research on the impact of nonverbal counseling skills regarding the impact of postural lean. In research conducted by researchers in New Zealand and Australia (Hermansson et al., 1988) studying the facilitative impact of postural shifts by evaluating the impact of forward, backward, and choice leans on the qualities of empathy, respect, and intensity, the researchers found that there were no statistically significant differences between the postures themselves and discussed the idea that for male counselors working with female clients adopting a forward lean, backward lean, or position of choice has no statistically significant impact on the levels of conveyed facilitative conditions as assessed by independent raters. They also found compensatory behaviors in their research. In other words, counselors who preferred to lean forward (as became apparent during the time when they adopted their posture of choice) demonstrated more compensatory facilitative levels, and when leaning forward there were decreased facilitative levels found. The counselors who preferred to move forward (as opposed to backward) were also assessed as most effective with respect to their empathy levels.

## E—Eye Contact

### Lie to Me

After teaching the counseling skills class the past several years, we began receiving the feedback from students that some of what we were doing in class was reminding them of a television show called, *Lie to Me,* and they urged us to watch the show.

The television show featuring the Lightman group capitalizes on the research of Paul Eckman and what facial expressions communicate, and has popularized the importance of reading nonverbal cues, emphasizing the idea that you are always communicating.

Furthermore, some of our students have given rave reviews of the show indicating, for example, "This show is awesome and does a great job at showing nonverbal behaviors. 10 of 10 recommend the show."

K. Wortendyke (personal communication, 2018, May 22).

One of the most critical of the nonverbal skills is represented by the **E, eye contact**. Eye contact is typically considered a steady gaze into the client's eyes with occasional breaks in gaze. However, the Goldilocks principle is at work here. Remember, in the story of Goldilocks and the three bears, when she went in to taste the porridge, the first one was a bit too hot, the second one was too cold, but by the time she found the third serving, she thought that was just right (Alperin & Daubney, 2015). We should try to achieve the right amount of eye contact so that the client has a sense that they are being heard and attended to, but not so much as the client feels that it is too

### To Hug or Not to Hug

Thoughts from Winnicott on how understanding and reflecting with the skills can have a greater impact than just a physical gesture of comfort such as a hug:

As written by Blackwell (1997):

intense or so little so that it feels as if the counselor is not attending.

## R—Relax

The R in the acronym represents the process of **relaxing.** I know it may be hard to think about remaining relaxed while you are trying to remember the skills in order.

> *A correct and well-timed interpretation in an analytic treatment gives a sense of being held physically that is more real than if a real holding or nursing had taken place. Understanding goes deeper.*

We do suggest leaning in to the discomfort and trying to adopt these nonverbals until they become second nature. Remember the first time you drove, or the first time you rode a bike. It was probably scary and required your full attention, engagement, and effort. However, have you noticed any changes? Maybe now you get home on autopilot. You drive home from work but are able to think about other things as you drive; it has become natural. Likewise, when first learning to adopt SOLER, it may feel uncomfortable, but on average, after 15 hours of practicing SOLER (and the other counseling skills), students report beginning to feel comfortable (both with the SOLER position and with limiting the use of questions). However, it is important to remember that this is not a military protocol and that a counselor's genuineness and warmth are valued. To hear a discussion from the authors on the R from SOLER and other aspects of nonverbal communication, please watch this video.

**Video**

**The Posture of Listening**

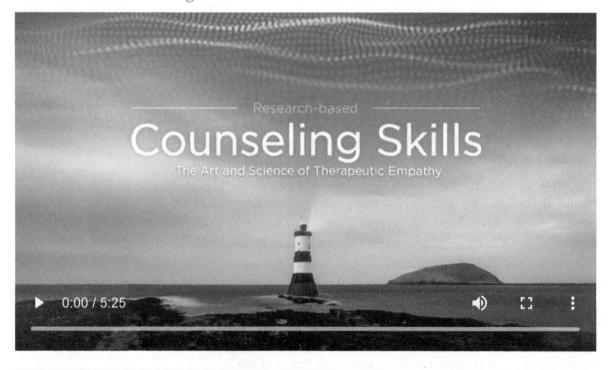

In addition to SOLER, other skills that help us stay tuned into our client may be represented by the following acronym: 3 V's + B (Ivey et al., 2018).

# 3 V's + B

## V—Visual

The first **V** of attending is **visual**, which represents eye contact. This is one of the most important indicators to others that we are listening and paying attention. It also allows the counselor to attend to the client's nonverbal communications and emotions transmitted through facial expressions, eyes (such as the welling up of tears), and energy shifts. Be sure to remember that good eye contact usually consists of a steady gaze with occasional breaks in gaze.

## V—Vocal Qualities

The second V in the sequence of attending skills here is "vocal qualities." Vocal quality is an important nonverbal communicator. When there is a lack of congruence and vocal tone and verbal message do not align, it is the vocal tone that is "given greater credence by the listener" (Duncan et al., 1968). Furthermore, vocal tone is a way of communicating emotion. For example, if my client indicates she is graduating this spring, then I may reflect the feeling that may be associated with that event and elevate my vocal tone while emphasizing, "That sounds exciting; you have set a goal, reached it, and now you are celebrating that milestone!" However, if a client reports they have lost a loved one, I may adopt a more hushed tone of voice and respond with, "It must be very painful to lose someone that has been such an important part of your life; help me understand what it is like to grieve this loss."

## V—Verbal Tracking

Verbal tracking is the third V of the attending skills. Verbal tracking is one way we show our clients that we are listening and seeking to understand what they are communicating rather than telling them that we are listening. When a client shares his or her story, we can pause and say, "I want to make sure I am tracking, it sounds like you said. . ." and then give a brief recap. Sometimes, a client will wonder if the counselor or listener is understanding, so they will give additional detail or tell the story again a different way to help the listener

*An important rule in counseling is **"show, don't tell,"** which refers to seeking to understand. If you have a client that has been struggling in a relationship that comes in and reports what happened with the breakup and their corresponding mixed feelings, let us look at a couple ways you could respond. Rather than saying, "Oh I understand what you are saying," we recommend saying something that includes a reflection of content and feeling: "It sounds like your experience has been mixed emotions; you are sad about the break up and will miss your girlfriend, but a part of you feels relieved that it is what is best for both of you." The latter is a reflection of content and a reflection of feeling that shows the client through the skill usage that* understand. Other clients may use brief phrases to check in such as "you know?" or "make sense?" Verbal tracking is one way we follow another rule in counseling, *show don't tell*.

*counselor is seeking to understand and approaching understanding of their situation. We say "approaching understanding" rather than understanding because we can never fully understand a person's experience because it is impossible to live life through another person's mind and spirit.*

## Attachment Illumination

© Shutterstock.com

This idea of "show don't tell" is consistent with developing a coherent attachment narrative. When we use the Adult Attachment Interview in our counseling work, and a client is asked the hallmark AAI question, "Would you provide five adjectives that describe your childhood relationship with your mother?" (George et al., 1985, p. 2). The client may list one adjective as "loving" but then when the interviewer asks the follow-up question, "Would you provide for me a specific autobiographical episode or a memory that illustrates how your relationship with your mother was loving?" (George et al., 1985, p. 3) the client may say, "Well, she was loving because she was caring, what is your next question?" This is not considered a coherent response, and we are not given a specific memory. It can be challenging for people to face the truth of their story and the idea that perhaps their relationship with their parent was not as loving as it could have been, or if it was even at times unloving or abusive. However, it is best for their development to face the truth of this story (Knight & Sibcy, 2018). As the counselor remains present and uses verbal tracking to paraphrase and help the client make sense of his or her story, the client can face the story with the empathic other and begin to make more movement toward coherence. So, this attending skill and the others to come (in subsequent chapters) may have powerful implications for attachment.

## B—Body Language

Body language is a very important communicator; as discussed previously, it can communicate even more than words. SOLER provides a helpful guide for how to be attentive to clients through body language, squarely facing them with an open nondefensive posture, leaning in and making eye contact while remaining relaxed. Remember that your body is often an outward communication of what your internal state is. If you are anxious, it may be difficult to sit still, or your facial expression might communicate an intensity or anxiety that you do not want to communicate. Consider taking time to relax before session, perhaps through prayer or meditation.

## Caveats

Remember that there are cultural variations and adjustments that need to be made. Demonstrating cognitive flexibility and the capacity to modify flexibly based on clients' cultural preferences is important. For example, when I worked with adolescent males struggling with substance abuse challenges at a Christian inpatient facility, I found that some of them preferred to interact through a therapeutic activity such as drawing their feelings and it was more helpful to sit side by side and discuss their art work and what feelings and thoughts they were communicating through that activity, than to sit squarely facing each other. Handshakes and touch are another area where there are lots of cultural considerations to keep in mind. For example, I (Anita Kuhnley) come from a Cuban and Italian heritage; my family can be very warm and affectionate; if you greeted my Italian grandmother with a handshake, she would say, "Oh, come here honey and give me a hug and a kiss!" She is 90 years young and lives in a retirement community; when I visit her, she introduces me to everyone we come across, and she always pats, touches, and hugs and calls them "sweet heart," "honey," "dear," "sweet girl" or some other term of endearment. I once said, "Mims [all her grandchildren have always called her Mims], I really like how tender you are and how you have these sweet terms of endearment for everyone." She replied, "Can I tell you something, honey?" I said, "Tell me something, Mims." She said, "It is so I don't have to remember their names!" We want to be cognizant of our clients' backgrounds and flexibly adapt to their interpersonal needs, and to also keep in mind that there are often as many differences within cultures as between.

## Handshake or Touch: Nonverbal Greetings

However, in counseling, it is important to avoid imposing intimacy and to be culturally sensitive to our clients. As counseling can be a very personal and intimate experience, it is better to err on the side of not using physical touch or a handshake in counseling if unsure. Given the pitfalls that can be associated with a counselor's use of therapeutic touch, it is best to use caution and seeking supervisor feedback and guidance. Part of our human tendency toward touch and helper's desire to use touch in session in a therapeutic way may be explained by some of the research on the therapeutic benefits of appropriate touch. See the section on attachment research for information on how Dr. Coan and his colleagues discussed their research that investigated (in part) the impact of hand holding (within a relationship with mutuality) on neural threat response.

# Use Caution with Opposite Sex and Those with a History of Sexual Abuse

> In counseling, we use progress notes and active listening skills in order to serve a similar function. At the end of the session, we use summarization skills (see Chapter 12), and at the beginning of the next session, we may again use summarization skills to check in.
> What is the shared purpose of the progress notes and active listening skills? This is unclear.

Although touch can be therapeutic, it is important to use caution with the opposite sex. Counseling can be a very intimate process. Clients are often opening up and sharing their story. Some clients may be sharing things for the first time, or you may be the only person they are self-disclosing at this level of depth. The counseling relationship can be deceptively intimate. One distinction that makes the counseling relationship unique from other relationships is that it is not reciprocal. In a friendship, one friend may ask the other, "How was your day today?" and the two may then take turns inquiring and self-disclosing. In a counseling relationship, although a client may ask how a therapist is doing, the client is typically paying by the therapeutic hour, and this exchange should remain brief. So, the nonreciprocal or one-sided nature of the counseling relationship typically means the client feels closer to the counselor than the counselor does the client. Although we greatly value and care for our clients, a counselor typically has many clients and a client only one counselor. This allows for the opportunity for the client to allow more cognitive room for the counselor or to think of the counselor more frequently. A counselor is served well by contemplating these dynamics as a reminder to use caution when interacting with the opposite sex in session, especially when it comes to touch.

Although physical touch such as a handshake, appropriate hug, or pat on the back may be therapeutic, there are also different situations in which they are not. Part of the difficulty with touch is that it is often associated with romantic relationships. Touch has even been called a "love language." Gary Chapman (2004) popularized the idea of love languages in his book, *The Five Love Languages*, and physical touch is defined as one of the love languages.

It is important to discuss any uncertainty in this area with a clinical supervisor, and as my dear friend used to say, "When in doubt, don't."

© YegoeVdo22/Shutterstock.com

## A CASE TO CONSIDER: THE CASE OF FREDDY

One of our colleagues shared a case that illustrates the potential pitfalls of physical touch. She shared she had a colleague who worked in a Christian private counseling practice. In

each session her colleague, Freddy (name changed for the purposes of confidentiality), joined hands with a couple he was working with at the beginning of each session, and the three of them then prayed together. One session the husband was not able to make it, so the counselor had an individual session with his wife. As was their custom, he held her hands and prayed as they began the session. Later that day he received a phone call from the husband who said, "Hey! What is the big idea?! I heard that you held my wife's hand while I was not there! That is not okay!" This created an unnecessary and difficult situation for all involved and is an example of why we need to use caution in these situations.

© antoniodiaz/Shutterstock.com

## Appropriate Touch or Handshake May Be a Ritual upon Greeting or Termination

Appropriate touch can have a healing impact. Dr. Gary Smalley and Dr. John Trent, in their powerful book entitled *The Blessing*, discuss the healing power of touch. They cite a study that indicates that hemoglobin can be released with the laying on of hands

*Inside our bodies is hemoglobin the pigment of red blood cells, which carries oxygen to the tissues. Repeatedly, Dr. Krieger has found that hemoglobin levels in both people's blood streams go up during the act of the laying on of hands.* (Smalley & Trent, 1986, p. 44).

They also discuss how it is the first of the five key elements of giving the blessing. Thus, a warm, appropriate handshake can communicate something important to the client. Smalley and Trent draw on scriptural references that illustrate how patriarchs of the Old Testament transmitted the blessing to their children and their children's children by the laying on of hands; for example, we see the picture of Israel blessing his grandchildren, laying his hands on them

[15]Then he blessed Joseph and said,

*May the God before whom my fathers Abraham and Isaac walked faithfully, the God who has been my shepherd all my life to this day,[16] the Angel who has delivered me from all harm—may he bless these boys. May they be called by my name and the names of my fathers Abraham and Isaac, and may they increase greatly on the earth.*

(Genesis 48: 15-16, NIV)

*A Concept to Contemplate*

© Shutterstock.com

See the call-out box entitled "How to give and receive 'The Blessing' (Smalley and Trent, 1986)." Take a moment to contemplate the passage above. What feelings bubble up inside as you contemplate Israel speaking these words to his grandsons? Can you imagine Israel as a spiritual father to you speaking these words of blessing? What would it mean to you if he laid his hands on you and blessed you?

Some clients have experienced trauma or physical abuse or sexual abuse, and touch has been something harmful in their lives. These experiences can be associated with shame, and a handshake can be an important communicator that they are "touchable." However, touch can also be a trigger for past trauma, so it is important to use sensitivity and consult with your clinical supervisor.

Moreover, it is important to think about what it means to have an appropriate handshake. A handshake is something that we often do, but rarely discuss. It is important not to impose intimacy. Although a handshake can be an example of how a counselor in the United States may demonstrate appropriate touch, it is important to make sure the client is comfortable with this (sometimes this can be assessed nonverbally, and sometimes it is helpful to ask the client). If the counselor and supervisor discern it is appropriate, then a handshake may become a tradition in counseling that the counselor can use to greet the client.

The family systems literature indicates that children who grow up with traditions, routines, and rituals tend to have better childhood behavior and adjustment (Fritz, 2004). Thus, a handshake may be a tradition that a counselor can use, if deemed appropriate by counselor and supervisor, to begin and end sessions. Other traditions of sorts may include beginning the session with a summary, scaling the client's mood at the beginning and end of session, scaling progress toward a goal, or scaling session satisfaction or productivity (see Chapter 13 for more on goal setting).

The call-out box given below illustrates some of the handshakes that we encounter. It is important to be sensitive to cultural considerations and talk with our clients or follow their cues about what may be appropriate for them culturally or with respect to their individual preferences. It is also important to be aware of counselor tendencies and to discuss discomfort in supervision. For example, if a counselor struggles with obsessive-compulsive disorder tendencies related to germs, or the flu is going around, and the counselor feels very anxious after shaking hands, and is feeling tense and fidgety with a compelling urge to use hand sanitizer immediately after the handshake, then it may be more therapeutic to avoid the handshake in this case. Due to client diversity and history, it is essential to use discernment and consult with supervisors when deciding whether or not to participate in a handshake.

Please discuss this with your supervisor or your counseling skills professor and solicit their feedback and recommendations for your current setting.

## How to Give and Receive "The Blessing" (Smalley & Trent, 1986):

Dr. Gary Smalley and Dr. John Trent co-authored a book called *The Blessing*; this classic book outlines five elements that they see as central to giving someone "the blessing" based on the Biblical blessing seen transmitted from patriarchs to their children and grandchildren in the Old Testament.

These elements of the blessing are defined as follows (Smalley & Trent, 1986):

1. *Meaningful physical touch*

2. *The spoken word*

3. *Expressing high value*

4. *Picturing a special future*

5. *An active commitment*

We highly recommend reading this book; it is powerful and we believe you and those you love will be blessed because of it. Moreover, if you have not received the blessing in your family of origin, this book also advocates and provides a strategy for being the one to give the blessing to your parents or loved ones, who also may not have received it.

## *A Concept to Contemplate*

© Shutterstock.com

If you prefer to avoid shaking hands, and your client initiates a handshake, how will you respond?

What would you share with your supervisor if asked, "What is behind this fear?"

Could you wait until after the session to use sanitizer? What would be some ways of approaching this with your client that may be appropriate?

## Types of Handshakes

In every class, I like to give students the opportunity to discuss the experiences they have had with handshakes, to practice their own handshake, and to get feedback from peers on what their handshake communicates nonverbally. We often begin counseling sessions, especially intakes, with a handshake and greeting as we welcome our clients. Take a moment to pause and think about the different types of handshakes that you have experienced in the past. We will use names that characterize the different sensations associated with the handshakes; some that have come up during class discussion include the following:

**The Knuckle Crusher:** As the name indicates here, pressure is applied upon the hand and there is a squeeze that can result in a feeling of pain and the hand being pressed too hard. This can be especially painful for those who have arthritis or other chronic pain and should be added to our "to don't list."

**The Wet Noodle:** This is the handshake that is very limp, and there is no firmness in the person's hand. Students have reported sensing that the person is not invested or really interested in the handshake. Women have sometimes reported feeling surprised when they shake a man's hand and encounter this type of handshake. Men have sometimes reported being socialized not to hurt a woman or shake her hand too firmly. This one often leads to a lively discussion with people of both genders having strong opinions.

**The Lingering Handshake:** This handshake involves what starts as a handshake and transitions into a handhold. Both parties are still hanging onto each other's hands, but the acceptable time period for a handshake has passed, and now there may be an awkward awareness that it has become more of a handhold. When children are learning to shake hands, they will often use this method.

**The Arm Shake:** Here one person is overly enthusiastic and may begin to vigorously shake the other person's hand and this may turn into shaking his or her whole arm.

**The Double HandShake:** This can be used to communicate warmth. Students have reported they have experienced others shaking their hands this way perhaps at a funeral, after a loss, and in a manner that seems to communicate a desire to comfort.

**The Pull in for a Hug:** Another type of handshake that morphs into something else is the pull in for a hug. Here this begins as a handshake but transitions into a pull-in for a hug and can seem invasive if the other party is not comfortable with a hug.

**The Fist Bump or Dap:** Teenagers often have sophisticated fist bumps that involve a sequence of hand gestures. I have had adolescent male clients teach me their fist bump patterns, and this has been a neat rapport-building experience.

The takeaway is it is important to really be intentional about how you greet someone and what your handshake communicates. As counselors we believe it is important to communicate a warm and professional welcome with a brief firm handshake and a pleasant, welcoming facial expression.

## Practice Activity

What do each of the gestures below communicate?

- Rolling your eyes

- Opening and relaxing

- Touching

- Not moving

- Crossed arms

- Slumping

- Leaning back

Consider Gottman's 5:1 (6:1 ratio) ratio and how each behavior is coded—would smiling be coded as a positive?

## Nonverbal To-Do List

- Please review this video vignette of Dr. Silvey counseling Bonnie and illustrating the posture of listening/SOLER.

## Video

**Bonnie SOLER: Justin Silvey & Bonnie Gould**

- Seek to make eye contact (first V + E from SOLER)

- Modify vocal tone to show excitement or joy when greeting the client and modify appropriately throughout (second V of attending, vocal quality)

- Verbally track—restate to the client key themes being heard

- Squarely face client (S from SOLER)

- Use open posture in session (avoid crossing arms or legs)

- Lean (lean in to communicate interest when appropriate)

- Pray before the client arrives to prepare my heart and to ask the Lord to help me R relax in session

## Recommended Reading

If you would like to expand your knowledge on the topics discussed in this chapter, we would recommend reading the following texts:

- Chapman, G. (2004). *The 5 love languages: The secret to love that lasts.* Chicago, IL: Northfield Publishing.

- Coan, J. A., Kasle, S., Jackson, A., Schaefer, H. S., & Davidson, R. J. (2013). Mutuality and the social regulation of neural threat responding. *Attachment & Human Development, 15*(3), 303–315. doi:10.1080/14616734.2013.782656.

- Smalley, G., & Trent, J. (1986). *The Blessing.* Nashville, TN: Thomas Nelson/HarperCollins.

## Chapter Summary

Chapter 6 explored the nonverbal communication skills. These skills include gestures, facial expressions, and proxemics or postural lean and have often been summarized by the acronym SOLER. Research literature has demonstrated evidence that nonverbal messages are responsible for more of the variance in how a message is judged than verbal. Moreover, nonverbals allow a counselor to communicate empathy and emotion. Suggested practices for counselors in nonverbal skills can be represented by the word SOLER. SOLER stands for squarely facing, open posture, learn in, eye contact, and relax. SOLER has also been adapted as SOLAR, where A is for aim rather than eye contact, which is more inclusive. It is important to remember that this is not a military protocol, and although SOLER is suggested, the counselor's genuineness, empathy, and warmth are important, and there may be times where leaning in may seem to aggressive or personal and times when adjustments need to be made. The 3Vs of attending include visual (which also represents eye contact), vocal tone, and verbal tracking. B has been added on and could include body language.

Touch has also been an important nonverbal communication skill, but it is important to use caution and err on the side of not engaging in physical touch; however, one appropriate greeting that involves touch is the handshake. Counselors are encouraged to seek supervision to discuss its implications and appropriateness. Often, it can be appropriate to use a handshake that meets the Goldilocks criteria of being "just right": not overly firm or too limp, but firm and accompanied by a pleasant facial expression. It is good practice to seek feedback from others on what one's handshake communicates as well as what the resting facial expression communicates. It is important to be congruent to ensure that verbal and nonverbal skills are in alignment and that nonverbals help to communicate a safe and facilitative environment. Counselors are encouraged not only to listen with their ears but also to their eyes, heart, mind, and body. Nonverbal communication allows counselors to communicate presence. This has spiritual implications; when believers are seeking connection with God and feel distant from him, but encounter a counselor who is fully present they can become more aware of God's presence and experience the healing power of presence.

## Chapter Seven

# Paralanguage and Minimal Encouragers

## Anita Kuhnley and Gary Sibcy

*Drawing on my fine command of the English language I said nothing.*

—Robert Benchley

### Chapter Learning Objectives

- To unpack how essential interviewing skills, such as encouragers, may facilitate movement toward a more coherent state of mind with respect to attachment (CACREP II.F.5.g, 2016, p. 12)
- To evaluate strategies for communicating presence in the therapeutic dialogue (CACREP II.F.5.g, 2016, p. 12)
- To identify appropriate use of paralanguage (CACREP II.F.5.g, 2016, p. 13)

## Chapter Overview

How does our body language communicate a congruent message that indicates that we are interested in listening and that we are listening? Egan's skilled helper model provides us with the acronym SOLER that helps us to communicate these things nonverbally. As we move on to verbal utterances, we have paralanguage, minimal encouragers, and key word encouragers to add to the tool kit. We will explore examples of paralanguage, how it can be helpful, and the purposes behind using it. We will also unpack other encouragers and add them to the tool kit.

## What Is Paralanguage?

Paralanguage is a term that was discussed by Trager in 1958. It was part of a very well-articulated taxonomy of vocalizations. Trager defines paralanguage as being divided into several categories. The two categories of paralanguage are "voice set as background for and voice qualities and vocalizations as accompaniments of language proper" (Trager, 1958, p. 278). Trager advocated that one could not study language without also studying paralinguistic and kinesics.

In the previous chapter, we discussed how much of the communication that occurs during a counseling session is nonverbal. We discussed nonverbal recommendations for counselors such as using the three Vs of attending plus B (see Chapter 6) and SOLER, appropriate handshake and greeting, and pleasant facial expressions. As much communication is nonverbal, these are all very important prerequisites to focus on the verbal skills. Once we have had a chance to practice these and develop a back-and-forth rhythm to the session (through the one verbal skill mentioned, verbal tracking), it is now time to start adding more tools to the tool kit. We will typically start the counseling session with an open-ended question (see Chapter 13 for more information). Then, as we practice our nonverbal communication skills and listen to the client's response, we can use paralanguage and encouragers to encourage the client to continue sharing. These are skills designed to facilitate safety and help our clients feel comfortable self-disclosing, which is necessary for effective counseling.

## Helping Clients Overcome Blocks to Self-Disclosure

When clients come to therapy, we invite them to share their story and to openly discuss their struggles from day one. This can be challenging for many people. Perhaps they have received messages in their family of origin or had rules (spoken or unspoken) imposed upon them that may have served to limit self-disclosure.

These rules may have included:

*Children are to be seen and not heard.*

*Turn that frown upside down.*

*Don't complain or I'll give you something to complain about.*

*If you don't have anything nice to say, then don't say anything.*

© Carolyn Franks/Shutterstock.com

These "rules" may have encouraged them during their developmental years not to share their feelings, especially the feelings associated with displeasure. They may have even influenced them not to share at all but to remain quiet so as not to displease the adults. Rules and norms that we experience during our developmental years can have a powerful impact on us. Even years later, there may be a negative association with opening up especially when it means disclosing uncomfortable and negative emotions. Some of the messages represented by these rules are as follows: do not speak, do not feel, and do not express feelings. However, when clients come to counseling, we are asking them to open up and to speak, to feel, and to share those feelings. In part, this is why we have a unique set of skills designed to create a safe atmosphere where we use skills intentionally to encourage clients to open up and share their story. For some, it may be an untold story, and facilitating it is an important task that requires specific skills.

## Facilitating Storytelling

*Not only is your story worth telling, but it can be told in words so painstakingly eloquent that it becomes a song.*

—*Gloria Naylor* (Montgomery, 2004, p. 11)

One of our goals as counselors is to facilitate the client's story and to help him or her to tell his or her story more coherently. Have you heard a coherent story? Maybe you recall a book from your childhood that included a very coherent story. There are clear themes, a sense of cohesiveness, a sense that you, as the reader, are also kept in mind. As counselors, we have the opportunity to help clients develop a coherent narrative and make sense of their past. This process of "making sense" has powerful implications, which will be more fully explored in Chapter 11 (Knight & Sibcy, 2018; Siegel, 2010a).

## Attachment Illumination:
## Encouraging the Client to Share His or Her Attachment Story

© Shutterstock.com

In the Adult Attachment Interview developed by Main et al. (2002), the interviewer asks the clients questions regarding their attachment history (George et al., 1985). The hallmark question of the AAI is, "Would you share with me five adjectives to describe your childhood relationship with your mother (or other primary early caregiver can be substituted for the word 'mother' here)?" The AAI has been described by Howard and Steele (2008), who teach at The New School in New York City, as "both a mainstay of attachment research and a uniquely valuable clinical tool" (p. 26). When used for research purposes, the interview is also coded by a trained coder using a rigorous coding system (Main et al., 2002).

Let us say you decide to use the AAI clinically. You ask the hallmark question and the client selects the adjective "loving" to describe his or her relationship with her mother. A subsequent question from the interviewer would be "Would you share with me a specific autobiographical episode that illustrates how your early relationship with your mom was 'loving'?" Now, this question can be tough as it has the impact of surprising the unconscious. However, this may give the client the opportunity, when this interview is used clinically, to move toward congruence. In other words, the counselor can use the listening skills to assist the client in articulating his or her attachment story. In this example, the attachment story begins with a description of how the client's early relationship with mom was loving. If the client struggles to find specific memories that are consistent with the adjectives that are chosen, then this is a lack of coherence. We will look at how each of the skills may be strategically used to help the client to develop a more coherent narrative. Minimal encouragers help the client continue sharing and help the client feel comfortable knowing the listener is interested and present. These may be especially helpful for those with a more dismissing state of mind, that are inclined to move away from discussing attachment as encouragers serve the purpose of encouraging them to continue moving toward the discussion.

## Minimal Encouragers: Being Present in the Conversation

Have you ever felt alone in a conversation?, Maybe you were sharing a story and as you shared, it was unclear as to whether your conversation partner was there with you or out to lunch. Although, in the counseling office, we want clients to be the primary speaker, we do not want to encourage them to have a monologue. Although the client may feel some relief to have gotten something off his or her chest, if there is not much dialogue, he or she may feel a sense of emptiness from pouring out but not receiving anything back. Encouragers help maintain some dialogue and a sense of intimacy, and minimal encouragers can offer counselors a user-friendly tool for preventing this phenomenon.

## Minimal Encouragers

Minimal encouragers are nonverbal or verbal counseling skills that can be used to encourage clients to continue on sharing their story but indicate to the speaker that the listener is present and engaged. Some important minimal encouragers include the following:

- Head nods
- Paralanguage (such as hmm, mm hmm, uh huh, huh. . .)
- One-word encouragers (such as "stressful" and "powerful")
- Phrases to encourage the client to continue (e.g., "tell me more". . .)

Using minimal encouragers allows the counselor to be more active as he or she listens; this active engagement and reflection of key words will set the stage for the counselor to smoothly move into other skills such as paraphrasing, reflecting content, reflecting feeling, and summarizing. Minimal encouragers are designed to encourage the clients to continue their story with minimal input from the counselor.

Imagine you have a client who shares the following, and you respond as the counselor does below:

**Client:**     Work is getting very stressful, we are short staffed, and I am having to carry the load of four employees.

**Counselor:** Mmm, stressful.

**Client:**     Yes, it is stressful! And those who are supposed to be helping me on projects are not contributing or doing their part, and to top that off they are not communicating. Why are people such jerks?

**Counselor:** Frustrating.

Notice that the counselor in the session above used minimal encouragers along with key word or one-word encouragers; this validation of the client's feelings prompted him to say more. What if the counselor had reflected using different encouragers? For example, if the counselor used "four employees!" as the first encourager, the client may have launched into a list of all the tasks he was doing that were originally assigned to the other employees who were not following through. With the skills in this chapter and subsequent chapters, the counselor is walking alongside the client seeking to understand; however, the way that the counselor reflects does influence the direction of the counseling session.

We supervised a doctoral student who was finishing up a prerequisite internship. We will call him Clark for the purpose of confidentiality. During supervision, I noticed that he was tuned in and listening, and although he exhibited some nonverbal encouragers on occasion, Clark did not typically use verbal minimal encouragers. We went over a few examples such as mm hmm, uh huh, hmm, huh, and uh huh. I challenged Clark to use these the next week during his sessions with clients. Thankfully, he was open to feedback and fine-tuning his skills. So, Clark did add more verbal encouragers to his sessions the next week! One of his long-term clients gave him some feedback on these skills. He shared that at the end of the session: She said, "I like it when you give me those words, like 'mm hmm.'"

## Paralanguage and Minimal Encouragers To-Do List

In my next practice counseling session, I will practice the following:

- I will pay attention to key words and use one-word encouragers such as "stress."

- I will combine one-word encouragers with minimal encouragers to communicate empathy such as: "mmm, stress."

- I will use the following minimal encouragers throughout the session as appropriate:

- Mmm hmm

- Uh huh

- Hmm

- Mmm

- Aww

## Recommended Reading

If you would like to enhance your expertise on the topics discussed in this chapter, we would recommend reading the following texts to expand your knowledge in this area:

© Shutterstock.com

- Siegel, D. (2010). *Mindsight: Transform your brain with the new science of kindness*. Oxford, United Kingdom: One World.

- Steele, H., & Steele, M. (2008). *Clinical applications of the adult attachment interview*. New York, NY: Guilford Press.

## Chapter Summary

Many people may come to counseling unaccustomed to self-disclosure and may find the first session difficult to adjust to. The mode number of counseling sessions is one, which means that after one session, most people terminate and do not return. So, one of the goals of the therapist is to create a safe environment where the client can explore. The nonverbal skills laid the groundwork for communicating presence through the use of strategies like SOLER and the three Vs of attending plus B. Chapter 7 is based on the nonverbal skills discussed in Chapter 6 and added two new skills to the tool kit including minimal encouragers such as head nods and paralanguage that communicates to the speaker that the listener is listening without "interrupting" the conversation, which may include sounds such as "mm hmm," "uh huh," "huh," "mmm," and other sounds that may communicate interest, agreement, compassion, and other supportive responses.

## Chapter Eight

# Reflection of Content, Paraphrasing, and Summarizing

### Anita Kuhnley and Gary Sibcy

*Understand this, my dear brothers and sisters: You must all be*
*quick to listen, slow to speak, and slow to get angry.*

—James 1:19; NLT

## Chapter Learning Objectives

- To learn essential interviewing and counseling skills such as reflection of content and paraphrasing (CACREP II.F.5.g, p.12)

- To explore the impact of spiritual beliefs on clients' and counselors' worldviews through the use of skills such as reflection of content and paraphrasing (CACREP II.F.2.g, 2016, p. 10)

- To identify a systems approach to conceptualizing clients when reflecting and exploring feelings (CACREP II.F.5.b, 2016, p. 11)

## Chapter Overview

It can be tempting for counselors and other helpers to jump into fix-it mode and begin conceptualizing, finding solutions, and seeking to "fix" the client before taking the time to be present and listen to what has brought the client in to see us. This chapter builds on the nonverbal communication skills discussed in Chapter 6 and the minimal encouragers in Chapter 7 and begins adding the verbal skills to the tool kit to show a client that we are present and seeking to understand. As we seek to understand a person using the skill of reflection (of content), we are also helping him or her understand himself or herself in a way that extends his or her understanding of himself or herself. Strategies for reflecting content, strategies for overcoming challenges with the skill, and implications for counseling are discussed here. This chapter is the first in a series of three chapters on the reflecting skills. These are part of the "essential interviewing and case conceptualization skills" that Council for Accreditation for Counseling and Related Educational Programs (CACREP) emphasizes for counseling and related educational programs.

## Reflecting Skills

*Most people do not listen with the intent to understand. They listen with the intent to reply.*

—Stephen Covey

Reflecting skills help clients process their thoughts and feelings and have the potential to facilitate and extend their understanding of themselves and their world in a clearer way. As a client hears a therapist rephrase his or her narrative from a new perspective in different words, sometimes new insights develop. Sometimes things that were blurry become clear. Reflecting skills are similar to peeling back the layers of an onion. The first layer involves reflection of content, the second layer involves reflection of feeling, and the third and final layer involves reflection of meaning. Increasing levels of self-disclosure often come with increasing levels of trust, safety, and respect in the therapeutic relationship.

## Reflecting Content

The first layer is the content. This usually involves a recounting of what happened or the story and may not include feelings and meanings. Some authors (Ivey et al., 2018) refer to this as a paraphrase, but a paraphrase may also include other layers of reflection, which we will discuss in subsequent sections.

Consider this "Autobiography in Five Chapters" by Portia Nelson:

Chapter One
I walk down the street.
There is a deep hole in the sidewalk
I fall in.
I am lost. . .
I am helpless.
It isn't my fault.
It takes forever to find a way out.

Chapter Two
I walk down the same street.
There is a deep hole in the sidewalk.
I pretend I don't see it.
I fall in again.
I can't believe I'm in the same place.
But it isn't my fault.
It still takes a long time to get out.

Chapter Three
I walk down the same street.
There is a deep hole in the sidewalk.
I see it is there.
I still fall. . .it's a habit. . .but,
I know where I am.
My eyes are open; I know where I am;
It is my fault.
I get out immediately.

Chapter Four
I walk down the same street.
There is a deep hole in the sidewalk.
I walk around it.

Chapter Five
I walk down another street.

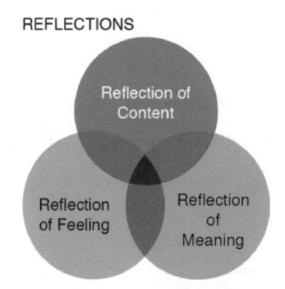

REFLECTIONS

Here in this autobiography, we may have feelings. In response, we may make meaning, but what we have within this autobiography is content. Perhaps the author has made meaning of experience through the lens of personal responsibility. We will revisit feeling and meaning in subsequent sections, but first let us take a look at the content or the "what" of the story. If we are reflecting content, we may say something like:

**Counselor:** "So as you reflect on your life's journey you see yourself starting off taking a particular road that included a hole that was tough to avoid. It sounds like the first time you got stuck and concluded that it was not your fault. It sounds like the second time you concluded it was your fault, and the third time you changed your route to include a new street altogether, so you did not encounter that hole again."

A shorter paraphrase may be:

**Counselor:** "It sounds like you have been on a journey and in each leg of the journey you have learned something. Tell me more about what this has been like."

One of the things you may notice here about this particular reflection of content or paraphrase may be that there is no more than a passing reference to the client's feelings or meaning or interpretations of the events. If we peel back this layer of content and look at the feelings that may lie beneath the surface, we may notice that no feeling words were used. However, if we used advanced empathy (discussed in greater detail in Chapter 3), we would start by thinking about this journey for a moment, and then do an empathy-building exercise that can be helpful in making the process of reflecting feelings easier.

## Empathy Is an Umbrella Skill That Needs to Be Used with Every Other Skill to Provide a Sense of Empathic Understanding to the Client

© Yuganov Konstantin/Shutterstock.com

If you feel comfortable doing so, let us do an empathy-building exercise together. You may have immediately imagined yourself in the author's shoes when reading the autobiography above, but let us do it again intentionally and pay special attention to feelings that bubble up.

First let us try to get into a comfortable position; if you are seated, rest your feet comfortably flat on the floor with hands resting on your thighs.

Let us imagine that you are on a journey, and as you progress along this path, you fall into a hole and get stuck there for a long time. Eventually, you do get out, and you conclude it was not your fault. What might you be feeling? Disappointment that this happened? Frustration that your plans were thwarted? Fear about being stuck? Lonely that you are in a hole alone? Some combination of these feelings?

**A Verse to Remember:** "Rejoice with those who rejoice; mourn with those who mourn." - Romans 12: 15

Some authors (Goleman, 2004) postulate that in order to understand and make sense of other people's feelings, we must first understand our own feelings. This is referred to as cognitive empathy (Goleman, 2006; Ivey et al., 2018). Cognitive empathy involves the prefrontal cortex (PFC; Ivey et al., 2018), which has also been called the executive command center of the brain or "the CEO in your brain" or "cop in your rearview mirror" (Amen, 2010, p. 157). As neuroscientist and single-photon emission computed tomography expert Dr. Daniel Amen indicates, the CEO in your brain or cop in your rearview mirror keeps you on task with goal-directed activity.

This is the same region of the brain involved with helping us to gain an understanding of the emotional state of another. However, Goleman adds we also need to be able to move into maintaining some distance from the other person to remain in the helping role (see Chapter 3 for a more detailed discussion on empathy). How does a counselor remain empathic while also maintaining distance from a client? In almost every counseling skills class, we teach this concept. It is natural to "feel with" another when they are struggling with pain. The scriptures indicate in Romans 12:15, NIV, " Rejoice with those who rejoice; mourn with those who mourn." Students often ask, "Is it okay to cry with your clients?" We suggest empathic listening and concern communicated through paralanguage and strong presence as manifested through the verbal and nonverbal skills, but if possible, avoid crying with clients because we do not want the client to feel pressure to do a role reversal and switch modes into the helper role to help the counselor deal with his or her emotions in the situation and/or to shut down for fear of upsetting the counselor. We believe it is helpful for each counselor to be able to have a time set aside to process feelings and thoughts regularly so that there is not a temptation to use the client's time to do that. Some helpful strategies may involve journaling, prayer journaling, sitting in the other chair by seeking out one's own counseling, or participating in a psychotherapeutic group for counselors.

If a client has heard messages from his or her family of origin that encouraged him or her not to feel or especially not to express negative emotions as discussed in the section, then the counselor may need to use a skill called "advanced empathy" here.

Recall from Chapter 3's discussion on advanced empathy that advanced empathy is defined as a skill that involves attunement to another person's emotion such that one may identify a client's emotion and reflecting it back before he or she is aware of himself or herself of exactly what he or she is feeling.

In these cases, the client's narrative may be barren of any emotional language or perhaps barren of any negative emotional content. Thus, tools such as a feeling wheel can be helpful.

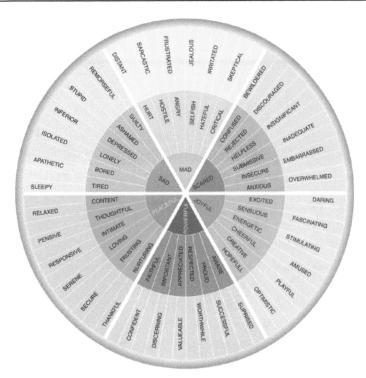

**Figure 8.1.** Feeling wheel.
© Kendall Hunt Publishing Company

Figure 8.1 shows the feeling wheel. This tool can really help clients who are not accustomed to using feeling vocabulary or dialoguing about their internal experiences. Some clients may not have a rich vocabulary of emotional terms. When you ask a client how a difficult conversation went, and they say, "It went fine," we do not stop there. As our colleague Dr. John Kuhnley likes to say, "A good clinician doesn't stop at 'fine.'"

Based on the scenario above, you may use your advanced empathy to pick up on a mixture of emotions that you believe one who experienced this sequence of events may feel and so you may reflect back to the client something similar to the following:

"So, it sounds like you found yourself on a journey and making your way down a street and then you fell into a hole. That must have been surprising and scary to find yourself in a hole and frustrating for it to take a long time to get out of the hole. Tell me more about what that experience felt like." The speaker may then clarify feelings or expand on feelings the counselor reflected.

## Caveats

It is important to remember to validate the client's feelings. If the client reports that his or her experience was different, then the counselor needs to accept and validate that. For example, if the client said, "Well, no it wasn't scary. I found a ladder and knew I would eventually get out it just might take a while to get it steadied," then the counselor would <u>not</u> respond, "Oh no, I know scary and you were scared!" Instead the counselor would validate what the client was saying with an attitude that conveys a curiosity about the client's experience. An example would be "Okay, so it was not scary, there was a sense of confidence that was aroused, but a sense that some effort or time was required. Tell me more."

## The Philosophy of Reflection

*Being heard is so close to being loved that for the average person, they are almost indistinguishable.*

David W. Augsburger, Caring Enough to Hear and Be Heard (1982, p. 12)

At first it may seem as if reflecting the client's content back to him or her is not important to beginning counselors or those unfamiliar with the listening skills. When we have a sense that we have heard and understood a person, it can be tempting to respond with a phrase such as "I understand what you mean," "I know what you mean," or some other iteration of this phrase. However, this may be counterproductive. Here we recommend the following guideline: "Show it, don't say it." This phrase may be reminiscent of the words commonly attributed to St. Thomas of Assisi (however, we do not know the original source of this quote, as this is not found in his writings). *"Preach the gospel at all times, use words only when necessary."* This sentiment is perhaps also captured by the words written in 1 John 3:18 (New Living Translation [NLT]): "Dear children, let us not merely say that we love each other, let us show the truth with our actions" or perhaps the more commonly quoted version (New International Version [NIV]), "Dear children, let us not love with words or speech but with actions and in truth." Spiritually, we are encouraged to take action to support speech. There is a value in showing something that can go beyond saying it. This concept resonates with many people, as demonstrated by the popular series of books stemming from the text by Gary Chapman entitled *The Five Love Languages* (2004) The premise of this text is that Chapman has found, anecdotally in his clinical work, that as he interacts with clients, some feel more loved by some expressions of love than others. He finds that these expressions of love tend to fall within five distinct categories, (order is not significant): (a) physical touch, (b) words of affirmation, (c) quality time, (d) gifts, and (e) acts of service. Chapman has developed a quiz for people to take to seek to identify their primary languages and encourages people to learn to speak their partner's language. In other words, instead of saying "I love you" in a way that is

**A verse to remember (1 John 3:18, NIV):**
*"Dear children, let us not love with words or speech but with actions and in truth."*

**The Five Love Languages:**

1. Physical touch
2. Words of affirmation
3. Quality time
4. Gifts
5. Acts of service

(Chapman, 2004)

**The Presenting Problem:** You may have heard the phrase before that "the presenting problem is often not the problem." When clients present for counseling, they may begin discussing a problem that they feel comfortable discussing at the time, and perhaps as trust is built and rapport is established within the therapeutic relationship, the client begins to feel more comfortable delving deeper into a deeper level of self-disclosure. Perhaps as this process unfolds, the presenting problem is seen through a new lens of depth and other underlying concerns emerge, or perhaps standard, people are encouraged to find out how their partner wants to be loved and show their love in a manner that is congruent. So, if Jim's love language is physical touch and Cara's love language is acts of service, Jim may be encouraged to do things like wash Cara's car and fix her a cup of tea to show his love for her. Meanwhile, Cara, although it may not be her natural language, she may be encouraged to give Jim a massage, hold his hand, or communicate her love through physical affection. These demonstrations may be more meaningful and may feel more congruent than the simple statement of the phrase, "I love you." Perhaps if Jim's primary love language is touch and Cara only is compelled to demonstrate affection toward Jim on rare occasions, her words "I love you" may leave him

as the rapport is built, the client feels more comfortable revealing and processing at a deeper level, making a more authentic connection possible. However, this phenomenon highlights further the sense of the therapeutic relationship and how important it is.

feeling empty. Likewise, in counseling, it can be tempting to just use the phrase "I understand," but our sense that we understand our client may leave him or her feeling empty or misunderstood. When the counselor takes the time to reflect the essence of what the client is saying through a paraphrase, then we are showing the client we understand by seeking to understand him or her and demonstrating that understanding. Perhaps we are able to identify a metaphor that aptly captures the situation.

Years ago, I was working with a client who was a female college student. She had met a young man that she was interested in, but they defined their relationship as a friendship. While she was visiting him, she indicated the thought of being a couple was always on her mind. I reflected, "So, it sounds like that ever-present romantic tension was like an elephant in the room no one was talking about" while you were interacting. She exclaimed very loudly and enthusiastically, "Yes, that is exactly what it is like! I did not know how to describe it, but that's it!" If the counselor were to say, "I understand what you mean," the client may be left wondering, "Does she really?" When the counselor demonstrates an understanding of the client through an appropriate reflection, then the client can trust this reflection because the counselor has shown the client rather than just telling the client. This is why we like the phrase, "Show it, don't say it."

# Attachment Illumination

© Shutterstock.com

## The Maxim of Quality in Conversation

Experience with the Adult Attachment Interview has given us a renewed appreciation for the linguistics behind storytelling and collaborative communication. Herbert Paul Grice, known as Paul, contributed the chapter entitled "Logic and Conversation" to the text *The Semantics-Pragmatics Boundary in Philosophy*, edited by Maite Ezcurdia and Robert J. Stainton. In this chapter, Grice discusses some of the components of collaborative communication. Grice's maxims of collaborative communication offer more insight into the need to show our clients we understand, rather than simply utter the phrase "I understand." Grice describes our conversational exchanges and points out that when we engage in a two-way dialogue (as we do in a counseling session), our conversational exchanges do not just consist of a series of "disconnected remarks, and would not be rationale if they did" (Grice, 1975, p. 49). Grice goes on to make the case that instead of a series of randomly disconnected remarks, our conversational exchanges are instead a collaborative effort working toward a common purpose or goal.

The idea that we are not talking at random about disconnected pieces of information, but working collaboratively toward a common or "mutually accepted" (Grice, 1975, p. 49) conversational goal, is especially the case in counseling, where a client often comes in with what we refer to as "the presenting problem" that they would like to work on, which is why we often discuss collaborative goal setting rather than unilateral goal setting. So, an implied objective is the desire to move toward resolution of the presenting problem. One of the skills we will discuss in Chapter 13 is the skill of goal setting and case conceptualization. As we identify what the client's goals are, counselor and client work collaboratively to design a treatment plan and an agreed-upon plan of action for accomplishing these goals.

Communication (especially therapeutic communication) is a collaborative process, the goals of communication may be formal or informal, and there may be varying degrees of flexibility within a dialogue depending on the requirements set forth by the commonly accepted goals. If one of the conversational partners, in this case client or counselor, moves beyond the accepted bounds, this could lead to risks to the relationship and perhaps deductions from the therapeutic bank account. We can use the metaphor of the therapeutic bank account here because the therapeutic relationship is indeed a relationship, similar to other forms of partnership, and interactions can be likened in some ways to deposits or withdrawals. Willard Harley (2011) in his text, *His Needs Her Needs*, discusses common relationship needs that men have in relationships including, (a) sexual fulfillment, (b) recreational companionship, (c) physical attractiveness, (d) domestic support, and (e) admiration and the needs women have in relationships including, (a) affection, (b) intimate conversation, (c)

*Herbert Paul Grice, known as Paul Grice, was a key player in the linguistics literature of his day and has heavily influenced our study of adult attachment. Grice was a British philosopher of language who taught for the latter portion of his life at UC Berkley. He is known for his development of Grice's Maxims of Collaborative Communication ("Paul Grice," 2017), and he has influenced the philosophy of language.*

*One principle of Grice's work that would serve counselors well is to remember the cooperative principle, which states:*

"Make your conversational contribution such as is required, at the stage at which it occurs, by the accepted purpose or direction of the talk exchange in which you are engaged" (Grice, 1991, p. 26).

honesty and openness, (d) financial support, and (e) family commitment. He indicates that each time that you meet your partner's need, it can be likened to making an emotional deposit in the bank account, and each time you do not, it can be likened to a relationship withdrawal. Clearly, just like with any account, the more deposits made and the larger deposits made, the less impact any withdrawal has on the overall balance. Each skill we have discussed so far in the text is designed to build rapport and thus can be categorized as a deposit in the therapeutic alliance account, which may have the impact of strengthening the trust in the therapeutic relationship and making self-disclosure and risk taking more likely. Dr. John Gottman's research may also provide us with some helpful information about the importance of making deposits in the therapeutic bank account. In the next section we will take a look at what Gottman's research says about this concept.

## Relationship Research and Implications for the Counseling Relationship

Drs. John and Julie Gottman are the founders of the Family Research Institute, affectionately called "The Love Lab," where they have researched and unfolded important dynamics that are associated with longevity or termination in relationships (Gottman & Silver, 2015). They have been able to identify with over 90% accuracy (which is very impressive with inferential statistics) whether a partnership will last or fail. Gottman and his colleagues have identified the four horsemen of the apocalypse, which are so coined because they are behaviors that serve as predictors that the end is near (criticism, contempt, defensiveness, and stonewalling). These behaviors are on our "to don't list" so to speak, because they usher in the end of a rapport or relationship. The goal of the majority of the skills that we are discussing in this text is to facilitate therapeutic dialogue and relationship rapport, not to usher in a premature termination to counseling.

Interestingly, researchers at the University of Nevada, Reno, and Florida Atlantic University have been conducting research on the therapeutic relationship, extending Dr. Gottman's and Dr. Paul Eckman's work to predict the longevity of the therapeutic alliance. They summarize the literature on the topic of dropout and indicate that it has been well documented that most clients (50%) tend to experience meaningful change after they complete eight sessions of counseling and two thirds tend to experience improvement after 26 counseling sessions (Howard, Kopta, Krause, & Orlinsky, 1986; Luedke, Peluso, Diaz, Freund, & Baker, 2017). Luedke and her research team draw on the work of previous researchers that indicate that the therapeutic relationship is one of the greatest predictors of clients indicating that therapy was successful and remaining in therapy; these clients rated their therapists as having empathic traits such as being caring, understanding, and respectful.

**New Frontiers in Counseling Research**
It is exciting to see counseling researchers applying the rigorous research methodologies to the therapeutic relationship. This is a great example of the importance of the right brain, left brain, corpus callosum discussion (see Chapter 12 for more information on this topic).

Luedke and colleagues have applied a coding system that was originally developed by John Gottman and Lowell Krokoff (1989).

## The Specific Affective Coding System and Implications for Counseling

Gottman and Krokoff (1989) were considering an important question: "What distinguishes a marriage that will become more satisfying over time from one that will become less satisfying over time?" The answer to this question may appear to be counterintuitive or even ironic when the answer is considered with regard to both present and longitudinal implications. For example, what is helpful for keeping the peace in the moment could perhaps leave unresolved roots of bitterness that will bear bitter fruit later on that may spoil the whole relationship in the long run. Gottman and Krokoff addressed this significant research question by observing behaviors between couples and analyzing them on a micro level. Their method of research was original and added great value to the literature because early iterations of marital research relied on more biased collections of data that could be influenced by a lack of self-awareness (Knight & Tetrault, 2018; Kruger &

*According to Gottman's research, what is helpful for keeping the peace in the moment could perhaps leave unresolved roots of bitterness that will bear bitter fruit later on that may spoil the whole relationship in the long run.*

Dunning, 1999) that is apparent in self-assessments and the subjectivity associated with some qualitative research. Social science research widely accepts self-report instrumentation and interview data, and of course self-perceptions are not without great value. Gottman and Krokoff acknowledge the contributions of this early research and stand on the shoulders of their marital research predecessors. As the research on martial satisfaction and dissatisfaction was adapted over the years, there were a few systems that were developed that focused on systematic observation of marital interaction and developed strategies for coding the interaction. Gottman and Krokoff used two previous coding systems in addition to the new coding system they introduced in 1989; these previous coding systems included the marital interaction coding system (MICS; Weiss and Summers, 1983; Gottman & Krokoff, 1989) and the couples interaction scoring system (CISS, Gottman, 1979). The system introduced with their 1989 study is known as the specific affective coding system (SPAFF; Gottman & Krokoff, 1989). The purpose of creating the SPAFF was to be able to take the construct of negative emotion and dissect it. The reason it is important to dismantle the variable of negative affect is not all negative affect is the same (Gottman & Korkoff, 1989; Gottman & Levenson, 1986; see Chapter 9 on reflecting feelings). Gottman's previous research with his colleague Robert Levenson confirmed that negative affect played a significant role in the marriages of dissatisfied couples. They found three patterns related to negative emotion in couples who were unsatisfied, (a) there is a greater quantity of negative emotion among couples who are dissatisfied with their marriages, (b) when comparing dissatisfied couples with those who are more satisfied, they found that the dissatisfied couples tended to experience more mutuality in negative emotion among partners, and (c) when couples were dissatisfied, their interactions showed more consistency and it was also easier to predict the way partners would respond to each other in dissatisfied marriages, and their interactions were also less autonomous, which makes sense in terms of attachment. So, since previous research by a variety of marital researchers had uncovered the role of negative affect (as a general category), Gottman and Krokoff wanted to unpack this construct of negative to identify how the various components of negative impact influence the couple relationship. The SPAFF dismantles negative affect into five: (a) anger, (b) contempt, (c) fear, (d) sadness, and (e) whining. In the study (Gottman & Krokoff, 1989) using the SPAFF when it was newly introduced, the researchers used the other two coding systems in addition to it to code 15-minute interviews where couples were discussing a conflict issue. The SPAFF added value to the other coding systems used because of its Gestalt focus on not only coding the verbal utterances but also considering the nonverbals. Recall from Chapter 6 the significance of nonverbal communication including the idea that nonverbal communication is not always congruent with verbal communication, and when there is a discrepancy, those judging a message tend to assign the nonverbal portion of the message with more weight. In counseling, after addressing the personhood of the counselor with respect to state of mind, habits, ethical foundations, and multicultural competencies, our model looks at intentional nonverbal communication. Thus, a coding system that considers the impact of nonverbal communication in addition to verbal components is considered of great value. The nonverbal components that Gottman and Krokoff's (1989) system evaluates included "voice tone, context, facial expression, gestures and body movement" (Gottman and Krokoff, 1989, p. 51). The major finding of this study in terms of practical recommendations is as follows:

*In terms of recommendations for marriage, our results suggest that wives should confront disagreement and should not be overly compliant, fearful, and sad but should express anger and contempt. Husbands should also engage in conflict but should not be stubborn or withdrawn. Neither spouse should be defensive.*

We recommend this article for further reading if you would like to learn more about their findings. Please see the recommended reading for more information.

Since this introduction of the third coding modality that Gottman and Krokoff used, the SPAFF, it has been widely used in research; Coan and Gottman (2007) indicated, "Since its debut, the SPAFF has, in one version or another, informed dozens of published scientific findings deriving from numerous laboratories" (Coan & Gottman, 2007, p. 267). Coan and Gottman (2007) wrote a chapter on SPAFF that was published in *The Handbook of Emotion Elicitation and Assessment* approximately 18 years after the original debut of the system. They seemed to emphasize that the importance of the coding system was not to break down infinitely miniscule aspects of communication for the sake of analysis but to serve more practical purposes such as determining what contempt looks like and what validation looks like with respect to interactions and to provide a measurement of these constructs. The model that the SPAFF system uses to measure affect has been described as a latent variable model. Coan and Gottman use the example of validation, one of the five different codes of positive affect (validation, affection, enthusiasm, interest, and humor) and indicate that one cannot see the variable "validation" but can see indicators of validation. They use the following model to illustrate this: it is a SPAFF code for the latent construct validation that can be "seen," if you will, by its indicators in the rectangles that the arrows point to below which include agreement or apology, summarizing, and head nodding and/or eye contact.

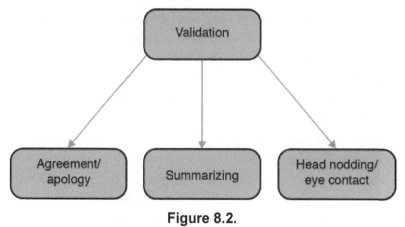

**Figure 8.2.**
© Kendall Hunt Publishing Company

Do some of these indicators sound familiar? In Chapter 6, when discussing the nonverbal counseling skills, you may recall learning about the importance of (SOLER and the 3Vs plus B, which include one of the most critical nonverbal counseling skills, eye contact. Head nodding is a minimal encourager, an important attending skill that was discussed in Chapter 7. Summarizing is also an important counseling skill, which falls in the category of reflecting skills that we will discuss further in this chapter. A SPAFF coder may see when we observe a counselor using these important counseling skills, we are seeing (if you will) the latent variable of validation (Coan & Gottman, 2007)!

Defensiveness is another latent variable that is coded on the SPAFF. Recall from Chapter 6 that defensiveness is one of the four horsemen of the apocalypse that indicates the end is near in a relationship or partnership! As we have previously established in this chapter, the strength of the therapeutic relationship is one of the most important predictors of longevity and efficacy of counseling, so we want to avoid affect that can evoke the dissolution of the therapeutic alliance. Let us look at what the indicators of defensiveness are on the SPAFF (Coan & Gottman, 2007, p. 275): (a) "yes-but" phrases, which can be identified when a listener agrees with a speaker briefly but then quickly disagrees, (b) cross-complaining, another indicator that involves responding to a speaker's complaint with one's own complaint rather than addressing the complaint that was shared, (c) minimization, which involves discounting the concerns of the speaker (e.g., if we consider a potential counseling application, a client complains the counselor was late for the session, and the counselor responds, "Yes, I am sorry that I was late, but most counselors only give 45 minutes for the therapeutic hour, so being 15 minutes late really doesn't matter since we still have 45"), (d) excuses, which involve the allocation of blame from the speaker to something or someone else (such as I could not help being late because there was road work down the street), and (e) aggressive defensiveness that just involves outright denial, for example, " I was not late." Also note that some of these latent variables have physical components; guess what the physical component for defensiveness is? Here is a clue: recall from Chapter 6 that the O from SOLER represents open posture and counselors are encouraged not to close or fold their arms across their chest. Yes, the physical indicator of defensiveness includes arms folded across the chest.

Thus it makes sense that Luedke and colleagues have applied this system to evaluating counseling sessions and the therapeutic relationship. They found that there were statistically significant differences in the areas of validation and defensiveness between those clients who terminated therapy prematurely and those who continued to return to therapy (Luedke et al., 2017). As far as counselor behaviors that were associated with client's return to therapy, they reported the following findings:

> *Regarding counselor behaviors, demonstrations of **tension and high validation** were significantly different between the counselors with clients who dropped out of therapy and counselors with clients who stayed. Unsurprisingly, counselors who provided **higher levels of validation and were more comfortable in the room** (e.g., fewer displays of tension) were **more likely to see clients return to therapy.** (Luedke et al. 2017, p. 131)*

This robust research using such valid, reliable, and objective measures with trained raters adds to the validity of research in counselor education. This also speaks of the importance of counselors working to develop and employ these foundational reflecting skills including, but not limited to, summarizing and reflecting content (as well as the R of SOLER, which is to maintain a relaxed state as opposed to uncomfortable state as referenced above), good eye contact, and minimal encouragers.

## The Validating and Staying Power of the Reflecting Skills

There are a range of reflecting skills, which may include key word reflections, feeling word reflections, reflections of content, and reflections of meaning, paraphrases, and summaries. We will explore each one in more detail.

Now we have established the importance of validating the client and showing the client that he or she is understood through the reflecting skills, which may be indicators of validation (or ways of seeing validation in a counseling session). This is a process that also serves in part to enhance therapeutic rapport; let us return to Grice's maxims for some important guidelines as to how we may apply that to our demonstration of understanding. Let us start by exploring Grice's cooperative principle, which states, "Make your conversational contribution such as is required, at the stage which it occurs, by the accepted purpose or direction of the talk exchange in which you are engaged" (Grice, 1975, pp. 49–50). In order to understand the specific maxims of collaboration that Grice identifies, it is necessary to go back further to the work of Aristotle and Kant (See the call out box). In Aristotle's work, *Categories*, he provides a framework for assigning every object to a category. His work has been described by authors such as Smith (1995, in *The Cambridge Companion to Aristotle* as "perhaps the single most heavily discussed of all Aristotelian notions" (p. 55). Aristotle indicated that those categories include substance, quantity, quality, relation, place, date, posture, state, action, and passion (Studtmann,

> Something to remember: "Make your conversational contribution such as is required, at the stage which it occurs, by the accepted purpose or direction of the talk exchange in which you are engaged" (Grice, 1975, pp. 49–50).

Kant.

2017). Kant introduced anthropology as an area of study at universities in Germany (Pitte, 1971).

Aristotle.

© A. Sych/Shutterstock.com

## Strategies for Reflecting Content

### The Key Word Reflection

Counselors can listen to a client's narrative and identify key words; Some of these reflecting skills overlap, and a key word reflection can also be a reflection of feeling. Feeling words are often key words. See the feeling wheel and complete the activity below to heighten your awareness of feeling words. As you complete the activity below, make a mental note that all of the words below, if used to describe a client's state of mind or emotional experience, are key words and can be reflected back with just a single word. These can be referred to as key word encouragers or one-word encouragers. They are markers for the client that validate feelings but invite the client to continue sharing. It is as if a friend told you she was working on a group project with three other people, and all three of the others did not contribute their part of the work, and your friend was left with all of it. If you were resonating with the friend's emotion, and they looked upset you may sigh and say, "Ugh, frustrating." This would be an example of a key word reflection.

### Practice Activity

What are some words that may be indicative of sadness? Add three more words to the list below:

- Melancholy
- Discouraged
- Blue

What are some other words that you could use that describe varying intensity of the feeling anger?

- Irritation
- Frustration
- Rage

What are some other words that could be substituted for dimensions of the feeling of joy?

- Happiness
- Glad
- Excited

## Enriching and Paraphrasing

Paraphrasing is one of the most frequently used and most important counseling skills. It shows evidence throughout the session that the counselor understands the client and is often a minimum competency for counselors in training.

In order to paraphrase a client's narrative, we must first use the skill of enrichment/enriching. Sometimes an early counselor-in-training will have a client that is verbose and has a lot to say. At first, students report feeling uncomfortable interjecting. They often report they feel as if they are interrupting the client. This hesitancy and discomfort make sense because socially we have been taught not to interrupt others. If a client was telling his or her story and a counselor interrupted to say, "Oh, I can relate to you I had a very similar experience let me tell you about it. . .," that would be an inappropriate interruption and probably an inappropriate self-disclosure. However, the purpose of a counselor's interjection in order to use a reflecting skill such as paraphrasing is not an interruption, but rather an enrichment to the counseling session because the counselor is enriching the client's experience by helping him or her feel understood and enriching his or her understanding of himself or herself as he or she hears things paraphrased in different words and possibly from a different perspective, as in the case when a counselor uses a paraphrase to reframe something or share it from another perspective. Therefore, we refer to the skill of interjecting to use a reflecting skill "enriching." Moreover, the counselor is socializing the client to counseling and teaching the client what it means to be a client. Counseling is a dialogue not a monologue; if the counselor were to let the clients talk the entire session without interjection (and some clients may approach doing this if the counselor does not interject), the client may leave feeling empty. They may feel a sense of relief because they were able to "dump" the feelings, concerns, and worries they were struggling with. However, they may feel empty because the counselor did not respond with what Coan and Gottman may call indicators of validation; we have to be able to see the validation and empathy manifest through the use of counseling skills such as minimal encouragers and paraphrases. Another way to think about the difference between an interruption and an interjection is to think of a GPS. When you are driving to your destination, your GPS may interject and say, "You are on the fastest route to your destination and you will arrive at 9 p.m." or if you are not on the fastest route to your destination, your GPS may interject and say, "There is upcoming traffic; there is a shorter route to your destination available." An interruption involves a break or redirect of a trajectory or intended direction. However, when a counselor breaks in to use a reflecting skill, the counselor, like the GPS, is seeking to help the clients clarify their direction and perhaps ensure they are on the route that suits them best and they are working together to move to a mutually agreed-upon destination just as it is with your GPS. So, give yourself permission to enrich the session, which is the first step to paraphrasing.

## Attachment Illumination and Violating Grice's Maxims

© Shutterstock.com

As you reflect on Grice's maxim of collaborative communication, note that when a person is violating a maxim such as quality and not providing evidence for what they are saying, this is an example of a lack of coherence. Recall from previous discussions in Chapter 1 that one of the most important predictors of attachment is coherence. Coherence and collaboration go hand in hand. However, we have found in our clinical work, which is supported by attachment research, when one has an interpersonal history characterized by rejection, he or she can manifest an emergence of a lack of Grice's maxim of quality. As we seek to demonstrate the maxim of quality through our counseling skills and congruence, we can help our clients move toward a more coherent narrative honoring the maxim of quality as well. Let us see how this may manifest in the case of Andy.

## The Case of Andy: An Avoidant Style

Andy was a 58-year-old senior associate pastor at a large church. For years he had struggled with occasional pornography use. Recently, his wife stumbled into his office while Andy was viewing images on his desktop computer. She was outraged, and Andy was engulfed in feelings of shame and depression. He and his wife went to a couples counselor and have been able to work things out in the marriage, but Andy became increasingly depressed and angry with himself for having to deal with the ongoing temptation to use pornography.

Andy grew up in a home with five children. He was the middle child and tended to feel like he had to "make it on my own." As many with a history of an avoidant attachment pattern, Andy did not really like talking about his childhood, and he tended to idealize his parents (with idealization, there is often no evidence for positive characteristics attributed to the parents). He portrayed his childhood years and his relationship with his parents in general, nonspecific aphorisms: "It was all good. My mom was a beautiful, caring, loving, hardworking, and an intelligent woman. She was always on the move, cleaning, cooking, and taking care of the household duties. My dad was a hard-working business man who did his best to make a good living for us kids. He loved us and was caring but he was all business. He would take us fishing and hunting but was a man of few words. He always made time for church on Sundays and we would always eat a big meal together."

When the counselor pressed Andy for some specific memories of his childhood experiences with each of his parents, Andy would push the questions aside without much reflection. For example, when the counselor asked for memories about his mother being caring and loving, Andy was slightly irritated, and his eyes glossed over with a sense of bewilderment. "I do not know. . .I can't think of anything specific. That was just the way she was. She was always loving and caring. . .that was just the way mom was." *(Note, here, this is a violation of the collaborative principle because Andy is not making his contribution as the generally accepted purpose of the interview requires, he is not providing a response to why his mom was the way she is, not providing evidence, this is characteristic of one who may have had to come to terms with a rejecting parent and minimized the pain).*

From an attachment perspective, Andy was organized like an avoidantly attached individual on several levels. First, he was disconnected from his feelings and had difficulty reflecting on his attachment history. In fact, he was annoyed by the therapist's inquiries into these issues, stating that he did not think that what happened to him as a child had anything to do with what was happening to him now. He just wanted the temptation to use pornography gone from his head so he did not have to deal with it anymore. Second, Andy and his wife, Debbie, had become entrenched in their roles; he spent much of his time on duty as a church pastor, writing sermons, counseling parishioners, consoling the sick in the hospital or at home, conducting funerals and weddings, and attending endless meetings with elders and others on his leadership team. His wife was more of a mother or grandmother than a romantic partner. She was busy taking care of their 15-year-old daughter, who needed to be taxied from one activity to another, and playing a role of a backup babysitter for their one-year-old grandson from their oldest daughter, Katlyn, and her husband Luke. Andy and Debbie had very little time together alone. And when they did, they had very little to talk about besides updating each other about the minutia of their day-to-day lives. There was no time or energy for sexual intimacy. When their heads hit the pillow, they were asleep. Third, Andy was a lonely man. Like many pastors, his role dictated that he always be in a position of authority over the people around him. So, he related to everyone as an employee, a subordinate. He did not have one friend he could relate to on equal terms, someone he could hang out with, play golf, fish, hunt, or do any of the recreational activities he used to enjoy when he was younger. He also had no one to confide in, and he preferred it that way. He felt far too vulnerable to trust others with his thoughts, feelings, weaknesses, and concerns. He had convinced himself that all he needed was God, the Bible, and a good concordance and he would be fine. But what he did not see—nor did he want to see—was that God had made him for relationships and that his lack of intimacy—lack of real friends and a few confidants—was fueling his sexual drives. Many with avoidant attachment deny their need for relational intimacy and instead turn to fantasy or some other substitute (drugs, alcohol, fame, power, money, etc.)

The key, however, for the counselor in the early stages of therapy, was to identify and respect Andy's avoidant defenses. So, it would be a mistake to be overly empathic and to overemphasize the need for Andy to identify and express his feelings. It would also be important to flex with intentional competence (Ivey et al., 2018) as discussed in Chapter 4, and if Andy did not respond well to attempts to reflect or validate his feelings, then to meet Andy where he is. A counselor appreciating the Gestalt flavor of counseling may even use the advanced skills of both immediacy and scaling, to have him gauge in the moment how uncomfortable he is or was feeling to measure progress and help Andy engage in the moment.

It is important for the therapist to maintain a sense of compassion and capacity to recognize and respect Andy's difficulties with acknowledging his vulnerabilities and relying on or confiding his concerns and vulnerabilities to the therapist, which should not be interpreted as resistance. In Cassidy and Shaver's *Handbook of Attachment* (2002), we learned that as early as age three some children with avoidant tendencies had learned to mask their physiological and emotional desire to connect with attachment figures. Note, this was an adaptive survival strategy that was a necessity for maintaining contact with a rejecting attachment figure.

The therapist would have to start at the "behavioral level" with Andy and help him identify triggers in his environment that activated his sexual urges. He would need to help Andy organize a plan to reduce his exposure to these triggers (which is called stimulus control) and to provide some methods for shifting his attention away from his sexual fantasies on to other, externally based activities and behaviors as a way of coping with the urge to use pornography. Finally, he would need to help Andy voluntarily limit his access to the Internet by placing filters on all his electronic devices so he could not easily access pornographic material whenever the urges arose. With some success, Andy may begin to trust the therapist more and then possibly consider how his loneliness fueled his sexual fantasies.

## How to Paraphrase

*There is a difference between listening and waiting for your turn to speak.*

Simon Sinek (2009)

If step one is giving yourself permission to enrich the session, then step two is determining the appropriate time to enrich. It is important to paraphrase and use minimal and one-word encouragers frequently throughout the session to let the client know that you are hearing and seeking to understand him or her. Sometimes, a client will pause to check in and may ask, "Does that make sense?" Or he or she may do a relatively brief, less direct check by very briefly pausing with a comment such as "You know?" or "So" and then look at you to shift the conversational turn. These are moments when a counselor could jump in with a paraphrase. If the client does not stop, then the counselor may need to rely on nonverbal gestures such as leaning forward or using louder paralanguage preceding an enrichment. Step three is combining the enriching moment with a leading phrase and then paraphrasing key content or affect in your own words to capture the essence of what the client has shared so far and to help the client feel understood. Remember the quote at the beginning of this section: when you focus on seeking to understand the client and seeking to experience his or her story and connect to his or her emotions and experience, then the words will be there when it comes time to paraphrase. It is important to focus on being present and seeking to understand rather than thinking about what to say in an upcoming paraphrase.

## Summarizing

*You compose because you want to somehow summarize in some permanent form your most basic feelings about being alive, to set down. . . some sort of permanent statement about the way it feels to live now, today.*

*Aaron Copland (Applewhite, Evans, & Frothingham, 2003, p. 289)*

Coan and Gottman (2007) report in the SPAFF that the latent variable validation is marked as positive (please recall, this is one of the coding systems used in Gottman's research; he is the clinical researcher who has been able to predict with over 90% accuracy which couples will stay together and which will divorce as discussed earlier in this chapter). They report several indicators of validation. One is called "back channels," which are attending skills that communicate (Coan & Gottman, 2007, p.15) "affirmative listening"; these include eye contact (which is part of our nonverbal configuration of skills captured in SOLER) and head nods and paralanguage, which we consider minimal encouragers. Direct expressions of respect or understanding are also coded as validation such as "that is a good idea." **Paraphrasing** is another indicator of validation, which can be a verbatim restatement or a restatement in the listener's own words. Paraphrasing is on the same continuum as summarizing; a summary is a longer paraphrase. These skills can be associated with building the therapeutic relationship just as validation is a positive indicator for a couple's relationship.

Summarizing is a counseling skill that involves an articulation of the central themes related to content, feeling, and, if explored, meaning from a client's narrative. It is similar to a paraphrase but longer in length. A summary is often used toward the end of a session to wrap up the session and pull out key themes. It can also be used at the beginning of a session to summarize the previous session so the counselor and client do not have to start from scratch but can pick up where they left off.

## Strategies for Summarizing

**<u>Step One:</u>** Listen for key themes throughout the session (make sure to listen for both key content and affect).

**<u>Step Two:</u>** Select a leading statement; consider the following examples:

- Some things that stand out to me from our time together today include. . .
- So, today we spent most of our time discussing. . .
- So, we are getting to the end of our time together, and I just want to recap some key themes from today. . .
- What stands out most to me from today's session is. . .
- Okay, it is time to wrap up for today, so the takeaway from today's session is. . .

**<u>Step Three:</u>** Paraphrase key themes and affect from the session.

**<u>Step Four:</u>** Add advanced skill of scaling and homework.

The summary is an exceptionally valuable way to start the session. It indicates to the client that you have spent some time preparing and thinking about the session. It helps orient the client to where to pick up. It prevents losing session time to small talk and provides continuity to each session when starting and ending with a summary.

Ending the session with a summary can also provide a nice rhythm to the session, and restating the homework can give a preview for the next session; it also allows for a micro consolidation of gains (we will discuss more on the importance of consolidating gains in Chapter 14 on termination).

## To Do List

**Paraphrasing**

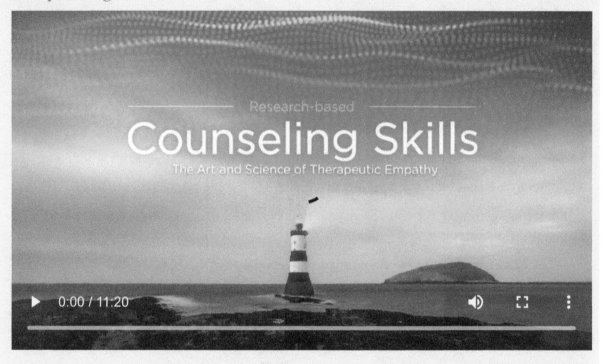

- First, please watch the counseling session with Alex, and listen for paraphrasing

- **Enrich:** Periodically interject during the client's narrative

- **Key word reflections:** Identify and restate key feeling words similar to minimal encouragers to prompt the client to continue and to recognize key feelings (e.g., mmm stressful!)

- **Paraphrase:** Restate in your own words the essence of what the client is saying, and pick some leading phrases from the following (or identify your own):

    ○ **It sounds like. . .**

    ○ **What I'm hearing you say is. . .**

    ○ **So, you are saying. . .**

- Please watch the counseling session with Alex for a summary of the previous session.

Summarizing

0:00 / 9:25

- **Summarizing:** A more lengthy paraphrase (use some of the following leading phrases or develop your own):

  ○ **A few things that stand out from today's session are. . .**

  ○ **We are getting to the end of our time, so let me take a moment to recap. . .**

- **Seek to be empathetic**

## Recommended Reading

If you would like to continue expanding your expertise on the topics covered in this chapter, we would recommend reading the following texts to expand your knowledge in this area. These are recommended literatures as they provided the basis of some of the research used for this chapter.

© Shutterstock.com

- Coan, J. A., & Gottman, J. M. (2007). *The specific affect coding system.* In J. A. Coan & J. N. Allen (Eds.), *Handbook of emotion elicitation and assessment* (pp. 106–123). New York, NY: Oxford University Press.

- Gottman, J. M. (2007). *Why marriages succeed or fail: And how you can make yours last.* New York, NY: Simon & Schuster.

- Gottman, J. M., & Levenson, R. W. (1986). Assessing the role of emotion in marriage. *Behavioral Assessment, 8*(1), 31–48.

- Leudke, A. J., Peluso, P. R., Diaz, P., Freund, R., & Baker, A. (2017). Predicting dropout in counseling using affect coding of the therapeutic relationship: An empirical analysis. *Journal of Counseling & Development, 95*(2), 125–134. doi:10.1002/jcad.12125

## Chapter Summary

In Chapter 8, we discussed the reflecting skills that include key word reflections, paraphrases, and summaries. We also discussed cutting edge research conducted by Leudke et al. (2017) on the use of Coan and Gottman's (2007) affective coding system called SPAFF for short. This coding system allowed Gottman et al. to extend the marital satisfaction research and to dismantle the construct of negative affect (largely associated with dissatisfying partnerships) into observable indicators, for example, a physical observation of defensiveness, which is the folding of the arms over the chest. However, positive interactive processes such as validation are also coded, and the reflecting skills are primary indicators, especially paraphrasing and summarizing. Furthermore, other counseling skills such as eye contact and a relaxed stance are associated with validation. Gottman's work has been applied to the therapeutic relationship, and researchers have found that counselors who tend to be high on indicators of empathy and validation tend to have clients who are less likely to drop out and more likely to remain in therapy. This confirms the importance of developing strong reflecting skills. Attachment implications are also discussed in this chapter. H. Paul Grice, a linguist who developed the collaborative principle that defines the maxims of collaborative communication, discussed the importance of quality or providing support for claims, which is necessary for collaborative communication. Reflecting skills allow counselors to show that they are seeking to understand their clients and are more powerful validations than statements such as "I know what you mean." The skill reflecting key words includes using one-word encouragers to validate a feeling such as "stressful." The skill of enrichment was also discussed and contrasted with interrupting. Enriching involves a counselor interjecting to help clarify the client's story and to seek to understand the client. Paraphrasing includes restating a client's words in the counselor's own words, and summarizing is a longer paraphrase that covers a longer portion of the session. Summaries are typically used at the beginning or end of a session to bring closure and consolidate gains, not unlike the chapter summaries in this book.

## Chapter Nine

# Reflecting and Exploring Feelings

### Anita M. Kuhnley and Gary Sibcy

*Feelings are much like waves, we can't stop them from coming, but we can choose which ones to surf.*

— Commonly Attributed to Jonatan Mårtensson

© Hayk_Shalunts/Shutterstock.com

## Chapter Learning Objectives

- To identify counselor characteristics and behaviors that influence the counseling process, such as using skills such as reflecting and exploring feeling to create a safe environment (CACREP II.5.f, 2016, p. 12)
- To learn essential interviewing and counseling skills such as identifying feeling and reflecting/exploring feelings (CACREP II.5.g, 2016, p. 12)

- To explore the impact of spiritual beliefs on clients' and counselors' worldviews (CACREP II.F.2.g, 2016, p. 10)
- To determine a systems approach to conceptualizing clients when using nonverbal behaviors (CACREP II.F.5.b, 2016, p. 11)

# Chapter Overview

In Chapter 8, we discussed the first of three reflecting skills, reflections of content. Content can be reflected through a paraphrase or even a key word reflection or one-word encourager (this skill overlaps both categories, serving as a reflection and a minimal encourager) and summaries that can facilitate the start of a session or provide a strategy for wrapping up and bringing closure to the session. Groundbreaking research on relationships and the therapeutic relationship shows how important these validating skills are. In this chapter, we explore another very important reflecting skill. This is the second reflecting skill in a series of three. Here we will discuss reflection of feelings. If reflecting is like peeling back the layers of an onion, the first layer fell off as we reflected key content, and now the second layer falls off as we reflect key feelings, As with chopping onions, our tear glands may begin to produce tears in response to the pulling away of another layer of onion. Likewise, as we reflect the client's feelings and he or she becomes more present with the pain in their lives, after peeling a layer of content away and labeling feelings, the tears and other emotions may begin to manifest in more powerful ways. The importance of reflecting and validating these feelings is discussed, and strategies for reflecting feelings are explored.

*According to a Spanish Proverb:*

*No hay peor sordo que el que no quiere oír.*

*There is no worse deaf person than someone who doesn't want to listen.*

*(as cited in Ivey, Ivey, & Zalaquett, 2013, p. 145)*

As the above Spanish proverb indicates, empathy involves being present in the moment with another person's emotional experience and acknowledging what it is in the here and now. There is a radical acceptance. If we are uncomfortable with a feeling state such as sadness or anger, then it will be difficult to stay present with clients and facilitate their discussion and processing of their feelings. It can be helpful to practice a mindful acceptance of feelings; on the interpersonal circumplex (Ivey et al., 2013), we want to be able to move to the neutral center and to observe feelings and be present with them.

## Where Does Reflecting Feelings Fit in with the Other Skills?

To begin a counseling session, we may use pleasant nonverbal communication such as a smile, a gesture to the client to sit down and make herself comfortable, and/or a warm and appropriate handshake. These nonverbal skills combined with SOLER or may communicate to our clients a congruent message that we are present with them and want to connect and collaborate with them to work toward mutually agreed-upon goals. Once the nonverbal communications have been clear, then we use a door opener; this is an open-ended question that opens the door to begin the session (unless we have been seeing this client for several sessions, in which case it is helpful to start the session with a summary of the previous session or the agreed-upon homework, see Chapter 8 to review the skill of summarizing and to review homework). A door opener may be an open-ended question such as the following:

- What brings you in today?

- What would you like to accomplish during our time together today?

- What prompted you to seek out counseling now?

- I see your intake says. . .tell me more about what brought you here.

- So, tell me about what would you like to work on in today's session

Next, we will use the minimal encouragers and paralanguage discussed in Chapter 7 to encourage the client to continue sharing. Once we have explored content and reflected key content in the form of a paraphrase, a summary, and/or key word reflections, the next layer of the client's narrative to peel away is feeling. It is important to reflect and validate others' feelings. Sometimes a client may not have a substantial vocabulary of feeling words. Some people struggle to articulate their feelings, whereas others are very fluent when discussing emotions. The client's capacity to discuss feelings is not the real matter here. The task of the therapist is to create an environment of safety such that the client feels comfortable and sufficiently safe to begin exploring feelings. As we transition to discuss the importance of validating and reflecting emotions, let us first begin with a discussion on difficult (that some may consider negative) emotions such as sadness that interferes with functioning and manifests as depression. Understanding how some mood disorders such as persistent depressive disorder (PDD; *DSM-5*; APA, 2013) develop may be helpful in developing empathy and understanding the importance of using skills such as reflecting feelings to help indicate validation and to create a sense of felt safety for the client. Understanding the why (Sinek, 2009), behind our skills is an important part of what fuels us to embrace them and refine them with zeal.

## Feelings and Emotion Dysregulation: Depression and Cognitive Behavioral Analysis System of Psychotherapy

*The walls we build around us to keep sadness out also keep out joy.*

—Jim Rohn (2006)

## Key Contributors in Treatment Research for Chronic Depression

Dr. James P. McCullough, Jr., is Emeritus Professor of Psychology in Richmond, VA, at Virginia Commonwealth University. Dr. McCullough is a key contributor because during a time (1970s and early 1980s) when persistent depression was considered to be a personality disorder (personality disorders were not considered to be responsive to either medication or psychological treatment), McCullough developed the Cognitive Behavioral Analysis System of Psychotherapy (CBASP) and tested the model using a single-case design research and published his findings. During his career, he has been refining his research using data from single-case studies and randomized clinical trials. His approach has now undergone multiple clinical trials, which has established CBASP as an empirically validated treatment, the gold standard in terms of treatment research (Knight & Tetrault, 2018; CBASP website: **www.CBASP.org).**

**James McCullough**

Copyright © 2018 by James McCullough. Reprinted by permission.

## Persistent Depressive Disorder (Advances in Psychotherapy: Evidence-Based Practice)

Dr. Jennifer Kim Penberthy, a certified clinical psychologist, has worked collaboratively with James McCullough on many research projects and publications related to the treatment of persistent depression. She has extended McCullough's work to group practice. She works at the University of Virginia Department of Psychiatry and Neurobehavioral Sciences. She is the author and co-author of multiple books on the topic including her forthcoming book (2019) *Persistent Depressive Disorder (Advances in Psychotherapy: Evidence-Based Practice).*

*CBASP as a Distinctive Treatment for Persistent Depressive Disorder: Distinctive features (CBT Distinctive Features) (2014),* and

**Dr. J. Kim Penberthy**

Copyright © 2018 by Jennifer Kim Penberthy. Reprinted by permission.

*Group Workbook for Treatment of Persistent Depression: Cognitive Behavioral Analysis System of Psychotherapy (CBASP) Patient's Guide.*

What brings people into counseling? There are as many different motivations as there are clients, so it is difficult to make broad generalizations. However, we do have data that indicate prevalence rates and common presenting problems (Rochlen & O'Brien, 2002). Oftentimes we see problems with emotion regulation, for example, struggles with anxiety, depression, post-traumatic stress disorder (PTSD), anger management, or other mood disorders that are interfering with functioning. One of the most common presenting problems that we have seen clients bring into counseling is depression and symptoms of depression (American Psychiatric Association, 2013, p. 165). The prevalence of depression as reported in the *DSM-5* is 7% of the population in a given 12-month period. There is some variation by age, with depression being three times more prevalent in individuals in 18 to 29 years old compared with individuals 60 years or older. Moreover, there are some gender differences in depression rates. In to the *DSM-5*, females are up to three times more likely than males to experience depression. Depression rates are also higher in terms of lifetime prevalence compared with 12-month prevalence rates. In a study on lifetime prevalence estimates of major depression using an indirect estimation method, Kruijshaar, Barendregt, de Graaf, Spijker, and Andrews (2005) found that in the Netherlands and Australia, the lowest number of men and women having a depressive episode was 30% of men and 40% of women.

Given the prevalence of depression and other mood disorders, it is important for counselors to explore feelings and emotions with clients. As the field moves away from schoolism and toward research-based treatments, helpful advanced interventions have been developed such as cognitive behavioral analysis system of psychotherapy (CBASP; McCullough, 2000), which is an research-based form of talk therapy that has provided much hope for clients with persistent depression, because positive outcome studies exist that demonstrate its efficacy (McCullough, 2000). Furthermore, CBASP provides a helpful explanatory model for the development and maintenance of chronic depression and structured procedures for conducting therapy.

Exploring emotions, including sadness, discouragement, and grief, that may be associated with depression, requires communication of empathy. In order for a therapist to be empathic, it is important to first understand emotions and emotional thinking. Although therapists are careful not to ask why questions in a way that evokes defensiveness, we do explore the rationale behind a feeling or the reasons behind a feeling. Let us look at Greenspan's model, for example. There are four levels: (a) regulating feelings perhaps through gestures (note if a client is overwhelmed and dysregulated emotionally it will be difficult to make any real progress in therapy); (b) two-way communications, which involves beginning two-way communication and overlap with the first level that involves gesturing; (c) labeling internal experiences, which is called "representational elaboration" (Greenspan, 1997, p. 225; Greenspan, 199) but is not limited not limited to only feelings but also includes desires, opinions, concerns, and other internal experiences; (d) ...

Persistent depressive disorder (PDD; dysthymia; which has been developed from a combination of the *DSM-IV*'s criteria for both major depressive disorder and dysthymic disorder) is described as "depressed mood for most of the day, for more days than not, as indicated by either subjective account or observation by others, for at least 2 years (American Psychiatric Association, 2013, p. 168)." Diagnosing this disorder requires the clinician to note the presence of two or more for the following symptoms:

1. "Poor appetite or overeating
2. Insomnia or hypersomnia
3. Low energy or fatigue
4. Low self-esteem
5. Poor concentration or difficulty making decisions
6. Feelings of hopelessness" (American Psychiatric Association, 2013, p. 168)

The *DSM* lists additional criteria regarding the time frame, the absence of manic episodes or hypomanic episodes, and ruling out other disturbances, and of course the symptoms cause clinically significant interference with other areas of functioning (American Psychiatric Association, 2013, For more information, see the *DSM* for a full description of all criteria; the purpose of including this abbreviated version is to give you an idea of how the disorder manifests and the feelings to listen for. Counselors need to listen for descriptions of feelings or emotional states that may suggest a client is manifesting symptoms of depression. Since depression left untreated can result in early death by suicide, it is of utmost importance to listen carefully, validate feelings, and explore feelings if there is an impression that the client may be depressed. Also, please review Chapter 5 for a discussion on suicide risk assessment, and please keep these procedures in mind as you explore feelings and symptoms related to depressive symptoms.

What feelings may you hear from the previous symptoms for PDD? Hungry, bloated, tired, exhausted, edgy, sluggish, discouraged, unfocused, distracted, unsure, and/or hopeless, may all be some feelings associated with symptoms of depression.

In previous editions of the *DSM*, persistent depression was not included as a diagnosis. McCullough, Schramm, and Penberthy (2015) report that in 2013, the APA's *DSM-5* added "a formal diagnostic category, PDD (dysthymia), to describe this unipolar patient." (p. xvi) One of the characteristics of PDD is interpersonal challenges and cognitive behavioral patterns that are not adaptive (Khanna, Penberthy, & Gioia, 2018; McCullough, 2000, McCullough et al., 2015). For example, one of the primary maladaptive patterns in the struggle of the client who is diagnosed with a chronic condition of this sort has been described as "pervasive interpersonal fear-avoidance" (McCullough et al., 2015, p. 18). Because this disorder is often misdiagnosed and is said to require experienced therapists, it may be something that you focus on later in your training; however, we will discuss it in this section because *CBASP has a lot to teach us about the importance of felt safety, which is one of the intentions behind reflection and validation of feelings.* Expressing feelings, especially vulnerable feelings, can be uncomfortable and scary for clients. Those with a background of attachment injuries may have been socialized through their attachment histories to engage in interpersonal avoidance or to engage in preoccupation, both of which may interfere with clear, coherent communication and state of mind (Knight & Sibcy, 2018). At that time, the manifestation of interpersonal fear-avoidance may have served to be an adaptive practice that may have protected a child from an abusive, harsh or rejecting caregiver. However, creating safety and providing an atmosphere where the client can begin to evaluate these responses and challenge these patterns and automatic thoughts or feelings can allow them an opportunity for what Clinton and Sibcy (2002) may call an emotionally corrective experience, or what CBASP therapists may call a shift toward perceptual engagement as a function of disciplined interpersonal involvement. For more on CBASP please see the recommended readings of Penberthy and McCullough.

## The Etiology of Persistent Depression

*Directions are instructions given to explain how. Direction is a vision offered to explain why.*

—Simon Sinek (2009a)

Since counselors will often be implementing these skills of reflecting feelings with clients struggling with PDD or attachment injuries, let us take a moment to consider etiology. So how does such unrelenting depression develop? McCullough et al. (2015) provide an explanatory model. The development of this chronic depression lies in interpersonal history. Note that the term "interpersonal" suggests relations between persons, which is what attachment theory is founded upon the first relationship between primary caregiver and child. James McCullough acknowledges the painful interpersonal story of the early chapters of these individuals' lives is often marked with childhood experiences characterized by neglect and abuse. In some of the attachment literature, we may refer to these experiences as attachment injuries (Knight & Sibcy, 2018).

Penberthy (2019, manuscript in preparation) eloquently describes the etiology and maintenance of PDD:

*PDD is viewed as a mood disorder ensuing from biopsychosocial factors, driven by learned Pavlovian fears of interpersonal encounters, and maintained by a refractory pattern of Skinnerian interpersonal avoidance; as a result, a disconnect between the patient and the environment ensues.*

*Thus, the CBASP approach is built upon the belief that effective treatment reduces symptomatology via cognitive, affective, and behavioral changes that enable patients to reduce interpersonal fear and avoidance, perceive the functionality of their behavior, reconnect to their environments, and increase their perception of control. The two primary goals of CBASP are (1) to quiet interpersonal fear-avoidance and replace it with felt emotional safety, and (2) to help patients acquire perceived functionality.*

## The Interpersonal Pavlovian Drivers of Persistent Depression

*The greatest motivator in life is not the pursuit of pleasure, but the avoidance of pain.*

—Gary Sibcy (personal communication, 2016)

Penberthy notes that what drives persistent depression is Pavlovian fears of interpersonal encounters. Recall, Pavlovian fears tend to develop when a neutral stimulus begins to be paired with a conditioned stimulus. For example, a neutral stimulus such as asking for what one wants is paired with a conditioned stimulus such as criticism and rejection. Eventually, one begins to pair the experience of expressing themselves with criticism and rejection. Sibcy has provided the visual explanatory model below (Sibcy & Knight, 2017b).

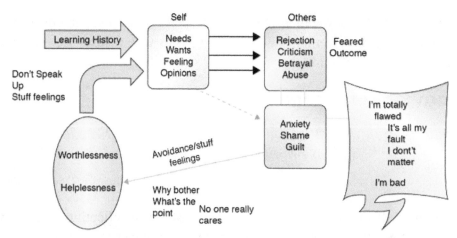

**Figure 9.1.** Interpersonal Leaning History of Persistent Depression
© Kendall Hunt Publishing Company

The graphic above (see Figure 9.1) starts with the client's interpersonal learning history, and how the client expresses his or her needs, wants, feelings, and opinions, then the person expresses these to another person and is met with a conditioned stimulus such as rejection, criticism, betrayal, and/or abuse. Thus, the neutral or unconditioned stimulus of expressing the self may then be paired with the conditioned stimulus of rejection and associated shame. When experiencing these feelings of anxiety, shame, and/or guilt, the person is likely to be meditating on thoughts, represented in the thought bubble above. These thoughts may include "I'm totally flawed," "It's all my fault," "I don't matter,' or "I'm bad,' among others. So the neutral stimulus of the self is paired with the conditioned stimulus of rejection, criticism, betrayal, and abuse and the associated feelings of shame and guilt. Thus eventually the sense of self becomes associated with anxiety, shame, and guilt, which may then promote the client to stuff or to use avoidance, which then points to a sense of helplessness and worthlessness that begins to be associated with the self.

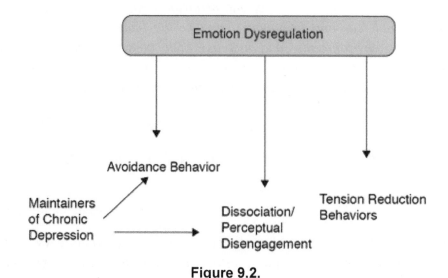

**Figure 9.2.**
© Kendall Hunt Publishing Company

176

This avoidance and stuffing of feelings are then associated with emotion dysregulation. In order to manage the dysregulated emotions, the client engages in avoidance behavior. This avoidance behavior can take several forms (see Figure 9.3, some of which include self-mutilation, sexual acting out, addictive behavior, and suicide fantasy). These behaviors temporarily relieve distress but in the long run help maintain emotion dysregulation.

## Maintaining Chronic Depression

In order for clients to remain persistently depressed, there are a few behavioral patterns that are required. One of the maintainers is avoidance behavior (interpersonal avoidance), another is a client's disengagement or dissociation of his or her interpersonal environment, and the last is engagement in tension-reduction behaviors, which essentially help maintain emotion dysregulation.

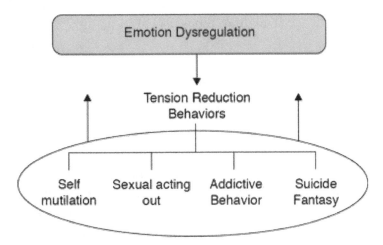

**Figure 9.3.** Behavioral patterns that maintain emotional dysregulation.
© Kendall Hunt Publishing Company

CBASP is one of the few forms of talk therapy that shows promise for clients with PDD. Note, one of the primary goals of CBASP involves replacing the relational fear-avoidance pattern with felt safety. Let us take a moment to explore felt safety (Penberthy, 2019) which is also a requirement for client vulnerability and exploration of feelings.

## Felt Safety

*Safety isn't expensive it is priceless.*

—Jerry Smith

One of the recommended readings for this chapter and subsequent chapters on advanced counseling skills is J. K. Penberthy's forthcoming (2019) text entitled *Persistent Depressive Disorder: Evidence-Based Practice*; she eloquently describes the maintenance of chronic depression;

"Good relationships with other people are antidepressants in their own right"
(McCullough et al., 2015, p. xiv).

she discusses the importance of **felt safety** as a primary goal in the treatment of persistent depression. McCullough et al. (2015) also indicate that CBASP is set apart from other forms of treatment in that it addresses interpersonal consequences. One of the aims of using the reflecting skills is to validate the client's emotion and also to strengthen the therapeutic alliance (which, when used with the skills in this text, should be a "good relationship" and may have an antidepressant effect as McCullough indicates).

However, as discussed above, those with a history of interpersonal trauma or attachment injuries (also referred to as psychological insults) often have a paucity of these relationships, and CBASP uses strategies like "disciplined interpersonal involvement" in order to facilitate an emotionally corrective experience (Knight & Sibcy, 2018).

## Reflecting Feelings and the Emotionally Corrective Experience

As the experience of people having their feelings rejected is likely to play a role in the etiology of chronic depression, the therapist seeks to be very intentional about validating and reflecting a client's feelings. This skill helps a client feel heard and understood. This is part of the reason reflecting and validating a client's thoughts and feelings (among other skills) are very important parts of positive outcomes. The therapeutic alliance also becomes a relationship that is safe and, as indicated above, is an "antidepressant in [its] own right" (McCullough et al., 2015, p. xiv).

Bettmann/Contributor/Getty

Who is B.F. Skinner? B.F. Skinner wrote the text *The Behavior of Organisms: An Experimental Analysis* and other books such as *Science and Human Behavior*. He was a psychologist and a behaviorist. He is credited with shaping psychology and especially behaviorism (Sobel, 1990).

*A Concept to Contemplate*

© Shutterstock.com

As we consider the model for how a *DSM* diagnosis such as persistent depression can develop, we see that an individual's expression of his or her sense of self, including his or her "feelings," is rejected or criticized. What are the implications for counseling? If a client has experienced rejection, betrayal, and criticism many times in their interpersonal learning history, then how may it impact.

## Attachment Illumination

Tim Clinton and Gary Sibcy (2002) in their popular text, *Attachments: Why You Love, Feel, and Act the Way You Do,* discuss the value of the emotionally corrective experience in healing attachment wounds. Clinton and Sibcy illustrate a path that has been paved by many before us that leads to an emotionally corrective experience. Thus, creating a safe place in counseling for clients to explore feelings and even experience new emotions within the therapeutic alliance is a very critical skill to hone.

## Milestones Along the Journey

*The walk of a thousand miles begins beneath your feet.*

—Lou Tzu, (2010, p. 116)

The starting point for the journey down this path is to first **remember your story**. In order to make sense or meaning of experiences, it is important to first remember those experiences. The next milestone along the pathway to healing is to **tell the story**; it is suggested that the story be told as a newspaper reporter would tell it, including the painful stories and the details that surround them. For example, if you sense your father was unloving and "let you down," explain a specific memory that describes this. Try to make sure this is a slice in time with a beginning, middle, and end. One helpful strategy may be to imagine a fly on the wall to tell your story. What would the fly on the wall see? Ensure your story is coherent and consistent. This can be difficult, especially when discussing painful experiences. Clinton and Sibcy (2002) provide a series of questions that should be asked to clarify your story and that are in keeping with Dan Siegel's and Kuhnley and Sibcy's suggestion (Knight & Sibcy, 2018; Siegel, 2010) that if one is able to "make sense" of his or her attachment history and face the truth of it (Knight & Sibcy, 2018), then they can move toward healing. As counselors, our role, in part, is to help the client become a dynamic and coherent storyteller. Clients need to be able to articulate the facts and then explore the feelings that correspond to them. The skills that involve using paraphrasing to reflect both content and feeling to the client can be very helpful here. For example, a therapeutic dialogue utilizing the skill of reflection of feeling to develop the story teller may go something like this (with the integration of modified AAI questions):

**Counselor:** Would you share with me three adjectives that describe your childhood relationship with your mother? (Skill used: question)

**Client:** Hmm, let's see. Well, it was sometimes disappointing, sometimes loving, and affectionate.

**Counselor:** So, sometimes disappointing, sometimes loving, and affectionate. (Skill used: key word reflection).

**Client:** Yes, I guess.

**Counselor:** Hmm, sometimes disappointing, sounds painful in a sense. Tell me more about what that felt like. (Skills used: reflection of feeling, advanced empathy, encourager)

**Client:** Hmmm, well, like, maybe I told her I really wanted her to come to my football game, and she never came. Well, one time she came, but then she just left a drink there for me and left after five minutes or so. So, it was like she was not there. You know, that is just like last week.

**Counselor:** (Skills used: enriching and redirection) So, it sounds like a part of you was encouraged to see that she came to a game, but it was so brief an appearance that it was almost as if she was not there. So, it sounds like it felt hurtful that you told her you wanted her there, but her involvement was still minimal. (Skills used: reflection of feeling, reflection of content)

**Client:** Yes, I guess it was hurtful. I guess I tried not to let it bother me, but now that you mention it, I guess it does hurt.

**Counselor:** So, looking back on it and talking about it, you can see that there is some pain and hurt attached even through you tried not to feel it in the past. (Skills used: reflecting feeling)

**Client:** Yes, but it feels intense, so I guess maybe it was there for a long time, and I just did not want to see it.

**Counselor:** What is it like to acknowledge the disappointment and the pain in this moment? (Skills used: reflecting feeling, question, and immediacy)

**Client:** It feels uncomfortable and maybe there is some guilt. I feel as if I should be recognizing all the positive things that Mom did. It is hard to acknowledge the hurt.

> A traumatic memory that is shared with an emphatic other as a story with a beginning, middle, and end then has less power.

Here, you can see how the counselor uses reflection of feeling, reflection of content, and other skills to help the client explore the story and develop a more coherent narrative. The counselor is facilitating the process of storytelling and helping the client to label the feelings and be present in the moment exploring the feelings (see Chapter 12 on the advanced skill of immediacy and for more on the skills of exploring the present moment with the client). When the counselor has taken the time to explore and unpack his or her own story, it can be easier to be empathic (Knight & Sibcy, 2018; Rubino et al., 2000) and to stay present with the client.

Clinton and Sibcy (2002) discuss the importance of helping the client retrace the path of pain through his or her story, and the skill of reflecting feeling is paramount here. The empathic other (Neborsky, 2006) is able to validate the client's feelings and experiences, and the story is then seen as finite with a beginning, middle, and end. In the cases of abuse, trauma, or other unloving experiences, the person has already experienced pain in the past. To continue to experience the pain and perhaps even repeat it robs the person of the experience to live in the present in its fullness.

Another step in the process of the emotionally corrective experience (Clinton & Sibcy, 2002) is to "recognize your pain and your need for healing." (p. 265) Herein lies the process of making meaning. Within this milestone is to see

> **A Verse to Remember:**
> 2 Corinthians 1:3: "Praise be to the God and Father of our Lord Jesus Christ, the Father of compassion, and the God of all comfort who comforts us in all our troubles **so that we can comfort those in any trouble with the comfort we ourselves receive from God.**"

the meaning or the purpose that is in the pain (Read more about the skill of reflecting meaning in Chapter 11). The Apostle Paul's letter to the church in Corinth represented one way he made meaning or saw purpose in pain and pondered his words (2 Corinthians 1:3): "Praise be to the God and Father of our Lord Jesus Christ, the Father of compassion, and the God of all comfort who comforts us in all our troubles **so that we can comfort those in any trouble with the comfort we ourselves receive from God**." Paul believed it was for the purposes of comforting others that he had experienced troubles and God's comfort.

Reflecting feelings can sometimes be difficult for counselors. It requires taking time to stay present with feelings. Oftentimes feelings are uncomfortable. However, remember the comfort that is offered to those that are broken hearted within the scriptures? Consider the following words from Psalm 34:18: "The Lord is close to the brokenhearted; He rescues those whose spirits are crushed." It is comforting when facing struggles to know

> **A Verse to Remember:**
> Psalm 34:18: The Lord is close to the brokenhearted; He rescues those whose spirits are crushed.

that we do not face them alone, that the Lord is with us (Knight, 2011). When our clients may feel alone, but they experience the presence of an "empathic other" (Neborsky, 2006), they may be more aware of God's presence, as the Living God dwells within us.

The next milestone is to "reframe the meaning of the story" (Clinton & Sibcy, 2002, p. 266). Part of the counselor's role in moving toward this milestone may be to help the client *reframe* his or her story. Reframing is a counseling skill that involves looking at a situation or an experience from a different perspective. when we see a picture in a frame that does not complement or accentuate its colors, and then we find a new frame and matting which complements the picture itself, it helps us see new colors emerge. If there is a light over the new frame, it may also help us truly see the picture in a new light. Likewise, when we reframe content a client may begin to see it in a new way. For example, here is a dialogue where the counselor and the client may begin reframing the client's narrative:

**Client:**    He [uncle] used to hit us, and it left marks, when he would lose his temper.

**Counselor:** Sounds like it was scary.

**Client:**    Yes, it was very scary! Sometimes, I am still scared of him and I don't know why because I am bigger than him and he can't hurt me. It is so stupid, and when I get anxious, which is almost always, I avoid. Just like when I was a little kid, I would run away and hide when he got mad, and now I still do except instead of going in the closet, I just stay away from him or withdraw myself from everyone. When someone is angry I avoid them too.

**Counselor:** So, when you were a little boy and scared, it sounds like the best way to keep yourself safe was to hide away from your unclease, especially if he was angry. So, you developed the coping mechanism to avoid dangerous situations to stay safe. However, now, I hear you verbally critiquing yourself a bit as you are engaging in self-awareness and acknowledging that avoiding may not be serving you well or it may no longer be necessary to protect yourself anymore—even though it was then. What is it like to notice this in this moment? (Skills: Reframing, reflecting content, immediacy/exploring feeling).

**Client:**    Well, it is embarrassing and pretty uncomfortable, to be honest.

**Counselor:** Yes, it is uncomfortable to face the pain and to look at the tools that worked back then and to acknowledge they are not working now. It sounds like as a young boy you were resourceful and you adapted and developed a strategy to deal with dangerous situations. Now as an adult I hear you being resourceful once again and acknowledging that an adjustment may be necessary because your old coping skills may not be serving you anymore. You also mentioned feeling embarrassed. Help me understand more about that.

You can see how the counselor in the scenario above used reframing in his reflection of content and feeling to help the client see his story from a different perspective. Clinton and Sibcy (2002) provide us with the caveat that reflecting is not an exercise in denying reality in order to focus on the positive. The only way effective reframing can occur is if at first the truth of the story is recognized. The truth in the story above is that the client experienced unloving behavior and anger from his uncle, and it felt scary. In an effort to stay safe, he adapted by avoiding the dangerous situations that were the source of fear and anxiety. Now, the fear and anxiety he feels in life trigger the same desire to take refuge and hide or avoid. However, he is aware of this now and can begin to see how he adapted and was resilient as a child, and he can once again adapt and be resilient as an adult. In order to reframe something, it has to first be framed and the frame it is currently in needs to be acknowledged. In the Adult Attachment Interview, a characteristic of a narrative that tends to be classified as secure is coherence and consistency. Secure is not synonymous with positive. Sometimes, the true story involves pain and heartache, and the truth is not always easy to acknowledge, but recognizing that someone was not there for you when you needed them and that it was painful is important for being able to experience healing (Knight & Sibcy, 2018).

Sometimes counselors in training ask about adaptive strategies for managing difficult emotions. It is beyond the scope of this text to discuss all the different theoretical approaches that address emotions such as emotion focused therapy or acceptance and commitment therapy, but we do appreciate these approaches and Dr. Everette Worthington's research and writings on forgiveness. Here is something to consider. Jesus did not deny that people hurt him; he recognized it, but he prayed for their forgiveness. When Jesus was at the end of his life hanging on the cross, he prayed for those who hurt him and forgave them, saying, "Father they know not what they do." Likewise, the narrative of the secure autonomous attachment style does not require us to deny tough experiences, but to acknowledge them. The secure narrative is also marked with forgiveness. Let us take a moment to look at one of our clients who demonstrated features of the secure autonomous attachment style.

## A Secure Case: Jamie

A case of secure attachment is seen in the case of Jamie, a first semester nursing student, in a local RN program. Jamie had made what she and her instructors believed was an inadvertent HIPAA violation. However, the hospital in which the student nurse was training did not see it that way and so banned Jamie and several other students from acquiring additional access to medical records. Consequently, this school of nursing had no option other than to expel Jamie and several other students from the nursing program. Jamie was, understandably, quite upset about being expelled from the nursing program and saw this as a major setback in her career aspiration. Her mother was a nurse, and Jamie always wanted to be a nurse herself. As would be expected, Jamie experienced a wide range of negative emotions: from sadness about the loss of an important dream she had about her career to anxiety about what she was going to do and, how this was going to affect her ability to work in health care, and to anger and frustration about feeling treated unjustly and unfairly (note she felt that she was able to articulate and share these emotions without minimizing them unnecessarily).

Jamie stated, "I can't believe that they just assumed that I was snooping around in a patient's records just to have a little fun. As if I would put my whole career on the line to look at a patient's record." Jamie went through the appeal process with the school, but as the hospital had made the determination to ban her from accessing medical records, the school's hands were tied.

From an attachment perspective, this stressor activated her attachment system, and she felt an understandable level of negative emotion. However, she was willing to seek help to try and find comfort and support, not only from family and friends but also from a counselor. Jamie had been through a number of challenges throughout her adolescence, from the sudden death of her grandmother from a heart attack, to her grandfather's recent diagnosis of a terminal medical condition, to the sudden death of a boyfriend due to a rare blood disorder. She had gone through a number of losses but was able to bounce back from them and continue with her education. This was just another, uncontrollable event in her life, and it brought her to a point of significant emotional dysregulation. She was able to talk to the counselor about all of these problems and make sense of them while allowing herself to feel the negative emotions that welled up inside of her as she talked about them. Note, it was important for the counselor to validate and explore those feelings with her so that she could feel them and process them, giving them less power. This was a sign of attachment security, namely the ability to experience negative emotions, talk about her thoughts and feelings, and reflect on them while also seeking help from others around her. This represents characteristics such as valuing attachment relationships, forgiving/avoiding blaming herself or others, and the capacity to coherently share her story as a series of events with a beginning, middle, and end.

She decided to seek counseling because, in part, she did not want to overwhelm everyone with her problems. She needed someone objective who could hear her or listen to her as she worked through these thorny difficulties. As she did, Jamie was able to also reflect on her relationship with God and to wonder how He was going to use these events in her life to make her a better person. What she did not do was think that God was out to get her or that He was trying to punish her in some way (blaming God, or blame in general, may be a more preoccupied tendency).

Jamie was able to benefit from the secure base provided by the therapist. They worked together to develop a list of problems and goals Jamie needed to find a way to effectively cope with all the feelings that she had. In many ways, she had come to terms with the losses she had experienced. She felt sad about losing her grandmother and her dear friend. It did not make sense to her why they were gone, but she also realized that death was a part of life. She also found that while going through these experiences, she could talk to others about them. She wrote poetry and music to help her cope. She was also able to seek closeness in her relationship to God believing that, ultimately, He could turn these events into something that would help her somewhere down the road although she wasn't sure how. She also knew that what she did was wrong, technically, even though she did not know it was wrong at the time. This kind of injustice made her angry in an appropriate way. She wanted to get vindication by proving to herself and others that she was a good person even though she had flaws. One of her most important benefits that she got from therapy was that she needed to turn these emotions into effective coping strategies. One of the most important strategies that she learned was not to get stuck inside her head ruminating about all that had happened because this would not solve anything. What she needed to focus on was problem solving.

Her main goal was to go back to school. Instead of going to nursing school though, she decided to enter into a four-year college and to set the stage for a future in either law or psychology, both of which she had an interest in. Her aunt was a lawyer and practiced family law where she helped families overcome many of the legal challenges they faced when going through difficult times such as divorce, separation, and other types of situations. She also had an uncle who was a psychologist, and she looked up to him because he seemed to really make a difference in people's lives. She was able to benefit from problem-solving and activity-scheduling exercises where she planned out the strategy for applying to schools in writing a letter that described the events leading up to her dismissal from the nursing program.

From an attachment perspective, Jamie was able to use the counseling relationship as a secure base as she explored these issues. Even though it made her nervous to think about the possibility of being rejected again, she continued and executed all the steps necessary to gain entry into a four-year college. She was eventually accepted and is now in the process of seeking a double major in psychology and pre-law. The last time the counselor talked to her, she had a 3.4 GPA, and although she was not sure what program of study she would pursue in graduate school, she felt confident that she would be able to do something that made a difference.

Her current plan was to graduate and then apply to law school. She was not overly confident in her abilities but felt that she had a reasonable chance of gaining entry into such a program. Her contingency plan was to apply to counseling programs, so if law school did not work out, then she would pursue a counseling degree.

You can see that Jamie was able to make sense of her experience without blaming herself, the hospital, or her academic program. It can be painful to take responsibility and accept something, especially when hurtful, but she took responsibility and was able to bounce back and adapt to the situation.

In contrast, a preoccupied narrative may include more blame. So, a counselor can help facilitate this forgiveness and coherence through the process of reframing and looking at the client's personal responsibility. The client cannot control life's circumstances, but some central questions that may help us unwrap some content that may lead to underlying feelings are as follows:

"How did you respond to the pain of your attachment story (or to the injustice? Or to the challenges you faced)?"

"How do you interact with this pain in your life now?"

The Adult Attachment Interview protocol is recommended reading, and the questions toward the end of the interview are in line with these questions and help a person to look toward the future and answer questions related to how childhood experiences impact his or her adult personality. Another important question is to look at what we have gained from our experiences in our attachment history. This is all a part of making meaning of the experience (see Chapter 11 for more on meaning making).

Clinton and Sibcy (2002) state the following, which eloquently describes how powerful the skill of reframing may be:

The objective of reframing your story is to see yourself, and your past in a different light. Where before you generally saw just your weakness and frailties, now you're able to see your strengths as well, along with your tenacity, your will to survive and your desire to thrive. More importantly, if you look you'll begin to see how God has worked in your pain to woo you closer to Himself and to bring healing moments throughout your journey. He works in every nook and cranny of our lives to win our hearts, to show us how safe we are with him. (p. 268)

The next milestone on the path Clinton and Sibcy outline toward the emotionally corrective experience involves repairing your story, which they describe as the most lengthy portion of the journey. If your attachment history involves an insecure attachment pattern such as dismissing attachment figures, getting tangled up in attachment relationships, or a disorganized pattern, it has been described as "broken" and perhaps the insecure strategies worked in the past but are no longer effective. This involves taking a look at the dynamics of the relationship or attachment rules and evaluating and revising them. The counselor can use reflection of feelings, and the more advanced skill of reflection of meaning (which we will explore further in Chapter 11) here to help the client makes sense of these experiences. For example, consider the following therapeutic dialogue:

**Counselor:** I hear you saying that you tend to worry your husband will not be there for you. Tell me more about this feeling of worry and how it impacts you. (Skills used: reflection of feeling and exploration of feeling)

**Client:** Okay, well it is just, um, well I get anxious thinking about it. It is a knot in the pit of my stomach and it burns. I think of the times he has not followed through in the past and wonder if it will be different or the same.

**Counselor:** So you feel the knots in your stomach, you get anxious feeling, and your thoughts move to times in the past when he has let you down. (Skills used: reflection of feelings and content)

**Client:** Yeah, it seems like this happens a lot.

**Counselor:** What does it mean to you when he lets you down?

**Client:** Well, it is just like how my parents were. It reminds me that you can just never count on anyone.

**Counselor:** So one of the things you learned about relationships from your experiences with your parents growing up is that when you counted on others you were disappointed.

Notice, the counselor reflected the client's feelings and content; now we are beginning to go into reflecting meaning as the counselor explores what the client learned from the experiences. Evaluating what we learned from an experience may be another way we explore how we made meaning of an experience. The rules that we take away from an experience such as "Don't trust others, and you won't be disappointed" can be designed to protect us from pain but can also be maladaptive and sabotage close relationships. When I went to physical therapy due to lower back pain, my physical therapist mentioned that she was doing some massaging of my back and pressing in different spots in order to calm down my nervous system and communicate to it that it is okay for those muscles to move. She explained that our muscles tense up in order to protect us from pain and injury, but she was just letting the nervous system know that it was okay, and trying to calm it down. Much like our nervous system may tense muscles to protect us from injury, our psychological fight-or-flight response may also activate to protect us from perceived threats. As we work to validate our clients' feelings through paraphrasing feelings, reflecting feelings, and using the other skills to help the client feel safe, heard, and understood, we are doing much like what my physical therapist does to calm the lower back pain. We are helping the client communicate to the nervous system it is okay to take risks and be vulnerable and approach feelings. Perhaps activating relaxation in the back muscles is akin to activating the opening of the walls constructed in response to interpersonal fear. In the past interpersonal avoidance may have been a protective practice to keep one safe, but it may not be necessary in the present.

Part of the therapeutic journey can be exploring meaning and revising relational rules. We will discuss this more in the next chapter, but here, let us take a closer look at how to reflect and explore feelings, as this is a central part of facilitating an emotionally corrective experience. We will start by reviewing the paraphrase.

## Reviewing the Paraphrase

Let us take a moment to review a skill discussed previously. Recall that a **paraphrase** includes *repeating back to a client what you have heard in your own words.* Sometimes it can be helpful to add word pictures here. For example, if a client talks about the stress involved in having a lot to do, we may say, "It sounds like you're juggling lots of balls and it is a lot of pressure to keep everything in the air." This adds a visual component.

Also, as we reflect back the content to the client, we are also adding, "and it is a lot of pressure," or we may say. "It is stressful to juggle all these balls." These statements include a reflection of feeling. We identify what the feeling or feelings are that the client is experiencing and then name them and articulate them verbally. As we share with the client the feelings that we are hearing coming through his or her story or content, we validate his or her feelings.

© Gino Santa Maria/Shutterstock.com

In its simplest form, the skill of reflecting feeling involves listening to a client's story and hearing his or her feeling. Then we state the feeling word back. Let us look at an excerpt from one of our recent counseling sessions:

**Client:**      Well, when my parents would fight, I would not know what to do. I remember my Dad yelling at Mom and getting very angry at her.

**Counselor:** It sounds like it felt scary whenever Dad got angry and started yelling at mom.

**Client:**      Yes, it was very scary and I did not want to be there.

Here, we may be able to then move into exploring feeling. If we have a client high in self-awareness, he or she may say something like, "I notice even talking about it I have knots in my stomach and tension in my chest." The counselor may then move into some advanced skills like scaling (which will be covered in Chapter 13) to measure the intensity of the feeling and use more immediacy (another advanced skill that we discuss in more detail in Chapter 12).

However, often clients do not have this high level of self-awareness. Counselors may sometimes use a skill known as "advanced empathy" (which is discussed in Chapter 3) in order to identify what a client is feeling even before the client is aware of the feeling. Counselors can also use tools such as feeling wheels to help a client pick up on feelings that are not as clear.

## Multicultural Considerations

There may be gender differences between males and females when it comes to the expression of emotions. Women are socialized not to express anger, and men are socialized not to express sadness, so when a man feels sad, he may feel discomfort with the feeling and it may instead seem to manifest as discomfort or fatigue. Women may feel less comfortable experiencing anger and it may then come out in unplanned situations, for example, road rage (Chaplin, 2015).

Feelings that are "against the rules" that a person learned to ascribe to in their family of origin such as "if you don't have anything nice to say don't say anything" or "turn that frown upside down" can also be associated with difficulty acknowledging, discussing, or exploring negative emotion. It is important for counselors to tread here with empathy and attunement.

## Exploring Feelings

Moving toward the pain is part of the exploration process. Remember when we discussed the circle of security in Chapter 1. Let us revisit that for a moment. When someone is on the top part of the circle and he or she feels safe, his or her "fully charged indicator wiggle light comes on" (Marvin, 2017 personal communication). When they are feeling safe, then they are more comfortable to explore feelings, be vulnerable, and explore their narrative. Thus, a prerequisite for exploring feelings and meaning is felt safety. All of the skills covered so far help to establish felt safety for the client, and empathy and congruence are of particular importance.

Furthermore, it is important for the counselor to have a sense of felt safety and the capacity to create what the early British-trained psycho-analyst, Donald Winnicott, may have called an "attachment holding environment." Winnicott, in his text entitled *Human Nature,* discussed the task of the psychoanalyst to bring the unconscious of the patient into consciousness (see section on "What About Self-Awareness in Relation to Effectiveness?" in Chapter 4 for more on this and the idea of "lowering the water line" p. 62) and the importance of the therapist to demonstrate understanding and tolerance of feelings through exposition in language. He also stresses the value of being present and understanding our clients' thoughts and feelings and how it can be even more powerful than seeking to physically comfort them. Consider his words (Winnicott, 1988,),

> A correct and well-timed interpretation in an analytic treatment gives a sense of being held physically that is more real (to the non-psychotic) than if a real holding or nursing had taken place. Understanding goes deeper, and by understanding, shown by the use of language, the analyst holds physically in the past, that is, at the time of the need to be held, when love meant physical care and adaptation.

The modern counselor's efforts to seek to understand the client in the form of a reflection of feeling and content can, as is in line with Winnicott's thinking, bring about a sense of feeling held that goes deeper than if the therapist were to physically hold or hug the client (see Chapter 6 for more discussion on this in the call-out "To Hug or Not to Hug"). In a sense, one way to think of the safety created here is that it is similar to a counselor giving a client a hug with words; as Winnicott put it, understanding goes deeper. As a matter of fact, it goes beyond a hug, and the desire to give a hug and the impact of a hug may seem to speak louder; however, the impact of an accurate reflection of content and feeling lasts longer.

So, after the counselor has conducted appropriate informed consent, used minimal encouragers and paralanguage, used an appropriate door opener, and reflected content appropriately through paraphrases and any other gestures to seek to create a sense of warmth and safety, then the stage is set for a client to move toward the top of the circle and begin exploring feelings.

As Winnicott's sentiments indicate, a well-timed interpretation, or perhaps reflection of content, feeling, and meaning, can help the client to experience a sense of "being held" and comforted where or when he or she really needed it and thus experience a sense of safety that can allow for exploration. Just as the man in the picture below is scoping out the terrain with his binoculars and preparing for exploration, cultivating a safe environment can help clients prepare for a period of exploration.

*As clients share their stories and have a sense of being understood by an empathic other, therapeutic processes are activated and movement toward healing begins to occur.*

Just as the client needs to sense safety, it goes without saying that the counselor needs to as well; the counselor needs to be prepared to walk alongside the client through the exploration of painful feelings. One of the counselor's tasks is to learn to be at peace in the midst of walking through pain with clients.

© Ollyy/Shutterstock.com

I once had a soccer coach who used to run laps with us in practice. He used to say (Deepan, personal communication, 1991), "I wouldn't ask you to do anything that I wouldn't do myself." As clinicians, it can be helpful to do our own work of moving toward grief, loss, and pain in our own lives.

This process of being present with our clients as they face pain is that process of walking alongside them through their journey with mindful presence (see section on "What About Self-Awareness in Relation to Effectiveness?" in Chapter 4 for a definition of mindful presence). As they recognize that they are not alone, it can be easier to take courage, take risks, and face pain. There is an old Swedish proverb that says "A joy shared is doubled and a burden shared is halved." (Ström, 1981, p. 251), As clients share their stories and have a sense of being understood by an empathic other, therapeutic processes are activated and movement toward healing begins to occur. It can be difficult to stay present with people in their painful emotions, but if you as counselor lean into the discomfort, then more therapeutic movement can occur.

What we usually tell students, in the form of a quote borrowed from one of our favorite storytellers, Brené Brown, is to try "leaning into the discomfort (Brown, 2010, 02:35)." It may be highly uncomfortable at first to explore painful emotions with a client. It is important to lean into the discomfort and be willing to go with the client as he or she moves toward the pain and the truth of his or her story. Do you recall taking the Presidential Physical Fitness Test in high school gym class? Just like the "sit and reach" (a stretch where a student strives to touch or reach past his or her toes as far as possible portion of the Presidential Physical Fitness Test, leaning into the stretch or discomfort allows us to reach

> *It is important to lean into the discomfort and be willing to go with the client as they move toward the pain and the truth of his or her story.*

further. Likewise, in therapy, as we are willing to move toward feelings, even exploring painful or negative ones with our clients (when the time is appropriate), we may find that the therapeutic reach stretches further or deeper.

In Dweck's book, *Mindset,* she discusses the fixed versus growth mindset. She shares how she worked with a group of four-year-olds who were given an easy jigsaw puzzle. They were then given a choice: to redo the easy jigsaw puzzle or try a harder one. Dweck reports those with a fixed mindset shared a theme indicating that "kids who are born smart 'don't do mistakes.'" (Dwek, 2007, p. 16) However, those with a growth mindset, those who selected option two, had a different perspective. They believed you could grow smarter and exhibited enthusiasm at the idea of figuring out harder jigsaw puzzles. Embracing a growth mindset is important for clinical mental health counselors seeking to help clients embrace change and growth.

## Crying in Counseling

*I understand now that I'm not a mess but a deeply feeling person in a messy world. I explain that now, when someone asks me why I cry so often, I say, "For the same reason I laugh so often because I'm paying attention.*

—Doyle Melton (2016, p. 225)

In every counseling skills class we teach the question comes up, "Is it okay to cry with your clients?"

A full-time private practice counselor that I used to teach with named Marilyn Harding once shared that she had the sense that when she was working with a client that she was on a mission from God to stay present with that client. So, she would tell herself that she could come back to her feelings later but right now in the moment she needed to be present with her client.

© Photographee.eu/Shutterstock.com

I once worked in a counseling setting where we ran math anxiety groups. We had a student who struggled with anxiety and one of the coleaders of the math anxiety group gave her feedback, "I notice that when you get anxious you start speaking really quickly and it hardly seems as if you take a breath between sentences and I can feel the anxiety emanating and so I feel anxious as I listen." She came back after the group and shared with me, "I must be in really bad shape because I made my counselor anxious today." The counselor had intended this feedback to the client to facilitate self-awareness; instead, the client became a bit defensive and began to worry about her influence on the counselor. Likewise, if the counselor begins to cry in session, it may in some circumstances be validating; however, it moves the focus from the client to the counselor and may work against the counselor's objectives. So, for the counselor, we add crying in session to the "to don't" list (we recognize that sometimes an involuntary watering of the eyes may occur as we are touched by our clients story; this is okay, and we advise seeking to regulate and limit it in most cases to maintain a focus on the client's feeling and state of mind). Of course, the client can express herself however she sees fit, so this guideline just goes for the counselors.

Those with a fixed mindset, Dweck shared, are interested in proving themselves. In contrast, those with a growth mindset are focused on stretching and growing. Adopting that mindset when learning skills can be helpful for clinical mental health counselors as we seek to help clients grow or move toward their goals.

The greatest motivator in life is not the pursuit of pleasure but the avoidance of pain (Sibcy, 2018). Leaning in or moving toward pain can be difficult. Avoidance is a powerfully deceptive strategy. Avoidance is one of the practices that serves to maintain chronic depression. When persons express their needs, wants, and opinions and are met with criticism, rejection, or abuse, then they experience shame and/or guilt (McCullough, 2000; Sibcy & Knight, 2017). So, the individual then avoids expressing himself or herself interpersonally, and the brain begins to shut down. This is yet another reason why reflecting and validating clients' feelings can be healing. For an individual's opinions, feelings and needs to be heard and understood by another, especially when one has often had a contrary experience, can be therapeutic. This is a necessary part of therapy, and later we will talk about how though these foundational skills are necessary, they may not always be sufficient. If rejecting or invalidating a client's concerns can help maintain chronic depression, when a therapist validates feelings and stays present with a client and helps him or her explore his or her feelings and perhaps disentangle thoughts, feelings, and behaviors through the use of these reflecting skills, perhaps in conjunction with some of the advanced skills (discussed in Chapter 3) movement toward healing can occur.

Avoidance, denial, and repression (Rolston & Lloyd-Richardson, 2017) are just some of the strategies used to move away from feeling, especially with feelings that may appear to be negative.

So, it is important to tread lightly but to be willing to stay with the feelings. Moreover, some clients may be struggling with what has been referred to as **thought-feeling fusion**. They may find it difficult to untangle their thoughts from their feelings. Thus, it is important **not** to allow clients to continuously **feel thoughts**. Feeling thoughts is the phenomenon that occurs when a client starts with the statement, "I feel _____," and fills in the blank with a thought rather than a feeling. For example, if a client says, "I feel like it has been a long day." What is wrong with this statement? Is "it has been a long day" a feeling? No, it is a thought. The problem is the two phrases being combined together. It may be associated with thought-feeling entanglement and can make the client's narrative less coherent. Part one of the phrase is "I feel like" and should be followed with a feeling word such as stressed, exhausted, overwhelmed, and so on, and "it has been a long day" is a thought, so a counselor may use the skill of paraphrasing or reflecting content to bring subtle clarity here. As the counselor uses the skill of reflection of feeling, the counselor can gently redirect and clarify feelings by rephrasing the phrase appropriately for the client when reflecting.

Consider the following therapeutic dialogue:

**Counselor:** How do you feel your day went?

**Client:** I had tests in both my classes, a project due at work, and tons of email today. **I feel like it has been a long day.**

**Counselor:** So, it sounds like as you think about the day, the thought you come away with is it has been a long one. Tell me more about what you **feel inside** as you meditate on this thought. (reflection of content, emphasis on the word feel to explore feelings).

Here we are paraphrasing the thought and inviting more exploration of feelings. This will be very important as we get to the later chapters on advanced skills (See Chapters 12 & 13), especially CBT interventions.

All of the skills we have been discussing so far in the text (such as door openers, nonverbals, minimal encouragers, key words, one-word encouragers, and paralanguage) are designed to help us seek to understand the client and to help them feel heard and comfortable sharing.

This rapport and safety that is established may make it easier for a client to feel safe and to begin exploring more vulnerable feelings. Now that we have discussed the importance of reflecting feeling, exploring feeling for facilitating an emotionally corrective experience, and sample dialogues for reflecting feelings, now let us turn to how to reflect feeling. We will first look at the structure of a reflection of feeling.

# The Structure of a Reflection of Feeling

## Caveat

It is important to note that although we seek to provide a structure or formula if you will, it is important to use empathy, flexibility, and variety and to develop a natural rhythm so that the reflections do not sound robotic. However, sometimes it can be helpful to have a recipe to start with. Consider a seasoned cook, who may use a pinch of cinnamon here and a bit of sugar there, and add other seasonings "to taste" rather than using a prescribed recipe. Likewise, a counselor may begin with a recipe of reflections and then move to improvisation, drawing upon a repertoire of phrases and feeling words. Use the examples here as a starting point and then develop your own rhythm.

**Step One: Identify a preparatory statement** (or use a one-word encourager, in this case also known as a key feeling word encourager. If you opt to use a key feeling word encourager, skip to Step Three):

- It sounds like you feel. . .

- I am hearing that you feel. . .

- I sense you are feeling. . .

- So, the feeling is. . .

**Step Two: Recognize feeling words or underlying emotion and keep them readily in mind.** This may involve increasing your repertoire of feeling words. The feeling wheel can be a helpful tool in increasing your vocabulary here (Wilcox, 1982). This can also be a helpful tool to use with clients, especially those who do not have as wide as a feeling vocabulary.

- **What are the core emotions?** The core emotions are in the center of the feeling wheel (see Chapter 7) and often include mad, sad, and glad, which are easy to recall as they rhyme, and peaceful and powerful.

It can be helpful to increase the feeling words, which are a part of counselors' vernacular. This may help with the process of identifying feeling words to reflect.

Core emotions are often identified as follows:

- Mad
- Sad
- Glad
- Peaceful
- Powerful

We like to use this list for a few reasons. Notice mad, sad, and glad all rhyme, and this has been used to help people recall those key emotions. Also, this particular list makes use of not only rhyming but also alliteration with both peaceful and powerful starting with a P. Considering this when exploring feelings and looking for core feelings.

Increasing the counselor's repertoire of feeling words to increase recognition of primary and secondary feelings can be accomplished through using tools such as the feeling wheel and feeling faces. It can also be helpful for the counselor to practice labeling his or her own emotions and identifying physical sensations that accompany said emotions, as well as thoughts that tend to correlate with those emotions; this self-awareness combined with mindful presence in session may help the counselor to readily explore feeling with the client.

In thinking of increasing one's feeling vocabulary, let us look at the core feelings on the feeling wheel. For example, what are some synonyms for mad, sad, and glad? Other feeling words that may represent different intensities of feeling mad may include irritation, frustration, anger, and rage.

**Step 3: After recognizing feeling words and identifying a feeling word to use in the reflection, select an appropriate time to enrich.**

Remember that enriching and interrupting are different. However, if the counselor enriches inappropriately, it may be experienced as an interruption. Interject with an acknowledgment of the feeling at an appropriate time. Consider the examples below:

Reflection of feeling phrases:

- It sounds like you are feeling frustrated.

- It sounds like you are feeling excited about graduation!

- I am hearing sadness in your voice as you talk about this transition.

- It sounds like you are feeling discouragement that things did not go as expected.

- I see sadness in your eyes as you talk about your new position.

- It seems like you are feeling excited about this next chapter of life.

Key word reflection of feelings:

- Hmm, stressful!

- Ugh, rough.

- Mm, painful.

- Frustrating.

You may be wondering when is it appropriate to use a key word reflection of feeling and a reflection of feeling phrase. If a counselor is working with a client who is verbose or who is in the middle of an important story, it may be difficult or inappropriate to enrich and shift the conversational ball to the therapist, and the counselor can use paralanguage and express the feeling word as a one-word or key word encourager.

However, it is important to continue to keep a rhythm of dialogue so that the client expects and experiences the counselor interjecting frequently throughout the dialogue. Otherwise, there is a danger of therapy becoming a monologue. Also, validating the client's feelings is a critical skill, so if a key feeling word encourager is not used right away, at the next pause, breath, check in, or enrichment, the counselor should interject a reflection of feeling phrase. This will help the client to develop a coherent narrative and to make sense of his or her feelings.

## Multicultural Considerations

Ivey et al. (2013) indicate feelings tend to be experienced in the native language, and they recommend learning the following key words when working with Spanish clients:

- Aguantar: endure
- Orgullo: proud
- Coraje: anger
- Miedo: fear
- Cariño: like
- Amor: love
- Sentir: feel

Ivey and Ivey share that for many counselors, reflecting feelings is the most important skill (Ivey et al., 2013, p. 151; see Chapter 15 for more on multicultural counseling skills).

### To Do list
### and within the next practice session: reflecting feelings

Review the feeling wheel and feeling faces to expand repertoire of feeling words.
Adopt a list of preparatory phrases for feeling words such as:

- It looks like you feel ___
- It sounds like you feel ___
- I hear ____ in your voice
- I see ___ in your eyes
- I sense you are feeing _____

Next, add an appropriate feeling word in the blank.
Practice this process through journaling or labeling the counselors' own emotions.

## Recommended Reading

If you would like to continue to develop your expertise on the topics discussed in this chapter, we recommend the resources indicated below:

© Shutterstock.com

- Clinton, T. & Sibcy, G. (2002). *Attachments: Why you love, feel, and act the way you do.* Nashville, TN: Integrity. (This is written by one of the primary authors of this textbook, Dr. Gary Sibcy, which unpacks concepts related to attachment style in a very compelling way that is easy to understand; it is also available as an audio book).

- Ivey, A. E., Ivey M. B., & Zalaquett, C. P. (2013). *Intentional interviewing and counseling: Facilitating client development in a multicultural society* (8th ed.). Belmont, CA: Brooks/Cole.

- McCullough, J. P., Schramm, E., & Penberthy, J. K. (2015). *CBASP: A distinctive treatment for persistent depressive disorder.* New York, NY: Routledge.

(Recall that McCullough is the developer of CBASP and this is his work, which has resulted in significant contributions in the field in terms of alleviating suffering associated with chronic depression).

- Showers, A. (2013). *The feelings wheel developed by Dr. Gloria Wilcox.* Retrieved from: http://msaprilshowers.com/emotions/the-feelings-wheel-developed-by-dr-gloria-willcox

- (The feeling wheel is a very handy tool that we recommend using in session with clients. It is especially helpful for those that do not have a ready repertoire of feeling words).

## Chapter Summary

The purpose of this chapter was to prepare counselors in training to manifest the skill of reflecting feelings. Here we discussed where reflecting feelings fits in with the sequence of other skills discussed so far in this text. We also discussed the reason it is so important to create an atmosphere conductive to a client's felt safety and how the validation of feelings is an important part of treating disorders related to dysregulated mood such as persistent depressive disorder (PDD). Recall, a session typically begins with a welcome and a warm greeting and/or handshake if appropriate, then the counselor uses a door opener (which is an open-ended question) to begin the session and uses appropriate nonverbal skills such as

SOLER, minimal encouragers, paralanguage, reflection of content, and then reflection of feelings. Problematic feelings such as persistent sadness or low mood in the form of depression often bring people into counseling. The processes that serve to maintain depression were explored. Key players in the treatment of mood disorders such as depression were introduced, including James McCullough and J. Kim Penberthy. Attachment theory implications are discussed, including the protocol that Clinton and Sibcy outline on how to facilitate an emotionally corrective experience and the role of reflecting and exploring feelings in helping a client tell his or her attachment story. The strategies for how to reflect feelings including starting with a preparatory phrase such as "it sounds like" or "I am sensing" and then expanding one's vocabulary of feeling words, selecting an appropriate feeling word and then identifying the appropriate time to interject are unpacked.

# PART THREE

# Advanced Skills and Advanced Techniques

As we have mentioned previously in the text, the foundational skills are necessary but not sufficient. The basic skills build a strong foundation upon which a solid structure can be built.

The foundational counseling skills are also atheoretical, meaning that these skills can be used with all different theoretical orientations. No matter what theory a clinician identifies with, it is important for the clinician to hear and understand their clients' stories.

Once a client feels heard and understood, proper rapport is established within the therapeutic alliance, a case conceptualization is formed, and a treatment plan is developed, then a clinical mental health counselor will want to begin considering which advanced techniques and interventions target the changes or the relevant aspects of their treatment plans. This also involves seeking to stay current with the research literature associated with evidence-based practices; we will talk about evidence-based practices more in Chapter 13. In order to identify the correct intervention, some clinicians advise identifying where a client is in DiClemente's stages of change (Prochaska & DiClemente, 1982) and which change process the counselor wishes to target with that particular intervention.

In the following chapters, some of the more advanced skills such as termination will be explored. Listen as Dr. Hawkins summarizes the process of counseling as we come alongside clients and move toward termination. Listen for ideas about how to both engage and finish well. Also, let his words inspire you to continue your desire to learn and read and embrace the recommended readings as he discusses the importance of reading broadly.

**Video**

**Engaging**

Research-based
Counseling Skills
The Art and Science of Therapeutic Empathy

0:00 / 9:40

# The Art and Science of Questions

## Anita M. Kuhnley and Gary A. Sibcy

*Good questions lead to excellent answers.*

—Robin S. Sharma (2008, p. 52)

© ESB Professional/Shutterstock.com

### Chapter Learning Objectives

- To explore counselor characteristics and behaviors that influence the counseling process, such as using skills such as asking open-ended questions, closed questions, and clarifying questions (CACREP II.5.f, 2016, p. 12)

- To determine essential interviewing and counseling skills such as learning to identify and ask different types of questions appropriately (CACREP II.5.g, 2016, p. 12)

- To explore the impact of spiritual beliefs on clients' and counselors' worldviews as could be explored with the use of questions (CACREP II.F.2.g, 2016, p.12)

# Chapter Overview

As we think about how to use questions in therapeutic dialogue, it is important to remember that there is both an art and science to the questioning process. For example, we consider the art to be the "how" behind the question. In other words, is the question placed well in the dialogue? Is it worded in a warm and supportive way? Is it gentle and not abrasive? Although the science that informs the questioning process may relate more to the intentionality of the question, if we are assessing the client's level of depression, did we remember to ask about changes in sleeping patterns and eating habits? Or, in the case of chronic depression, we may use a situation analysis that includes a series of questions to guide the session. There is a great deal of intentionality behind a good question; good questions do not happen on accident. Let us explore how therapeutic questions may be different from questions in social dialogue.

## Questions in Social Conversation versus Questions in Therapeutic Dialogue

Questions are a common tool used in social conversation to generate conversation, to rescue the conversationalists from silence, and to satisfy a curiosity. However, in clinical dialogue, questions should be in the best interest of the client and for a specific purpose, rather than just to generate dialogue. Remember the phrase "a pregnant pause"? This signifies that the speaker is "pregnant," so to speak, with a thought and about to give birth to an idea. Often times, people are not given the conversational space to let their wheels turn as they formulate a thought and interject it into the conversation. Have you ever been in a dialogue where you are sharing information and about to expand on information, when the listener delivers a question that asks just what you were about to disclose? In therapeutic dialogue, we want to be very

© Janek Sergejev/Shutterstock.com

intentional about the questions that we use. They are not used to fill space, but rather to open up dialogue in a goal-oriented direction or to make an inquiry that prompts the client to explore something that is in keeping with the agreed-upon goals of treatment (see Chapter 13 for more on the advanced skill of goal setting).

## Caveats of Misusing Questions

We often wait to introduce questions to our students because we want to ensure that they have mastered the previous listening skills first. If a counselor is using skills such as minimal encouragers, paraphrasing, and summarizing, he or she is validating the client while also inviting the client to expand. The use of these skills helps the client clarify their story and share it in a more coherent way.

### Questions as interrogators

Questions, if misused, may interrupt the flow and not be additive; at worst they may make the session feel like an interrogation with counselor in the role of detective firing off an arsenal of questions trying to fulfill his or her own agenda. Winnicott discussed how the therapist using the therapeutic session to satisfy his or her own needs (which may include curiosity) is one of the gravest pitfalls of therapy (Winnicott, 1988). One way to do this is to reflect on our "why." When our students ask, "Is it okay to ask this question?" our response is often, "Are you seeking to understand or to be understood?" Recall that one of the primary rules of counseling is to seek to understand.

*One way to identify whether or not a specific question or statement is helpful to the therapeutic dialogue is to ask oneself,* "Am I seeking to understand or to be understood?"

### Advice-giving in disguise

If a counselor is tempted to ask, "Well, have you ever tried journaling your discouraging thoughts?" or "What about keeping a to do list, and delegating tasks; have you ever thought about that?" this is actually a counseling faux pas, advice-giving in disguise. It is important for counselors to be prepared for those moments when they will be tempted to play the role of the "sage on the stage" and to give advice, and to recognize this in oneself and instead to redirect efforts to seeking to understand and walking alongside clients as they identify the answers that are best for them. We are in a sense working ourselves out of a job, because rather than cultivating dependence we are seeking to help clients develop confidence in their decision making and to make decisions that are best for them.

### Being overly directive

Sometimes a client will need some conversational space to make sense of an experience or share an update although we want to ensure that we are participating in purposeful counseling (see Chapter 13 for more on goal setting). Asking questions inappropriately may move clients away from content that needs to be shared to properly formulate treatment goals and to remain mindfully present.

## Failing to listen

Researchers have found that especially with counseling children, listening skills are more important than questioning skills ( Erdman & Lampe, 1996; Hughes & Baker, 1990). The other skills discussed up to this point serve to create a safe and supportive atmosphere to help the child feel comfortable to open up and share.

## Defensiveness

Another caveat to consider, is that if questions are asked in such a way that here is an implication that the client needs to provide a reason or rationale for a particular course of action, then the client may feel defensive. One key example of a question that can trigger defensiveness is a why question. A counselor may ask, "Why did you come in today?" "Why is perfectionism such a struggle?" The why questions probe for an answer or rationale that may be associated with defensiveness. Recall from Chapter 6 where we discussed Gottman's work using the SPAFF (specific affect coding system) to predict the dissolution of a marital relationships that just like defensiveness may be a predictor or one of the four horsemen that signifies the end of a romantic relationship may be near, it may also signify the end of a therapeutic relationship. Therefore, we want to avoid questions that begin with "why."

## Autobiographical bias

Also, a counselor may be looking at a client's story through his or her own lens rather than seeking to understand the client's story from the lens of the experiences and history of the client. This can lead to projections and misunderstandings and of course the misuse of questions. When asking questions, it is important to use empathy and to seek to understand. Carl Rogers described one of his goals in treatment as seeking to get a sense for what it is like to walk around in the client's world and experience life through their eyes (Covey, 2004; Rogers, 1965).

## Training the client to rely on questions

Another reason why it is important not to develop an overreliance on questions is that this dynamic may lead to the clients answering a question and then waiting for the next question rather than expanding on their statements and discussing content as needed. This would require the counselor to have to work much harder and not as effectively.

Despite these reasons not to ask questions, there are some types of questions that can be more useful than others, and an appropriate well-timed question can be a useful intervention. Let us explore the different types of questions next.

# Identify the Different Types of Questions and When to Ask Them

*Questions underpin all aspects of therapeutic assessment and intervention and are a vital component of the clinical process.*

—James, Morse, and Howarth (2010, p. 83)

Although questions should not be overused or misused, there are times when questions are necessary. McGee, del Vento, and Bavelas (2005) indicate there are different types of questions used in therapeutic dialogue, as a variety of theoretical approaches such as brief therapy and narrative therapy use questions for specific therapeutic purposes. McGee et al. extended the work of the Milan associates and others that advocated for the use of questions as interventions and analyzed the impact of questions in therapy. McGee et al. share that questions should involve some common ground so that the client can understand the therapist's question to begin with. Additionally, as the client makes sense of the question being asked, the process of co-construction begins to take place (see the recommended reading for information on where to read more about the nature of questions and a microanalysis of them).

One type of question that can be helpful in session is a door opener or to help the client move toward **purposeful counseling**, counseling that is in alignment with the agreed-upon goals of therapy. Different theoretical approaches to therapy may encourage different usages of questions. For example, those with a cognitive orientation may use questions in order to accomplish several objectives; one objective may be to collaboratively explore struggles from different perspectives. Another way cognitive therapists may use questions is to create a sense of cognitive dissonance. **Cognitive dissonance** involves an awareness of conflicting thoughts. For example, we had a client who said, "I really want to quit smoking. Yet, I do not want to quit smoking because I like how calm it makes me feel." These two conflicting messages can lead to a state of internal tension or turmoil. This cognitive dissonance is associated with a feeling of unpleasantness that triggers a motivation within the individual to bring the two thoughts into alignment and to reduce the discrepancies that separate them (Fischer, Frey, Peus, & Kastenmueller, 2008). The more relevant to a personal value these thoughts are, the more intense the experience of cognitive dissonance. Questions may help provide an opportunity to highlight and explore cognitive dissonance. Here is an example from one of our previous sessions:

**Client:** So, since the divorce I have met this man, and we have been dating for a few months and sleeping together, but since he lives an hour away I have been taking my kids to his place to stay with him every weekend. I feel bad then knowing what I am doing, like it doesn't feel right. Yet, I want to do it and do not want to lose him. (Client disclosure of cognitive dissonance in the form of conflicting thoughts about competing values, the value of relationship and the value of doing what she believes is right).

**Counselor:** So, it sounds like you have met someone that is special to you and you value the relationship and don't want to lose it, but you also don't feel right about the kids knowing you are sleeping together. What do your values say to you in this situation? (**Skill usage:** Counselor asks a question to invite the client to explore cognitive dissonance here: Desires and fears are encouraging her in one direction, and values are pulling in another. This brings the focus to the discrepancy and invites exploration).

**Client:** Well, I am a Christian, so I do believe that sex outside of marriage is wrong. Hmm, maybe that is why it feels wrong.

**Counselor:** So it sounds like your values tell you that you want to wait for marriage to be sexually active, and it feels wrong not to. Tell me more about this.

**Open-ended questions** are designed to open up the discussion and help the client expand on important content. They give the clients the conversational space and freedom to go where they see fit in response to the question. Open-ended questions are sometimes used at the beginning of the first session in order to invite the client to share openly. The first question used to begin the first session is sometimes referred to in the counseling literature as a "door opener" (Young, 2017, p. 73) because it opens the door to the therapeutic dialogue. One example of an open-ended question that is often used as a door opener is, "What would you like to accomplish from our time together today?" Or, "What brought you into counseling today?" Open-ended questions are typically not answered with a one-word response but instead help the client to open up the dialogue and share. Here is a sample therapeutic dialogue that may stem from a door opener.

**Counselor:** What brings you in today? (skill usage: door opener/open-ended question)

**Client:** Well, I have been having some stressors at home with my family that I wanted to talk about and get some help figuring out what to do about a situation.

**Counselor:** So, it sounds like things at home are weighing on your mind and causing some stress (skill usage: reflection of content and reflection of feeling).

**Client:** Yes, this all started when. . .

Notice, that the counselor gave the client the freedom and conversational space to share what brought him in; then the counselor used the skill of enriching and reflection to validate the response and invite more elaboration. It is important to try to limit the use of questions so that they are not overused. Notice, here the counselor did not follow this answer to the first question with a follow-up question but instead the counselor reflected back to the client. If the counselor were just to ask a series of questions, then the counselor may be training the client to rely on questions rather than freely expanding. If questions are phrased in a skillful manner that promotes client thinking and exploration, then the process of using questions in counseling can facilitate client increased self-awareness. Questions can help a client develop a more coherent narrative and integrate common themes or seek to make dissonant thoughts more congruent.

# Attachment Illumination

© Shutterstock.com

On the Adult Attachment Interview (George, Kaplan, & Main, 1985), of course the mode for gathering information to assess one's attachment style is via interview questions. The AAI includes the hallmark question, which involves asking the individual to provide five adjectives (or words) to describe one's childhood relationship with his or her mother and father. Later participants are also asked to elaborate upon these adjectives (or words) with specific autobiographical memories that illustrate what lead them to select these adjectives. Other questions (or prompts) on the AAI involve the following (Steele & Steele, 2008): describe separation illnesses and what happened when an attachment figure was upset as a child. The questions also explore any experiences that involve loss and/or trauma. Participants are eventually asked to respond to the question about why they believe their parents behaved as they did, along with questions regarding several other experiences (see Main et al., 2002; Steele & Steele, 2008)

One of the purposes of the AAI questions is to activate the attachment system. Steele and Steele (2008) discuss this phenomenon

It is helpful to appreciate that the AAI questions serve as an activation of the attachment system in the adolescent or adult respondent (see Dozier & Kobak, 1992) by taking the adult back in his or her mind, to childhood and earlier life circumstances, when the attachment system was previously activated. Thus, the AAI can be seen in this light as a test of the extent to which one can remain balanced and coherent when thinking about previously occurring attachment-related events or circumstances that were emotionally upsetting, while showing understanding and/or valuing of the persons and relationships concerned. One of the aims of the AAI is to "surprise the unconscious" (George et al., 1985) by posing in a calm but persistent way a series of questions that serve invariably to take the interviewee back to highly emotional events in early childhood that he or she will not ordinarily have discussed or reflected upon, and to which, in some cases, he or she may not have conscious access (p. 8;).

Dozier and Kobak (1992) indicate that the goal of the AAI interview questions is to test interviewees' capacity to process attachment-related memories and experiences and integrate them with their feelings, thoughts, and memories.

As you can see, in order to assess a client's attachment style or what has been referred to by Main et al. (2002) as their state of mind with respect to attachment, it is important to look at how they process and integrate attachment-related information.

When using the AAI clinically, a client may disclose that he or she had experienced abuse by a caregiver early in life. For example, perhaps they mentioned that their father hit them with an object and it left a bruise or cut (this is a clear definition of abuse based on the AAI system), but then in another portion of the interview, they said, "Well, my dad was not really abusive, he just had a bad temper," which demonstrates a lack of coherence and consistency and may be associated with cognitive dissonance and internal turmoil. Here, the therapist may use questions to address this incoherence and cognitive dissonance. The most prominent characteristic of a secure narrative is coherence (the capacity to consistently tell the truth about your interpersonal experience), but other important characteristics include forgiveness and valuing of attachment figures, so it is important to note a coherent narrative is not characterized by blame. For example, the therapist may combine the skills of questioning and challenging while supporting (an advanced skill to be covered more in Chapter 12); consider the therapeutic dialogue below.

**Counselor** (modified clinical use of AAI): Was there ever a time when your parents were abusive?

**Client:** So, when he would get really angry he would sometimes throw plates or canned goods at me. One time he repeatedly rammed one into my knee so that it felt like he hammered one into my leg and it bled through my jeans. That is one memory that stands out; there were also other similar experiences. But I mean he was not abusive; he just had a bad temper.

**Counselor:** So, I am hearing you say that there were times when he would hit you with objects or in other ways that would leave bruises and/or make you bleed on the one hand, yet on the other hand, I am hearing you say that he was not abusive. Help me understand. How is it that your father would leave you bruised and bloodied at times, but was not abusive?

This is a scenario, which includes a question that directly addresses the cognitive dissonance and the incoherence in the attachment narrative. It is very difficult to acknowledge that primary caregivers and those that were supposed to love us may have been unloving and even abusive at times. However, in order to develop a secure relationship style, it is important to develop a coherent narrative or story that allows one to make sense of

*Making sense of your story involves facing the truth of your story.*

experiences. That requires facing the truth of the story (Knight & Sibcy, 2018). One important warning is to remember all of the skills up to this point have been designed to strengthen and build rapport. However, challenging skills and uncomfortable questions that highlight cognitive dissonance and incongruence can feel confrontational or unsupportive and risk disrupting rapport. Thus questions should be used sparingly, only when strong rapport has been established. You can see that questions used in this scenario can be very powerful and can help the client move toward a more coherent-integrated narrative, which is healing and characterized by forgiveness (recall: to forgive requires to first acknowledge there is something to forgive, and forgiveness is a feature associated with a secure style of processing).

In addition to exploring struggles from a variety of different viewpoints and bringing focus to cognitive dissonance, another reason for asking good questions may be to build thinking styles that serve the individual better and are more adaptive in nature. Now let us look at some of the types of questions that may be used and how and when they may be appropriate to use.

## Closed-Ended Questions

Closed-ended questions and/or clarifying questions are typically questions that stop the flow of the therapeutic dialogue and invite one-word (or brief) answers. These questions can be important when the counselor needs to clarify some information, and the counselor jumps in to enrich and pause the client's story.

For example, a closed-ended or clarifying question may be, "How many siblings do you have?" "Did you say you were the oldest?" These invite responses such as a number ("two") or a binary response such as "yes" or "no." These questions can be used when the counselor needs to clarify important information for seeking to understand the client and the goals of treatment.

Another reason not to use closed questions too generously is the findings indicated in a study on the impact of motivational interviewing on college students' drinking levels: "Results indicated that a higher number of closed questions was related to less contemplation and a higher number of open questions was related to more contemplation post intervention" (Tollison et al., 2007, p. 183). So, perhaps asking open-ended questions provides more opportunities to generate thoughts and contemplation outside of sessions.

## Leading Questions

Leading questions are questions that are typically governed by an agenda. As discussed previously in the text, often beginning counselors tempted to give advice may fall into the trap of asking the client if they have ever tried some particular strategies in order to disguise their efforts at advice giving. Some examples of advice giving in disguise include, "Have you ever tried to pick one day of the week for rest?" "What would it be like if you were to start journaling?" These are efforts at advice giving in disguise and are typically not appropriate, unless perhaps used to schedule the next session. Consider the example below:

**Counselor:** Did you say you would like to keep the same appointment time each week?
**Client:** Yes, that would be nice.
**Counselor:** Okay, then same time next week?
**Client:** Yes.

This may be an appropriate use of closed/leading questions.

Consider the example below, which would not be an appropriate use of a leading question:
**Client:** I am just not sure if I should tell my best friend what happened with my boyfriend.
**Counselor:** Have you ever considered writing her a text instead?
**Client:** No, not really. I don't really text. I have a dumb phone not a smart phone. It is an old flip phone.
**Counselor:** Have you ever considered getting a new phone to stay current with technology?

These leading questions may be experienced as patronizing to the client and may be advice giving in disguise and should typically be avoided.

## How to Craft Powerful Questions

Now that we have discussed the difference between the use of questions in a social dialogue and a therapeutic dialogue, the different types of questions, and when to use them, let us turn our attention to how to craft powerful questions. Powerful questions often lead to client insight and meaning making. Consider the therapeutic dialogue below:

**Client:** I do not know what to do. I am working so many hours that I am tired all of the time and it is difficult to stay awake in class, but I need to work in order to make at least some money to keep from having to take out student loans and going into great debt.
**Counselor:** So, it sounds like you are feeling stuck. You don't want to sleep in class, but you feel like you need to work in order to be able to come to class (skills used: reflection of feeling, reflection of content, challenging while supporting).
**Client:** Yes, I mean I wish I did not have to work; sometimes it seems like it would be nice to just focus on school and enjoy the process and not have to work so many hours and struggle to stay awake and focus on school work.
**Counselor:** So, there is a longing you feel to be free to just focus on school and not work while in school.
**Client:** Yes, that is what I long for!
**Counselor:** Who do you want to give you permission? (Note, the use of a powerful question that prompts the client to reflect and gain insight).
**Client:** (Long pause) Hmm, I guess there is a part of me that wants my parents, or you, or someone else that would take care of me financially, if I could not, to give me permission, but I guess I am realizing that now as a college student and adult, I am the only one that can give myself permission. Hmmm. . . (wheels turning).

This is an excerpt from one of our colleagues' sessions. Here, the counselor is noticing the client expressing a desire to focus on school and take out loans rather than working full time but seems stuck. When asked about permission, the client went on to indicate an insight that developed, and you could see the client's expression of surprise and epiphany when reflecting on this powerful question.

Powerful questions tend to be purposeful, in keeping with the agreed-upon goals of treatment. They tend to promote thought and often engage clients in thinking from alternate or new perspectives. Powerful questions also may relate to one's values, triggering a depth of response that goes beyond what is typical in social dialogue, and they may lead to transformation.

## Double Questions

Another type of question to be careful to avoid is the double question. If we ask clients multiple questions at the same time, then they may not know which question to answer. Often they will feel overwhelmed or just go with the first question or the last question. It can be difficult for a beginning counselor, especially if anxiety levels are high, to resist the urge to use a double question. However, one helpful strategy can be to begin with a question and then to use reflecting skills to facilitate the client's answer to the question.

**To Do List**

- First, please watch this counseling session with Dr. Silvey and Kristen, where he explores questions regarding responsibility with Kristen.

**Video**

**Exploring the Question of Responsibility**

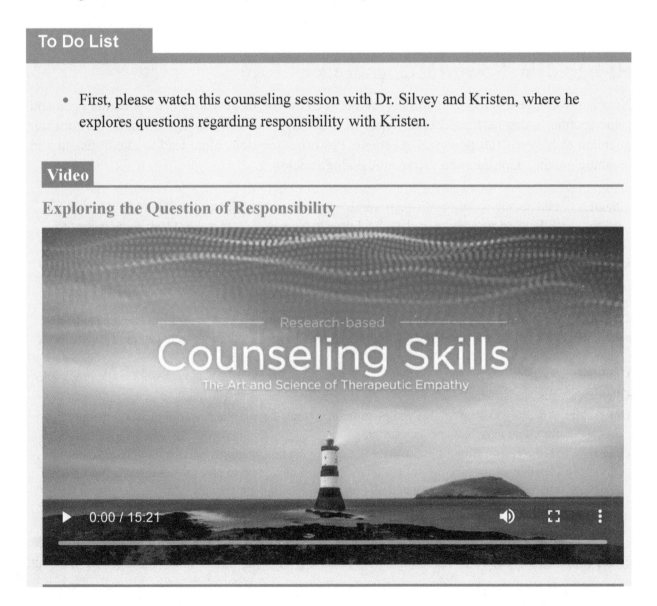

- Consider beginning the session with a door opener such as "What would you like to accomplish during our time together today?"

- Practice using the reflecting skills to validate client's answers to questions.

- Remember not to use questions inappropriately as strategies for advice giving or just to generate conversational filler.

- Consider asking questions that relate to client's values.

- Identify what is most important to you of the different challenges you face.

- Use clarifying questions or closed questions sparingly but when needed.

## Recommended Reading

If you would like to enhance your expertise on this content, we recommend the sources below:

© Shutterstock.com

- Fischer, P., Frey, D., Peus, C., & Kastenmueller, A. (2008). The theory of cognitive dissonance: state of the science and directions for future research. In P. Meusburger, M. Welker, & E. Wunder (Eds.), *Clah of knowledge: Orthodoxies and heterodoxies in science and religion* (pp. 189–198). New York, NY: Springer.

- Main, M., Goldwyn, R., & Hesse, E. (2002). *Adult attachment classification system.* Berkeley, CA: Regents of the University of California.

- McGee, D., Del Vento, A., & Bavelas, J. B. (2005). An interactional model of questions as therapeutic interventions. *Journal of Marital and Family Therapy, 31*(4), 371.

## Chapter Summary

Chapter 10 discussed the potential pitfalls of asking questions. Some of these include a bias toward interpreting the clients' story through one's own autobiographical perspective, seeking to lead through questions, and shutting down the dialogue by asking closed-ended questions. Next, the various types of questions such as open-ended questions, closed questions, clarifying questions, leading questions, and the subsequent impact of each were explained. In addition, the benefits of door openers and open ended questions were explored. The Adult Attachment Interview also includes helpful questions that can help clients make sense of their story; these were discussed as potential questions for use in session to explore background. Powerful questions exploring concepts such as permissions are used to help the client challenge existing thought conditioning.

## Chapter Eleven

# Reflecting Meaning

### Anita M. Kuhnley and Gary Sibcy

*When we are no longer able to change a situation, we are challenged to change ourselves.*

—Viktor Frankl (2000, p. 112)

## Chapter Learning Objectives

- To identify strategies for getting to meaning values in face-to-face counseling sessions (CACREP II.F.5.d, 2016, p. 11)
- To learn essential interviewing, counseling, and case conceptualization skills
- To discuss counseling skills on how to reflect meaning (CACREP II.F.5.d, 2016, p. 11)
- To discuss essential aspects of neurobiology (CACREP II.F.3.e., 2016, p. 10)

## Chapter Overview

In Chapter 10, we discovered how to use intentional and well-timed questions to explore our clients' thoughts and feelings. In this chapter, we will develop reflecting skills, which bring the session to a deeper place through reflection of meaning. We will explore meaning-making tasks, such as assessing values and identifying attachment-based relationship rules. For example, by using the skill of reflecting meaning, we may help a client discover how his or her values and relationship rules are impacting his or her current relationships. The importance of reflecting meanings to take the session to a deeper level of self-disclosure and transformation is discussed, and strategies for reflecting meanings, such as identifying values, are explored.

# Reflecting Meaning

*Deep calls unto deep.*

—Psalm 42:7

The verse above, "Deep calls unto deep..." (Psalm 42:7), provides us with a concept to contemplate as we begin to explore meaning. We find that engaging in and leading a client to deep reflection can begin to lead to connecting with deep meaning. The first two layers of reflection we discussed were content and feeling. Once a counselor has used the nonverbal skills, the 3 Vs, the minimal encouragers, paralanguage, and the reflection

© iQoncept/Shutterstock.com

of content and feelings, it is time to delve deeper and to seek to get to the meaning of the client's story. We want to engage in purposeful counseling and move toward greater levels of self-disclosure. Now, let us look at the pathway that leads to the deepest level of self-disclosure out of the listening skills. This pathway involves reflecting meaning. **Reflecting meaning** is a very important skill because it helps clients go through the process of "making sense" of their experiences.

## A Key Player in Meaning Making

### Viktor Frankl

© Imagno/Contributor/Getty Images

Dr. Frankl was an Austrian psychiatrist and Holocaust survivor who developed logotherapy and has influenced much thinking on the process of meaning making through his reflections on his experiences. Frankl (2000) believed that for many individuals who suffer, part of the source of their suffering is a failure to find meaning in their experiences and suffering. Frankl's approach to treatment, logotherapy, is considered one of several forms of existential therapy. Meaning making was seen to be the key to progressing from living to surviving. It is important to note that survival was of utmost importance to those like Frankl who spent time in the concentration camps. Here is an inspiring quote from his text on the phenomenon: "It is here that we find the central theme of existentialism: to live is to suffer, to survive is to find meaning in the suffering" (Frankl, 2000, p. 9). Here is another concept to contemplate: If, as Frankl says, to live is to suffer, and to survive is to find meaning in suffering, what does it mean to thrive?

212

# Attachment Illumination

© Shutterstock.com

The role reversal where the client tends to feel responsible for the counselors' feelings, is often seen on the Adult Attachment Interview in the transcripts of people with a history of interacting with parents that were inconsistently available and who engaged in role reversal. This is why it can be very useful for counselors to explore their own attachment histories and to seek to work through the insecure relationship rules in order to be fully present therapists to their own clients.

Recall, when we are using reflecting skills, we first reflect content, then feeling, and then meaning. Although we typically encourage our students <u>not</u> to ask questions in the beginning of their counseling skill development, in order to leave room to develop all of the other listening skills, we actually want to move toward getting at the answer to one question, a question that we do not ask directly because it will not have the desired outcome (for a full discussion on questions, see Chapter 10). That question is "Why?" If we can understand the meaning, the why behind the what and how of our client's story, and help him or her to make sense of his or her story in a way that extends his or her understanding of himself or herself, then we may be able to help him or her move toward what Rogers called "congruence," what attachment theorists call "coherence or secure attachment," what high-performance coaches call such as Brendon Burchard "clarity," and what neuroscientists, like Dan Siegel, call "integration." This is a movement toward wellness and in a direction of the client's goals. In a TED Talk that Dr. Silvey introduced me to, Simon Sinek, author of *Start with Why*, discusses how important our "why" is and draws on the field of biology and more specifically neuroscience to explain this phenomenon. Sinek has popularized the concept of the golden circle and the phrase "begin with why" (see Chapter 2 for a full discussion on these concepts). He explains that the brain is divided into two different regions, and he lists those as the neocortex, which is associated with logic and reasoning, and the limbic brain, which is associated with emotions, trust, and decision making (Sinek, 2009a). He shares that the gut level is where decisions are made. So when clients say, "It doesn't feel right," but they do not have the words to explain why it does not feel right, or perhaps they say, "I don't know why I do this; it is not in line with my long-term goals," it may be because the limbic system, which is the part of the brain associated with our emotions, feelings, and decision making, is responding. So, if we start with these feelings that arise, then we can move to the why. Sinek suggests moving from the inside out: This is the "why," and why can inform what. So, although we start with reflecting content, we may then be able to move backward once we uncover meaning and help clients make sense of their script (or content) in a manner that is informed by their "why" or the deeper meaning and purpose.

As we discussed earlier, in Chapter 8, when we are reflecting the essence of the client's story back to them, we often do it in layers. The first layer is the reflection of content, the second layer is the reflection of feeling, and the third layer is reflection of meaning. Reflecting and exploring the meaning of a client's story can help us to go deeper.

The ironic law of timing is at work here, and it is important to remember this in order to get to meaning. The irony of the time it takes to get to meaning is we get there faster by going slower. This is ironic because if you are flying, for example, this may not be the case. I am currently traveling on an airplane as I write these words; we are traveling 501 miles per hour as we fly over the Atlantic Ocean just south of Florida. We have 788 miles left until we arrive in Atlanta. Most likely, the faster we travel, the more likely we are to arrive sooner. So, the law of timing in counseling is ironic because progressing in counseling can be very

© somsak mungmee/Shutterstock.com

different from progressing in an airplane. As a counselor uses skills and seeks to understand and reflect components of the client's story, the counselor may pick up speed in the session (perhaps using minimal encouragers such as a head nod that is constant and the use of paralanguage such as "mm hmm," "uh huh," and "mm"). The client may have finished explaining the sequence of events or the content (surface-level information of the session) but may not have a chance to make sense of related feelings, meanings, and conflicting or confusing parts of the story. Therefore, it is best to slow down, seek to understand and reflect while allowing time for the client to explore feelings, meanings, conflicts, and coherence in their narrative. So, in counseling, it is better to be the tortoise than the hare. Recall in Aesop's fable of the tortoise and the hare, the hare jested with the tortoise and asked if he could ever make it anywhere, and the tortoise assured the hare he did and challenged him to a race. The hare, wanting to prove the tortoise was ridiculous, lay down to take a nap. The tortoise, meanwhile, continued progressing slowly and steadily and was near the finish line when the hare awoke. It was too late for the hare to catch up. The moral of the story is captured in the last line, "The race is not always to the swift" (Aesop, 1919, p. 96). So, when we dig in to explore the meaning behind the story and the relationship rules, it may feel like the session slows down. Ironically though, as we slow down, we arrive at our treatment goal sooner in many instances. Let us explore a sample counseling session Where is this?. In the session where Dr. Sibcy was doing a sample counseling session with Alex, he began unpacking her interpersonal history to explore the relationship rules underlying her decisions and meaning making. As he spoke with her about her belief that she could not tell her parents she was feeling down because they may worry, he asked her where she learned this. Alex began sharing about how she did not want to be a burden. Here, Dr. Sibcy could have had Alex go on sharing about the content of her situation and more on what made her sad, but instead he began digging deeper into the meaning behind her relationship rules. This was the beginning of a discussion on Alex's relationship rules, or attachment rules.

So, if the counselor and client are moving too fast, they may not be exploring what Paul Harvey may have called, "the rest of the story," unless, like the tortoise, they progress slowly and steadily allowing for time to process not only the content, but the feelings and deeper meanings of the client's narrative. So, let us consider some strategies for identifying meanings.

There are exceptions when we can sometimes move quickly to meaning. Our colleague, psychiatrist John Kuhnley says, "When you build a strong rapport, it gets you in the door more quickly." All the skills we have discussed up to this point are designed to help build rapport. However, the therapist needs to gauge and discern whether the client is ready to explore meaning.

## Relationship Rules and Identifying Meaning

Relationship rules relate to how one perceives the self and others, whether one is worthy to receive love and in terms of whether others are competent and capable of giving love (Clinton & Sibcy, 2006).

Let us discuss some cues that may help us to identify meaningful components of the client's story as they relate to the Adult Attachment Interview (AAI) and relationship rules. On the AAI, there are four primary patterns of responses or processing styles with respect to attachment. These attachment classifications include the secure autonomous, the preoccupied, the dismissing, and the unresolved (for loss or abuse). In our attachment research using the AAI we have found that in the insecure-preoccupied pattern of processing attachment-related information (which is labeled E for enmeshed), the speaker seems to be flooded or overwhelmed by emotion and unpleasant reminders from their autobiographical memories. Dr. John Gottman, in his research on marital success and in his book entitled, *What Makes Love Last? How to Build Trust and Avoid Betrayal,* states that flooding can be measured by pulse oximeters. Pulse oximeters are tools that use information from heart rate and oxygen to measure physiological arousal. Flooding is physiologically measured by two markers: a heart rate above '00 beats per minute and an oxygen concentration that falls below 95% (they do specify that although 100 bpm is standard, that for athletes there is a lower threshold of 80 bpm; Gottman & Silver, 2012). So, if a client is discussing memories or experiences that are or were distressing and becomes flooded, then we may see manifestations of that in terms of repetition of words or exaggerative language. This may signify that the individual is hurt, angry, or upset about the topic of discussion. When a client starts repeating three or more times certain words, phrases or themes, this could be an indicator that the client has some preoccupation, and perhaps even preoccupying anger regarding a particular situation, or perhaps some preoccupying fear (Steele & Steele, 2008). This may be an indicator of some underlying relationship rules. Clinton and Sibcy (2002) discuss how each attachment style is associated with particular relationship rules; in preoccupied attachment styles, the relationship rules may indicate "others are able to show love, but the self is not worthy of love"; these relationship rules may be associated with how the person then makes sense of his or her experiences.

Looking at meaning making through an attachment lens, if there is a dismissing pattern of movement away from talking about attachment relationships, subject changes, less elaboration, or discomfort, this may be an indicator of underlying relationship rules that suggest the self is worthy of love, but others are not able to or willing to show love (Clinton & Sibcy, 2002; Steele & Steele, 2008). This may manifest in a lack of examples to support overall estimates (e.g., my relationship with my mother was loving because it was caring; no specific example).

Likewise, with the secure autonomous attachment style, there may be a manifestation of relationship rules that indicate the self is worthy of love and others are able to show love (Clinton & Sibcy, 2002). Indicators that may demonstrate manifestations of these relationship rules may include a way of speaking about one's attachment history that sounds fresh and coherent and demonstrates a valuing of attachment relationships.

Other relationship rules could represent the idea that "the grass is dead on both sides of the fence" (Clinton & Sibcy, 2002, p. 95), indicating a belief that the self is not worthy of love and others are not able to show love. This is typically associated with an attachment style that is unresolved for loss or unresolved for abuse. These relationship rules may manifest with incoherence. Perhaps there is not a clear message about what exactly happened in the speaker's background that was traumatic, or perhaps trauma is mentioned and then discounted. Likewise, maybe a person who died is discussed in present tense. These are linguistic indicators that there may be some lack of resolution. Consider the therapeutic dialogue below:

**Client:** My husband and I got divorced ten years ago.
**Counselor:** Okay, so you have been single for ten years.(early in session) Later in session:
**Client:** Yes, but my husband says he thinks I'll never remarry. (recall divorce occurred ten years ago)
**Counselor:** Your ex-husband says he thinks you won't remarry?
**Client:** Right.

The client may not be aware that she is speaking of a spouse that she divorced 10 years ago in the present as if they are still married calling him her "husband" rather than her "ex-husband." This may indicate that the client has not come to terms with the divorce and made the internal adjustments, or perhaps it is just a slip of the tongue because she was accustomed to speaking this way for many years.

An indicator that meaning making is lacking may be a difficulty facing the truth of one's story (Knight & Sibcy, 2018). If a client tends to violate relevance and when asked about feelings or meanings related to a given experience, if they go off topic, this can be an indicator that the pain of seeking to make sense of a difficult story may be present either consciously or subconsciously (Knight & Sibcy, 2018). If the client's narrative begins to move in a confusing direction with contradictions, exaggerations, or irrelevant information, this could also indicate the difficulty a client may be having in the pain of facing the truth of his or her story. In these cases, this process of helping a client to make meaning of his or her experience can be very transformative.

## Earned Secure Attachment Style

*In some ways suffering ceases to be suffering at the moment it finds a meaning, such as the meaning of a sacrifice.*

—Viktor E. Frankl, Man's Search for Meaning

When taking a difficult narrative that may involve abuse, trauma, or loss and unpacking it coherently, an earned secure narrative could emerge (Knight & Sibcy, 2018; Siegel, 2010b). John Bowlby, the father of attachment, discussed this concept; he emphasized that it is very difficult for an individual to admit they were unwanted by their parents. Yet he emphasized that "if it is true, it is true and they are better off if they recognize that is what did happen" (Lifespan Learning LA, 2009).

If the therapist can help the clients explore what it means to them that these difficult things happened and if they can integrate this into a coherent narrative, they can move to what we call an "earned secure attachment style"; this may reflect that despite an early history characterized by unloving experience, they still learned to distinguish between loving and unloving experiences and to talk about them coherently. This concept reminds me of God's redeeming love, and his "adoption" of us as his children and his love as our Heavenly Father, our ultimate attachment figure. His word indicates in Galatians 4:4–5, "[4]But when the set time had fully come, God sent his Son, born of a woman, born under the law, [5]to redeem those under the law, that we might receive adoption to sonship." Christ followers may make meaning of their experiences, by remembering who

> *A Verse to Remember*:
> Galatians (4:4–5), "But when the set time had fully come, God sent his Son, born of a woman, born under the law, to redeem those under the law, that we might receive adoption to sonship."

they are, children of the Most High God, and that they came from God and are returning to God (see Chapter 1 on the circle of security) and interacting with God as the ultimate attachment figure may help some to make meaning of their stories (Knight & Sibcy, 2018). Dan Siegel has discussed this process of developing a coherent narrative and facing and integrating the truth and called it "making sense." We could perhaps also call it "making meaning of our attachment story," and Siegel has mentioned that parents who do this wind up having children more secure than any other classification, including the prototypical secure.

## Star Wars on Meaning Making

© Yuri Turkov/Shutterstock.com

Even in the popular film, *Star Wars: The Last Jedi,* we see depth of conversation emerge about meaning making. Kylo Ren and Ray have a discussion about the influence of parents (Kennedy, Abrams, Kasdan, Bergman, & Kinberg, 2017):

**Rey**: Why did you hate your father? Give me an honest answer. You had a father who loved you; he gave a *damn* about you!

**Ren**: I didn't hate him.

**Rey**: Then *why?*

**Ren**: "Why" what? *[pauses]* "Why" what? Say it.

| Rey: | *[sobbing]* Why did you...why did you kill him? I don't understand. |
| --- | --- |
| **Ren:** | No. Your parents threw you away like garbage. |
| **Rey:** | They *didn't*. |
| **Ren:** | They did, but you can't stop needing them. It's your greatest weakness. Looking for them everywhere, in Han Solo, and now in Skywalker. Did he tell you what happened that night? |

Kylo Ren recognized the impact of Rey's past on her present. As Kylo suggests to Rey that she let the past die or kill it as one way of dealing with the impact it has had on her, he is getting closer to the meaning in Rey's story. Therapists also look at the impact of the past, but they do something different. They help clients process through the negative impact of the past by making sense of it, processing it, talking through it, and facing the pain of the story. Rather than killing the past, there is a movement toward healing it. As we explore underlying meanings and the process of making sense, this is where healing and a revision of relationship rules can take place.

## Areas of Importance

Another pathway for getting to meaning is to identify what is important to the client. This can be done by attending to the client's vocal tone. When does he or she get more excited and exhibit an increase in vocal pacing? Do you notice a raised vocal tone? Do you notice more enthusiasm, and his or her eyes light up when talking about something? These may be indicators that the client is talking about an area of importance that could be a pathway to meaning.

So, how do we get to meaning? We discussed one pathway being exploring attachment history and relationship rules. Let us discuss another pathway: identifying the client's values. Reflecting and exploring our clients' values may help us to identify meaning. For example, if a client's values consist of a Christian worldview, then a loss may be processed differently from someone who does not have a Christian worldview. Belief in heaven or afterlife and the hope of reunion may be associated

© sondem/Shutterstock.com     with a sense of hope during the grieving process. At the same time, someone without a Christian worldview may process the loss differently. Even within groups, there are large variations in beliefs, so part of the process of reflecting and exploring meaning may involve identifying what a client's values are and reflecting those and examining how they influence the lens through which the client processes his or her experiences.

## How to Reflect Meaning

The words the client use may represent the 20% of the ice berg that is above the water line, and the meanings may represent the other 80% that underlies the client's words. So, the first step to reflecting meaning is to examine what the client may be communicating beneath his or her words. For example, consider the therapeutic dialogue below:

© Arcady/Shutterstock.com

**Client:** It is like she never considers the other person. I always have to do what she wants, and she just doesn't seem to take time to think about you. I hate it when people are like that.

**Counselor:** So, it sounds like when your wife is focused on her own needs and not thinking about how her actions hurt you it is frustrating because you value consideration, and when people behave in an unpredictable way it seems they are not being considerate. It sounds like this frustration is compounded by the experiences you have had with your wife over time.

**Client:** Yes! And I am seeing that she is not the only one that is like that. It feels like I am surrounded with these people who are selfish, but then sometimes surprise you and will be considerate, but then they may go back to being selfish at the blink of an eye. It is like you cannot count on them.

**Counselor:** So, it sounds like you value consistency and thoughtfulness, and when people act in an inconsistent or thoughtless way it is frustrating. What kind of messages do you take away about other people when these things happen? (Skill: Reflecting values to get to meaning; with a direct question)

The client's relationship rules begin to emerge; as he struggles to make sense of inconsistent behaviors, a preoccupation follows. The client tries to make sense of the source of the unloving behaviors. So, this can help us fine-tune our listening to look for how a client's relationship rules are related to perhaps something in the client's interpersonal history. We also want to listen for and reflect statements that involve generalizing these behaviors to others.

Here we are moving toward meaning by reflecting values and asking direct questions about the meanings or messages the client takes away about people when they behave in ways that are inconsiderate and inconsistent.

Sometimes, a counselor can use a direct, open-ended question to assess meaning such as:

- What does it mean to you that _____ happened?

- What does it mean about you that your parents were not here for you?

- What does it mean about others, that you could not count on your parents?

Any similar range of questions may elicit meaning from a clients story. Some clients may not be as accustomed to contemplation and pondering things in their hearts; thus, it is important to be patient and stay with the client as they struggle to face the crudeness of reality apart from coping mechanisms that may have served to numb them when facing questions about meaning (such as alcohol, drugs, and sex). The counselor needs to use discernment and tread carefully when seeking to begin to move toward meaning.

The following table shows a list of triggers or possible times when it may be appropriate to reflect meaning and then also some formulas for how to reflect meaning.

| When to reflect meaning (when any of the following occur, it may point to meaning) | Methods for reflecting or exploring meaning |
|---|---|
| • When a client is repeating a theme more than once in session<br><br>• When a client is expressing relationship rules such as the following:<br><br>• Others are not dependable or available when you need them<br><br>• Others are inconsistently available or inconsistently loving<br><br>• Perhaps they did something wrong to invite maltreatment or the self is not worthy of love<br><br>• The self is worthy of love<br><br>• Others are able to show love<br><br>• When a client mentions their values or something is important to them<br><br>• When a client mentions that his or her values have been violated | • What does it mean to you when ___?<br><br>• What do you tell yourself that ___ happened?<br><br>• How do you explain the reasons behind ___ to yourself?<br><br>• You feel upset when your colleagues do not work hard on a project because you value hard work.<br><br>• Tell me about what it means to you when others _____<br><br>• Tell me more about what it means to you about_____ |

## To Do List

- Listen for themes or content that is repeated

- Listen to vocal tone for emphasis on what is important

- Listen for relationship rules and relational themes

- When identifying a pathway to meaning, reflect or ask a direct question

- Consider and use the following formats for reflections:

  - What does it mean to you that ____?

  - How do you make sense of ___?

  - What messages do you take away about others due to ___?

  - It sounds like you feel ___ because ___ is important to you

  - It sounds like you feel ____ because you value ___ and ____

## Recommended Reading

If you would like to enhance your expertise on the topics discussed in this chapter, we would recommend reading the following texts to expand your knowledge on the topic or related to the topic of exploring meaning in counseling:

© Shutterstock.com

- Clinton, T., & Sibcy, G. (2006). *Why do you do the things you do: The secret to healthy relationships*. Nashville, TN: Thomas Nelson.

- Ivey, A. E., Ivey, M. B., & Zalaquett, C. P. (2018). *Intentional interviewing and counseling: Facilitating client development in a multicultural society* (9th ed.). Boston, MA: Cengage Learning.

- Knight, A., & Sibcy, G. (2018). *Redeeming attachment: A counselor's guide to facilitating attachment to God and earned security.* Dubuque, IA: Kendall Hunt.

- Young, M. (2016). *Learning the art of helping: Building blocks and techniques.* New York, NY: Pearson.

## Chapter Summary

Chapter 11 explored the counseling skill of reflecting meaning. Making meaning is adaptive for surviving and thriving. Viktor Frankl, who is one of the key players in the literature on reflecting meaning. Frankl, who survived the Nazi concentration camps and wrote about his experiences, emphasized the role of meaning making in survival. He also developed the therapeutic approach called logotherapy. Some processes that may help lead us to meaning include exploring values and attachment-based relationship rules. There are relationship rules introduced by Clinton and Sibcy (2002) that apply to each of the different attachment styles. Those with a preoccupied style may believe that the self is not worth of love (although others are able to demonstrate it), while those with a dismissing style may believe others are not able to show love. From those with a dismissing style, we may hear a movement away from or avoidance of discussing attachedment-related subjects. Likewise, if a client has experienced loss or trauma, we may hear indicators that it is yet to be resolved. These can all be pointers to meaning. There are different strategies for reflecting meaning, such as the direct question or the reflection.

## Chapter Twelve

# Challenging Skills and Immediacy

## Gary Sibcy and Anita Kuhnley

*A ship in harbor is safe but that is not what ships are for.*

—John A. Shedd (Shapiro, 2006, p. 705)

### Chapter Learning Objectives

- To add more essential interviewing and counseling skills to the tool kit including reframing confrontation as challenging while supporting (CACREP II.F.5.g, 2016, p. 12)

- To evaluate when it is appropriate to use challenging skills (CACREP II.F.5.g, 2016, p. 12)

- To identify a strategy for using confrontation (i.e., challenging while supporting) (CACREP II.F.5.g, 2016, p. 12)

## Chapter Overview

Now that we have discussed the essential skills that help a person feel heard and understood, we can move on to the necessary skill of challenging. Note, this is the first skill that is a risk to the relationship. If we use this skill prematurely before using empathy and the other skills, we may risk the client feeling misunderstood and alienated. Thus, it is important to continue seeking to understand and using the basic skills throughout the course of therapy. Although some texts call this skill confrontation, as I learned from one of my clinical supervisors and mentors, Dr. George Jefferson, it is important to balance every skill with lots of support. Hence, it is more accurate to call this skill "challenging while supporting." An example of a statement that challenges while supports is, "On the one hand I am hearing you say that you want to play more tennis and improve your game, on the other hand I am hearing you say that you have been feeling tired and just want time to relax and rest after work instead of hitting the courts. Help me understand what this internal tension feels like to have two parts of you leaning in different directions" Notice, that the challenge includes a reflection of both parts of the self; thus, challenges are sometimes referred to as "double reflections" and simply involve using your reflecting skills to challenge an area of inconsistency.

> *There is a reason why I think it is of greatest help to assist a patient to discover their own past, and to recognize how it comes about that they cannot do it or won't do it or don't want to do it. . . or whatever it may be, either it is too painful, no one wants to think that their mother never wanted them and always really rejected them, it is a very painful situation to find themselves in, and yet if its true, its true, and they are going to be better off if they recognize that is what did happen.*
>
> —John Bowlby

As we explore meaning with clients, one thing that becomes apparent is that at face value, words may disguise underlying meanings, and it is important to unpack what the unspoken messages and relationship rules are that clients have been operating under.

## Reframing Confrontation

Confrontation can take many forms; sometimes it involves a confrontation with oneself that requires one to seek to bring disparate thoughts and feelings into alignment. Consider the above quote by John Bowlby. He discusses the idea that it is difficult to acknowledge the unloving behaviors of one's parents. Perhaps there is something within the human heart that longs to believe that one's primary caregivers love them, and to be confronted with the unloving behavior that may not align with that belief can be painful. Yet, this pain can be an important and necessary part of healing. Confrontation can have a negative connotation; when thinking about people getting into a confrontation, what comes to mind? Do you think of people having an argument or an altercation? Challenging while supporting has a more positive connotation than confrontation. Challenges promote growth but are often positive and welcome. A challenge is defined an invitation to engage in a competition; it may be associated with visions of winning,

> **A Quote to Remember. . .**
> Perhaps there is something within the human heart that longs to believe that one's primary caregivers (often one's parents) love them, and to be confronted with the unloving behavior that may not align with that belief can be painful. Yet, this pain can be an important and necessary part of healing.

victory, and game playing. Support, likewise, has a positive connotation, and the term may be accompanied by visions of warmth and kindness. **Challenging while supporting** is often used whenever a client is experiencing cognitive dissonance or a lack of congruence between two parts of the self. Challenging is a strategy for bringing the two parts of the self into the light and bringing them into the light. So, the skill challenging while supporting is defined as reflecting two aspects of the self that are not congruent and inviting the client to consider these parts.

Remember that each time a challenge is used, it is a risk to the relationship. The client may feel misunderstood when the counselor seeks to confront or challenge them on a matter. The client may become defensive if challenged before the relationship has developed. So, the counselor also needs to use care with determining when an appropriate time to implement this skill is at hand.

## When It May Be Appropriate to Use Challenging While Supporting

This skill should only be used after the majority of the other skills discussed up to this point have been used. Recall, we often begin the session with ethical informed consent and then use minimal encouragers, paralanguage, key word encouragers, paraphrasing, reflecting content, reflecting feelings, asking appropriate questions, and reflecting meaning. Once these other skills have been used and a sufficient therapeutic relationship has been established, then, if an opportunity presents itself and if the counselor discerns the client may be open and prepared for the challenge, then the time may be appropriate. Once all of this has set the stage, there are a few other occurrences when it may be beneficial to use challenging.

Sometimes clients may indicate that their values tell them to do one thing, but their desires are pulling them in another direction. For example, in the famous sessions between Gloria and Carl Rogers (https://www.youtube.com/watch?v=24d-FEptYj8), Gloria shared that she was concerned that when her daughter, who was nine years old, asked her if she had ever slept with anyone besides her daughter's father, Gloria said, "no" However, she had slept with someone else and felt bad for not telling the truth to her daughter. Gloria felt torn because she did not want to tell her daughter the truth and her daughter to think she was awful or think worse of her. In contrast, she also did not want to keep it from her then for her daughter to later find out the truth, in which case keeping it from her may negatively influence their relationship. This is a perfect example of when to use challenging. Carl Rogers used his hands to form a triangle and indicated the different parts of Gloria; this was one method of not only challenging her to deal with the conflicting thoughts and feelings but also providing the support of the therapeutic relationship and the validation of the different parts of the self.

So here are some situations where (after using most of the other skills discussed so far) it may be helpful to use challenging while supporting:

- **Lack of congruence or discrepancy between feelings and goals.** For example, a client may say, "My goal is _____ (e.g., to graduate as quickly as possible), but my feelings are _____ (they feel tired and in need of a break from school and want to take a term off)."

- **Lack of congruence or discrepancy between behaviors and values.** For example, a client may say, "I value _____ (e.g., purity), but I have been _____ (e.g., sexually active with my partner)."

- **Lack of congruence between thoughts (cognitive dissonance).** For example, a client may say, "I sometimes think I should ____ (e.g., marry him), and I sometimes think I should not _____ (e.g., marry him)."

*A Concept to Contemplate*

## Automatic Negative Thoughts

© Shutterstock.com • **Another time when it may be appropriate to use challenging while supporting, especially when using a CBT approach, is when there are automatic negative thoughts present such as:**

- He always _____ (absolutist thinking).

- She never _____ (absolutist thinking).

- I don't think _____ likes me (mind reading).

- Oh, everything is going to be awful (awfulizing).

- He should know better! (what Dr. Sibcy calls, "What is it like to live in Realville." How does taking responsibility for negative thoughts and redirecting them feel different?).

## Strategies for Using Confrontation

One way to use challenging skills is to refer to one's hands as an explanatory model. For example, a counselor may lift her right hand and say, on the one hand "I hear you saying _____" (e.g., that you would like to quit smoking), "and yet on the other hand I hear you saying _____" (e.g., that you really crave that cigarette to relax after work). The counselor may then prompt the client to explore this lack of congruence with a statement such as, "Help me understand what it feels like to be torn like this." This allows for the opportunity to explore the internal tension created by the incongruence.

## Another Strategy or Formula Is to Appeal to the Part of the Client Wanting Growth

Breunlin, Schwartz, and Kune-Karrer (2001) wrote a text entitled, *Metaframeworks: Transcending Family Therapy* and discuss the power of using language that appeals to the different parts of the person and creating a safe atmosphere. They indicate that rather than focusing on diagnosis and directives, it is often best "to create an atmosphere in sessions in which the fearful or angry parts of people are calmed and their resources can emerge. When this happens therapy becomes a kind of collaborative discussion" (p. 5). We have also found that using parts language can be very helpful for collaborative exploration. Even if the parts are at odds with one another (as is often the case), this type of challenge (calling the client's attention to the discrepancy) is very supportive and collaborative. Now, let us look at some examples that illustrate how we may use parts language in a session. It sounds like a part of you wants to _____ (e.g., wake up earlier and get an early start on work), but the other part of you_____(e.g., wants to sleep in and catch up on sleep). Help me understand how these two parts co-exist. (This can be further combined with good questions down the road, such as "What would the part of you that wants to wake up earlier say?" This allows us to appeal to the part of the self that the client desires to change.)

## Attachment Illumination

© Shutterstock.com

In this chapter, we have been discussing the idea that sometimes the counselor challenges the client to examine ideas that are not congruent. This helps the client to develop a more coherent narrative, and a more coherent narrative may be associated with moving toward developing a more secure state of mind with respect to attachment. Sometimes, it is a lack of congruence within a client's state of mind that may be making it hard for him or her to come to terms with his or her attachment story. For example, when we lose an attachment figure, there is a loss that takes place that is disorganizing. Bowlby (1980) said the following about loss:

*Loss of a loved person is one of the most intensely painful experiences any human being can suffer. And not only is it painful to experience but it is also painful to witness, if only because we are so impotent to help. To the bereaved nothing but the return of the lost person can bring true comfort; should what we provide fall short of that it is felt almost as an insult.*

—(pp. 7–8)

When a person loses an attachment figure, he or she faces the task of making adjustments in his or her internal world to bring his or her internal sense of orientation to attachment figures into alignment with a change that has been made in the external world. In other words, he or she needs to come to terms with the loss of the attachment figure by making shifts internally to acknowledge, grieve, mourn, and accept that the lost person is no longer available and present. When a person denies or suppresses feelings and thoughts related to the loss, it can make it more difficult to develop the coherent narrative, which is often characterized by a relative acceptance of experience. How can one discuss his or her attachment-related experiences coherently unless he or she is first willing to accept and acknowledge them? (Knight & Sibcy, 2018). Some authors believe that the Adult Attachment Interview (AAI) coding system, which assesses a speaker's state of mind with respect to loss, can give insight into how the bereaved mind operates, and that these insights may serve to guide clinical treatment approaches (Thomson, 2010). Sometimes in the AAI (Main et al., 2002) when a speaker has not come to terms with a loss, he or she may indicate at one point in the narrative that a loved one has died, but then later speak of him or her in present tense as if he or she is still living. Thomson (2010) reflects that it is considered an important part of the healing process to acknowledge that the death of the loved one is permanent and not reversible. Of course, Christians maintain the hope of being reunited in heaven; however, it is important to come to terms with the idea that the person is no longer present in this world, and one's internal beliefs, thoughts, and communications need to reflect this in a coherent way. When the external world (the person being dead) and the speaker's internal world (struggling to acknowledge the permanence of the loss) are at odds, this is considered incoherent (Main et al., 2002 as cited in Thomson, 2010). Thomson suggests that one aspect of coming to terms with the loss, also known as resolving the loss, may involve taking comfort from developing an "internalized sense of the existence of the loved one" (Thomson, 2010, p. 904).

When listening carefully to a speaker, we may notice that one may slip into present speech when talking about someone who is no longer living; for example, a speaker may say, "My dad is a lifelong Steelers fan" after having previously noted the speaker's father died some years ago. This may be an area to explore further in session, and if the counselor notices the client using speech that may be indicative that the internal shift and awareness that the loved one is gone have not become fully coherent as manifested by monitoring discourse as above, then this may be an area for very gentle challenging while supporting. For example, the counselor may use a reflecting statement to clarify, "So your dad passed but was a Steelers fan, or you mean your stepfather, who is still living? Help me understand." As the speaker allows humself to talk about the loss, grieve the loss, and come to resolve the loss (in terms of acknowledgment and acceptance), he may move toward a more coherent narrative when telling his attachment story.

## Defining Immediacy

Another advanced skill is immediacy. For the purposes of the skills to be mastered throughout this text, we will define immediacy as follows: being present with the person in the here and now and exploring what is going on in the moment. Sometimes, this includes exploring what is going on within the client's body. For example, in a session Dr. Sibcy spoke with his client, Alex, about her interpersonal history, and she at some point expressed feelings of sadness. Dr. Sibcy then asked Alex where she felt the sadness in the current moment, and Alex replied, "In my head." Dr. Sibcy went on to ask her a question that went something like this: "Where in your head do you feel the sadness?" This would be an example of immediacy. Please review the companion website to view this video.

## Types of Immediacy

Immediacy has been divided into two types (Egan, 1976). One type of immediacy has been labeled "here and now immediacy," and another is called "relationship immediacy." For the purposes of this text, we want to emphasize here and now immediacy.

Relationship immediacy involves having the capacity to have a dialogue with a relationship partner about where you stand within the relationship. here and now immediacy involves discussing what is going on right now, in the present moment, within the interpersonal interaction (Egan, 1976). We extend this to being able to discuss what is going on within the intrapersonal relationship, so we may also invite the client to explore what is going on within their interactions with themselves. Exploring immediacy may involve how their feelings are manifesting physically in their body, the influence their thoughts have on their feelings, and other intrapersonal processes.

## Obstacles to Immediacy

It is easy to avoid the present moment by thinking about the past. When we think about the past, we may contemplate things we wish would have been different that may manifest as regret. Another way to avoid experiencing the present may be to think about the future. Thoughts about the future may be associated with feelings of anxiety and dread and a general sense of impending doom. Another obstacle to immediacy could be fear of judgments of one's intentions; it can be difficult and risky to share one's thoughts, feelings, and intentions and there is the risk of misinterpretation. Thus, it is important to establish rapport and a sense of safety for the client so that they may launch out onto the top half of the circle and take the risk of exploring the present in the context of a safe supportive and empathic other.

## Strategies for Using Immediacy in Session

Let us look at how the counselor used immediacy with Chuck.

Relationship immediacy can involve the counselor assessing the unspoken messages being communicated, seeking to put them into words, and then inviting the client to explore the interpersonal dynamics through dialogue. Likewise, here and now interpersonal and intrapersonal interactions can be discussed.

**Counselor**: Chuck, as you talk about connecting with others, I notice that your eyes light up.

**Chuck:** Yes, this is good stuff! I like to be able to talk about these things with no fear of repercussions. I guess it feels good because I have not talked about it this freely before.

**Counselor**: It sounds like you are feeling relief as you share this with me and you feel safe within this therapeutic relationship and free to open up (relationship immediacy).

**Chuck:** Yes! Here's the thing, my buddy Cooper and I were just telling each other jokes the other day and I felt relieved! Then, I thought I want to feel like this more, and that is how I feel now.

**Counselor:** Chuck, as you become aware of this feeling of relief, where in your body are you experiencing it in this moment (intrapersonal here and now immediacy)?

**Chuck:** I think I feel it in my face, like I can't contain the smile.

**Counselor:** Sounds like you feel joy manifesting in your face coming out in your smile! So, recently you have found yourself wanting to feel relief, and even right now, in our interaction, you find yourself feeling relief and smiling as you reflect on the safety and the sense of freedom to talk about the situation (interpersonal relationship immediacy and here and now immediacy).

## To Do List

- Review the discussion on challenging while supporting and the concept of using the challenging "recipe" of you feel ___ on the one hand, and __ on the other hand. Please watch for challenging and other skills as you watch the video below.

## Video

**Challenging Skills**

- First, use the majority of the other skills discussed up to this point (door opener, ethical informed consent, minimal encouragers, paralanguage, key word encouragers, reflection of content, reflection of feeling, and reflection of meaning)

- Assess whether rapport has been established sufficiently for challenging

- Identify a lack of congruence, automatic negative thought, or other appropriate item to challenge

- Use a formula such as, "On the one hand I hear ___ and on the other hand I hear ___" or "It sounds like a part of you wants ___ and a part of you wants ___"

- Use reflecting skills to support the client as he or she responds to the challenge

## Recommended Reading

In order to learn more about the skills of challenging and immediacy, attachment-related incongruence/disorganization, and the other topics discussed in this chapter, we recommend the texts below for further study:

© Shutterstock.com

- Egan, G. (1975). *The skilled helper: A model for systematic helping and interpersonal relating.* Pacific Grove, CA: Brooks Cole.

- Egan, G. (1976). *Interpersonal living: A skills/contract approach to human relations training in groups add to references.* Belmont, CA: Brooks Cole.

- Thomson, P. (2010). Loss and disorganization from an attachment perspective. *Death Studies, 34*(10), 893–914.

## Chapter Summary

Confrontation is a term that has often had a negative connotation. We prefer to reframe confrontation as "challenging while supporting." It is appropriate to use challenging while supporting in some circumstances; however, it is a risk to the relationship so it should be used sparingly and only after "strong rapport has opened the door," as our colleague Dr. Kuhnley would say. All of the skills discussed up to this point should be often used to increase rapport levels and build the relationship (except perhaps questions if used wrongly); challenging should be used more sparingly. If challenged prematurely, the client may feel misunderstood, so ensure it is used appropriately. Challenging should always be balanced with support, as communicated by the other skills used up to this point. Times when it may be appropriate to use challenging include when there is a lack of congruence between thoughts and feelings or goals and behaviors, or perhaps when there are automatic negative thoughts. A formula for using challenging is, "A part of you wants ___ and a part of you wants ___" or "On the one hand you want ___ and on the other hand you want___." Immediacy is another advanced skill introduced in this chapter. Immediacy helps bring the client into the present moment. There are different types of immediacy. One type is relationship immediacy, which involves each person discussing where in the relationship they are with respect to one another. A second type of immediacy is "here and now" immediacy, which can be intrapersonal or interpersonal and may involve discussing feelings one is experiencing within himself or herself in the present moment and/or what he or she is experiencing with respect to the counselor in the present moment.

## Chapter Thirteen

# Case Conceptualization, Scaling, and Preliminary Goal Setting

### Anita Kuhnley and Gary Sibcy

*Goals allow you to control the direction of change in your favor.*

—Brian Tracy (Fasano, 2015, p. 32)

## Chapter Learning Objectives

- To identify a model of case conceptualization (CACREP 11.F.5.g, 2016, p. 12)
- To explore strategies for developing measurable outcomes for clients using scaling and SMART goals (CACREP II.F.5.i, 2016, p. 12)
- To include a focus on interpersonal relationships and a systems approach to conceptualizing clients (CACREP II. F.5.b, 2016, p. 11)

## Chapter Overview

The skills discussed in the previous chapters are necessary but not sufficient. If we end with reflecting skills and do not progress to setting goals and challenging the client to participate in purposeful counseling, then the client may feel understood but may stagnate. Thus, we also use intentional empathy as a vehicle for goal setting. For example, we had a family session at a private practice, where the husband was very angry, and he was eating the clinician's lunch. After some time of this, the clinician went to get his supervisor. His supervisor turned up the empathy and said things like, "That makes sense that you would feel angry about that' "That sounds frustrating," etc. The client was then eating out of his supervisor's hand so to speak. Then, the supervisor went on to say, "And you want us to help you with this, right?" and began setting goals after validating the client's feeling and expressing empathy. Remember that empathy is an important precursor to goal setting. In this chapter, we will explore case conceptualization, a model for case conceptualization, strategies for using scaling to assess the intensity of feelings, and unpack the SMART (specific, measurable, attainable, realistic, timely) goals goals acronym for goal setting. Moreover, some insight into the change process is explored through attachment theory.

Just as clients can get overwhelmed by the therapeutic process and facing life's challenges, therapists can also feel overwhelmed. This is why, in part, training programs divide up the process of training master's level clinicians into different courses such as counseling skills and techniques, psychopathology, and diagnosis and treatment planning. In the diagnosis and treatment planning course, you will learn more about case conceptualization, treatment planning, and goal setting. However, in order to engage in purposeful counseling, it is helpful to have agreed-upon goals that direct the session. So, we will discuss strategies for advanced skills such as case conceptualization and preliminary goal setting. Note, it is beyond the scope of this text to cover these topics fully, so take some time to explore the recommended reading and stay tuned for more on this in the diagnosis and treatment planning texts and course.

## Case Conceptualization

Len Sperry and Jonathan Sperry wrote a text entitled *Case Conceptualization: Mastering this Competency with Ease and Confidence* (2012), which has promulgated a systematic approach to case conceptualization among counselors. Sperry, along with several of his colleagues, shared his approach at the 2018 American Counseling Association Annual conference in Atlanta, GA, with a large group of clinical mental health counselors and other helping professionals.

The increased focus on case conceptualization in a more systematic way is in part due to the influence of third-party payers, which are companies that often pay for medical expenses for individual clients and include Medicare, Medicaid, Anthem, and so on. These third-party payers impose an accountability that is facilitated by case conceptualization (Sperry & Sperry, 2012). Sperry and Sperry report that the past 20 years have been a very fruitful season in terms of a proliferation of psychotherapy research, and this increase in the number of scientific studies and even randomized controlled trials has led in part to an increase in accountability for clinical mental health counselors, who should go beyond staying up to date on the current research being conducted on effective treatments and should begin to apply it to their work. Case conceptualization provides a framework for doing just that (Elles, Sperry, & Sperry 2002).

Sperry and Sperry's (2012) approach to case conceptualization has its roots in several different theoretical orientations including the following: cognitive behavioral therapy, dynamic therapy, Adlerian therapy, and solution-focused therapy, as well as a number of other theoretical approaches. It is beyond the scope of this book to explore comprehensive models of case conceptualization because practitioners cannot learn all the different components of providing sound psychotherapy in one text or course. These processes are divided into bite-size pieces (or book-size components), and the purpose of this book is to explore some strategies that the beginning counselor learning counseling skills can use to inform their skill usage until they complete this portion of training. Later, the counselor in training can move on to a full immersion in the process of learning to diagnose and develop treatment plans and conceptualize cases. We recommend Sperry and Sperry's textbook entitled *Case Conceptualization: Mastering this Competency with Ease and Confidence* for a more comprehensive discussion on the topic.

What is case conceptualization? **Case conceptualization** may be considered a tool in the counselor's tool kit that helps with the process of treatment planning and identifying the best interventions to facilitate client movement toward treatment goals. One of the approaches to case conceptualization we like to use is BASIC ID.

# Video

Please take a moment to visit the companion site to view the video where Dr. Sibcy discusses the BASIC ID model for case conceptualization and applies it to the sessions conducted with Alex.

In this video, Dr. Sibcy explains how he was conceptualizing the case with Alex. Here is a recap of the session he is referring to: Alex noted that she had been feeling down since she graduated from college and her friends moved away. He assessed her depression levels by assessing changes in things like sleep, appetite, mood, etc. He also assessed for suicidal thoughts or fantasy and ruled out suicidal ideation. Alex noted she was staying in bed quite a bit to avoid going to work or going out because she did not feel like getting up. Please watch this video to hear Dr. Sibcy's thoughts as he was conceptualizing this case.

BASIC ID is a model that explores: behavior, affect, sensation, imagery, cognition, interpersonal relationships, and drugs. In the video Dr. Sibcy also explores an advanced skill set/approach and discusses how you might decide whether to use behavioral activation, interpersonal forms of therapy, cognitive therapy, or interpersonal therapy. He also explores how behavior activation can be as effective as medication in some situations, but how referral to a psychiatrist for medication evaluation may be indicated if needed. He explains a three-stage approach that he may use to help the client.

# A Case Conceptualization Model: BASIC ID

One of the purposes of this chapter is introduce some case conceptualization models. The tools that counselors need to have available to them go beyond just one theoretical perspective—one lens for trying to make sense of complex clinical cases—but rather an understanding of evidence-based practices and theory. The field of mental health used to be dominated by an approach, some call **schoolism**. In schoolism, one takes the last name of a theorist and turns it into an adjective and identifies themselves with that theorist's approach. For example, many therapists in the past may have described themselves as Rogerian, Freudian, Beckian, and so forth. Our field is now, in the era of managed care, moving toward **evidence-based practices**. Evidence-based practices are integrative approaches to decision making in clinical work that weave together three different components: (a) client preferences, (b) therapist expertise, and (c) research evidence (Spring, 2007). Thus, given client preferences, therapist expertise, and research on effective practice, it is necessary to have multiple lenses rather than just the lens of one theoretical perspective. It is important to see that there are multiple ways of looking at the same problem.

It is ironic to see how our field is sometimes slow to adapt to changes in research and findings related to what works (and changes in technology), despite the fact that one of our purposes is to help our clients change, adjust, and adapt to transitions. There is a tendency in the field of mental health to be rather archaic in the way that we think about psychological, emotional, and biopsychosocial problems. In medicine, interestingly, physicians recognize that there are multiple systems that operate within the body. Although each system in and of itself is crucial to human survival and biological survival, at the same time, they all need to work together (notice the theme of integration not only spiritually but also in other ways throughout this text). Sometimes complex clinical diagnoses in medicine require physicians to understand how the different systems within the body operate together, for example, how the heart can influence the lungs, the lungs can influence the heart, the kidneys can influence the heart, and the kidneys can influence the liver. They all have ways of influencing each other, and when one system goes awry, then it can affect all the others.

Well, in many training programs, especially counselor education programs, people are still taught to think like schoolists; sometimes a counselor will enjoy his or her supervisor's methods and use those same methods when training his or her supervisees—they may then go on to share: I am from the Adlerian school, or I am from the Freudian school, or I am from the behaviorist school, or the cognitive school, or the emotional school—as if all these are different systems and one of them is true and all the other ones are false. This is outdated thinking, if you will, and "schoolism" is dead. In medicine, it would be absurd for physicians to say, "I am a cardiologist, and cardiology is all that matters. It is the heart of the matter anyway," or for a pulmonologist to say, "The lungs are the breath of life, and without the lungs no one could live, so they are the most important organ." They all recognize the importance and context or role within the body (take a moment to review the introduction and the corresponding video to hear the words of Dr. Hawkins for more on the importance of context). Although a physician may specialize in one system, that does not mean that he or she devalues other areas of medicine. So, likewise, we need to take this approach in the bio-psycho-social-spiritually integrated models of human functioning.

A case formulation model that we sometimes used is derived from one articulated by Arnold Lazarus called **BASIC ID** (Lazarus, 1981, 1989). Lazarus was in agreement with other colleagues that therapy could be thought of as "coping skills training" (Lazarus, 1989, p. 224) and that many different sets of coping skills are needed for different areas of life; thus he offered his model BASIC ID, which we will unpack here. BASIC ID is an acronym of the following:

- **Behavior**

- **Affect**, which referred to emotions

- **Sensations**, primarily referring to physical sensations that people experience

**(BASIC ID) Model**
an acronym that Arnold Lazarus used to define personality and his multimodal approach to treatment, seeking to address the discrete aspects of personality and the intersection between them. Lazarus approach "multimodal therapy" consists of comprehensive

- **Imagery**, images that come into people's heads

- **Cognition**, having to do with not just the content of what a person is thinking or the beliefs that they may hold but also the processes of cognitive thinking or cognition

- **Interpersonal Relationship** concepts in a personal context in which some problem may unfold

- **Drugs**, which refers to the biological or somatic aspects of what may be occurring for an individual, which could include exploring whether one is on any medication or experiencing any physical problems (this also relates to nutrition, exercise, and any physiological ailments; Lazarus, 1989).

Imagine that these are all puzzle pieces that make up a personality, and all require considerations for treatment (see Figure 13.1).

assessment and treatment of a client using the BASIC ID, which addresses client behaviors, affect, sensations, imagery, cognitions, interpersonal relationships, and physiological needs including psychopharmacological drugs (see **Chapter 16** by Dr. Kuhnley for more on the topic of psychopharmacology), nutrition, exercise, and physiological challenges.

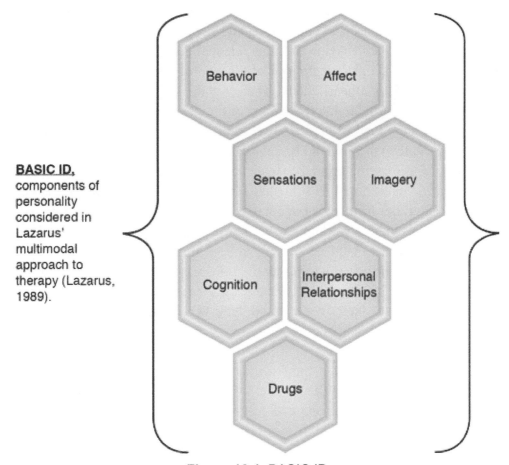

**BASIC ID,** components of personality considered in Lazarus' multimodal approach to therapy (Lazarus, 1989).

**Figure 13.1.** BASIC ID.
© Kendall Hunt Publishing Company

Lazarus looked at therapy primarily in terms of analyzing a specific problem. For example, if our client has a diagnosis of panic disorder, and she experiences a panic attack, one of the methods used across multiple treatment approaches is a situation analysis. Using a situation analysis, you would ask a person for a specific time and place where she had a panic attack, and in this you will conduct an analysis of these different dimensions, these different aspects of functioning. Lazarus at the firing order—in other words, which aspect, which dimension, comes online or fires first. You may counselor a person that says she had a panic attack on her drive home from her job as a teacher. In this scenario, it has been a stressful day—the kids were behaving in an unruly fashion in her classroom, and she has been pretty stressed out. As she drives home, she starts feeling her heart racing, and she feels her chest tightening. She thinks, "Oh my gosh, this is terrible. I am having a cardiac event. I might be having a heart attack. What in the world is wrong with me? This is terrible." The next thing you know, she starts sweating, and her breathing becomes more labored. She starts to think that maybe she needs to go to the hospital and get some immediate medical attention, so she drives to the hospital and on the way she calls her husband and tells him what is happening. He says, "You're just anxious, and you've had a bad day. Don't go to the hospital; you're going to be fine." She hangs up on him, furious about the fact that he ignores the severity of these events and does not take them seriously, and she goes to the ER. Using the BASIC ID model from Lazarus's perspective, you could break this thing down and ask, "What was the firing order of these events?" One thing that may stand out is that she was driving down the road after a long day of work. Behaviorally, she was in her car, and she was coming home from a hard day of work. Interpersonally, she was working with kids and with a classroom full of noise and commotion and stress and she may be primed for anxiety. These experiences address the behavior and interpersonal components, if you will. She noticed her heart racing and her chest tightening, physical sensations. The sensations came first, and then she had this thought: "This is a heart attack. There's something really wrong with me. This is dangerous." These are catastrophic interpretations of the physical sensations. (On a side note, if in fact she does have some kind of cardiac disease or some kind of physical problem that has already been diagnosed, then these would be catastrophic cognitions. If you are driving in the car and you have these kind of symptoms, then you start sweating, and cardiac concerns have not been ruled out already, then it might be something that you actually do want to get checked out. However, we know from her history that she has been to the ER four or five times for this and has had an EKG and a medical workup, so we know that she does not have any underlying physical biological issues that could be causing these symptoms. This is important to keep in mind). To go further then, she called her husband on the phone while she was driving to the ER, which is another behavior. This action also encompasses the interpersonal dimension. The spouse appeared to minimize the, at least in her mind. She perceived him as being unhelpful and uncaring; thus her emotional reaction to this was that she became angry, which actually intensified these symptoms even more.

If we look at this scenario within the Lazarus BASIC ID framework in *the Multimodal Theory: A Primer*, we can get an idea of the firing order of these different dimensions of functioning. And this can be very important as we think about treatment planning and what kind of interventions we may need to utilize. It may also give us some more information about areas to explore, for example, the nature of her job and how it is that she has experienced it as being stressful. There may be changes at her work. She may have a new boss. She may have another teacher she is having conflict with. She may find that some of the constraints on teachers due to standardized testing have impacted her job satisfaction. She may have originally gone into teaching because she wanted to make a difference in kids' lives and teach them at the same time, but now there is an emphasis in education on standards of learning the need for testing. Additionally, she is now primarily evaluated on how well her kids do on tests, not how well she actually teaches them or deals with their special concerns that may come into the classroom. This may be a shift, whereas before she was able to not get so stressed out about having kids that were not doing as well or kids that were having behavioral problems or emotional dysregulation-type problems. However, now these kids dominate most of her time and attention and she cannot really teach the material. The only way to learn what is really underneath this is to explore this with her using the basic skills of paraphrasing, reflection of content, reflection of feeling, and eventually reflection of meaning, but remember skills are important to understand her stress.

Second, age may be a factor; this woman is between 35 and 40 years old and has no history of heart disease, but it is a good question about whether or not there has been someone in her life who has died from a heart attack or that she has heard of somebody who has died of a heart attack or if she has for years been concerned with somatic symptoms and catastrophizes but now has focused on her heart. These are important considerations. Then if you are going to treat panic disorder from a cognitive-behavioral perspective, you are interested in the fact that when she gets these physical sensations that are very common physical sensations when people are stressed in normal ways, but when she gets these physical sensations, she **catastrophizes** them. Note, catastrophizing is a type of automatic negative thought; it has also been referred to as "awfulizing" and involves predicting the worst. Now, this is an important way of conceptualizing panic disorder within a cognitive-behavioral tradition and represents the core types of strategies that would be utilized in a treatment plan using cognitive-behavioral therapy and a specific adaptation called panic control treatment developed by David Barlow (Barlow & Craske, 2006). In the treatment, helping her see the relationship between her physical sensations, her catastrophic interpretations of those sensations, and the worsening of her panic symptoms would be important. Looking at the behavioral components, one important aspect has to do with the safety behavior—the need, desire, the drive to go to the ER, as she has already been there numerous times and has already found that she does not have anything that can fulfill a physical diagnosis.

So, BASIC ID may help us conceptualize the different areas of personality a problem behavior is influencing and in what order. Furthermore, some more advanced skills such as scaling can be used to assess the severity of the symptoms; for example, perhaps this client could report her average anxiety that week on a scale and we could use this self-reported information to help monitor her progress. Scaling can be a helpful tool, and now we will turn our focus to discussing this strategy.

**Video**

## Case Conceptualization (Gary Sibcy)

**Video**

## Using BASIC-ID

## Scaling

Many times, clients come into counseling and report that they are feeling overwhelmed. They may complain of having too much stress, too much to do, too much debt, too much tiredness, or some other "too." There is an advanced skill set that can give us the tools to begin helping clients measure progress in small, bite-size pieces. You have heard the saying, "How do you eat an elephant? One bite at a time" (never mind that we have never wanted to eat an elephant). However, before employing any of the advanced skills we will discuss here, it is important to remember that the client's thoughts and feelings need to be validated and that the client may find the idea of attacking the current goal or problem daunting. (Barlow et al., 2017). Once a client feels understood by the empathic other and validated, it can be easier to begin forward movement in the stages of change.

In this chapter, we will introduce the advanced technique of scaling. This goes beyond listening to listening that is intentional, purposeful, goal-oriented and gives the counselor the resources to do a basic form of assessment to measure progress. Oftentimes, clients present to therapy with a concern about stress, sadness, low mood, and so on. Scaling can allow a client to assess the degree of overwhelm they are experiencing and identify a small step they can take to move even a quarter of a point up or down the scale, or scaling can sometimes make things that are abstract, more concrete, and easier to measure.

The solution-focused approach to counseling is a good theoretical framework for conceptualizing the goal-setting process. In the solution-focused approach to treatment, the therapist seeks to help the client formulate his or her goals in positive terms (De Shazer, Dolan, & Korman, 2007). For example, if a client came into counseling and shared, "I would like to not feel so stressed out all the time, like I have no peace," the counselor using a solution-focused framework for goal setting may respond by saying, "So, I am hearing you say that you would like to increase the level of peace that you are experiencing." This allows the client to approach peace and scale this experience and to have a positive goal to approach; the approach goal can be a powerful motivator in therapy.

Scaling involves identifying a continuum. One commonly conceptualized scale during graduate school is stress; some people may portray it something like this.

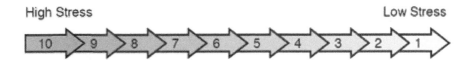

Counselors may use the continuum to identify a baseline level of stress and then to measure progress at intervals throughout therapy. Both ends of the spectrum are defined and are often referred to as anchors. The challenge with this particular example is that it emphasizes avoidance rather than approach. The client is avoiding high stress or seeking to move away from something rather than to move toward something. How could you transform this scale to edit the goal to emphasize an approach goal?

**One suggestion is to ask the question:** If I am moving away from _____ (fill in the blank by inserting the feeling that is troubling the client or the feeling that needs to be decreased), then what am I moving toward?

In this case, the client may be moving toward a sense of peace as he or she is moving away from stress. In order to create an approach goal, the counselor may revise the scale to look like this:

Psychologically, moving toward peace fits with subconscious thoughts related to progress and the inclusion of forward movement rather than backpedaling. Consider the various metaphors that we use to describe progress: "forward momentum," "moving on up," "rising to the next level," "up-leveling," "building upon what was learned," "progressing to the next level," and "rising to new heights." In keeping with the idea of forward movement we seek to identify approach goals.

Recall in science classes long ago learning about potential and kinetic energy. potential energy is energy at rest. and kinetic energy is energy in motion. As clients take even small steps and make slight movement toward their goals, then the momentum and the synergistic cycle can begin. Similarly, when you have a row of dominoes standing up in a line and you 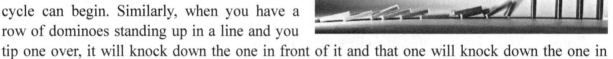 tip one over, it will knock down the one in front of it and that one will knock down the one in front of it and so on.

Likewise, life is systemic, and when one shift or change occurs, it can cause a ripple effect in the system that can lead to other changes.

Although we want to be selective and intentional about the questions used in therapy, scaling questions can be valuable and a good use of a question. They can also double as immediacy and can allow us to check in to assess where a client is in the current moment on the particular scale.

Sometimes, we will encounter clients who have a very difficult time articulating their

© Alison Coles/Shutterstock.com

goals in positive terms; one option in these cases is to use a strategy form the solution-focused school of thought called "the miracle question." The miracle question involves allowing a client to use his or her imagination to picture what things would be like if the problem was not present. The miracle question can be validating to clients, especially those who are struggling with a problem that they would assess to be intense or unsolvable, chronic, persisting, and/or unrelenting. In these situations, imagining a miracle occurred gives the client the opportunity to imagine what life would be like with the manifestation of solutions without challenging his or her thoughts related to the pervasiveness of the problem at hand.

There are different variations of the miracle question, but we suggest starting with asking permission. The counselor may say, for example, "Would you feel comfortable with me asking you a question a little bit out of the ordinary?" Or, "Do you mind if we do an exercise that is a bit different?" We have never had a client say no before, although sometimes their yes may be a bit tentative. The most frequent response we have heard from clients is, "Okay, is it bad?"

If the client gives permission to proceed, then we typically begin with helping him or her imagine a scenario. The script may go something like this: "Imagine that you go home tonight and you put on your favorite pajamas, and then you fall into a deep sleep. While you are asleep a miracle happens. However, no one else knows that the miracle has happened except for you. When you wake up in the morning, what do you notice is different about the first thought that you have?" We then add a series of other questions after using the reflecting skills to validate each answer. So, after we ask what is different about the client's thoughts, we may ask, "What would you notice was different about your behaviors?" In other words, what may you do after this miracle that you may not normally do?

We may then go on to explore other differences or changes that may be present in thoughts, feelings, or behaviors that are under the client's jurisdiction, for example:

- What would be different about how you are feeling? (consider who is in the client's inner circle, and who they come into contact with on a daily basis to tailor this question to your specific client).

- What would your spouse notice was different about you?

    Or

    What would your roommate notice was different about you?

    What would your neighbor notice was different about you?

    What would your parents notice was different about you?

    What would your siblings notice was different about you?

    What would your coworkers notice was different about you?

    What would your classmates notice was different about you?

    (If the client is a spiritual person) What would be different about the way you interact with God?

- What would be different about your environment (modify to home, office, care, etc.)?

## Caveats

Notice that when implementing the miracle question, we tend to specify the particular differences we are looking for. A caveat is to avoid questions that encourage the client to focus on someone else changing. Namely, we could be assessing for differences in thoughts, feelings, behaviors, interpersonal interactions, and so on. Instead of just asking a general question about what is different, we name specifics because sometimes a client may want someone else to change and may focus on that instead of on what is under his or her jurisdiction.

David Burns emphasizes the options that people have when facing interpersonal conflicts. In Burns's text entitled *Feeling Good Together* (2008), the author describes a case he dealt with where the client was having marital problems and was presenting for individual therapy (Note, this is a highly recommended text). He noticed that the sessions had begun to form a pattern of the client reading a litany of complaints about his spouse from his journal. Burns realized the therapy did not seem to be goal directed or productive, and so Burns pointed out to the client, that he had three choices regarding what to do about the problem he was experiencing with his wife. The options Burns laid out were the following:

1. File for divorce or separation.

2. try couples therapy to save his marriage.

3. continue what he is presently doing, venting, and maintaining the status quo

In other words, Burns describes the three interpersonal options as follows:

1. Leaving the relationship

2. Working to make the relationship better

3. Maintaining the status quo

Of the three possibilities, leaving and working on the relationship are not the most popular. Burns (2008) indicates that the most popular option is maintaining the status quo. However, the challenge is that inherently the maintenance of the status quo is at odds with treatment goals and movement toward change. Using scaling may help clients to take responsibility for their emotions or stressors and can help with purposeful counseling. Purposeful counseling helps clients choose options that will lead toward the development of an internal locus of control. **Locus of control** refers to the degree to which an individual expects that he or she is responsible for an outcome or a behavior and is thought to be a somewhat stable trait that does not change considerably over time (Kim & Lee, 2018).

Locus of control is also closely linked to a person's motivation that fuels their behaviors (Kim & Lee, 2018). There are two types of locus of control, internal and external. **Internal locus of control** relates to a person's effort and abilities. It can be defined as one's sense of responsibility over behaviors under his or her jurisdiction. However, **external locus of control** includes behaviors or processes that are out of the direct control of the self, such as powerful others. If a client has an external locus of control, then this may manifest in more passive behaviors. In contrast, if a client has a more internal locus of control, then this may manifest in an enhanced tendency to take responsibility for life's challenges and engage actively in problem-solving activities. Internal locus of control has been a positive predictor of success outcomes such as career adaptability.

Thus, as we work with clients on developing goals using strategies such as SMART or scaling, it is important to focus (and redirect focus in a gentle and appropriate manner) on outcomes that are within the client's internal locus of control. In order for clients to accomplish their goals, they may have to give up blame. Recall from the opening quote in this chapter, profound achievement comes from taking full responsibility for one's life, and this requires giving up blame.

*A Concept to Contemplate*

Take a moment to contemplate the concept of locus of control. If a client is able to move toward an internal locus of control and take responsibility for his or her own future and struggles rather than waiting for important or powerful others to change, then he or she is more likely to be successful in reaching therapeutic goals in treatment. As you contemplate the two types of locus of control (internal and external), take a moment to consider your life and experiences. What are some of the experiences that you can control and what are some that you cannot? See the circles below and list out in bullet point format the items that you can control in the circle on the left and the ones you cannot in the circle on the right.

© Shutterstock.com

**Activity**

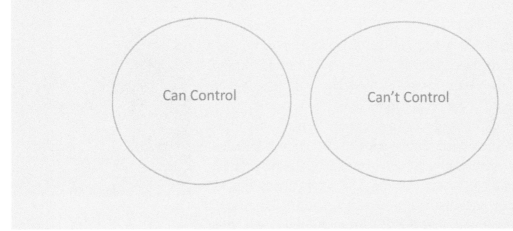

## The "Formula First Session Task"

Another advanced skill that comes to us from the solution-focused school of thought is the formula first session task. (Adams, Piercy, & Jurich, 1991). Research shows that when the "formula first session task" was used with some families and the problem-focused approach with others, those families who experienced the formula first session task "were significantly higher on measures of family compliance, clarity of treatment goals, and improvement in the presenting problem" (Adams et al., 1991, p. 277). Anecdotally in our own practice we have seen some benefits associated with the use of this intervention as well. So let us now explore the intervention.

Like the heading implies, this intervention typically comes at the end of the first session and is designed to help the client change out his or her sunglass lenses. The question as we like to use it is as follows:

- I would like you to think about the following question, between now and out next session:

- What is going on in your life, right now, that you would like to see continue to happen?

This question helps clients to shift their paradigm of thinking and helps them to change out their lenses. If they have had sunglasses with blue lenses, for example, and have been focused on everything that is blue in their present life circumstances and everything that is problematic, this helps them to shift focus to rose-colored glasses or solution-oriented glasses (this reminds me of the sunglasses made by Oakley that are called "The Unstoppables") in order to move toward solutions.

## Conceptualizing Change Based on Theory: Secure Model of Change

*Effective therapy is like the art and science of cooking.*
One of the reasons people seek out counseling is that they are seeking change. Clients present to counseling when they are feeling stuck, experiencing pain, or needing relief (and in some cases when referred or required to come by someone else). The definition of insanity is doing the same thing over and over again and expecting different results. In order for counselors to help clients facilitate change and reach agreed-upon goals, it may be helpful to understand how changes can be facilitated. In this section, we will discuss a model called "The Secure Model of Change." (Clinton & Sibcy, 2012).

© BGSmith/Shutterstock.com

In the quote that introduces this section, there is a parallel made between counseling and cooking. We do not consider ourselves to be great chefs, but we can appreciate the fact that cooking is both an art and a science. The science may include factors such as the fact that it may take about 7 to 10 minutes to brown ground beef, and that it is important to make sure there is no remaining pink to confirm it has cooked. The art may involve factors such as using an array of different-colored bell peppers, corns, and various colored beans to create a medley of colors and flavors. We enjoy making chili. Like any other dish, you need to know some essential ingredients for the recipe to turn out well, for example: beef (or chicken or another source of protein), chili beans, onions, tomatoes, and different seasonings. The chef needs to know how the ingredients interact and complement one another. The chef also needs to appreciate how the ingredients can behave differently depending on their quality (e.g., using fresh tomatoes from the garden vs. store-bought tomatoes vs. canned tomatoes).

However, a good recipe requires more than just the right ingredients. A chef cannot just take all the ingredients and toss them in a bowl like a salad. Preparing chili involves a process: a sequence of steps. You need to know which ingredients to start with and how long to cook each one and at what temperature. A good cook is acutely aware of the importance of temperature: when to turn the burner on the stove on high and when to bring it down to just a simmer. In the good chef's arsenal of tools, he or she probably has a meat thermometer, helping him ensure that the meat is cooked to the proper temperature. Likewise, the good counselor appreciates the therapeutic power of emotion. The difference is that the chef simply has to turn the knob on the stove to adjust the heat, whereas the counselor requires great skill in regulating emotional activation (see Chapter 9 for a detailed discussion on how to validate a client's feelings through the process of reflecting, which can sometimes help decrease the intensity of the feeling as the client feels understood by the empathic other). There are several steps a counselor must use in order to engage in the process of regulating a client's emotion. Let us look at the systematic process involved here. First, the counselor must understand the mechanisms involved in turning up versus turning down emotional intensity or energy, as there are no dials on our client's foreheads for adjusting emotional intensity. For example, one strategy for decreasing the intensity of emotion involves using termination or closing skills, such as summarizing, consolidating gains, homework, and goal setting, which may be used to help bring closure to a session and allow the client to disengage in a more positive state of mind and emotion than if the session were to abruptly end while engaged in a strong negative emotion or discussion on something very painful and sad.

© ARENA Creative/Shutterstock.com

For example, we may be talking with a client about a transition, and emotions of stress are dialed up. Consider the therapeutic dialogue below as a strategy for using these closing skills to lower the emotional intensity and bring closure to the session:

- **Bella:** Yes, all my friends back home are tough to keep in touch with since I moved away to graduate school, and I feel so stressed. I don't know which friends to invest in here, or whether or not I should spend time trying to work on those relationships since my friends live far away. If I knew I would move back there, then I definitely would! But since I do not know where I will be, I am not sure I want to do that (5 minutes remaining in session). It is just kind of overwhelming and stressful because I don't know what to do.

- **Counselor:** So, it sounds like this has been a time of transition and you are sorting through the question of how your friendships will transition as you transition (reflection of content). There is some uncertainty about the future, and you are feeling stress (reflection of feeling) right now as you face these questions. If we were to scale your stress versus peace on a scale of 1-10, 1 being no peace/highly stressed and 10 being very peaceful where would you be on the scale? (advanced skill of scaling)

- **Bella:** Well, right now I guess I would be at about a five. I mean it is not killing me, but it is something I do think about and worry about. I guess. I worry some days more than others.

- **Counselor:** Okay, so it is a concern and you are right in the middle of the stress/peace continuum at about a five (reflecting content).

- **Bella:** Yes, right in the middle I guess.

- **Counselor:** Okay, well, it looks like we have about seven sessions remaining, and I am wondering by the end of our time together where would you like to be on that scale (preliminary goal setting)?

- **Bella:** Eventually I would like to be at about a ten, but at least maybe a 7 would be better.

- **Counselor:** Okay, so we are aiming for as much peace as is possible, but about a 7 would be an improvement (reflection of content).

- **Bella:** Yeah.

- **Counselor:** Okay, so as we reach the end of our session (preparing client to transition), what is one thing we can do between now and next time that may help you move just a half step up the scale to a 5.5 (collaboratively seeking to agree on a next step/homework assignment)?

- **Bella:** Hmmm, let me think for a minute (24-second pause). Well, I used to journal and whenever I would journal I would feel so much more peace. So, I guess I could journal about the situation and ask the Lord to give me direction.

- **Counselor:** Okay, so between now and next time you plan to journal and take some time to pray and seek wisdom from God about how to transition your friendships (reflection of content; validation of goal, preparing client for follow up in next session).

- **Bella:** Yeah! I used to journal a lot. It has been a while, but I think it will help!

- **Counselor:** I look forward to talking with you in our next session about your journal entries and how they impacted your level of peace.

© vectorfusionart/Shutterstock.com

Now that we have discussed one of the requirements for a counselor to engage in skilled emotion regulation with a client, which involves dialing down intensity through the use of closing skills, let us now look at a second skill. The counselor must be highly skilled at detecting changes in emotional activation: this includes noticing when a client's emotions change and enhancing the client's awareness of these feelings (this enhanced client awareness is sometimes achieved through the use of skills such as reflecting emotion and using scaling to assess the intensity of emotion), appreciating their meaning (exploring meaning and asking a client to examine what it means to them to experience a particular emotion in a given situation can help the counselor assess meaning), andregulating emotion (identifying the emotion, scaling the emotion, using

**The Metaphor of the Good Chef and the Art and Science of Cooking** Just like cooking is both an art and science, the art involving the additions of a pinch of one ingredient or another to add flavor and the variety of gradients to add color and flavor (such as bell peppers in different colors) The temperature or length at which meat has to cook is part of the science of cooking. Likewise, counseling is both an art and science that involves both knowing what research based strategies and skills are helpful to the client for a given presenting case, and the art of flexing with intentional competence and helping clients dial emotion up and down as appropriate.

immediacy to locate how the client is experiencing the emotion in the body, and using goal setting. Collaborative homework can help clients identify strategies for regulating and decreasing the intensity of emotions). Another function of collaborative homework is to facilitate growth and change (identifying the meaning behind the emotion, and perhaps asking what the emotion is telling the client, that is, sometimes sadness tells a client they have lost someone or something that was of great value to them).

We will refer to this metaphor of the good chef and the art and science of cooking throughout this text to help you appreciate some of the nuances involved in being a good counselor and the art and science of effective counseling and psychotherapy.

**A Verse to Remember:**
*Matthew 28:19:*
*"Go therefore and make disciples of all nations, baptizing them in the name of the Father and the son and the Holy Spirit."*

Now we want to build on the concept of secure base (recall, in Chapter 1, we discussed the theoretical foundations for counseling and also discussed the concept of the secure base. We also discussed how articulately Jesus emphasized the idea of launching out to explore from the secure base in Matthew 28:19, "Go therefore and make disciples of all nations, baptizing them in the name of the Father and the son and the Holy Spirit." Note, the secure base represents the place of security and safety that a child may experience in the presence of a sensitive caregiver from which he or she launches out and explores his or her environment). Remember, Bowlby (1988) defined the secure base in counseling as a springboard that the clinician provides for the client as place to launch into a discourse on emotion that is free flowing (Bowlby, 1988; Holmes, 1993), which is a characteristic of the narrative of one with a secure autonomous attachment style.

The secure base is a concept that can be applied, and we can use it to understand a transtheoretical model (TTM) of change, **which has also been called the behavior change model (Prochaska & Prochaska, 2016).** The TTM of change is based on the work of Prochaska and DiClemente (1982); they developed this model in an effort to move toward a more integrative model of change at a time when many different theoretical models were emerging. Prochaska developed the model out of an integration of over 18 different therapy systems (Prochaska, 1979). The theory of transtheoretical analysis developed out of four original tenets. The first was that there are preconditions for therapy, the second processes of change, the third that there is content to be changed, and the fourth the therapeutic relationship. The client's belief that therapy will be efficacious is one of the most important of the preconditions (see Chapter 2 for more on the important role that belief plays in counseling, both for the client and the therapist). Back in the 1980s, Prochaska and DiClemente indicated these beliefs and/or expectations could be problematic if a client's beliefs were not met, as then there was a greater likelihood of premature termination. At that time, this was thought to be one of the most important predictors of premature termination, and we believe it still is today. Prochaska identified common themes among the approaches such as increasing consciousness and catharsis. The TTM of change developed out of a focus on the process of change among groups of smokers who were seeking to kick the habit (Prochaska & DiClemente, 1982); some did so on their own and some through the course of therapy; however, there were common change processes that each of the groups engaged in. These processes were identified as follows:

1. Thinking about the idea of stopping smoking

2. Making the decision or determination to stop smoking

3. Actively making changes in habits and environment

More current work by Prochaska and Prochaska (2016) indicates six stages of change:

1. **Precontemplation**—not ready, not intending to take actions in the next 6 months

2. **Contemplation**—getting ready, intending to take action in the next 6 months

3. **Preparation**—ready to take action in the next 30 days

4. **Action**—have made the behavior change but for less than 6 months

5. **Maintenance**—doing the new healthy behavior for at least 6 months

6. **Termination**—confident with the change, not tempted to relapse (p. 215)"

It may be helpful to think of the TTM of change as a cycle (see Figure 13.2):

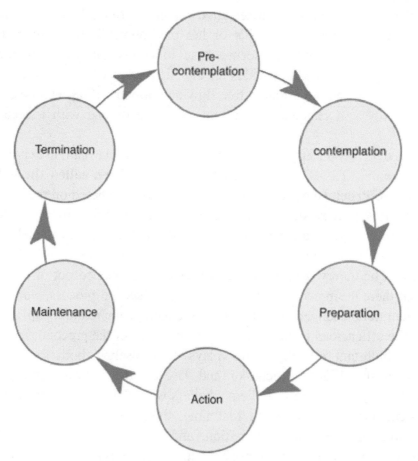

**Figure 13.2.** Six stages of change.
© Kendall Hunt Publishing Company

During the precontemplation stage of change, people may be thinking about change. Here people may feel stuck. They may not know how to change, or they may feel discouraged by failures in past efforts to change (Prochaska & Prochaska, 2016). Prochaska and Prochaska discuss how to facilitate clients' movement from a posture of defending habits to movement toward coping, thus making the transition from the precontemplation stage of change to the contemplation stage of change. It is important to meet clients where they are and validate their struggles and feelings as we discussed in Chapter 9 on reflecting feelings. Prochaska and Prochaska (2016), some of the greatest experts on change, indicate that the idea of moving from precontemplation to contemplation is like moving from the idea of wanting to buy oceanfront property to actually intending to buy oceanfront property. In peak vacation season, mid-July, in Virginia Beach, a hotel at a Marriott on a Monday night goes for $550.00 a night (as of July 2018) moving from desiring the view of the ocean for a day to actually intending to reserve a room at the Marriott on the

*Researchers have found that although some tend to label clients who are not ready for change "resistant," it may actually be the therapist or helping professional that is resistant to meeting a client where they are.*

oceanfront requires intentionality and the willingness to pay the price involved. Likewise, it is so with changes that clients may want to make therapeutically. Sometimes considering the challenge of making personal changes such as avoiding hitting the snooze button, giving up caffeine, giving up chocolate, fasting, or other common habits can give counselors the ability to empathize with clients in the precontemplation stage associated with making difficult changes.

## A Concept to Contemplate

© Shutterstock.com

Contemplate a change that you would like to make in your life that would likely increase the quality of your life in some way. For example, if you were to wake up about 10 minutes earlier each day to have some time for inspirational reading, if you were to avoid hitting snooze, if you were to add two hours a week of time spent volunteering, or some other changes you have been considering, what price would you have to pay?

Take a moment to contemplate answers to the following questions:

**What change may you want to think about thinking about making (a change if made would make your life better in some way, however small)?**

**If you were to make the above change, how would it improve the quality of your life?**

**What would it cost to make such a change? Consider time costs, financial costs, energy costs, and any other costs associated with the change.**

**On a scale of 1 to 10, where 10 = very certain and 1 = very uncertain, how certain are you that you would like to move from desiring to make this change to intending to make this change?**

**What would it be like if a researcher said you would never be 100% certain, so you cannot wait for your train to come in but have to drive it into the station?**

**Please contemplate the reasons that lead you to evaluate yourself at the particular number on the scale you selected.**

**What would it take to move from the place you are on the scale to a 1/4 of a point closer to certainty?**

**Would you be willing to make this change?**

If you answered yes in the questions above, who would you feel comfortable asking for accountability?

Based on your experience contemplating these questions, how difficult do you think it will be on average for clients to go through such a process that may be somewhat like the path of moving from precontemplation to contemplation?

on a scale of 1 to 10 with 1 representing extremely difficult and 10 representing very easy, how would you rate yourself on the scale?

Now, please rate your perception of the average client's level of difficulty changing very ingrained habits.

One of the unique aspects of the TTM of change or the stages of change model is that it brings this evidence-based therapeutic factor into the equation, which is "hope" (Prochaska & Prochaska, 2016). When people have perhaps reached contemplation or other stages of change in the past and then failed at the change process, they may become discouraged and thus begin to experience decreases in the hope of change.

You may have heard well-meaning friends, parents, or teachers, give a well-known recommendation to someone considering making a decision, that they were unsure about. What is this most common advice? "Have you thought about making a list of pros and cons regarding the situation?" The metaframework's approach involves using parts language (Breunlin et al., 2001), and if we were using strategies from that approach to help clients move from precontemplation to contemplation, we may appeal to the part of them who wants to change. Consider the following case:

Background: Casey would like to stop smoking, but she knows that smoking helps her feel relaxed and deal with stress. She worries that if she does not have her cigarette to look forward to each day that she will not be able to relax and may fall into a deep depression. How might you appeal to the part of herself that wants to change? Would it be ethical despite her concerns regarding depression? Take a moment to contemplate this.

| | |
|---|---|
| **Ms. Pondering:** | Since my boyfriend said he really wanted me to quit smoking because it is expensive, I have started thinking about the possibility. |
| **Dr. Change:** | It sounds like his words spurred you to begin considering making this life change. |
| **Ms. Pondering:** | Yes, well, maybe. I am actually scared that it could really mess me up. I mean, how will I deal with all the stress that I face, and what will I have to look forward to? The thought of life without having the relief of a cigarette to enjoy seems bleak. |
| **Dr. Change:** | It feels very scary to think about giving up something that has really helped you relax and deal with lots of stress. There is a part of you that is really not ready and concerned about even thinking about making the change. And at the same time you mentioned that there was a part of you beginning to think about thinking about it after your boyfriend mentioned it. |
| **Ms. Pondering:** | (laughs) Yes, I guess I am just thinking about thinking about it. I am not sure if it is really as great an idea as he thinks. I mean how would I deal with the stress? I guess part of me is scared. |
| **Dr.** | Okay, so part of you is scared. If that part of you had words what would it say? (Notice, Dr. |

**Change:**   Change is using parts language & working on calming and addressing the fear)

**Ms. Pondering:**   Well, I guess it would say that you have been smoking for a long time, You have tried to quit before and it has worked for a little while, but then life gets busy and stressful. It is something that helps you deal with the stress and taking care of five kids and working from home. Without that, that part of me is afraid at coming apart at the seams.

**Dr. Changes:**   So it has long been a part of the way you have managed stress, and it has helped bring relaxation in some ways. Giving that up would be hard, and there is a fear that it could cause other problems.

**Ms. Pondering:**   Yes, this is what I am feeling I guess.

**Dr. Change:**   Okay, let us take a look at other part of you the part that your boyfriend sparked and you told me about earlier that is thinking about thinking about it. Tell me about what that part of you would say.

**Ms. Pondering:**   Well, that part of me would say, I guess that there are other ways to relax such as taking a walk to clear my head, listening to some of my favorite music, being artistic, being out in nature, playing with my kids and dog (well sometimes) and that I could save some money and my boyfriend would be happy with it.

As the session continues, Dr. Change goes on to reflect both parts of Ms. Pondering's struggle. As she weighs the pros and cons, Dr. Change will encourage reflection and exploration of the part of her that wants change, and the hope that may be associated with the stages of change.

The contemplation stage of change involves thinking more fully about making changes and moving toward the preparation and action phases of change. It may involve confronting fears and other road blocks. Once one has contemplated the change process and need for change, there is a preparation stage that helps bridge the gap from thinking about change to acting to make changes in the action phase.

Once clients make it to the action phase and implement the changes, it is important to maintain change, which can be very difficult given the pressures and stresses of daily life, and the idea that many difficult or problematic behavior patterns begin as attempts to cope with various sources of stress. Eventually, therapists can work with clients to facilitate movement from action to maintenance to termination.

Identifying where clients are in the stages of change and meeting them where they are, validating, and working together to establish agreed-upon goals are an important part of the case conceptualization and change processes (we highly recommend Prochaska and Prochaska's text entitled *Changing to Thrive: Using the Stages of Change to Overcome the Top Threats to Your Health and Happiness*—see the section on Recommended Reading for more information).

This model of change can be applied across many different theoretical approaches. Throughout the text, we have drawn on the tenets of attachment theory to illuminate components of the therapeutic dialogue and the impact of the aptly used counseling skills. The TTM of change can be integrated with attachment theory (Clinton & Sibcy, 2012; Sibcy, 2007).

Our conceptual model involves at least six core attachment-based counseling tasks, each rooted in biblical principles and consistent with a wide range of theoretical orientations. They can be applied to clients with both common, uncomplicated problems and those suffering from more complex, serious clinical mental health disorders such as chronic depression and various types of trauma-related disorders. The acronym SECURE—safety, education, containment, understanding, restructuring, engagement—is used to aid memory of the six core tasks. For the purposes of this chapter, we are going to focus on the S, which represents safety. (Recall in Chapter 9 we discussed the importance of facilitating an atmosphere that allows for the development of felt safety within a client)

**Safety.** As noted previously, safety and a felt sense of security are important keys to therapeutic change. Just as it is difficult for individuals to move from precontemplation to contemplation without feeling they have the resources to pay the price or that they are understood and cared for in therapy, it can be difficult for a child or client to launch out to explore and make changes in the environment without coming from that sense of safety associated with the secure base and safe haven.

Also, we mentioned that various theorists have different terms to refer to the same concept: McCullough referred to this as "the safety zone," Winnicott called it the "holding environment," Bion, the "container," and of course, Bowlby termed it the "secure base" (see Figure 13.3).

All of the skills we have discussed so far with the exception of challenging are designed to increase the client's sense of felt safety and the therapeutic relationship. The task of safety involves a number of therapeutic skills and strategies. These are outlined in more detail below:

1. **Promoting a sense of felt security.** As you recall from Chapter 8, from the first few minutes of therapy, clients are assessing the therapist in terms of his or her ability to help them deal with whatever concerns motivated them to seek help from a qualified professional. Of course, there are situations where clients are not necessarily seeking help under their own volition (e.g., some outside party is forcing the client to get treatment, such is the case for clients who are court ordered or whose spouse is

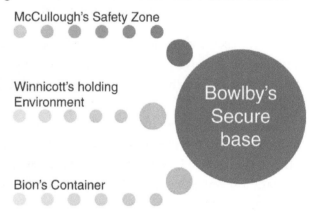

**Figure 13.3.**

Source: Anita Knight

giving them an ultimatum). Skilled therapists have a way about them that promotes a sense that they are trustworthy and helpful. This may involve a number of the skills we have discussed throughout this book, such as SOLER, empathic listening, reflection of content, reflection of feeling, summarizing, scaling, and purposeful counseling. However, in general, you must ask yourself if you have a knack for helping people feel at ease and comfortable when they are talking about their problems and concerns. In Chapter 3, covered many of the skills needed for fostering a sense of felt security, as many people decide what their impression of a person or in this case, a therapist, is within the first 500 to 1000 milliseconds of exposure to them (Willis & Todorov, 2006).

2. **Acceptance:** The therapeutic relationship is unique and powerful in many ways. Because of the characteristics of this relationship, it is different from most other close relationships. First, it involves a legal and ethical contract. What is discussed in therapy is confidential, with only a few statutory limits (e.g., the duty to report child and elder abuse, court orders, harm to self, or harm to others. See Chapter 5 for more on this topic). Second, the client is disclosing a great deal of sensitive, possibly shame-inducing material (e.g., affairs, drug use, and pornography use). Third, the therapist is committed to the acceptance of the client

as a person, independent of his or her behavior. This is a difficult task, especially when the client's behavior violates the values and beliefs of the therapist, and in some cases, the client himself or herself. Acceptance does not mean the therapist endorses these behaviors and beliefs (the difference between acceptance and endorsement is very important), but she accepts the client and works to remain warm, sensitive, open, and engaged. Finally, the therapist is committed to behave in a reliable and predictable way: starting and ending sessions on time, being available for appointments, being willing to discuss difficult, sometimes painful topics (e.g., the tragic death of a child), and so on. Skills we have discussed in previous chapters such as validating and reflecting clients' feelings, paraphrasing key content, using minimal encouragers, and exploring meaning can all communicate a sense of acceptance when used appropriately with empathic, mindful presence.

3. **Helping clients tell their story.** This quality takes on different forms over the course of therapy. Initially, it involves helping clients *tell their story*, starting with the chief presenting problem that brought them into therapy. This involves helping the client describe the factors that led up to this appointment, exploring the who, what, when, where, and why (although we do not directly ask why, we use the other skills to ascertain this information. See Chapter 11 on questions for more information on this) that prompted them to decide to pick up the phone and schedule an appointment. For many it takes a momentous event, a final straw as it were, for someone to decide, "I've got to get some help." As we will see, some clients are motivated primarily because of psychological symptoms, such as panic attacks, anger, depression, addictive behaviors such as drug use or pornography, or avoidance behaviors such as procrastination. These types of clients tend to have some insight, meaning they realize they have painful psychological symptoms and they want help or support overcoming them. As we will see, the counselor wants to explore and understand these symptoms and then explore the possible links between these symptoms of various life stressors; in order to do this, the counselor needs to use the listening skills such as minimal encouragers, key word encouragers, paraphrasing, and summarizing discussed in previous chapters (see Chapters 6–12). Other clients are motivated to seek help because of stressful life events: financial problems, loss of employment, conflicts in relationships, loss of loved ones, health problems, and so on. In these situations, the counselor seeks to understand (recall seeking to understand is the first rule of counseling) the nature of these problems and then inquires about how these stressors may be connected to painful psychological symptoms, such as depression, anxiety, and/or addictive behaviors. In Chapter 10, we covered some of the key skills involved in the first interview. Although we are not focusing directly on building your diagnostic skills per se, you will need to learn these counseling skills, also known as interviewing skills. These skills are used in order to successfully engage your clients in the first session of therapy, where you build, engage, and forge the basic foundation of the therapeutic alliance.

4. **Establishing a therapeutic alliance.** This is considered one of the most important common factors in counseling (Wampold, 2015). It contains three basic components (Bordin, 1979): (a) the bond, (b) an agreement on the goals of therapy, and (c) and an

agreement on the tasks or methods of therapy. We will discuss each of these components that contributes to the therapeutic alliance.

The *therapeutic bond* essentially refers to the affective quality of the relationships, meaning the sense of mutual trust, respect (as noted above), liking, and caring between both the patient and the client. The importance of this was drilled into us early in training. For example, Dr. Sibcy encountered a client whom we will refer to as Samantha, who really triggered him in a deep, guttural dislike. Whenever he saw her on his schedule, he would groan. He would hope and pray that she would not show up. There was so much about her and her way of being that irked him, for example, her lack of self-care, her inability to stay on topic, her raspy smoker's voice, and her mind-boggling ability to rattle on and on about apparently irrelevant topics. They made little progress in therapy and every time he tried to get her to define a problem and work on goals, she would find a way to circumvent his efforts and take the conversation down yet another dead-end pathway. Dr. Sibcy felt frustrated and

*As we will see, some clients are motivated primarily because of psychological symptoms, such as panic attacks, anger, depression, addictive behaviors such as drug use or pornography, or avoidance behaviors such as procrastination.*

© VGstockstudio/Shutterstock.com

helpless because internally he would conceptualize this client as being able to tangle up a conversation like the line on a backlashed fishing reel.

The good news was that Dr. Sibcy had some awareness of how this client was triggering him emotionally, and he shared his response with his supervisor. In supervision, Dr. Sibcy vented his frustrations about this case and hoped his supervisor would encourage him to make a referral. Instead, much to his dismay, his supervisor introduced him to the concepts of transference and countertransference. Transference is the way in which a client can project perceptions and feelings about earlier relationships (usually those of parents and peers) onto a therapist, and countertransference is how a therapist can attach feelings from previous relationships onto a client. Countertransference has traditionally been viewed in a negative light, implying that the therapist has unresolved issues with his or her family of origin. There is some validity to this observation: If you have not resolved conflicts and negative feelings about important past relationships, these feelings will very likely leak into and contaminate your therapy relationships. This is where supervisors often advise supervisees to be careful when tempted to go with their gut because it is always possible that one's gut is contaminated due to countertransference! Recall, in Chapter 2, we discussed the journey of becoming and how important it is to unpack your own struggles and "sit in the other chair" so to speak to do your work as a client.

However, more modern views of transference or countertransference consider the therapist's feelings about the client to be an important assessment tool for the therapist. The assumption is that many clients like Samantha have a knack for generating the same feelings in nearly all their relationships. In other words, Dr. Sibcy was probably not the only person who felt this way about Samantha. Her interpersonal behavior may alienate others in her life. She has become accustomed to others feeling negatively toward her and retreating. This behavior only confirms her low self-esteem and her sense of being defective or flawed, which reinforces her retreating or isolating behavior and develops into a negative cycle.

So Dr. Sibcy's helpful supervisor pointed out that this information is crucial to the case formulation and treatment planning process. The relationship is the most important therapeutic factor. The therapist cannot do anything to help Samantha (or any client) until first strengthening the relationship. Dr. Sibcy's first thought was to intervene by helping Samantha see just how annoying her behaviors were and teaching her some communication skills. Notice how Dr. Sibcy first started with changing her and not himself? This is a natural response but is precisely the problem for most beginning counselors. We think that the "difficult client" is difficult in a vacuum, ignoring the complex interplay between how they behave and how we react. We want to teach them how to take responsibility for their behavior, but in order to do so we must start with taking responsibility for our own reactions. We have to take ownership for our own part of the equation, and it can be painful to take responsibility for the challenges and struggles we face in life, especially when doing something so well intentioned as trying to help a client accomplish therapeutic goals.

*We want to teach our clients how to take responsibility for their behavior, but in order to do so, we must start with taking responsibility for our own reactions.*

As Joyce Meyer once said in her teaching on the power of thought, one way to terminate a relationship is to think about everything wrong with that relationship and then "think about it, talk about it, think about it, talk about it ..." Meyer went on to say, "Your mind affects your mouth and your mouth affects your mind. It's difficult to stop talking about a situation until you stop thinking about it" (Meyer, 2010). This resonates with Dr. John Gottman's research that contempt is the sulfuric acid of love, and criticism is one of the four horsemen that brings about the end (see Chapter 1 for more on this), but fondness and admiration are practices that grow love and are antidotes to the four horsemen (Gottman, 2007). As we discussed in Chapter 6, the therapeutic relationship is, of course, a relationship, and some of the same principles apply. So, Dr. Sibcy's job was to find something about Samantha that he liked. This was no small challenge, but what he came to realize about himself was that he was so focused on improving Samantha's mental health functioning that he forgot about the therapeutic relationship itself. As he learned to set this important goal aside, he began to see things about her that were good. Importantly, he began to empathize with how lonely and fearful she was when around other people. She expected rejection and her social awkwardness alienated her from others, including her therapist. As he appreciated these feelings and began relating to her more warmly, his eyes opened and he could see other things about her that he liked: She cared about people and longed to be able to touch their lives in meaningful ways. She loved her grown children and tried to love and support them and was deeply hurt by the rift that had developed between her oldest daughter and herself.

Samantha also noticed a change and perked up more in therapy. Eventually Dr. Sibcy was able to work with her to get back on track and work on some positive changes in her life. Once she felt more secure in the relationship, she began to venture out on the top of the secure base cycle (recall the circle of security discussed earlier in Chapter 1, and note, when the child is feeling secure, and the fully charged indicator wiggle is "on," then he or she is able to move out and explore and launch out into the world, or in therapy, able to take more risks and engage more fully in therapy due to the felt safety in the therapeutic bond) and was able to make some concrete changes she felt good about. For example, she wanted to work on healing the rift with her daughter and was now willing to focus in and work on her communication skills. Although it took several months of challenging work and a willingness to be vulnerable with her daughter, Samantha was able to resolve the conflict with her daughter, which helped improve her mood a great deal.

Dr. Sibcy, now a clinical supervisor himself, continues to use this framework when working with counselors in supervision; he often asks about the quality of the relationship and teaches counselors in training skills for strengthening the therapeutic bond, especially with more challenging clients. Learning these skills is a centerpiece to this text and the core focus of introductory counseling courses. The skills we have covered in this textbook all facilitate therapeutic rapport and are central to creating a strong bond between the client and the counselor; you will find that therapists from all different theoretical orientations use these skills.

**Agreement on goals** is another essential quality of an effective therapeutic alliance. On the surface, this task of goal setting sounds straightforward and simple; however, it is not. People do not generally come to therapy with a list of goals (and sometimes we need to use the miracle question because it is hard for some clients to even conceptualize life without the problem). Instead, clients typically come to therapy with problems: problems defined in global, negative, and rigid terms: For example, a client may say, "My life is in shambles," "My marriage is falling apart," "I am in a dead-end relationship," "My spiritual life is dead," "I feel horrible all the time," "Anxiety rules my life," "I am a slave to food (or alcohol or pornopgraphy)," or make any other of an array of similar global complains.

The challenge for the therapist is to help the client translate problems into goals that are realistic and attainable. The translation problem involves a number of steps or subtasks. First, these global descriptions must be broken down into specific problems. For example, for the client who feels "ruled by anxiety and worry," one place to start is asking for examples of specific times when anxiety had a grip on his or her life. Once we can identify specific behaviors or interpersonal exchanges to focus on and target with our goals, we can move toward creating SMART goals. So, this process is a prerequisite that involves funneling global negative complaints into goals that can be transformed into specific, measurable, attainable, realistic, and timely goals. Let us now turn our focus to this next stage of the process.

## SMART Goals

In order to make abstract goals more measurable, we often use the acronym SMART. There are many different descriptions of the words represented by this acronym (e.g., some used S for strategic, and some for specific) and this acronym has been around for several decades and used in business and the helping professions (Conzemius & O'Neill, 2005). The concept of SMART goals was originally introduced by George Doran in a November 1981 article entitled "There's a SMART way to Write Management Goals and Objectives" (Conzemius & O'Neill, 2005; Devoir, 2014), which was developed to stand for specific (identify a specific area to focus on); measurable (find a strategy for measuring progress); assignable, (identify what person would accomplish what goal; in counseling this is already determined to be the client so we have modified this to attainable, which addresses having the resources needed to accomplish the goal) realistic, (look at whether the goal can be accomplished given the resources at hand, and if not how or when can more resources be obtained or created); and timely, (set a deadline for accomplishment). **SMART** is a tool that has been used by counselors, business persons, and other helping professionals to facilitate the development of specific, measurable, attainable, relevant, and timely goals to help people set goals they are more likely to accomplish.

## Specific and Measurable

If a client comes in with the problem of stress or worry, we may use a scale of 1 to 10 and identify the lack of peace (or degree of stress, in the case of nonapproach goals) and then assess where the client is on the scale currently and where he or she would like to be. This can then allow us to measure progress from session to session; this scaling progress will then be especially important to draw upon later during the termination phase of counseling. Using scaling makes the goal more specific and measurable, for example, if the client says, "I am experiencing very little peace due to this anxiety and am at a 2 on the peace scale, but I would like to be at a 7." We then need to explore with the client using the reflecting skills what it means to be at a 2 and what it means to be at a 7.

## Attainable

As we explore attainability, we can look at activities and thoughts that are associated with peace. We may ask questions such as, "When do you remember feeling most peaceful?" Clients we have had in the past have said things like, "when I am journaling my prayers," "when I am near the ocean," "when I am out in nature," "when I am listening to worship music," and "when I am thinking about all the things I am grateful for." Here we examine, the price the client needs to pay to make the changes or the resources that are needed to make the change. For example, what would be involved in spending more time near the ocean? How far do you live from the beach? What would it require of you to renew the habit of keeping a prayer journal? What were you doing in the past that helped you keep your thoughts on topics such as what you are grateful for? The counselor works with the client to determine whether the necessary resources are available.

## Realistic

Realistic goals are goals that can be achieved based on the resources that are available. If the resources are not sufficient for accomplishing the goal, is there a plan in place to obtain or create more resources? It is important to explore this or to explore modifying the goals. It is helpful to set goals that can be accomplished or develop strategies for obtaining resources to avoid the discouragement and disillusionment discussed previously that can be characteristic of the preconception stage of change when people have made efforts to accomplish goals and have not been successful.

## Timely

Interestingly, when people have a deadline for completing a goal, they are more likely to accomplish it than if they can do it anytime they wish (Damgarrd & Gravart, 2017). Researchers found that when there was a deadline put on charitable donations, there was a now or never effect, so people either gave right away or not at all. We believe in counseling there is no time like the present; there is never going to be a perfect time to work on a goal. One may never feel ready to face a challenge; thus you cannot wait for your train to come in. You have to drive your train into the station. So, it is important to explore with the client questions such as "When would you like to accomplish this goal?" Or "How long do you believe it will take to accomplish this goal?"

Thus in the situation described above, a SMART goal would involve assessing where the client is on the scale in terms of anxiety or peace. If she rates her current level of peace as a 2 and wants to get to a 7, and we explore what this means, then we have a measureable and specific area to work on.

To determine if this goal is attainable, we may ask, "I am hearing that work has been stressful, and the thoughts that you have during your drive home seems to be a trigger to the anxiety to escalate to panic. Do you remember a time when you felt at peace? What was different?" She may tell us she had a different job, or different focus at work, or a different housing situation. We then need to explore with her what resources she needs to return to or create an environment conductive to more peace and less anxiety and assess whether this is attainable with current resources. In order to set a realistic goal, we need to assess the resources discussed under attainability. If the client reports her stressful job is the source of the anxiety and robbing her of peace, but she needs to stay at her current job, we may begin looking at what the factors at work are contributing to her stress levels and seek to modify them or rather the client's response to them; as discussed previously, often times the challenge is in taking responsibility. Then, we need to set a timeline to determine when she wants to accomplish this goal, or what her deadline is.

Returning to the BASIC ID and Lazarus' influence on our work, we can also tease out a manner for conceptualizing the case with each one of the examples discussed previously into different categories of experience: the situation (time, place, context; e.g., "Last Wednesday I was driving to work, running late, and stuck in traffic, and the next thing I know anxiety [feeling] hit me like a freight train") and the accompanying thoughts, feelings, behaviors, and resultant consequences ("I thought, 'Oh no I am going to have a heart attack right here and can't do anything about it [thought]. So I pulled my car over to the shoulder of the highway and started crying uncontrollably. I called my husband on the phone and told him to come and get me [behaviors]. He told me to get myself together and go to work or drive myself to the ER. If I could not do that, then just call 911 [relational consequence or also another trigger]. I was livid [feeling]. I cannot believe he would just abandon me on the side of the highway [thought]. I drove the car along the shoulder of the highway and got off at the next exit. I drove myself home and called into work sick [escape behaviors]. The anxiety eventually went down, but now I might lose my job because I am out of sick time [reduced anxiety is a consequence of escape behavior and as is job instability, which is also another trigger]."

Rarely does a client so vividly and succinctly describe a problem situation. The counselor must skillfully and sensitively probe for this kind of information. The reflecting skill and paraphrasing allow the counselor to do just that and to identify each aspect as they go. For example, "So, I hear you saying that at the time you started to feel panicked and your anxiety increased, the thought, 'I am having a cardiac event; this will be awful' is on your mind, and then your behavior is. . .." Here with this example, the counselor has successfully broken the problem down into more specific problems; this combines the active listening skills such as paraphrasing, reflecting content, reflecting feeling, and reflecting meaning with case conceptualization. The subproblems include running late in the morning, getting stuck in traffic, translating emotional stress into physical symptoms, and then catastrophizing them (e.g., "Oh no, I am having a heart attack. . .I am going to die"), and safety and escape behaviors (pulling over to the side of the highway and calling her husband, and driving home). Also notice the cascade of consequences (husband's frustration with her anxiety and avoidance, negative feelings and thoughts about husband, the reduction of anxiety as a result of escape behavior, new anxiety and worry about work), due to avoidance behavior. Notice how consequences can also become triggers for yet another iteration of thoughts-feelings-behavior-consequences. Thus, you might begin to see how problems can turn into a vicious cycle. Later we will discuss the skills and tactics involved in helping clients see these vicious cycles and how to translate this discovery into more specific goals.

Based on this example (and perhaps others that are similar to it) some more basic concrete problems emerge, and as we will see, problems have goals attached directly to them (they are two sides of the same coin).

1. Problems in the morning getting ready for work. The counselor will need to explore this more:[1]

   - What factors interfere with her getting reading in the morning:
     i. gets up late
     ii. low energy
     iii. low motivation
     iv. poor organization, and so on
     v. Also, is traffic a common problem?
     vi. What time does she need to leave to make it to work in plenty of time?
     vii. Leaving late increases her basic level of anxiety and frustration

2. Client interprets her physical symptoms of emotional stress as signs of catastrophic physical crisis (heart attack). This interpretation exacerbates her physical symptoms, creating a vicious cycle

3. Avoidance behaviors

4. Relationship problems at home and at work

## Agreement on Treatment Methods

Also, and very importantly, the client's understanding of the interconnection between triggers, thoughts-feelings-behaviors, and consequences sets the stage for the counselor to provide a rationale for the treatment plan and the specific kinds of methods and strategies used to help the client achieve his or her goals.

### Identifying specific examples of problems

One of the challenges centers on the fact that the goals of the client might be somewhat different from the goals of that the therapist may be inclined toward. Examples might include the client who wants to feel less depressed but does not want to improve the quality of his relationships or reduce the amount of alcohol he consumes. Another challenge is that in some cases, the client's goals are not actually attainable in therapy (see the section on SMART goals for more information). Examples might include the depressed client whose goal is to change her husband's attitude about life or the angry client who wants life to go his way: for example, "I just want things to work out the right way instead of having to always deal with roadblocks and dead ends."

The other side of the equation has to do with the therapist's gut felt reaction to the client; consider the example of Dr. Sibcy and Samantha. Her way of relating to him was such that he felt annoyed, frustrated, and somewhat disengaged. Also, once he had developed this negative feeling toward her, he developed a negative bias toward her such that he selectively attended to her negative traits and characteristics and selectively ignored anything good. This becomes a self-fulfilling prophecy because the more he found unpleasant about her, the more annoyed and disengaged he became. Of course, Samantha could sense his unpleasant feelings toward her; they were just like those of everyone else she knew. Dr. Sibcy was just like all the other people she encountered over the years, except he had to see her because she was his client. It is important to remember that we do not have the clients that we want; we have the clients that God sends us. It is important to remember that they are created in the image of God and should treated as such!

So, Dr. Sibcy's challenge from his supervisor was to search and find something about Samantha that he liked. At first this truly seemed like a pointless search expedition. He might also been given the task of finding the proverbial needle in a haystack. But much to his surprise, as he searched, he found, and this improved the therapeutic relationship and made it easier to establish and move toward agreed-upon goals.

> **A Verse to Remember:** Matthew 7:7: "Ask and it will be given to you; seek and you will find; knock and the door will be opened to you."

A scripture to remember that resonates with this case is Matthew 7:7 (New International Version) "Ask and it will be given to you; seek and you will find; knock and the door will be opened to you."

## Other Advanced Skills

*Using natural gates and smooth transitions.* This is a key skill for the effective counselor. The basic idea is that the counselor fosters collaboration as she or he creates a steady, easy flow to the session. Natural gates and smooth transitions involve using the skills such as minimal encouragers, paraphrases, summaries, and asking questions that slowly build tempo and explore important and, sometimes, sensitive information.

For example, for those clients seeking help for symptoms, the counselor explores their symptoms, asking meaningful, relevant questions that reflect the counselor expertise. For example, the counselor may ask a depressed person the following questions (or probing in the form of statements):

- Are you having difficulties with sleep? Or: Tell me about what your sleep has been like lately.

- Have you had low energy and fatigue lately? Or: Tell me about your energy levels lately.

- Have you had any difficulties with concentration and decision making? Tell me about what your focus and concentration levels have been like lately.

- Sensitively asking these kinds of questions implies that you have a deeper understanding of their concerns than the average, empathic listener. Recall, from Chapter 10 on questions, that we discussed the importance of using questions sparingly. When you get into diagnosis and treatment planning (in future classes), you will find out more of the key questions to ask depending on the presenting problem. These questions are good questions and are strategic and allow the clinician to better assess the client. However, the reflecting skills can also be used in place of some of the questions (as demonstrated above), and this may be associated with a more conversational tone, rather than a question-answer dynamic, where the counselor asks a question and the client answers and then sits quietly waiting for the next questions. Saving questions for these strategic items rather than for simple time fillers allows the therapist to add more value to the session. In the example above, the counselor will then explore how these symptoms have affected other areas of life: family, relationships, work, recreation, and so on.

For those with life stressors, the counselor explores the nature of these problems and then links these problems to possible psychological symptoms and may ask questions such as the following:

- When did these problems with your boss start? Or: Tell me about when you first recall these problems with your boss starting.

- How have they changed the time? Tell me about how these problems with your boss have changed over time.

- How did you try to handle the situation? Or: You mentioned that you have tried everything; tell me more about the strategies you used.

- Did these efforts help or make things worse? Or: I am wondering how your efforts impacted the situation.

- You also said something about some conflict with your wife about how to deal with your teenage daughter who was struggling at school. When did these struggles start? Or: (Same beginning sentence). Tell me more about when these struggles first began.

- Are the difficulties at work and at home connected in any way? The counselor may then inquire about how these stressful events may have resulted in unpleasant psychological, emotional, and physical symptoms.

- For example, "Joe, it sounds like you've been really stressed trying to cope with stress at work and dealing with the conflicts between you and your wife about how to handle your teenage daughter. Has this stress affected your mood?" Or: "It sounds like this has been a stressful season between work and home life. Tell me about what your mood has been like."

- How about your level of interest in doing things? (these are two screening questions for depression). Have you been struggling with feelings of anxiety or worry (screening for anxiety symptoms)? Or: Tell me about what your anxiety and worry levels have been like.

- When you feel this way, how do you try to cope? Sometimes people try to ease the tension by doing other things like drinking (normalizing a behavior). (Or, replace the first sentence with, "Tell me about how you cope with tension.")

- Is this something that you do (screening for alcohol use)?

Although this book is not designed to be a diagnostic interviewing text, it is important to understand some of the basic concepts involved in clinical interviewing. As we learn the core skills of the effective counselor, we want to help you understand the different counseling contexts in which these skills are used. You will learn more about how to ask strategic questions related to diagnosis and treatment planning in the Diagnosis and Treatment Planning course and text. It may be beyond the scope of this text to diagnosis and formulate a comprehensive treatment plan, but using BASIC ID for conceptualization, scaling, and SMART goals is movement in that direction. One other important advanced skill is homework.

## Collaborative Homework

After conceptualizing where the client is using BASIC ID and listening skills to help the client parse out the various parts of the problem and connect the dots to see how they overlap, it is then important to assess where they are on a scale (later, in the diagnosis and treatment planning portion of your training, we will add other assessments to use in treatment). Then, toward the end of counseling, a clinician can ask the client to identify one step he or she may take to move a fourth of a point up the scale, just one step forward in a positive direction. For example, the counselor may say, "Jen I hear you saying that you have been having some anxiety lately and would rate yourself at about a 4 on the peace scale, with 10 being perfect peace. What is one thing you could do between now and next time we meet to move up the scale just a quarter of a point form a 4 to a 4.25?" Often the client will have something in mind, but sometimes the client will say, "Well, I am not sure. I feel stuck." In this case the clinician can join the client in taking a closer look or using a solution-focused approach that searches for an exception. Here, we draw upon our training in solution focused therapy, and we may ask, "Can you recall a time when the problem was not occurring? If so, what was different? If not, what has helped you to cope with so much courage?"

## To Do List

Consider the presenting problem your client brings to therapy and try to:

- Conceptualize it in terms of behavior, affect, sensations, imagery, cognition, interpersonal relations, and drugs or physiological aspects.

Please watch this video on the use of scaling in session with Alex.

## Video

**Scaling**

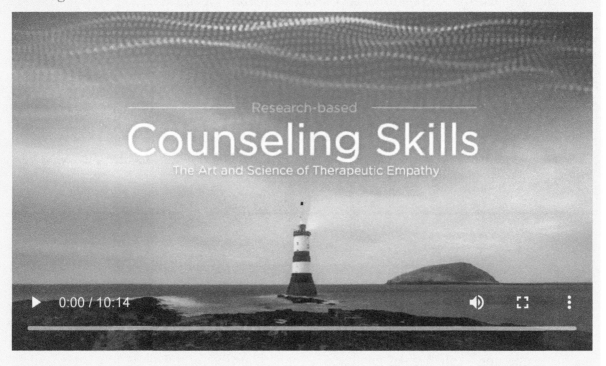

- Use scaling with anchors to identify where a client is on the scale in the present moment.
- Work collaboratively with the client to discuss agreed-upon SMART goals (ask strategic questions for moving toward identifying a specific area of change, a measurable method for assessing progress, etc.).

## Recommended Reading

For additional reading on case conceptualization and related information, we would recommend reading the following texts to expand your knowledge in this area. These are recommended as they provided the basis of some of the research used for this chapter. Moreover, these texts add to a counselor's repertoire of resources in the field:

© Shutterstock.com

- Kim, N., & Lee, K. (2018). The effect of internal locus of control on career adaptability: The mediating role of career decision-making self-efficacy and occupational engagement. *The Journal of Employment Counseling 55*(1), 2–15. doi:10.1002/joec.12069

- Barlow, D. H., Farchione, T. J., Sauer-Zavala, S., Murray Latin, H., Ellard, K. K., Bullis, J. R., . . . Cassiello-Robbins, C. (2017). *Unified protocol for transdiagnostic treatment of emotional disorders: Therapist guide* (2nd ed.). New York, NY: Oxford University Press.

- Prochaska, J. O., & Prochaska, J. M. (2016). *Changing to thrive: Using the stages of change to overcome the top threats to your health and happiness.* Center City, MN: Hazelden Publishing

## Chapter Summary

Purposeful counseling involves working together with clients to form collaborative goals that the client and the counselor agree on. Some advanced skills that you may use to accomplish this task include conceptualizing cases using BASIC ID, scaling, using the miracle question where needed, and seeking to facilitate the formulation of SMART goals.

Part of the therapist's skill is being able to listen, be empathic, understand, help the client translate his or her global problems into smaller problems, and then formulate those agreed-upon goals. Although the mental health field used to be more aligned with different schools of thought related to theoretical orientation, there is currently a movement in the field toward more evidence-based treatments. It is important to use strategic questions or probes based on the client's presenting challenges. The questions or probes the counselor uses also help the client to understand himself or herself better. Strategies like the BASIC ID, created by Arnold Lazarus, can be used to look at discrete parts of the client's personality.

---

[1] As it turns out, the client had to get her three kids ready for school in the morning because her husband leaves an hour before she does.

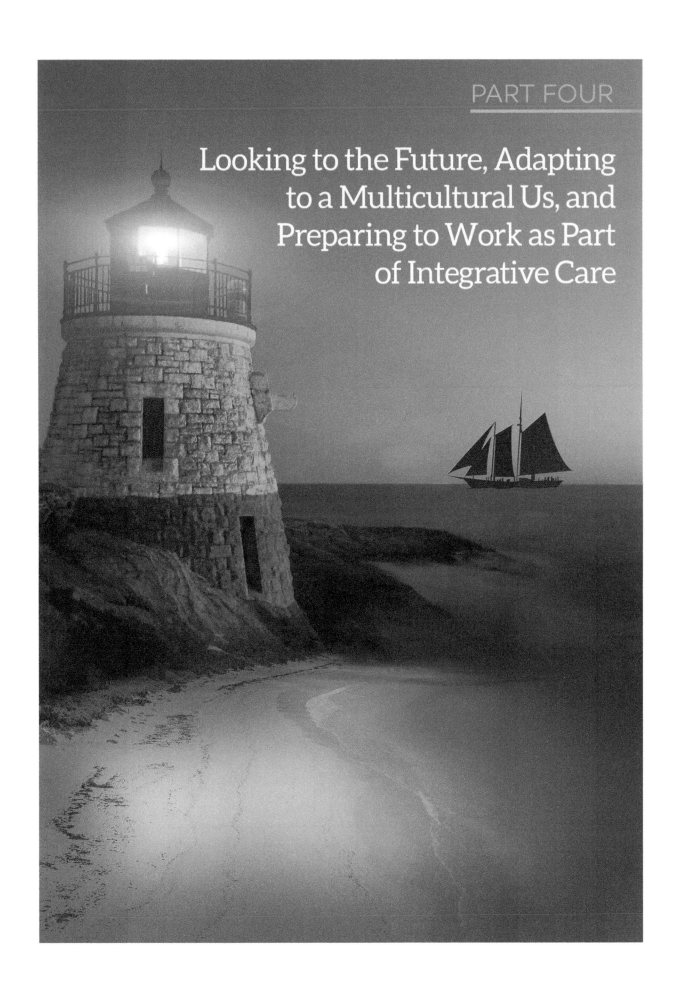

# PART FOUR

# Looking to the Future, Adapting to a Multicultural Us, and Preparing to Work as Part of Integrative Care

In Part Four of this text, we turn our focus to adapting to changes in our field and our world. Our world is becoming more of a melting pot and multicultural society. So, it is important for the effective counselor to not only have appropriate skills and be empathic but also be prepared to work in a multicultural environment with the knowledge that all people are created in the image of God and are to be treated as such.

There are also changes in terms of the way care is integrated from practitioners along the continuum of care from LPCs, school counselors, psychologists, and psychiatrists. In this section, we will explore more deeply multicultural counseling considerations and psychopharmacology, including what to listen for when using the skills as clients discuss medications and symptomology. In this segment of the book, we also have contributions from guest authors Drs. Elias Moitinho and John Kuhnley.

Chapter Fourteen

# Strategies for Preparing for Termination

Anita Knight and Gary Sibcy

*It's okay how some stories leave off without an ending. Life doesn't always deliver the one you would expect.*

—Adam Silvera (2015, p. 283)

## Chapter Learning Objectives

- To identify strategies to promote client understanding of and access to a variety of community-based resources (CACREP II.F.5.k, 2016, p. 12)
- To address losses and endings in the termination phase of counseling (CACREP II.F.5.k, 2016, p. 12)
- To learn termination skills (CACREP II.F.5.d., 2016, p. 11)
  - Summarizing
  - Assessing progress
  - Exploring loss
  - Planning for maintenance
  - Planning for relapse prevention
  - Open door or follow-up appointment
  - Assessing accountability or support system

267

# Chapter Overview

Recall from our chapter on understanding emotions that sadness is always tied to perceived loss. Termination may be perceived as a loss of a relationship, that is, the therapeutic relationship. It is an ending of sorts that can be associated with loss. We need to prepare our clients for this and help them consolidate gains to be aware of what they have accomplished. Sometimes a client may have reached the appropriate stage of change such that termination is appropriate, or sometimes insurance no longer reimburses for sessions, or perhaps job changes or moving out of the area results in early termination. Regardless of the reason for termination, ending well may not be easy. However, there are some termination skills or closing skills that counselors can use to make endings easier. Some of those skills include summarizing (discussed in Chapter 8), consolidating gains, identifying an accountability or support system, planning for relapse prevention, and including a transitional object (TO).

## Preparing Our Hearts for Facing the End

Sometimes when we move toward termination, we realize that there are still things left undone, as indicated in the introductory quote, "life does not always deliver" the ending that we would expect. However, the theme scripture indicates that there is one thing that we can be confident in. God is not finished with us and is not finished with our clients. We can trust that He will see them through to completion. We have been on a journey with our clients, the journey of becoming; now we may be approaching our exit, or they may be approaching their exit. It is a time of parting ways, but God continues to walk alongside each of us for our full journey. Things may not have gone as expected, and we may not have accomplished all our therapeutic goals (as in cases where third-party payers or external circumstances require early termination).

> And I am certain that God, who began the good work within you, will continue his work until it is finally finished on the day when Christ Jesus returns.
>
> —Philippians 1:6

This process may bring up thoughts about past endings, loneliness, losses, and existential loneliness. It is important to create an atmosphere that allows clients to explore these thoughts and feelings. Recall, in Chapter 6, we talked about SOLER, in which the counselor is encouraged to maintain a relaxed atmosphere and the core feeling that underlies relaxed is "peaceful." It may help to have a strong conviction that, as the poet Robert Browning wrote, "the best is yet to be." Consider the first four lines of Robert Browning's poem "Rabbi Ben Ezra:"

*"Grow old along with me!*
*The best is yet to be,*
*The last of life, for which the first was made:*
*Our times are in His hand"*

Remember the instillation of hope is an important therapeutic factor (Yalom, 1980), and the belief that with effort and intentionality things will continue to get better is an important attitude to retain. My clinical supervisor, Dr. George Jefferson, used to use quips, anecdotes, and poetry to make the crudeness of reality easier to bear. After all, pain and heartache are quite poetic, and poetry tends to be beautiful. We also know that humor is some of the best medicine, so maintaining perspective is essential, and using strategies to prepare the heart of the counselor to maintain peace and perspective is important for walking alongside clients facing endings of any sort. Proverbs 17:22 (NIV) states, "A cheerful heart is good medicine, but a crushed spirit dries up the bones." Dr. Jefferson would often say about painful experiences, "Just like kidney stones, this too shall pass." This is funny to just about anyone, except someone who has had a kidney stone.

*A Verse to Remember:* Proverbs 17:22 (NIV): *A cheerful heart is good medicine, but a crushed spirit dries up the bones.*

In the face of heartbreak, the comfort the Bible offers comes in the form of God's presence. Psalm 34:18 in the New Living Translation (NLT) says, "The LORD is close to the brokenhearted; he rescues those whose spirits are crushed." So, we can take comfort in knowing that we are never alone and our clients are never alone in approaching the end of treatment. Often, termination can be positive. For example, some substance abuse rehabilitation facilities where we have worked have had graduation ceremonies. It may often feel lonely, especially for clients who may be giving up one of the few relationships they retained with someone they could trust and with whom they feel safe. Even clients with a strong spiritual life may question God's presence. It can be helpful to remember the poem entitled "Footprints."

© Ozerov Alexander/Shutterstock.com

It is with the peace of knowing that there is One who will be with us to the end that will complete the good work in our lives and the lives of our clients. We can walk with our clients as they face losses or endings of any kind and retain the important therapeutic factor of hope and an attitude and willingness to seek to instill hope in our clients. We may not be in the appropriate context to draw upon spiritual truths or may be working with clients who do not wish to integrate spirituality within their treatment. However, we can always pray for our clients outside of treatment and bring an attitude of hope and conviction that the best is yet to come.

> **A Verse to Remember:**
> *"But as it has been written: 'What no eye has seen, and no ear has heard, and has not entered into the heart of man, what God has prepared for those loving Him.'"*
> 2 Corinthians 9, Berean Literal Bible.

## Preparing Our Clients for Termination

Termination is the final phase of counseling, not a single session but rather a process. One of the responsibilities of the counselor is to prepare the client for termination. Our colleague, Dr. Kuhnley (personal communication, June 2017), discusses the importance of employing the BDA, which is preparation **before-during-after (BDA)** important events. Dr. Kuhnley shared that he used the acronym BDA to help his patients understand themselves and situations, organize their thinking, and learn from everything to prepare for more effective function and success in subsequent situations. He believed that it helped to increase understanding, and one of the themes discussed in this text is that counselors seek first to understand their clients. To understand clients and help them to understand or make sense of their feelings, we can use BDA in the termination phase and talk about termination before it comes and during the termination phase and leave the door open for them to return to process after or to identify an outlet such as journaling or talking with a trusted friend with whom they can process feelings after terminating sessions.

As discussed in Chapter 6, the bond that develops between the client and the therapist, referred to as the therapeutic alliance, therapeutic relationship, rapport, and a variety of other terms, is indeed a relationship. Although it is a professional relationship, it is still a relationship and may be the only safe relationship for the client where the client can open up, be vulnerable, and share. So, it is important to prepare clients for the termination stage and to let them know the number of sessions available. Much of therapy is time limited. However, in some cases, such as in the case of chronic depression, a client's third-party payers may allow for ongoing therapeutic support.

## Avoiding Premature Termination

Recall, from Chapter 6, that we discussed Gottman and Levenson's (1999) research on relationship termination and the factors that contribute to the therapeutic relationship and likelihood that clients will return. Recall that high validation behaviors were associated with a higher likelihood that clients would return, and defensiveness was a negative predictor. It is important to use the skills throughout the book to validate and build therapeutic rapport. It can also be helpful to check in with clients and perhaps to scale their satisfaction with the treatment process.

Researchers interviewed clinicians at an eating disorder clinic regarding the causes of premature termination (Masson & Sheeshka, 2009). Factors they identified as important in predicting client's completion of treatment include "motivation to be in the program, work on recovery and ability to establish trusting relationships" (Masson & Sheeshka, 2009, p. 109). Considering the work of Prochaska and Prochaska (2016) on the stages of change, it may also be helpful to acknowledge the stage of change the client is in and meet them where they are. Many clients may present to treatment still in the precontemplation stage, which could be interpreted as resistance. The active listening skills including paraphrasing, minimal encouragers, validation of feelings, and summarizing, along with advanced skills such as immediacy and scaling, can be used to meet clients where they are and validate them as they consider the costs and benefits associated with change. Challenging while supporting can also be used when appropriate rapport is established and the session calls for it.

Researchers studying counseling in college counseling centers have also reported that premature termination is a problem and that most clients only come to a handful of counseling sessions before ceasing treatment. After reviewing the literature, Hatchett (2004) found that a dose–effect relationship exists in counseling, meaning "greater client improvement is associated with the completion of more therapy sessions" (p. 15). However, many students prematurely terminate counseling before any clinically meaningful changes occur. This is a problem. Hatchett scoured the peer-reviewed research literature and put together a collection of eight different specifically designed strategies that clinicians can use to prevent premature termination. We recommend reading the full article (see the recommended reading section) for more information on this topic. These strategies include the following:

1. **Increase awareness of risk factors for early termination**

   According to Hatchett (2004), there have only been two risk factors for early termination that are considered client factors. The first is racial or ethnic minority status. The second risk factor is low socio-economic status. Suggestions include developing more multicultural competencies and reaching out and keeping these students engaged in the process (see Chapter 15 for more on multicultural competencies).

2. **Seek to prepare clients for the therapeutic process**

   As discussed in Chapter 5 by Dr. Kuhnley, counselors should provide their clients with a document that discloses information about the counseling process, called a "disclosure statement." Remley and Herlihy (2007) state, "Every counselor should have a professional disclosure statement that can be given to clients. A complete and signed professional disclosure statement will fulfill a counselor's legal obligation to obtain informed consent from a client" p. 101. They emphasize that it is important to remember to have a dialogue with clients regarding the disclosure statement. Although disclosure statements are necessary, they are not sufficient. Disclosure statements are considered legal contracts (Remley & Herlihy, 2007). Remley emphasizes including the items discussed for informed consent in the ACA code of ethics (ACA, 2014, section A.2.b., 2014) and indicates the following should be included:

   - The purposes, goals, techniques, procedures, limitations, potential risks, and benefits of services

- The counselor's qualifications, including relevant degrees held, licenses and certifications, areas of specialization, experience, and approach to counseling

- Arrangements for continuation of services if the counselor dies or becomes incapacitated

- The role of technology

- The implications of diagnosis and the intended use of tests and reports

- Fees and billing information, including procedures for nonpayment of fees

- Confidentiality and its limitations

- Clients' rights to obtain information about their records and to participate in ongoing counseling plans

- Clients' rights to refuse any recommended services or modality change and be advised of the consequences of refusal. (Remley & Herlihy, 2007, p. 97)

In addition to the elements addressed by the code, various writers have recommended that the following additional topics be included:

- A description of the counselor's theoretical orientation, in lay language that the client can understand (Corey & Corey, 2015), or a brief statement of the counselor's philosophy (how the counselor sees the counseling process)

- Information about logistics of the counseling process, such as length and frequency of sessions, procedures for making and canceling appointments, policies regarding telephone contact between sessions, and how to reach the counselor or an alternative service in an emergency (Haas, Malouf, & Mayerson, 1995)

- Information about insurance reimbursement, including the fact that any diagnosis assigned will become part of the client's permanent health record; what information will be provided to insurance carriers and how this limits confidentiality (Welfel & O'Donnell, 2013)

- Information about alternatives to counseling, such as 12-step groups or other self-help groups, books, medications, nutritional or exercise therapy, or other services (Bray, Shepherd, & Hays, 1985). (p. 97)

Remley and Herlihy's text (2007) also includes sample professional disclosure statement documents, and we recommend reading the text for a thorough discussion on professional disclosure statements as a strategy for guarding against premature termination and for also meeting ethical best practices (see Chapter 5 for more on the informed consent process and professional disclosure statements).

3. **Develop agreed-upon goals and expectations for therapy.**

It is important to focus on agreed-upon goals and interventions in treatment (Hatchett, 2004). This was discussed more extensively in the context of case conceptualization and SMART goals in Chapter 13.

4. **Implement procedures for the intake interview that are "client friendly"** of counseling sessions makes this prohibitive (with many clients coming to less than three sessions), Hatchett (2004) suggests beginning treatment right away, and having the client plan to come in about a half an hour early to complete intake paperwork. This way the time in

session is spent on treatment, and the therapist can still obtain some background information.

We have found that assessments such as the spiritual life map (a subjective assessment where the counselor invites the client to draw a time line across a page, with the starting point representing the first spiritual experience that was significant to a client such as coming to know Christ as savior or baptism and continuing to later experiences that are significant to the individual) or lifeline (a life line is similar to a spiritual life map; it involves inviting someone to draw a line where they place markers that represent different events that have been significant to them along the time lines of their lives) for clients that do not come from a Christian worldview are helpful. This allows the client to share the events that have occurred in their lives that they believe have been formative and spiritually significant. This may allow the therapist to move with the client toward meaningful processing and meaning making early in the counseling relationship.

## 5. Plan for termination early and include it in the treatment plan

Hatchett (2004) also suggests that counselors should talk with clients early on about the number of sessions that they will have and contract for a specific number of sessions (counselors may want to consider including this as a part or an attachment to the informed consent document or professional disclosure document). For example, a therapist may say to a client, "I believe we can address your presenting concern of test anxiety and work on some relaxation exercises and other coping exercises in about five sessions. At that point we can re-evaluate and determine whether more sessions are needed to reach your treatment goals. Depending on other variables or what happens between now and then, how much homework you do outside of treatment, etc., we may find the length of treatment is impacted." The counselor may go on to ask, "What are your thoughts about how long treatment should take or the number of sessions we have together?" We suggest that clinicians talk with their supervisors about this process and agency and third-party payer requirements may influence duration of treatment as well.

## 6. Act and plan for therapy to be brief in duration, with the knowledge that it can be extended later if needed

Often clients believe that therapy should take less time, and counselors believe it should be lengthened. While working in college counseling settings, we have found that short-term solution-focused therapy was often effective and, in some cases, we had to use different approaches depending on the needs of the client, the expertise of the counselor, and the resources available. We found many of the interventions of the solution-focused brief approach to therapy to be helpful including: the formula first session tasks, the miracle question, scaling, and the search for exceptions.

© Ditty_about_summer/Shutterstock.com

### 7. Continuously monitor progress throughout counseling

Scaling, an advanced skill we discussed previously in Chapter 13, provides an intervention for monitoring progress in counseling as well as client satisfaction. However, other more formal assessments can also be used to provide methods of valid and reliable feedback.

### 8. Reminder emails for appointments

It has also been suggested that appointment reminders are helpful (Hatchett, 2004). If you think about your last medical appointment, did you receive a reminder call? Was the reminder call helpful? Hatchett suggests that, since it can be difficult to reach clients by phone, counselors can include in their informed consent a document requesting permission to provide reminder emails, which he states may be more conducive to confidentiality than phone calls as a roommate, family member, spouse, or other person could potentially answer the phone.

© VectorKnight/Shutterstock.com

We have found in our practice that reminder calls, texts, or emails are helpful. However, we recommend having the front desk use this system from a "no-reply" email or an auto-reply that gives a suicide prevention hotline and suggests clients call 911 in the case of emergency as counselors cannot typically be available to provide support services via email. Be sure to discuss with your supervisor your method for reminders and obtain feedback about your population and what works best. When I first began working at a college counseling center, my clinical supervisor, Amy Beldon, encouraged me to conduct reminder calls and follow-up calls, both of which were very helpful with client retention as well as maintaining regular attendance for our ongoing *math anxiety group*.

## Termination and Loss

Remember the iceberg principle that Dr. Silvey discussed in Chapter 4? This principle indicates that what we see above the water line is only the tip of the iceberg, but there is much more under water than we cannot see. Termination, which can be viewed as a loss, may remind clients of past losses or bring up unresolved losses. So, it is important to use strategic questions or probes here. Consider the following possibilities:

- So, we have about three sessions remaining together, and we have been working together for over a year. I am wondering what feelings are bubbling up inside of you as you think about the end of our time together?

- As we approach the end of our time together, how are you feeling about terminating the therapeutic process?

- Sometimes endings can be hard (normalizing); what is it like for you to think about ending this process?

## Attachment Illumination: Transitional Objects

Photo credit: Anita Knight

275

## What Is a TO?

Just like the lighthouses throughout this text have represented the idea of a secure base and safe haven with respect to attachment, a transitional object (TO) can be used to represent maternal nurturing or the mother in the mother's absence. Some have applied the idea of attachment and support that the therapeutic relationship provided and have investigated the attachment bond or therapeutic alliance between the client and the counselor.

A popular example comes to us from a well-known cartoon. If you have ever read *Peanuts*, you probably remember the character named Linus. There is one thing that Linus is well known for and that is what he carried around with him. When you think about Linus, his name may even conjure up an image of something blue in your mind's eye. You may envision a Peanuts character standing around with slightly disheveled hair, sucking his thumb, and holding something blue—his security blanket.

The security blanket is a good example of what early British medically trained psychoanalyst, Donald Winnicott, called a "transitional object." A TO is usually defined as a soft object (although sometimes hard), such as a blanket, a cloth, a doll, or a stuffed animal, that begins to represent to the child the mother or the nurturing of the mother when the mother is not available (Winnicott, 1953).

PEANUTS © 1954 Peanuts Worldwide LLC. Dist. By ANDREWS MCMEEL SYNDICATION. Reprinted with permission. All rights reserved.

© catwalker/Shutterstock.com

PEANUTS © Peanuts Worldwide LLC. Dist. By ANDREWS MCMEEL SYNDICATION. Reprinted with permission. All rights reserved.

Children are comforted by the security blanket, TO, or comfort object as it is sometimes called. However, adults can also be comforted by such objects that represent the care of a loved one in their absence. Winnicott discussed the holding environment sometimes created in therapy. Consider the following quote:

*A correct and well-timed interpretation in an analytic treatment gives a sense of being held physically that is more real...than if a real holding or nursing had taken place. Understanding goes deeper.* (Winnicott, 1988, pp. 61–62)

In this text, we have talked about skills such as validating or reflecting feelings and exploring meaning. We could substitute here that the idea of a well-timed reflection of meaning from a therapist with empathic presence for a well-timed interpretation. This may give the client a sense of feeling understood and supported to such an extent that he or she may feel emotionally "held" or embraced by the therapist although no physical touch takes place.

Put another way, the client may feel the empathic presence of the therapist as the therapist and client face the moment when the client needed that support or holding and did not receive it (Winnicott, 1988). Yet this time that same event is encountered and verbally processed in the presence and with the support of the safe and empathically present counselor. The counselor is in a sense creating a holding environment for the client. This can be associated with the felt safety discussed in Chapter 13.

In discussing the attachment bond, we sometimes talk about separation anxiety or the tension that arises when a child experiences separation from the parent. Given that termination involves an ending or separation from an attachment-holding environment between the client and the counselor, this may trigger unresolved feelings or familiar feelings of attachment-related anxiety. In the strange situation performed by early attachment researchers such as Mary Ainsworth, the researchers watched what happened when mothers left their child in a nursery with a stranger; they watched the children at departure and then again at reunion. Many of the children sought proximity to their parents (e.g., chased after them as they left the room or banged on the door and cried). When the child chases after the parent and seeks closeness to them upon reunion when the parent returns to the nursery in the strange situation experiments, we call this proximity-seeking behavior (Salter Ainsworth & Bell, 1970). UVA professor and neuroscience researcher Dr. James Coan indicated in his chapter "Toward a Neuroscience of Attachment" (2008) that this behavior helps to serve an emotion regulation function. In other words, during times of distress, it is natural to seek out an attachment figure for comfort from distress. Adult attachment works in much the same way. So, sometimes in counseling when our clients accomplish key goals or "graduate" to termination of counseling, we use TOs to help them physically carry with them a small token that represents the support or progress they have made throughout the course of counseling. When we work with clients who have had a history of substance abuse, those who also participate in AA often have a token that represents the time that they have been sober. This may be considered a form of a TO that represents the bond and support that the AA group offers and helps the individual internalize that support during times when the other members are not present to show support. When I served as the head counselor in Teen Challenge, when an adolescent completed the program, we would have a graduation ceremony and a certificate of completion that represented all they had accomplished. Another example of a transitional object can be seen from an intervention that was implemented when we took a group of students to Zhytomyr, Ukraine, to work with orphans and were told that the orphans often were very attached to teddy bears or other stuffed animals and that they brought them comfort. These objects help make separations easier and help internalize to internalize the comfort and support they have received and take it with them literally.

## Using TOs at Termination

Based on Bowlbian and Winnicottian principles, we tend to use the TO in our clinical work and encourage our students and supervisees to do the same, when appropriate.

## An Important Caveat

It is important to remember that the TO is not a gift but a token or a symbol to represent therapeutic progress. Some examples we have used in the past include highlighters to indicate a client coming to embrace his style and unique attributes, a notepad with a symbol of an eagle to represent soaring above life's circumstances, and a quote to represent the acceptance of life's unanswered questions. So, it is important not to introduce any ethical dilemmas by giving the client something that is associated with a high price, perceived as a gift, or with any implication that he or she should reciprocate. The value of the token comes from what it represents and its meaningfulness to the client and counselor about the client's therapeutic journey and the therapeutic relationship.

## Advanced Skill, TO: Strategies for Using the TO

We have often and easily used TOs when running psychoeducational groups, in the form of graduation certificates or certificates of completion. First, the therapist must identify what the themes of the client's journey have been. In the Savickas career style interview (1998), when interviewees are asked to identify their favorite movie and their favorite character within that movie, the interviewer often asks them to describe the plight that their favorite movie character had faced. This is said, based on Adlerian psychology, to represent the plight that the client faces and a strategy for dealing with it. The career style interview allows the therapist to help identify themes. For example, we had a client whose favorite movie was *The Terminator*, and his favorite character was Arnold Schwarzenegger because of the strength and mental toughness that he represented. This gave him a template for dealing with some situations in his life where he felt powerless. Looking at the interview questions and the accompanying guidelines for interpretation may offer some helpful guidance to identify a central theme or problem a client has faced and strategies that may have been used to address the problem. Similar to attachment theory and the Adult Attachment Interview, assessing a person's state of mind with respect to attachment in terms of how coherently he or she tells his or her story (to some extent), Savickas (2011) emphasizes the importance of the client's narrative. Savickas shares that the term that is often used by career constructivist counselors is "narrative identity development. page number? Let us look at what can be learned from Savickas to integrate into the intervention already informed by the principles of Bowlby, Savickas, and Winnicott.

Key words in career construction are narrative, plot, and themes. We want to help the client unpack his or her narrative and seek to identify key themes. We also want to identify the plot; Savickas distinguishes a plot from a story indicating that a story tells what happened, but a plot tells why it happened. Here is how Savickas (2011) describes what a theme is:

The pattern weaved by the golden thread of a through line may be called a theme. The golden theme is the controlling idea implicit in the plot. The thematic pattern woven by this central idea provides the primary unit of meaning used to understand the plots of the occupational plot. (para 1)

The idea of a theme relates to how one makes meaning of experiences and keeps a sense of order and coherence. Savickas emphasizes that sometimes one's narrative will not be coherent. He draws upon the words of Whitman (Savickas, 2011; Whitman, 1855) in "Song of Myself":

*Do I contradict myself?*
*Very well then I contradict myself*
*(I am large, I contain multitudes).*
*(Stanza 51 lines 6-8)*

Savickas (1998) developed the questions in the career style interview over the course of three decades and used his practice with his clients to inform his theory.

The interview begins by asking clients to express their sense of self by describing the people they admired growing up (although this is not explicitly stated, so clients do not necessarily have to focus on this task and are free to perhaps be more open). Questions that are more central to understanding the golden thread that is weaved through a person's story may include:

- What is your favorite story?

- If the client does not recall a favorite story, it can be helpful to ask: What is your favorite television show or movie?

- Next, we ask the client, "Would you tell me the story in your own words?"

- Or "Would you share with me what the plot of the movie or TV show is?" (this is important to ask even if you have already seen it, because it helps explain to us in the client's own words what the struggle is or story is that he or she can perhaps relate to).

These questions, although designed to assess one's career story, may be helpful in identifying the client's theme (or golden thread) that has been worked on in counseling. For example, if a client who admires Wonder Woman addressed in counseling a central theme of how to maintain her femininity with strength and assertiveness while working in a male-dominated environment, an appropriate TO could be a small (inexpensive) Wonder Woman figurine that represents the progress she has made throughout the course of treatment and will continue to make on her "journey of becoming."

We recently had a supervisee whom we will call Arnold for the purposes of confidentiality. Arnold was a very intelligent, attentive, and skillful early career clinician. He had taken extra care to learn his counseling skills and worked with his supervisor on gaining extra opportunities to practice just to refine those skills. Once, he had a client whom we will call Tanequa. She struggled with chronic anxiety and depression and wanted to go to a "depressive center." However, there were no depressive centers available, and depression was only treated in an inpatient facility on a short-term basis until a person with suicidal ideation was stabilized and then they were referred to a counselor and psychiatrist for outpatient treatment. Well, Tanequa was very upset about this and wanted more time to stabilize, and her partner had struggled with substance abuse and had received treatment in an inpatient facility. So, she was outraged. She could not believe, as she put it, that her partner who "chose" her struggle could receive the help she needed and Tanequa, who indicated she, of course, did not choose her struggle, could not receive the help believed that she needed.

So, Arnold and I discussed the process of termination for Tanequa and what would help her to terminate well. We determined that we needed to do the following:

- First, Tanequa needed to work on **consolidating gains** (being able to identify what she gained from treatment was important, so that when she left she felt that she gained the coping skills needed to face her stressors).

- Second, Tanequa needed **assurance of support,** so another objective was to assist her in making contact and scheduling her first appointment with her outpatient counselor and psychiatrist, so she could begin receiving outpatient care right away. Another objective was to identify a support group she could join in the community.

- And third, a **transitional object** to help Tanequa, in concrete terms, carry with her what she had gained throughout the course of therapy. Arnold used a notebook that had an image of an eagle soaring above the clouds to represent Tanequa soaring above her circumstances. The notepad happened to have Arnold's university name at the bottom of it in light grey, and Arnold attended a Christian university, which got Tanequa excited as she thought back on the support she had felt at church and started up a conversation about seeking that out again. The TO in this case was very helpful in a variety of ways.

## *A Concept to Contemplate*

© Shutterstock.com

If you were to implement the changes discussed in Chapter 13 (related to the stages of change model) and make progress, how would you conceptualize the theme or script of your story?

If you were to work with a counselor on this journey, what do you think may be a good token or TO for your counselor to use?

## Summarizing

In addition to identifying central themes and scripts and an appropriate TO that symbolizes the work that has been done throughout the course of treatment, another skill to bring closure is the skill of summarizing. Recall that we discussed summarizing in Chapter 8.

In this case, we suggest starting the summary with the clients' gains. Think back to the original presenting problem that brought the client into treatment and what has happened since then, including the crises the client has faced, the crises the client has overcome, the new coping skills the client has learned, the new insights the client has had, and so on. A sample summary may go something like this:

Today is our last session, and it may seem just like yesterday that you came in reporting having regular panic attacks two years ago this month. When you first came in your peace level was at a 1 or a 2 on a scale of 1–10 where 10 was a high level of peace. For the past couple months, it has been between a 7 and a 9. You identified your triggers, participated in systematic desensitization, practiced your breathing exercises, and have also incorporated your stress management or peace-inducing behaviors into your routine such as prayer journaling, meditating, and spending time in nature. When you first came in you reported the coping mechanisms you typically used were alcohol and escaping with Netflix. You have reported that spending more time in nature and mediating has helped you develop a greater sense of peace and well-being. What stands out to me most was that you were able to take time to reflect on what has been happening and implement strategies that work and turn them into habits.

## Assessing Progress

You may have noticed that in the summary above, we used the scale and indicated where the client was on the scale when she first came into treatment and where she has been on the scale recently, which involves an assessment of progress. It can be this simple or it can be more elaborate (depending on the needs of the client and what the presenting problem and treatment calls for). Once you take the class on diagnosis and treatment planning and the assessment class, you will learn about many additional tools you can use to measure progress and let clients know how much they have improved on a scale such as the Hamilton Depression Scale (Hamilton, 1960). For now, we will focus on using scaling for this. Furthermore, it is important to help clients identify their own gains and progress. This is a closing skill used at termination in addition to each individual session during treatment. The question I like to ask in each session after summarizing is, "If you could take away one thing today, what one thing would you take away?" As clients get used to this question, sometimes midsession they will even say things like, "Ah! That is going to be my takeaway today!"

In order to help clients to assess their own progress at termination, after summarizing and reporting the progress that I have seen, I ask them to share with me what changes they have noticed or what stands out to them. Some strategic questions to get at this are:

- What stands out to you most from our time together over these past two years?

- What do you think are the major changes or gains that you have seen throughout the course of treatment?

- If you could take away three key things from all of our time together what would they be?

## Exploring Loss

As mentioned in the introduction to the chapter, the therapeutic relationship is a very important relationship in the lives of most clients. Termination means a loss of that relationship. In this case, it may bring up feelings about past endings and losses, so it is important for the therapist to check in with the client regarding these feelings. Consider some of the following questions or prompts:

- So, we are approaching the end of our time together. I am wondering what feelings bubble up inside of you as you think about the end of treatment?

- We have been working together in treatment for a few years, and I wanted to check in with you and see how you are feeling about the ending of this therapeutic relationship.

- We are approaching the end of our time together, and you mentioned in the past you have experienced some loss and unexpected endings; I am wondering what comes up for you as you think about being at the end.

After using these questions to open the door to conversation about loss, the clinician then uses the reflective listening skills including paraphrasing or reflecting content, reflecting feelings, and reflecting meaning to track with the client and validate his or her feelings related to the loss. Scaling could be used here as far as the client's level of comfort with termination or another scale that may be more appropriate, such as peace or preparedness.

## Developing a Plan for Maintenance

I used to work with adolescent males at a substance abuse rehabilitation facility. Upon completion of the program, they would be discharged back home to their same stressors, family dynamics, friend groups, and school systems. It would be tough to maintain the gains they had made when in treatment where they had a lot of support and prevention from access to substances. It was very important to develop a plan for how to maintain the progress that had been made.

Here are some questions to consider asking to accomplish this:

- You have made _____ and _____ (fill in the blanks with whatever major progress the client has made). What can you do after treatment to continue to progress or maintain this progress?

- What will you do to maintain this progress after you have completed treatment?

- What will you continue to do on your own to maintain _____ that you have accomplished while in treatment?

It is important to use the active listening skills to paraphrase and reflect feelings and key content during this phase just as in every other phase of counseling. These questions listed above are strategic questions, and the number of paraphrases, reflections of feeling, minimal encouragers, and other skills must outnumber the number of strategic questions.

## Relapse Prevention

You may think of relapse prevention when you think of substance abuse treatment, and it is certainly an important part of that treatment protocol. However, we consider relapse prevention with any treatment. It is easy for clients to regress to a previous stage of change or return to their previous coping mechanisms when life begins to feel overwhelming or when they face distress.

So, here it can be helpful to identify triggers. For example, we worked with a client who struggled with addiction to pornography and was able to make progress but found every few months or so, he would have a strong temptation to go back to it. So, we asked, "What are your triggers? What situations may make it difficult to abstain?" He shared that when he felt stressed or alone and had not had intercourse with his partner for some time, he would be tempted to use pornography, and once he started, he would use it for hours at a time and sometimes more than once per day. It was important to work collaboratively with him to identify his plan to avoid relapse. Here are some questions that can be used when planning for relapse prevention:

- What triggers may prompt you to want to _____ (use pornography, lose your temper, drink, panic, ruminate on absolutist thoughts, etc.)?

- What are some ways you can set yourself up to be more likely to use other coping mechanisms when you face ____ triggers?

- Who is in your support system (family, friends, church members, neighbors, AA, etc.) that will be in support of your goals? Could you identify an accountability partner to hold you accountable?

## Open Door or Follow-Up Appointment

When you visit your family doctor, what does he typically say at the end of the appointment? In many cases, he will say, come back and see in ____ (three, six, etc.) months. It can be helpful to do the same with our clients. The knowledge of access to support and formal accountability in checking in to report maintenance of progress or a new crisis, or to restart therapy if needed is helpful. However, as we are always working ourselves out of a job, it is important to ensure that the client has a support system set up outside of treatment as well.

## Accountability or Support Systems

Another important task to complete in preparation for termination is to evaluate the client's support system. Ideally, this occurs throughout therapy and the therapist would be working with the client to identify safe, supportive relationships. It is important for the client to identify who will be a part of his or her ongoing support system. Is there an accountability partner available, or someone that the client feels safe and comfortable to talk with about his or her challenges and goals? If not, can this support be sought in other places? Is the client a member of AA? Does he or she have a sponsor? Does the client have a trusted mentor at work, a friend at church, etc.?

## Referral to Appropriate Community Agencies

It is the counselors' ethical responsibility to provide appropriate preparation for termination and to provide referrals as necessary. Dr. Ted Remley is trained both as an attorney and a counselor, so we appreciate his unique perspective (Remley, personal communication, 2010). Remley also states that ideally the termination date is set by both the counselor and the client. However, this is not always possible, and sometimes the date may even be set by a third party (such as an insurance provider; see the earlier section on premature termination for more on this topic. We recommend Dr. Remley's text entitled *Ethical, Legal, and Professional Issues in Counseling*. See the Recommended Reading section for more information). We encourage our interns to maintain a list of providers in the community to refer to. For example, in our community, there is a health department where clients can sometimes obtain sliding scale health services. We also have several churches that offer free counseling services from clinical mental health counseling interns and a private practice that allows clients to see a counseling resident for a discounted rate. We encourage students to begin creating a database of available resources within the community for potential referral. We recommend counselors continually strive to compile a database of community resources and share the findings with clients as appropriate to help them access the needed services available. In additional courses taken within your counseling program, you may have the opportunity to develop a resource guide. A full discussion on community resources is beyond the scope of this text; however, we do suggest beginning to take notice of resources and compile a database so that you have some readily available when you encounter a client's need.

## Attachment Illumination

© Shutterstock.com

From an attachment perspective, termination can trigger feelings of past losses and unresolved loss as discussed earlier in the chapter. Loss can also be difficult for those who may have had an interpersonal history characterized by inconsistency, which is often the case for those with a preoccupied style. Their narratives typically tend to be longer, more entangled, and call for more time. Unfortunately, counseling is nearly always time sensitive, and there is a termination time for individual sessions, typically 45 minutes to an hour and then again the number of counseling sessions that comprise the course of treatment. The closing skills used in this chapter can be especially helpful to seek to bring closure and wind down a session with a client who has a more preoccupied style.

## The Case of Monica

### A Case Study of Preoccupied Attachment

Monica was a 28-year-old case manager at a residential home for at-risk adolescent girls. She enjoyed her job but often felt overwhelmed and besieged by anxiety and tension. She was drawn to the mental health field by her love of helping others. She earned a bachelor's degree in social work and has worked with struggling teens since graduating five years earlier. She relayed that recently, "One of my girls from the group home ran away Is there a word missing here? the run for several weeks until they found her strung-out on heroin and prostituting on the streets" in a town over a hundred miles south. Monica was stricken by feelings of guilt, anxiety, and anger. Even though her supervisor and the facility's director assured Monica that the young lady's decision to run away was not Monica's fault, she felt totally responsible for the girl's actions, blaming herself for not "seeing the signs that she was getting ready to bolt. I should have known. I feel like it is all my fault." To complicate matters, Monica's boyfriend had become increasingly emotionally unavailable. Because she was so engrossed in the happenings at the group home—even before the runaway incident—he began pulling away and spending more time with his buddies. Monica felt abandoned by him. "I don't think he cares about me and all I am going through. I need him to help me understand me and my feelings." The difficulty was that Monica did not just talk about her feelings; she gushed them. "It's like standing defenseless in front of a firehose," reported Angie, a seasoned therapist, as she briefed those on her supervision team regarding Monica's case.

When Angie administered parts of the AAI (Adult Attachment Interview), Monica became entangled in her descriptions about the past. Her father abandoned her mother before her second birthday. Her mother never remarried but had another child, Jannice, when Monica was five years old. Her younger sister suffered the same fate as Monica when the girl's father refused to marry her mother and permanently exited her life. Monica produced a mixed bag of adjectives to describe her relationship with her mother: loving, unfair, out of control, a mess, and childish. The challenge was following Monica's narrative. She was so flooded and overwhelmed by her emotions as she described her childhood relationship with her mother, she violated many of the basic rules of effective, collaborative conversation. It was as if she completely lost track of Angie's questions. For example, when Angie asked if Monica could give an example of her mother being "unfair" when Monica was a child in elementary school, Monica started out with:

> Well, just the other day she brought my sister's kids over to my house, all dressed up in new clothes she had just bought them. She never buys new clothes for my kids. It's like she always babies Jannice. That's the story of my life with mom; she always is there for my sister but never me and when she is in trouble and her life falls apart like it always does, then she expects me to be there for her, to help her. . .it is just not right. . ..don't you agree with me? Don't you see how messed up she is about stuff?

Notice how Monica does not answer the question. Angie asked for an example of Monica's mother being unfair when Monica was a child, but she launched into a present-day example. She simply mixed the past with the present as if they were the same thing. Then she went on to describe her mother's life as "falling apart" and was trying to get Angie to take her side by asking Angie if she agreed with her assessment that her mother was "messed up." Angie felt overwhelmed and confused by Monica's conversational style, a telltale sign of attachment preoccupation.

Like Monica, some clients are so entangled or preoccupied with their childhood attachment figures they cannot step back from the experience and describe it objectively and coherently. Instead, emotionally they are tied up in the experience. Instead of describing how she felt "then," she was actually feeling the experience and spewing it onto the counselor. Aptly, Angie said to the supervision group: "When Dr. Sibcy was a kid, his dad would take him fishing and he would make him use those old reels that would get backlashed. It was almost impossible to get them untangled. Monica can backlash a conversation like an old fishing reel."

Monica's attachment style was important to understanding her current concerns as a case manager. She had difficulty disentangling herself from the girls she was trying to help. She was preoccupied, as it were, with them and found herself feeling overwhelmed, anxious, and angry about their choices. Interestingly, she grew up in a home where she was always expected to take care of her mom and sister, whom Monica felt were out of control. She ended up in a job that required her to take care of a houseful of girls who were just like the ones she took care of as a child. And just like when she was a child, Monica was angry about the fact that she was always the one giving and caring for others, but no one was there to take care of her. What she did not see was that unlike her childhood, Monica was the one who had orchestrated her life such that she was in a position of being a compulsive caregiver. She did not know how to turn it off.

However, Monica could benefit from processing these feelings in session as her counselor works with her to make sense of her experience. Advanced skills like immediacy may be helpful to bring Monica back to the present moment when she gets preoccupied with the experiences she had with her mother. In terminating, it will be very important that her counselor use the closing skills, help her to identify a support system, and make a community referral, since not experiencing care is a theme for Monica, which is something to address as well.

## TO Do List

- Identify a key theme or script the client has been facing and has made progress with

- Identify a small token or TO that may be used to represent the progress the client has made throughout the process of counseling

- Summarize gains made throughout counseling

- Provide opportunities and an atmosphere to discuss the client's feeling about the end of treatment and any feelings of loss that may come up

- Assess progress made in counseling using scaling or other measure

- Ask the client who is in their support system or who will serve as an accountability partner or person they can talk to regarding progress

- Make appropriate referrals to the community as needed

## Recommended Reading

If you would like to gain more expertise on the topics discussed in this chapter, we would recommend reading the following texts to expand your knowledge in this area:

© Shutterstock.com

- Coan, J. (2008). Toward a neuroscience of attachment. In *Handbook of attachment: Theory, research, and clinical applications* (5th ed., pp. 241–258). New York, NY: Guilford Press.

- Hatchett, G. T. (2004). Reducing premature termination in university counseling centers. *Journal of College Student Psychotherapy, 19*(2), 13–27. doi:10.1300/J035v19n02_03

- Remley, T. P., Jr., & Herlihy, B. (2007). *Ethical, legal, and professional issues in counseling* (Updated 2nd ed.). Upper Saddle River, NJ: Pearson Merrill Prentice Hall.

- Savickas, M. L. (1998). Career style assessment and counseling. In T. Sweeney (Ed.), *Adlerian counseling: A practitioner's approach* (4th ed., pp. 329–360). Philadelphia, PA: Accelerated Development Press.

## Chapter Summary

It is important for the clinician to prepare his or her heart for being fully present with the client, especially when a client is facing endings of any sort. As a Christian counselor, the counselor has a sense of comfort and hope beyond what is transient. This is manifested in the words of a poem entitled "Footprints in the Sand." Next, it is important also to help clients prepare their hearts for the end of treatment during the termination phase; this involves preparing the client using the before-during-after or the BDA approach/principle that Dr. Kuhnley recommends. Prepare for termination beforehand through establishing treatment guidelines including duration, address termination issues during the final session, and determine resources for the client to use after the termination of therapy. A TO offered at the end of therapy can help smooth the transition from treatment to life without treatment. The idea of using a TO or a token to represent therapeutic gains comes from Bowlbyian, Winnicottian, and Savickasian principles. Other termination skills can also be integrated in order to have a successful termination with the client.

Another consideration is premature termination. Premature termination has been a problem in both inpatient and outpatient settings. Hatchett (2004) has researched and scoured the literature on eight different strategies that may help counselors prevent premature termination such as knowledge of risk factors, multicultural competence, reminder emails, informed consent or professional disclosure, planning for brief treatment, and so on. Moreover, important termination skills such as consolidating gains from counseling, identifying a support system, evaluating progress, and making appropriate referrals were addressed in this chapter.

Chapter Fifteen

# Multicultural Considerations for Counseling Skills

### Elias Moitinho, PhD, LPC-S, LMFT, LPC

*There is neither Jew nor Greek, there is neither slave nor free, there is no male and female, for you are all one in Christ Jesus.*

—Galatians 3:28 (ESV)

## Chapter Learning Objectives

- Explore multicultural considerations for using counseling skills with an ethnic diverse client population
- Understand the impact of different heritages, attitudes, and past experiences on an individual (CACREP II.F.2.d, 2016, p. 11)
- Learn that multicultural can include race, ethnicity, or religion and that each has an impact on the client (CACREP II.F.2.g. 2016, p.12)
- Identify the Multicultural and Social Justice Counseling Competencies (MCSJC)
- Explore a distinctive biblical anthropology
- Describe how core counseling skills can be used in various clinical contexts with an ethnically diverse client population
- Learn to lower barriers found in a multicultural setting (CACREP II.F.2.h, 2016, p.12)

# Chapter Overview

United States has become ethnically and culturally diverse, and consequently, unselors need to become competent in providing services that meet the needs of clients their context. This chapter will examine key essential multicultural considerations for unseling skills with an ethnically diverse client population. It will discuss how culture influences interpersonal relationships and communication and briefly review the Multicultural and Social Justice Counseling Competencies (MCSJC) adopted by the American Counseling Association (ACA). This chapter will also present a distinctive biblical anthropology to help future counselors view people from a biblical worldview, thus minimizing ethnocentrism, stereotyping, discrimination, and potential cultural conflict in counseling. This chapter will cover several elements regarding culture in counseling that address the Council for Accreditation of Counseling and Related Educational Programs (CACREP) standards about the multicultural counseling setting. Finally, the chapter will demonstrate how core counseling skills can be used in various clinical contexts with an ethnically diverse client population.

## Key Essential Multicultural Considerations

*Take a look at this picture.* What are some potential differences between the counselor and the client? Probably, you will notice two obvious differences, race and age. Let us examine this scenario more carefully.

Counseling always takes place in a cultural context. Therefore, whenever there is racial tension in the country and, obviously in the media, counselors and clients may experience some

© Monkey Business images/Shutterstock.com

tension in the counseling room as well. The counselor is the person responsible for bringing up and addressing potential racial or cultural differences and any tension that may exist. Furthermore, in this scenario, the client may wonder if the counselor will understand him or if he can fully trust the counselor. It is important to note that addressing cultural differences does not need to take place in every new multicultural counseling encounter.

*Now imagine that the counselor is a member of the minority culture* and also younger than the client.

Some of the same concerns may be present in this scenario. Again, it is the counselor's responsibility to initiate the discussion about their cultural differences in the counseling session. The field of multicultural counseling includes multiple areas such as culture, racial or ethnic identity, social justice and advocacy, social class and

© Monkey Business Images/Shutterstock.com

socioeconomic status, disability, age, gender, religion, and spirituality. Due to the brevity of this chapter, the focus will be on cultural and ethnic diversity.

**Addressing Religion and Spirituality**

## A Growing Ethnic Diversity in the United States

This section will examine briefly some of the demographic changes in recent decades and will describe a few of the ethnic minority cultures in the United States. However, future counselors need to be careful not to overgeneralize this information to every person of a minority group. You also need to remember that to be culturally sensitive and competent, you need to get to know each client well.

**TIP:** Do not overgeneralize the information you learn about a particular culture to every member of that cultural group. Make an effort to know each client well.

Racial and ethnic identities are a significant variable in counseling. Consequently, an important issue in counseling with members of ethnic minorities is client self-identification. Racial and ethnic identities are a complex concept, and multiple theories exist to explain how individuals select their cultural identity.

© Ollyy/Shutterstock.com

Moreover, identification with a particular ethnicity or cultural group is a process. As a counselor, you may be unsure of how to address or refer to your ethnic client. In the counseling literature, experts recommend that is preferable for a counselor to allow clients to share how they self-identify (Moore-Thomas, 2018). This can facilitate rapport building, and it shows respect toward the client.

A brief exploration of some ethnic minorities in the United States is given below.

## African American/Black and African Descent

According to the U.S. Census Bureau (2015a), the African American population was 45 million in 2015 and is projected to grow to 74.5 million by 2060.

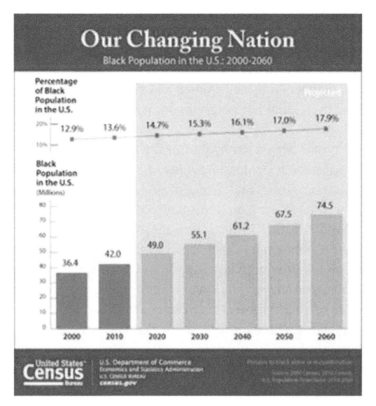

*Source*: https://www.census.gov/newsroom/facts-for-features/2015/cb15-ff01.html

The African American or Black population represents about 13% of the U.S. population and has a long and traumatic history in the United States. This overview will emphasize some characteristics of the African American population including within-group diversity, family structure, spirituality, and the stigma associated with mental illness. Regarding the appropriate terminology to address this group, the client's self-identification is important. Some African Americans prefer the term *Black* whereas others prefer *African American.* Colorism has also been an issue for this community where people of lighter skin tones are perceived more positively better and may discriminate against people of darker skin. Matthews and Johnson (2015) note, "It can be substantiated that African-American women who have darker tones experience a disproportionate amount of social and cultural pressure and are impacted by the pervasiveness of the prejudice" (p. 264).

The history of slavery, segregation, discrimination, and eventually the Civil Rights movement influence how African Americans perceive their interaction with the American society at large, particularly with the White population. Our nation has made tremendous strides toward racial reconciliation. However, we must acknowledge that there is a lot of work yet to be done, and that, unfortunately, racial tension still exists to various degrees.

It is essential for counselors to be aware of the diversity that exists within the African American culture. For example, such diversity can be seen in the family and socioeconomic status. Counselors need to be aware that there is no typical African American family (Boyd-

Franklyn, 2003). Unfortunately, a large number of African Americans live in poverty as the poverty rate in 2014 for Blacks was 26.2%, while the national rate was 14.8% (U.S. Census, 2015a).

The family structure in the African American community is collectivistic and includes relatives, extended families, and others who are not necessarily blood relatives (Bounds, Washington, & Henfield, 2018). The African American family has been described as matriarchal, and there is also a large number of single parent households (Sue & Sue, 2016). Therefore, the network of support is largely the extended family and community. Moreover, "counselors need to be sensitive to the larger numbers of Black women and single parents, as well as Black men who may be involved with their children but not living in the same household" (Bounds et al., 2018, p. 267).

Historically, spirituality has been a strong part of the African American culture. According to Masci (2018) of the Pew Research Center, "Roughly eight-in-ten (79%) African Americans self-identify as Christian." He points out that "While most Africans brought to the New World to be slaves were not Christians when they arrived, many of them and their descendants embraced Christianity, finding comfort in the Biblical message of spiritual equality and deliverance. In post-Civil War America, a burgeoning black church played a key role strengthening African American communities and in providing key support to the civil rights movement." As part of a biopsychosocial-spiritual assessment, you may need to assess the role that religion and spirituality play in the life of your African American client.

There is a stigma associated with mental illness within the African American population, and consequently, many individuals avoid seeking mental health services (Fripp & Carlson, 2017). Furthermore, other barriers to accessing and receiving mental health treatment for this population include "misdiagnosis, overutilization of emergency and inpatient care services, isolation and lack of social support, and disempowerment in treatment" (Kawaii-Bogue, Williams, & MacNear, 2017, p. 23). Thus, a large number of African Americans tend to seek help from their religious community rather than mental health counselors. From a counseling perspective, building trust with any client is essential, particularly with African Americans. This is especially important for White counselors, because "skepticism or suspicion of European Americans is pervasive among African Americans" (Gladding, 2016, p. 175).

## Hispanic/Latino/a Descent

According to the U.S. Census, the Hispanic/Latino population in the United States in 2014 was 55 million people, making up 17% of the U.S. population, the largest minority group. People of Mexican descent make up the majority of this population with almost 64% (U.S. Census, 2015b). Therefore, counselors must be careful to avoid the stereotype that all Hispanics are Mexican.

The Hispanic/Latino population in the United States is a multiethnic and multicultural group including individuals of diverse racial or ethnic, educational, political, economic, and religious backgrounds. Nevertheless, several cultural values including collectivism, familism, and personalism, to name a few, bind Hispanic/Latino individuals together, in addition to the Spanish language. It is important to note that Brazilians speak Portuguese. Therefore, most Brazilians would accept the term *Latino* to refer to themselves rather than *Hispanic*.

**Collectivism,** a strong core value of this culture, emphasizes the group rather than the individual. The collectivistic orientation is expressed throughout the culture in many ways including *familism*, which emphasizes family loyalty and interdependence. Other family-centered values incorporate hierarchy and clearly defined gender roles within the family (Falicov, 1998; McGoldrick, Giordano, & Garcia-Preto, 2005). Familism emphasizes providing for the family emotionally and financially. Some believe that the needs of the family supersede the needs of the individual, and decision making is family centered. A study also found support for "the notion that *familism* respect and obligation values are important for Latinos across all levels of SES" (Stein, Rivas-Drake, & Camacho, 2017, p. 112).

*Personalism* is another essential value that denotes personal dignity of each individual. It emphasizes warm and pleasant interactions and harmony in relationships. This value focuses on the importance of making other people feel welcomed and respected. Thus, I believe that personalism is consistent with a biblical worldview that emphasizes the intrinsic worth of each person as made in the image of God (Gen. 1:31).

Assessing levels of acculturation is an essential task when counseling minority individuals. Acculturation is "the changes in behavior, cognition, values, language, cultural activities, personal relational styles, and beliefs that a cultural minority group undergoes as it encounters the dominant culture" (Hays & McLeod, 2018, p. 6). Consequently, a person may be *high acculturated,* meaning the individual lives by the norms and values of the American culture and often speaks English as the first language. A person may be *bicultural* and therefore able to function in both cultures (American culture and the culture of the country of origin) and is usually bilingual. A person may be *low acculturated* due to having a high affiliation to the culture of the country of origin. Thus, it is important for the counselor to determine early on in the counseling process the level of acculturation of a Hispanic or Latino client. Usually, the low-acculturated client needs the services of interpreters.

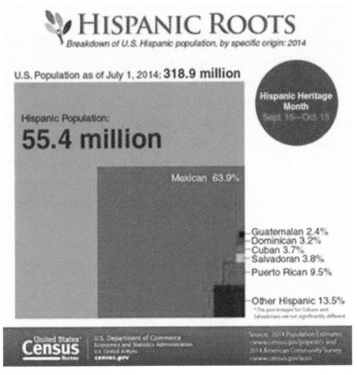

*Source*: https://www.census.gov/content/dam/Census/newsroom/facts-for-features/2015/cb15-ff18_graphic.jpg

## Asian Descent

According to the Pew Research Center, the U.S. Asian population is the fastest-growing minority group in the United States (López, Ruiz, & Patten, 2017) with an estimated population of 21.4 million in 2016 (Census.gov). This population is also very diverse because people of Asian descent come from multiple countries of origin. "As of 2015, 24% of Asian Americans (4.9 million) were of Chinese origin, the largest single origin group. The next two largest origin groups are Indian-origin Asians, who accounted for 20% of the national Asian population (4.0 million), and Filipinos (19%, or 3.9 million). Those with roots in Vietnam, Korea and Japan easily clear the 1 million mark as well" (López et al., 2017). Therefore, multiple cultures and languages are represented among people of Asian descent.

Another element that counselors need to consider when counseling people of Asian descent is the fact that the Asian cultures are collectivistic and place strong emphasis on the family. Lee and Mock (2005) point out that Asian families "emphasize harmonious interpersonal relationships, interdependence, and mutual obligations or loyalty for achieving a state of homeostasis or peaceful coexistence with family members or other fellow beings" (p. 274). Thus, counselors would do well to "consider family dynamics, and other related factors such as individual and family immigration history, adaptation experiences, cultural values, and generational differences in acculturation experience" (Luu, Inman, & Alvarez, 2018, p. 330). Similar to the Hispanic or Latino culture, a collectivistic orientation and a strong emphasis on the family are central values in the Asian American culture. Therefore, it is important for counselors to learn about the hierarchy and filial piety within this cultural group.

The *model minority* is a label that has been applied to this population because of the strong emphasis placed on educational achievement, and consequently higher income levels by people of Asian descent. "Asians overall are the highest-earning racial and ethnic group in the U.S., but it is not a status shared by all Asians. In 2016, the median annual income for Asian adults was $51,288, compared with $47,958 for whites, $31,082 for blacks and $30,400 for Hispanics" (Kochnar & Cilluffo, 2018). However, Chou and Feagin (2014) assert that Asian Americans continue to face discrimination and oppression, and feel stressed because "significant educational and economic achievement do not effectively shield them" (p. 4).

Emotional restraint is a value of many Asian cultures that may affect the therapeutic relationship (Lee & Mock, 2005). Therefore, a low-acculturated client of Asian descent will present less self-disclosure and less emotional expression in session. Although Asian Americans underutilize mental health services, you will probably encounter them in your counseling career. Therefore, as previously mentioned, when working with minority clients of Asian descent, the counselor will need to determine the client's level of acculturation. Such assesment will help the counselor know how to interact with the client effectively. Lee and Mock (2005) also recommend that the counselor take a "therapeutic stance of naivete, along with knowledgeable curiosity [to facilitate] a positive working relationship" (p. 282).

*Source*: https://www.census.gov/library/visualizations/2018/comm/api.html.html

## Other Ethnic Minorities

Other smaller ethnic minorities in the United States include the Native American population and people of Arab descent or families the Middle East. Native Americans made up about 2% of the U.S. population in 2016 with 6.7 million people (Census.gov). According to the Bureau of Indian Affairs (2017), currently, 567 tribes are recognized and eligible for funding and services. Native Americans face several challenges including low employment, substance abuse, and mental health issues including depression and high suicide rates (Herne, Bartholomew, & Weahkee, 2014).

Counselors who work with Native Americans need to be culturally sensitive and aware of the values espoused by this cultural group. Some of the Native American values that are particularly relevant for interpersonal interactions include expecations to "speak softly, at a lower rate, avoid singling out the listener, interject less, use less 'encouraging signs' (uh-huh, head nodding), delay response to auditory messages, and nonverbal communication" (Garrett et al., 2018, p. 412). Therefore, as a counselor, you may need to adjust your use of the active listening skills.

According to Brown, Guskin, and Mitchell (2012) of the Pew Research Center, "In the 2011 American Community Survey, the U.S. Census Bureau reported there were close to 1.8 million Arab Americans living within the United States, an approximately 47% increase in population size from 2000. Some believe, moreover, that this dramatically undercounts the population. For instance, according to the Arab American Institute, the number of Arab-Americans is increasing at an even greater rate, with a total population closer to 3.7 million" (p. or para. ##).

Finally, it is also important to note that the number of interracial or interethnic marriages in our society is increasing gradually. According to Livingston and Brown of the Pew Research Center (2017), "one-in-six newlyweds are married to someone of a different race or ethnicity" (p. 5). Therefore, more children will be biracial or multiethnic. Counselors will be dealing with various cultural dynamics in the counseling setting. My colleagues and I contend that mental health professionals need to be aware of some unique dynamics and challenges faced by interracial/interethnic married couples (Moitinho, Moitinho, Freyre, & Freyre, 2018).

## Understanding Culture

Axelson (1999) defines **culture** as "the totality of learned, socially transmitted behaviors that emerge from its members' interpersonal transactions" (p. 4). He furthers points out that "objective culture refers to the more obvious features of any group of people-the tangible, visible aspects such as artifacts, clothing, food, greetings, and festivals that may be readily observed by outsiders. Subjective culture refers to the invisible, less tangible, and less generalized aspects of group life-the deeper inner layers of personal attitudes, beliefs, feelings, values and norms of

© stoatphoto/Shutterstock.com

behaviors, and roles" (p. 3). Thus, counselors in training must be aware that culture is a broad concept that encompasses multiple elements that influence each person.

## Multicultural Counseling

Multicultural counseling involves acknowledging cultural elements and the client's cultural identity and integrating them in the counseling process. It includes a counselor's willingness to adapt a counseling approach to make it relevant and effective to a client's cultural context. As above mentioned, several elements have contributed toward these developments, including "changing demographics and a growing awareness of prevailing social and economic problems that greatly impacted the well-being of racial/ethnic minorities groups" (Casa, Suzuki, Alexander, & Jackson, 2017, p. 15).

From a Christian perspective, Christ is our model for race relations and work with a multicultural population. Hiebert (1985) asserts, "Christ provides us with God's model for ministry. In Christ, God became fully human to save us. But, in doing so, He remained fully God [Phil. 2:5–8]. We, too, must identify ourselves with people without compromising our Christian identity" (p. 108). Thus, a Christian counselor needs to be incarnational. In other words, the counselor needs to enter into the client's world

© Andrey_Popov/Shutterstock.com

and seek to understand life from the client's perspective. Doing so does not mean that the counselor agrees with the client.

## Becoming Culturally Competent

Developing multicultural competencies is a requirement in the counseling profession. Sue and Sue (2016) point out that "multicultural counseling competence is defined as the counselor's acquisition of awareness, knowledge, and skills needed to function effectively in a pluralistic democratic society" (pp. 65–66). These competencies have been advanced by the ACA. Moreover, the CACREP requires that counseling program objectives "reflect current knowledge and projected needs concerning counseling practice in a multicultural and pluralistic society." Counseling programs are required to cover elements that address social and cultural diversity, which includes multicultural counseling competencies.

The MCSJC include the following:

- **Counselor self-awareness**—the goal is for counselors to develop self-awareness and explore their worldview including beliefs, attitudes, and biases they may have.

- **Client worldview**—the goal is for counselors to become knowledgeable and aware of their clients' worldviews.

- **Counseling relationship**—the goal is that counselors become aware of how their worldview and the clients' worldview influence the counseling relationship.

- **Counseling and advocacy interventions**—the goal is for counselors to seek to work with and on behalf of their clients (Hays & Erford, 2018).

These competencies have certainly expanded the initial multicultural competencies developed in 1992 (Sue & Sue, 2016). The thrust of these competencies is for counselors to expand the focus of treatment intervention from the client (microsystem) toward the client's context and society at large (macrosystem). This paradigm shift does emphasize an ecosystemic perspective. I agree that such approach is more challenging and time consuming for counselors. However, this perspective is seeking to address the client within his or her broader sociocultural context.

I agree with Diller (2015), who asserts that becoming multiculturally competent "does not occur as a result of a single day of training, a few consultations with experts, reading a book, or even taking a course. Rather, it is a developmental process that depends on the continual acquisition of knowledge, the development of new and more advanced skills, and an ongoing self-evaluation of progress" (p. 18). So, in your counseling program, you will take a multicultural counseling course and work on developing these competencies. Then, in your practicum and internship, you may have an opportunity to work with a diverse population. In your postgraduate internship, you will continue to develop your multicultural competencies. As you become a licensed professional, you will still continue to work on improving your competencies. You will make all these efforts because you want to be an agent of healing in your clients' lives. Interestingly, Thomas and Schwarzbaum (2017) contend that "therapists who do not address cultural meanings in their clients may engage in oppressive practices rather than therapeutic ones" (p. 3).

# A Biblical Anthropology and Implications for Multicultural Counseling

When we interact with people of other cultures, we may bring our own cultural assumptions, biases, and stereotypes. Therefore, we need to ensure that we see people from a distinctive biblical worldview rather than from our distorted cultural lenses. A biblical worldview provides a framework for us to view all people, including our clients, from a distinct vantage point that values people and the worth of each individual. This worldview can be conceptualized in three significant teachings in Scriptures: creation, fall, and redemption.

© Romolo Tavani/Shutterstock.com

- **Creation**

    The Bible clearly states that God created every person in his own image (Gen 1:27; Acts 17:26), and consequently, everyone has intrinsic value and worth. Theologians have examined the meaning of *Imago Dei* for centuries. The meaning of *image of God* implies that human beings are relational, rational, social, and spiritual beings (Garrett, 1990).

- **Fall**

    The fall has distorted God's purposes and marred the image of God in humanity. Grudem (1995) notes that the image of God in man was marred and distorted by sin; however, it was not eliminated or lost. All humanity has been affected by sin; consequently, every culture has elements (worldview, norms, behaviors, etc.) that have been distorted by sin. For instance, many cultures sanction behaviors and expressions that are contrary to biblical teaching. Furthermore, sin has affected us immensely to the point that instead of unity and harmony among people, there is a

© MichaelJayBerlin/Shutterstock.com

    tendency toward dissent, conflict, and discrimination. Nevertheless, all cultures have elements of *common grace,* an expression of being made in the image of God. For instance, valuing family, honoring the elderly, and practicing hospitality are values found in many cultures that are consistent with a biblical worldview.

- **Redemption**

    Because of the fall, the main emphasis throughout Scriptures is that God loves every person and wants all to be saved (John 3:16; Matt. 28:19-20; 1 Tim. 2:4; 2 Pet. 3:9). Furthermore, the Bible declares that "God does not show favoritism" (Acts 10:34–35,

NIV). I believe that there is hope for all humanity because the Gospel reveals God's grace through the sacrifice of Christ on the cross and makes us new creations (2 Cor. 5:17).

**The Church becomes God's redemptive paradigm for race relations. In the Church, there should be unity in diversity.** Jesus prayed "your will be done on earth, as it is in heaven" (Matt. 6:10, NIV). We may ask, what is God's will in heaven? Regarding relationships, we can see that God desires for people to be united before Him, "After this I looked, and there © Romolo Tavani/Shutterstock.com before me was a great multitude that no one could count, from every nation, tribe, people and language, standing before the throne and before the Lamb. They were wearing white robes and were holding palm branches in their hands" (Rev. 7:9, NIV). Furthermore, the New Testament message emphasized love. Jesus taught that the greatest commandment is to love God, and the second commandment is "Love your neighbor" (Matt. 22:39). Moreover, God wants us to put love in action as it is exemplified in the Parable of the Good Samaritan (Luke 10:25–37). Finally, to the church, Paul proclaimed that there is no superior culture in God's kingdom (1 Cor. 12:13).

In the project Racial Reconciliation and Healing 2.0 (2017) of the American Association of Christian Counselors (AACC), I used the acronym RACE to help clarify some of the actions that I believe we, as Christians, need to engage in. I proposed that we need to:

**R**ecognize our biases

**A**ccept people of other ethnicities as created in the image of God with intrinsic worth

**C**onnect with people of other ethnicities by taking the initiative to build bridges

**E**mpower people by equipping them to be culturally sensitive

© goofyfoottaka/Shutterstock.com

# Attachment Illumination

© Shutterstock.com

*With Anita Kuhnley and Justin Silvey*

One of the CACREP standards related to diversity involves exploring spirituality with clients, specifically, "the impact of spritiaul beliefs on clients' and counselors' worldviews" (CACREP, 2016, Section II, F, 2. G). Moreover, the ACA code of ethics mentions the term "spiritual" or "spirituality" at least four times. Thus, there is some level of agreement within the profession that spirituality is important to consider in counseling. Dr. Stephen Parker and Dr. Glenn Moriarity, counselor educators at Regent University, have researched God image and interventions related to God image in counseling. God image relates to a person's emotional experience of God and can impact God attachment. Kirkpatrick and Shaver's research (1990) identifies two hypotheses that highlight how people relate to God. One is sometimes referred to as the correspondence hypothesis, indicating our relationship with God can correspond to our relationship with primary caregivers. The other is the compensatory hypothesis that indicates that our relationship with God can compensate for a harsh childhood. We believe the latter is more adaptive and have extended the work of Parker and Moriarty (2007) to conduct short-term workshops designed to facilitate God attachment (Knight, Sibcy, Gantt, Carapezza, & Macon, 2018), participants reported that the God Image Automatic Thought Record was the most impactful counseling intervention on their attachment to God out of all of the interventions used.

Here is a sample of a God Image Automatic Thought record chart from Parker and Moriarty's publication entitled, "Working with God Images in Therapy" (2007) this was published as Chapter 18 in the text entitled *What Do we Imagine God to Be? The function of "God Images" in our Lives.*

| Situation | Feelings | Automatic Thought(s) | Real God Response | Outcome |
|---|---|---|---|---|
| Actual event leading to feeling God's Disappointment | Specify sad, anxious, angry etc. | -Write irrational God image automatic thought(s) that preceded emotion(s) | (Drawing on your experience of prayer and scripture)<br><br>-Write real God response to irrational God image automatic thought(s) | -Re-rate belief in irrational God image automatic thought(s)<br><br>0 to 100% |
| | -Rate 0 to 100% | -Rate belief in irrational God image automatic thought(s), 0 to 100% | -Rate belief in real God response 0 to 100% | -Specify and rate subsequent feelings, 0 to 100% |
| I didn't put much time into that presentation. As a result, they weren't interested and they didn't understand me. | Worthless: 95% | God Image Response: "You always cut corners, You can't even take the time to put together a decent powerpoint. I am ashamed of you" 85% | "Sandra, I do not judge you based on your performance, I love you and am proud to be your Father. You are finite and cannot always give 100%" | Belief in God image Irrational Response: 40%<br><br>Degree of Feeling Worthless: 50% |

**Figure 15.1.** God image automatic thought record.

Notice how Figure 15.1 allows a therapist to explore with a client a situation and then to examine the client's feelings about the situation including a rating of those feelings. Then the intervention moves toward identifying the client's own narrative or automatic thought process that corresponds to the feelings and situation. It is rated in terms of how rational it is. Then, the client and counselor examine how God may truly respond to this situation or thought. This relates to God attachment, in that as the person challenges irrational negative beliefs about God, one may have a more positive and loving image of God and feel a greater sense of safety, allowing one to move toward God as a safe haven or secure base.

## Core Skills in Multicultural Counseling

If clients perceive that the counselor does not understand their situation or is not able to assist them, they will probably not return. Premature termination is a "no-win" situation for both client and counselor. Particularly, in cross-cultural counseling situations, the potential for misunderstanding increases significantly. The counselor's failure to make a good first impression combined with the client's lack of familiarity with counseling may contribute to this premature termination.

The counselor must be careful not to overlook, ignore, or perhaps even deny cultural factors. This mistake may be committed by those who may not experience many cross-cultural encounters and may not be sensitive to cultural differences. They may be unaware of the importance of considering cultural differences when counseling others. For example, some time ago, one of my students told me that he knew a Christian leader who proudly stated, "When I see people I do not see color, I only see the blood of Jesus." Although such statement that reflects color blindness may sound very spiritual, it is inaccurate. People are different due to their ethnic and cultural backgrounds. They tend to behave differently due to their diverse worldviews and cultural norms. Moreover, when a cross-cultural encounter occurs, many people will be inclined to reinforce their *ethnocentrism*, which is a tendency to evaluate another person's behavior according to the norms of one's own culture. Thus, a counselor needs to avoid viewing or interpreting all situations from his or her own cultural lenses.

Sue and Sue (2016) contend that the counseling profession has a Eurocentric perspective. Therefore, it reflects and emphasizes European values and norms that may be contrary to values and norms of other ethnicities. For instance, counseling emphasizes self-disclosure, so in counseling, clients are expected to share their feelings and verbalize their thoughts. However, many cultures such as the Asian culture value keeping one's thoughts and feelings inside as a sign of strength. Thus, self-disclosure is discouraged. Sue and Sue also point out that patterns of communication influence the counseling relationship. For instance, counseling emphasizes verbalization of feeling and emotions. Therefore, the client is expected to talk more than the counselor in the session. However, many cultures view the counselor as an authoritative expert. Consequently, clients come in and expect the professional to speak and provide a solution.

It is important to remember that emotions are universal. We all experience a wide range of emotions. Additionally, cultures dictate how emotions and feelings may be expressed. However, we must consider that each individual is unique. Therefore, the way a person may prefer to express and process his or her emotions may be different from how most people in his or her culture express and process emotions.

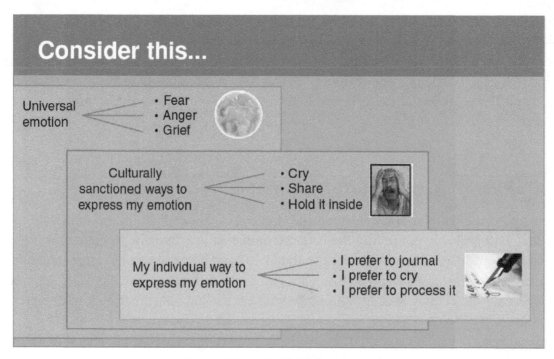

© Kendall Hunt Publishing Company

Becoming culturally competent includes becoming aware that ethnic clients may have been victims of **microagressions**. Sue et al. (2007) define **racial microaggressions** as "brief and commonplace daily verbal, behavioral, or environmental indignities, whether intentional or unintentional, that communicate hostile, derogatory, or negative racial slights and insults toward people of color" (p. 271). Therefore, counselors seek to be culturally competent and avoid making statements, even unintentionally, that could be considered and perceived by the client as such. Hook et al. (2016) conclude that counselors need to demonstrate cultural humility and "should educate themselves on the various types of racial microaggressions and be aware of the "racial microaggressions that are most common in counseling. Overall, the most common racial microaggressions were related to (a) denial of stereotypes or bias about cultural issues and (b) avoidance of discussion of cultural issues. Thus, at least from clients perspective, counselors often err on the side of denying their biases or minimizing cultural issues rather than validating the client's experience" (pp. 275–276)."

## Core Counseling Skills in a Multicultural Context

As a future counselor, you will need to master the core counseling skills to become clinically competent. You will also need to consider how to implement the skills in a way that shows that you are culturally sensitive. This section will examine the basic counseling skills and how they may be implemented in a multicultural counseling context. The counseling process starts with the first encounter between the counselor and the client. So, let us examine some important concepts and practices that may facilitate rapport building.

# Greeting, Welcome, and Hospitality

Effective counseling starts well when the counselor builds a solid therapeutic alliance with the client. This rapport is essential throughout the counseling process. Therefore, some important considerations need to be in place for the first encounter. Here are couple of important keys:

1. **Appropriate greeting and welcome set the tone for a positive encounter**

   Most cultures have specific ways to greet and welcome others. Obviously, you are not expected to know all the ways in which different cultures greet one another. However, if before your first meeting, you know what your client's cultural background is, it would be wise and beneficial for you to research and learn greeting behaviors and norms of the client's culture. For example, Asians tend

© pikcha/Shutterstock.com

to view the counselor as an authority and expert. Therefore, it would be important for the counselor to demonstrate professionalism and have credentials visible in the office. Depending on the country of origin and the level of acculturation, the client of Asian descent may bow. However, many websites that address the topic note that a handshake is common. In contrast, Hispanic or Latino clients, due to personalism, may expect the counselor to be warm, friendly, and relational. Consequently, the use of small talk may need to be maximized. Because of your own cultural background, you may think that engaging in small talk may be a waste of time; however, for many Latino/a clients, such practice creates a friendly interaction and sets the tone for a successful therapeutic relationship. Nevertheless, it is always important to note that you cannot overgeneralize a cultural practice to every member of that culture due to the variable of acculturation.

2. **Acknowledging ethnic and cultural differences that may be relevant in counseling**

   Discussing cultural differences at the beginning of the counseling process is recommended (Ivey et al., 2018). How would you address ethnic and cultural differences in counseling? You may say something like, "I am aware that there are racial and cultural differences between us. Do you have any concerns or thoughts about it that you would like to share?"

© Asia Images Group/Shutterstock.com

Hopefully, this will create freedom for the client to verbalize his or her thoughts or concerns about the counseling encounter. Several of my African American students have noted that especially in situations where a client is African American and the counselor is White, a major issue will be trust. Again, this is an indication that the counseling relationship can be seen as "a microcosm of racial relations in our larger society" (Sue & Sue, 2016, p. 138).

**Addressing Cultural and Gender Differences**

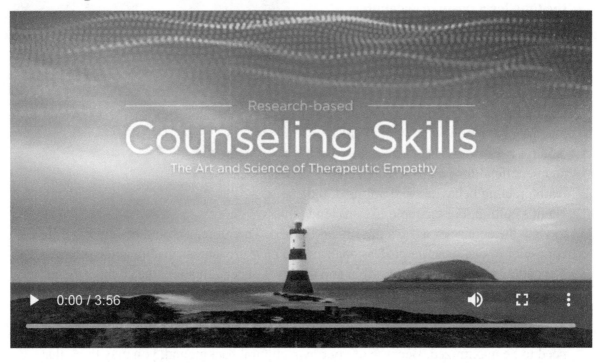

## Active Listening with Core Skills in Multicultural Counseling

Attending skills are essential for counselors to demonstrate that they are fully present psychologically in the session. The physical dimensions of attending are behaviors that include a posture of involvement, listening, and proxemics. These have been discussed in previous chapters. Here, I want to emphasize some nuances in multicultural encounters.

## Attending Skills

Murphy and Dillon (2008) wisely point out that "attending behaviors are culture-bound. What is considered attentive in one culture might be offensive in another" (p. 95). For instance, eye contact is very important in European cultures, whereas in the Native American culture, it is usually avoided. In some cultures, making eye contact with a person of authority may be a sign of disrespect. Therefore, clients may avoid making eye contact with the counselor.

The counselor's eye contact should be spontaneous and natural, and at times breaking eye contact is appropriate. As it has been described in other sections of this book, the counselor should avoid behaviors that interfere with effective listening such as looking down, writing notes, or looking away from the client. Again, you are not expected to know all cultures, but it is essential that you monitor your clients' reactions to your attending skills.

## Active Listening

It is imperative that counselors listen well to their clients. "To answer before listening—that is folly and shame" (Prov. 18:13). This truth of Scripture is relevant for counseling. As you are eager to help your clients, you must first listen carefully to understand their story, struggles, and pain before you can offer any help. Only when you listen will you be able to empathize with them and show care and Christlike concern. To emphasize the importance of listening, as a counselor educator, I have told my students multiple times, **"Give them your ears and they will give you their hearts."** What I mean by this is that when a counselor truly listens and empathizes with clients, the clients will trust the counselor and will open up and have more meaningful self-disclosure. Listening well is an essential task to build rapport and earn clients' trust. Through listening, a counselor enters the client's world and begins to understand the client's worldview and how he or she makes sense of his or her reality.

As explained in this book, when engaging in active listening, you will be using the skills of paraphrasing, reflecting, and summarizing. However, in a multicultural setting, counselors need to be mindful that they will encounter clients with various levels of acculturation and different levels of English language proficiency. In case of bilingual clients who prefer to share or express certain events or emotions in their first language, a recommendation is for the counselor to allow the client to share it in his or her first language and then share it in English (Ivey et al., 2018). The counselor can then use the skills of paraphrasing and reflecting to help the client process what has been shared.

© wavebreakmedia/Shutterstock.com

## Reflecting Skills

Empathizing with clients communicates that you as a counselor care and have a genuine concern for their well-being. Thus, reflecting feelings with a statement such as, "It sounds like you feel disappointed" demonstrates to the client that you understand the extent of his or her emotional struggle. Since reflecting skills have been explained well in previous chapters, here I want to highlight a couple of items. First, usually cultural norms dictate how people express their emotions and feelings, and these norms vary tremendously. Some cultures may value emotion regulation or restraint. Therefore, they discourage self-disclosure and self-expression and may view emotional expression as a potential sign of weakness. Hence, people in these cultures may appear more stoic. In contrast, some cultures may sanction emotional expression and view it as a strength. Consequently, people feel free to express their feelings openly. Second, counseling as a profession emphasizes openness, self-disclosure, and self-expression in the sessions. Sue and Sue (2016) point out that many diverse clients come from cultures where personal sharing in encouraged only in the context of family and long-term friendships. Therefore, counselors need to be sensitive to these clients; otherwise, a counselor may "erroneously conclude that the person is repressed, inhibited, shy, or passive" (Sue & Sue, 2016, p. 228). Realizing that it may take a while for the client to share, reflecting skills will need to be used carefully and with cultural sensitivity.

## Nonverbal

Proxemics is part of the nonverbal communication, and it refers to the interpersonal distance that is considered appropriate between people. As cultures vary in what is considered appropriate personal space, counselors will need to be attentive to what personal space is comfortable for the client. Counselors may need to avoid one of two extremes: being physically distant from the client or being physically too close from the client. However, what a counselor perceives as too close may be what a client feels comfortable with. I remember well dealing with proxemics when I first began to see clients as part of my counseling training over 20 years ago. As a Latino person who grew up in a culture with minimal personal space, I thought that my Anglo or White clients were sitting too far away. At first, this bothered me, and I was tempted to move my chair near them. Eventually, I came to the realization that the session is about the client. Hence, seating arrangements must be set in a way that make the clients feel comfortable.

## An Important Word About Using Professional Interpreters in Counseling

In a multicultural counseling setting, the potential for a language barrier exists. In your future career, you will probably face situations when you encounter clients who are not fluent in English. Furthermore, you may not speak the client's language. The counseling literature discourages the use of family members, including children, as interpreters (Paone & Malott, 2008). Therefore, in order to provide effective counseling services, you will need to rely on professionally trained interpreters. I have seen many Hispanic children translate for their parents in various settings such as at a store or in a church. Although this practice may be helpful to the family in those settings, it will certainly not work in the counseling setting, especially due to the personal nature of what is shared in counseling and the dynamics in the session.

Paone and Malott (2008) discuss best practices when using interpreters in counseling. They conceptualize the process in three parts: *presession briefing, within-session collaborative work,* and *postsession debriefing*. In the presession briefing, the counselor works with the interpreter in preparation for the session and emphasizes confidentiality. Within the session, the counselor and interpreter work collaboratively and follow specific guidelines to maximize understanding between the counselor and the client. In the debriefing session, the counselor hears the interpreter's impression of the session, including how culture may have influenced the content of the session. Costa (2017) recommends a similar process and emphasizes that in preparation for the session, the counselor needs to make the interpreter aware of any technical terminology that the counselor will be using during the session.

Furthermore, Costa (2017) recommends the following "good practice principles when working with interpreters" (p. 67):

* Meet with the interpreter before you meet with the client for a briefing. Explain your method of work and expected outcome to the interpreter. Let the interpreter know if you will be using any complex terminology.

- Meet with the client.

- Thank anyone from the family who wants to interpret so that they feel validated but explain that you are required to have a professional interpreter for your work. You may want to suggest that you would appreciate their support with other aspects of care if they are willing. It is important that the family member does not feel rejected or humiliated, for the well-being of everyone involved (Hadziabdic et al., 2014).

- Introduce yourself and the interpreter. Think how you will manage beginnings and endings of sessions.

- Set the ground rules, including confidentiality, and the fact that everything spoken in the room will be translated.

- Arrange seating so that everyone can see each other within the constraints of the room.

- Speak directly to the client.

- Work collaboratively together with the interpreter to form a team.

- Speak in small chunks so that the interpreter can translate accurately.

- Avoid having a private conversation with the interpreter in the client's presence.

- Allow enough time for de-briefing with the interpreter at the end. (p. 67)

## Multicultural Counseling Considerations and Telemental Health

Telemental health, also referred to as e-therapy or technology-assisted counseling, is a reality that is here to stay. Due to multiple advances in online technology, the fields of mental health counseling and medicine are making significant advances in using online technology to provide clinical services to clients and patients (Luxton, Nelson, & Maheu, 2016). CACREP emphasizes that ethical and culturally relevant strategies for establishing and maintaining in-person and technology-assisted relationships must be addressed by counseling training programs. Moreover, "The codes of ethics within the ACA, the IAMFC, and the AAMFT have increased clarity regarding the use of technology and providing counseling services" (Teufel-Prida, Raglin, Long, & Wirick, 2018, p. 140). Some potential limitations or concerns regarding technology-assisted counseling have already been covered in Chapter Five. Such considerations also apply to telemental health in a culturally diverse context. Suffice it to say, the use of technology limits the observation of nonverbal behavior. For example, a counselor may only be able to see a client's facial expressions while missing the client's overall posture and movements with the arms, hands, and legs.

1. **Case study**

A Hispanic couple sought counseling from a professional counselor. According to the wife, the main problem was that her husband was drinking excessively and was not fulfilling his roles as husband and father in the family. In the first session, the counselor allowed the wife to complain about her husband's behaviors, to put him down, and to attack him and his character verbally. She shared many examples of how her husband had failed her and the family because of his drinking problem. In the following two sessions, the counselor confronted the husband openly and challenged him to stop drinking and change. The couple did not return to counseling.

Many reasons may have contributed to this premature termination. First, many Hispanic/Latino individuals are not familiar with counseling. This couple, especially the wife, may have come seeking a quick solution to the situation. In this case, the counselor should have taken time to educate the clients that counseling is a process and, consequently, would involve multiple sessions. Second, it takes time to build rapport and to develop a strong therapeutic relationship with clients. Thus, the counselor should have focused on hearing from both and should have assessed the acculturation levels of each client quickly. While the wife shared openly, probably out of frustration, the husband felt blamed and not understood by the counselor since the counselor used confrontation too early in the counseling process. Additionally, due to the values of *machismo* and personalism, the husband may have felt devalued and perceived that he lost his authority and leadership in the family. Third, because first impressions are extremely important, counselors need to demonstrate care and concern for their clients and seek to understand their problems right away. In this scenario, the counselor may have used the skills of paraphrasing, reflecting, and empathizing poorly with the clients. The counselor allowed the wife to dominate the session and did not build a therapeutic alliance with the husband, who is the leader in most Hispanic/Latino homes, even though the husband's leadership in this scenario was questionable due to his drinking problem.

## Recommended Reading

If you liked the content of this chapter, we would recommend reading the following texts to expand your knowledge in this area. These are recommended literatures as they provided the basis of some of the research used for this chapter. Furthermore, these texts add to a counselor's repertoire of resources in the field:

© Shutterstock.com

- Hadziabdic, E., Albin, B., Heikkilä, K., Hjelm, K., Linnéuniversitetet, Institutionen för hälso- och vårdvetenskap (HV), & Fakulteten för Hälso- och livsvetenskap (FHL). (2014). Family members' experiences of the use of interpreters in healthcare. *Primary Health Care Research & Development, 15*(2), 156–169. doi:10.1017/S1463423612000680

- Kirkpatrick, L. A., & Shaver, P. R. (1990). Attachment theory and religion: Childhood attachments, religious beliefs, and conversion. *Journal for the Scientific Study of Religion, 29*(3), 315–334. doi:10.2307/1386461

- Malott, K. M., & Paone, T. R. (2008). Using interpreters in mental health counseling: A literature review and recommendations. *Journal of Multicultural Counseling and Development, 36*(3), 130–142. doi:10.1002/j.2161-1912.2008.tb00077.x

- Parker, S., & Moriarty, G. (2007). Working with God images in therapy. In P. Hegy (Ed.), *What do we imagine God to be? The function of "God images" in our lives* (pp. 255–269). Lewingston, NY: Edwin Mellen Press.

## Chapter Summary

Undoubtedly, every counseling session is a cultural encounter. In some encounters, the counselor and the client may be of the same ethnic background. Nevertheless, they may still have cultural differences. Due to the growing ethnic diversity in the US, counselors will work with clients of a diverse ethnic and cultural background more frequently. Building a solid therapeutic relationship by using the core counseling skills described in this text is key for effective counseling. This chapter provided you with an overview of elements essential to consider and implement in your counseling career to be culturally sensitive and multiculturally competent to work effectively with an ethnically and culturally diverse population.

## Chapter Sixteen

# What Counselors Need to Know about Psychopharmacology: What to Listen For

E. John Kuhnley, MD

*Medication is of course important but do not conclude that a pill dissolving in your stomach is necessarily more powerful than a healing thought in your mind.*

—Norman Vincent Peale (2007, p. 153)

## Chapter Learning Objectives

- To understand the role of prescription medication for the treatment of mental health conditions
- To identify barriers to effective diagnosis, medication decision making, and medication management (CACREP II.F.5.k, 2016, p. 12)
- To develop a plan for integrating counseling with medication management by prescribers
- To identify four major domains of diagnosis and relevant medications (CACREP II.F.3.e, 2016, p. 10)

# Chapter Overview

This chapter will examine the role of medications in the treatment of patients. Optimal prescription of medication requires careful, comprehensive evaluation, diagnosis, and ongoing management. Prescribers often do not have sufficient time to address these aspects of care, much less to create a safe atmosphere in which the patient will disclose information necessary for full understanding and management. Although counselors do not prescribe medication, they are in position to integrate the care of patients with professionals who do. The counselor facilitates an emotionally corrective experience for the patient. From this secure base, the counselor may help patients understand the role of medication, incorporate medications into their lives, and communicate with the prescribers regarding response and side effects. In this chapter, I refer to clients as patients, as this is the term used in the medical arena.

## Psychopharmacology

**Psychopharmacology** is the study of drugs (medications) to treat psychiatric or mental conditions. Psychiatric medications have psychoactive effects on brain function, especially the function of nerve cells or neurons. This impacts mood, thinking, behavior, sensation, and the physiology (function) of the brain and body organs (Figure 16.1). **Pharmacodynamics** refers to the effects of medication within the body. Pharmacokinetics refers to the processes by which the body responds to medication. **Pharmacokinetic processes** include absorption, distribution, metabolism, and excretion of a medication by the body.

Brain and body function require regulation or control resulting from communication among neurons or nerve cells. A synapse is a space or junction between nerve cells across which neurotransmitters (chemical signalers) produce impulses to communicate and stimulate actions. Although neurotransmitters provide communication between cells, hormones are chemical messengers that affect communication between body organs. The brain and body work together to produce homeostasis or balance in response to internal and external changes. Examples include breathing, consuming food, adjusting to temperature changes, interacting with

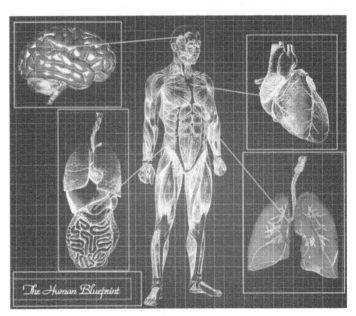

**Figure 16.1.**
© Digital Storm/Shutterstock.com

the world, and surviving danger. Illness or disease results from disruption of homeostasis and function within the brain and body.

Medications have desired effects to improve function and restore balance. However, they may have undesirable or adverse effects also known as side effects. Although side effects may be serious and require discontinuation or adjustment of the medication, most often they are transient while the brain and body are adjusting to the presence and impact of the medication. **Neurotransmitters** may exert different effects in various parts of the brain and body. When the medication affects one or more neurotransmitters, all areas impacted by the neurotransmitters must adjust. The goal of medication is to exert desired effects, which may include stabilization of mood, reduction of anxiety, improvement of concentration, and/or improvement of reality testing. Some medications are more specific, whereas others have broader potential impact.

# THE SYNAPSE

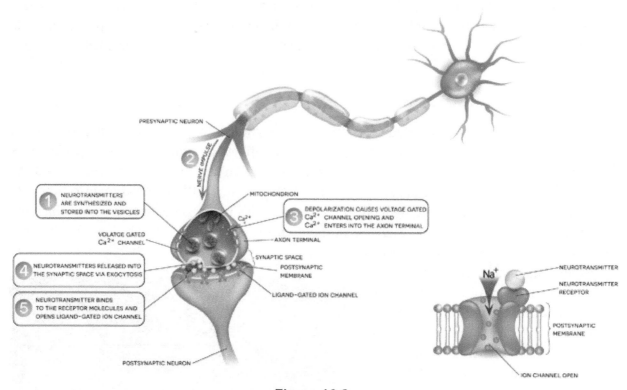

**Figure 16.2.**
© Tefi/Shutterstock.com

The axon of the presynaptic neuron forms a synapse (Figure 16.2) with the dendrite of a postsynaptic neuron. The axon releases neurotransmitters into the synaptic cleft to excite receptors on the postsynaptic neuron.

At the level of the neurons and synapses between neurons, psychoactive medications have one or more pharmacodynamic effects such as:

- Serving as a precursor in the cell's production or synthesis of a neurotransmitter

- Increasing, decreasing, or inhibiting the production or synthesis of a neurotransmitter

- Impacting storage of the neurotransmitter in the presynaptic neuron

- Increasing, decreasing, or inhibiting the breakdown of the neurotransmitter

- Stimulating or inhibiting the release of the neurotransmitter into the synapse

- Stimulating or blocking the postsynaptic receptors

- Blocking reuptake of the neurotransmitter by the presynaptic neuron

- Affecting other aspects of neurotransmitter and/or cellular function

Prescription of medication requires an evaluation to achieve an understanding of the individual who will take the medication. The prescriber must identify the condition or conditions with which the patient presents. An understanding of the actions of medications under consideration to treat the conditions guides the medication selection by the prescriber. The prescriber must match the pharmacodynamic effects of a medication with the symptoms and conditions presented by the patient. Pharmacokinetic effects of medications vary based on numerous factors within the individual taking the medication. Rational prescription of medication requires identification of the target symptoms or conditions and an understanding of the biological, medical, psychological, social, and spiritual attributes or characteristics of the individual taking the medication. For example, bupropion is a medication approved by the U.S. Food and Drug Administration (FDA) for treatment of depression. It also has approval for treating nicotine addiction. However, it is contraindicated or inadvisable if a person has a history of seizure disorder, a recent head injury, anorexia, or bulimia.

Numerous factors can influence or impact a person at any moment and over time. Whether counseling a patient or prescribing medication for a patient, it is wise for the provider to understand as much as possible the world of the patient. For a child, it is important to consider home factors, school factors, and the child's development and perceptions. Figure 16.3 illustrates many of the important elements of the world of the child. For an adult, it is important to consider home factors, work factors, and the adult's function and perceptions. Figure 16.4 illustrates many of the important elements of the world of the adult.

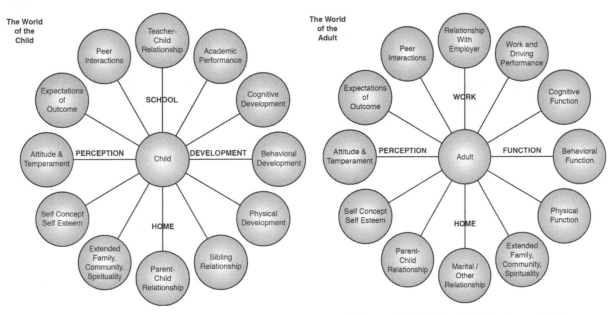

**Figure 16.3.** The World of a Child
© Kendall Hunt Publishing Company

**Figure 16.4.** The World of an Adult
© Kendall Hunt Publishing Company

The more a prescriber understands about the patient and the world of the patient, the better the prescriber can develop a plan for effective treatment. Although the patient is an important source, information from collateral sources (including family, significant others, employers, and records of previous treatment), as well as communication and collaboration with counselors and other health care providers increases the likelihood of having a better vision of the world of the patient.

A full psychiatric evaluation includes collection and documentation of identifying information about the patient; chief complaint or presenting problem prompting the patient to seek help; current and past psychiatric, medical, medication, developmental, social, and spiritual histories; medication and environmental allergies; psychosocial stressors including relational, educational, occupational, financial, and legal; strengths (attributes such as intelligence, motivation, and communication ability) and assets (resources such as family, friends,

© Photographee.eu/Shutterstock.com

clergy, and employment); assessment (summary of findings); formulation (theoretically based explanation); diagnostic profile including principal, accepted, and provisional diagnoses; and comprehensive treatment plan. A prescriber must consider these factors before recommending psychoactive medication for a patient. For optimal management and response, the prescription of medication must be part of a comprehensive treatment plan. Prescribers of psychiatric medications may include psychiatrists, other medical doctors (primarily family doctors and pediatricians), nurse practitioners, physician assistants, and, in some states, "appropriately trained" psychologists.

A prescriber must determine whether there is an indication or target (such as severe depression or anxiety) for medication. This includes review of other interventions undertaken by the patient, including counseling. The prescriber must disclose to the patient the indications, precautions, potential risks, and side effects possible with the medication, as well as potential drug interactions with other medications the patient may be taking. This prepares the patient to provide "informed consent" to take the medication as directed in the prescription. In many cases, the patient signs consent for the medication. The prescriber schedules follow-up sessions to review response and side effects, to determine whether to continue or discontinue the medication, to make necessary adjustments to the dose to strive to achieve optimal response, to determine whether it is necessary to switch to an alternative medication, or to add another medication to the initial medication.

There are basic guidelines with medication management. In the best scenario, the prescriber will increase the dose at appropriate intervals (which vary according to the specific medication and individual response of the patient) until the patient achieves optimal response in reduction or elimination of target symptoms with no side effects or at least tolerable side effects. As an example, dextroamphetamine and methylphenidate are medications for attention-deficit hyperactivity disorder (ADHD) to improve focus of attention and reduce impulsive and hyperactive behaviors. A common side effect is appetite suppression. If the patient achieves optimal response at a certain dose and has appetite suppression that is manageable, then the medication continues at that dose. Adjustment of daily routines such as meal times may be necessary.

In a second scenario, the prescriber increases the dose, but intolerable side effects occur. If there is no appreciable benefit, then the prescriber must discontinue the medication. As an example, selective serotonin reuptake inhibitors (SSRIs) are beneficial for treatment of anxiety, depression, and other conditions. Many individuals will experience sexual side effects including a disturbance of desire, excitement, and orgasm. Most patients want to discontinue the medication if this occurs. Another example is the weight gain that may result from treatment with atypical antipsychotic medications (such as **olanzapine** and **risperidone**) for conditions including schizophrenia and bipolar disorder. Although dietary manipulation and exercise may counter much of the weight gain, for many patients it becomes unhealthy and prompts discontinuation and review of alternative options.

Another scenario results when a patient experiences some, but not adequate or sufficient, beneficial response to a medication at a low dose without adverse effects. This prompts dose increase. If intolerable adverse effects occur at the next higher dose, the prescriber may return to the lower tolerable dose and consider additional or alternative measures, medication and nonmedication, to strive for better response. Adding a second antidepressant may achieve remission or elimination of symptoms from the combined effect of the two antidepressants. Lower doses of two medications may produce fewer or less severe side effects than higher doses of either medication.

Medication augmentation is a choice. Augmentation involves adding a second medication to boost the response to the first medication. For example, if unable to achieve full response to an antidepressant, the prescriber may increase the response by adding another agent. Lithium, thyroid hormone, stimulant medications, and other strategies have produced mixed results. Atypical antipsychotic medications such as aripiprazole have the best evidence to support use for antidepressant augmentation.

Finally, it is appropriate to discontinue a medication if it fails to produce any effect (positive or negative) despite adherence to the medication by the patient, achievement of adequate dosing (known to be clinically effective), and at least four to six weeks of continuous administration. In this case, it becomes necessary to consider an alternative medication and/or nonmedication strategies to address the depression.

Adherence to medication involves a collaboration between the patient and the prescriber achieving agreement wherein the patient incorporates the prescriber's recommendations into an integrated plan for achieving health improvement. Ideal patient–prescriber engagement involves the empathic understanding and interaction of the prescriber with the patient; individualized education of the

© ALMAGAMI/Shutterstock.com

patient toward understanding the treatment, targets of treatment, desired outcomes, and benefits for the patient; confirmation that the patient understands the use of the medication; and enthusiastic enrollment by the patient to choose to embrace and incorporate the treatment plan. Adherence transcends simple medication compliance in which the patient is obedient in following the prescriber's plan. Adherence enhances response and outcome because of the active participation of the patient and the power of the patient–prescriber collaboration.

Many factors affect medication adherence. Patients, and/or their significant others, may be resistant to considering medication or believing in medication. They may or may not communicate this with the prescriber. They may not understand the directions about how and when to take the medication. They may have trouble in getting the prescription filled, paying for the prescription, or remembering to take it once they have it. Some patients will be on multiple medications and have complex dosing schedules. Incorporating a medication regimen into already-stressed life circumstances may be overwhelming for some patients. There are a multitude of barriers, and it would be ideal for the prescriber to assess, identify, and address each one. This rarely happens.

Poor adherence often leads to a cycle of poor disease outcomes, higher utilization of services, higher health cost to the patient, and further poor adherence. The result is a higher disease burden on the patient and family, a lower quality of life, and even premature death.

According to Mayo Clinic (2013):

Nearly 70 percent of Americans are on at least one prescription drug, and more than half take two, Mayo Clinic and Olmsted Medical Center researchers say. Antibiotics, antidepressants and painkilling opioids are most commonly prescribed, their study found. Twenty percent of patients are on five or more prescription medications, according to the findings, published online in the journal Mayo Clinic Proceedings. (para. 2)

In addition, Brown and Bussell (2011) note:

The treatment of chronic illnesses commonly includes the long-term use of pharmacotherapy. Although these medications are effective in combating disease, their full benefits are often not realized because approximately 50% of patients do not take their medications as prescribed. Factors contributing to poor medication adherence are myriad and include those that are related to patients (eg, suboptimal health literacy and lack of involvement in the treatment decision—making process), those that are related to physicians (eg, prescription of complex drug regimens, communication barriers, ineffective communication of information about adverse effects, and provision of care by multiple physicians), and those that are related to health care systems (eg, office visit time limitations, limited access to care, and lack of health information technology). (p. 304)

**Psychiatrists** specialize in the diagnosis and treatment of mental health conditions including prescription of medications for those conditions. However, there are many barriers to obtaining psychiatric evaluation. Unfortunately, there is a severe shortage of psychiatrists and an uneven distribution geographically. Although referral to a psychiatrist may be ideal, it may take many months to obtain an appointment. Many patients are reluctant to see a psychiatrist due to stigma and other factors. Most often, patients must seek treatment from primary care providers who have some knowledge of mental health conditions. The result is that primary care provides 80% of psychiatric medication prescriptions.

In the case of physicians, many health insurance providers allocate 15 minutes for a session with a patient. Sinsky et al. (2016) published a study in the *Annals of Internal Medicine* that revealed that doctors spend about eight minutes of each session for interview and examination of the patient. The rest of the time is predominantly spent on the electronic health record. The primary care providers have limited time to conduct an evaluation and determine a treatment plan (Sinsky et al., 2016).

If a referral to a psychiatrist is successful, time constraints are still a factor. Depending on the site (clinic, hospital, private office, etc.), a psychiatrist may have 45 to 90 minutes to conduct a psychiatric evaluation and 15 to 30 minutes for a medication follow-up visit (Lipsitt, 2010). Often, there are many months in between visits. This is scant time to establish and maintain a provider–patient relationship.

Although the prescriber has limited time to collect and assimilate clinical information, the patient often provides a small part of the

© adike/Shutterstock.com

information. The patient may be reluctant to disclose information or may not think to disclose unless the provider asks a direct question relevant to the patient's condition. Consequently, the provider has available a small piece of the clinical picture for the patient. It is but the tip of an iceberg.

Although counselors do not prescribe medications, they have a valuable role in the treatment of a patient who is taking medication. A counselor may be the guiding light for the patient to navigate the stresses of life and engage in the interventions for improvement of health and well-being. Prescribers are wise to refer patients to counselors who have time to establish a collaborative relationship with the patient based on empathic listening and development of an understanding of the world of the patient. The counselor may provide valuable information and insights with which the prescriber may make a more informed decision regarding the possibility of medication

"Anxiously you ask, 'Is there a way to safety? Can someone guide me? Is there an escape from threatened destruction?' The answer is a resounding yes! I counsel you: Look to the lighthouse of the Lord. There is no fog so dense, no night so dark, no gale so strong, no mariner so lost but what its beacon light can rescue. It beckons through the storms of life. It calls, 'This way to safety; this way to home.'"

—Thomas S. Monson (2012)

management. Counselors who understand medications and their management can facilitate a patient's acceptance, understanding, and adherence to a prescribed medication regimen, as well as assist in monitoring for response and adverse effects encountered by the patient.

A comprehensive treatment plan starts with identification of the patient's needs and the changes the patient is willing to make. The clinician offers available resources to assist the patient in making changes. Medication is only part of the total treatment plan. Lifestyle changes are essential in mental health improvement. They are also important in adjusting for any side effects produced by the medications. For example, mood-stabilizing medications are necessary to manage episodes of bipolar disorder. Many of these medications carry the burden of potential weight gain and

West Quoddy Head Lighthouse Photo by E. John Kuhnley, MD (personal photo)

risk of metabolic syndrome, also known as insulin resistance, which may lead to cardiovascular disease and type 2 diabetes. Counselors may assist patients in understanding and adopting lifestyle changes in their sleep, diet, exercise, and stresslevels, all of which are valuable measures to improve physical and mental health even in the absence of medication treatment.

According to Bennett, Bennett, Sylvester, Roth, & Cataldi (2014):

> The counselor can play a significant role in ensuring concordance by building a strong working relationship with the medical professional, providing supportive education to the client and caregiver regarding the client's medical condition and the medical regimen as prescribed by the medical professional, supporting the client in adhering to the medical regimen, and encouraging the client to report side effects and symptoms to the medical professional in a timely fashion. (p. 1)

Lynne Shallcross is a senior writer for *Counseling Today.* In an article by Shallcross (2012) entitled "Client, Counselor, Prescriber," the role of the counselor in integration of care with prescribers was addressed. Shallcross cited Dixie Meyer, an assistant professor in the Department of Counseling and Family Therapy at St. Louis University, who engages in research on and teaching psychopharmacology. Meyer's message is that counselors need to know about the medications taken by their clients. Counselors are in a better position than their prescriber colleagues to take the time necessary to create a secure relationship within which to encourage adherence to all aspects of treatment. This includes taking medication as prescribed and communicating with the prescriber regarding response and adverse effects to assist in medication adjustment and management.

When addressing medication with a patient, a counselor must be aware of many factors. This provides an opportunity for better understanding and effective intervention. These factors include the following:

- The importance of the <u>counselor's awareness</u> and understanding of the patient's various medical and mental health conditions and the treatments, including medications and how they influence the patient's presentation, attitudes, and behavior

- The importance of the <u>patient's awareness</u> and understanding of the patient's various medical and mental health conditions and the treatments, including medications and how they influence the patient's presentation, attitudes, and behavior

- The patient's personal opinions and bias about medication

- The counselor's personal opinions and bias about medication

- The identity and credentials of other providers of the health care of the patient, especially the prescribers of any medications

- The patient's understanding of his or her medical and mental health conditions and the prescribed treatments and how they impact his or her function day to day

- Understanding the power of the patient's thought—whatever the patients think will help them, they may perceive as helping them

- Legal ramifications of discussion regarding medications

With a basic knowledge of psychopharmacology, a counselor may facilitate the patient's understanding of the role of the medication in treatment. Through weekly sessions with the patient, the counselor may provide close monitoring of the patient's response and any adverse effects. A basic knowledge of psychopharmacology enables the counselor to assist the patient in understanding:

- The psychiatric diagnosis or condition requiring medication intervention

- How the medication works and the specific symptoms that may respond and others that may not respond, assisting the patient in having realistic expectations for the medication

- Why it is important to take the medication consistently as prescribed

- What side effects may occur and how to address them as some tend to be transient and others require communication with the prescriber

- What to expect in terms of long-range planning with taking the medication and why it is important to work with the prescriber collaboratively

- That the counselor may facilitate the collaboration through direct interaction with the prescriber

- That adherence to the total treatment plan provides opportunity for ongoing adjustments that create more opportunities for better health and wellness for the patient

*A Verse to Remember. . .*
Proverbs 11:14: "Where there is no guidance, a people falls, but in an abundance of counselors there is safety,"

It is important for the counselor to have a full view of the world of the patient, including medications. This provides the counselor with the ability to encourage the patient to communicate with prescribers of both psychiatric and nonpsychiatric medications. However, counselors will encounter patients who are not on medications but appear to require evaluation for consideration of medications. It is wise for a counselor to know when (and to whom) to refer a patient and assist the patient in overcoming any reluctance or resistance in seeking referral.

Counselors may engage in consultation or collaboration with prescribers of medication. Consultation involves one professional providing opinions and recommendations regarding the care of a patient to another professional who then chooses a course of action. Collaboration involves two professionals communicating and working together as a treatment team. In collaboration, a counselor and a prescriber share the tasks of diagnosis, treatment plan formulation, and delivery of care. The prescriber and the counselor each provide services that may not be rendered by the other and some that may overlap.

The purpose of collaborative guidance is to maintain the safety of the client, to prevent fall into worsening illness, and to promote improved spiritual, physical, mental, and emotional health and well-being (Kuhnley, 2013).

Integrated care involves linking mental health services with primary care services. For more information on integrated care, refer to the National Institute of Mental Health webpage (https://www.nimh.nih.gov/health/topics/integrated-care/index.shtml).

Individuals with mental health and substance abuse conditions have higher rates of medical conditions. Patients select "gateways" or entries into care from many possible sources. Primary care is a common gateway. Counselors provide a valuable gateway. Duke Integrative Medicine (n.d.) states, "Integrative medicine is an approach to care that puts the patient at the center and addresses the full range of physical, emotional, mental, social, spiritual, and environmental influences that affect a person's health" (para. 1).

Integrated care increases the likelihood that the patient will receive a more comprehensive evaluation and treatment plan. It provides the opportunity to address the patient and the patient's conditions (mental health, medical health, and substance abuse) within the world of the patient. The desired outcome is the improved health and well-being of the patient. It promotes the active involvement of the patient in the improvement of health and addresses prevention of illness.

In summary of this section, please watch Dr. Kuhnley discuss medication management and other aspects of psychopharmacology with Alex, a client.

## Attachment Illumination

© Shutterstock.com

My colleague, Anita Kuhnley, LPC, PhD, offers reference to Winnicott, who indicates that the concept of the attachment-holding environment can be extended to the clinical relationship. A well-timed intervention where the therapist seeks to understand and helps the client feel understood can be even more therapeutic than if a physical holding takes place. Being heard communicates a sense of respect and valuing that is not unlike what love communicates.

**Psychopharmacology: (John and Alex)**

0:00 / 7:56

In conducting a psychiatric evaluation or medication follow-up session, a prescriber must demonstrate respect, employ empathic listening, and seek to understand the patient. The patient can tell when a provider values what the patient feels and says and cares about the patient's well-being. Patients tell me that they feel heard and understood when I listen and reflect what I hear them saying. Years ago, I conducted an evaluation of a woman referred to me to determine whether she had a problem. She was exquisitely composed and denied any problems. I sensed her denial but had no definitive evidence of psychopathology. I used proverb interpretation to assess abstract ability and listened to the content of the interpretation because it often revealed information indirectly. One proverb I like to use is "You don't judge a book by its cover." Her response was, "A person can seem composed on the outside though she is suffering on the inside." She realized what she had just said and quickly added "or he." I did not react to this but continued with the mental status exam. At the end of my assessment, I provided her with a synopsis including that observation that she is trying to convince herself and the world that she is okay but does not feel okay. Her internal world was not congruent with her external expression to present to the outside world. Within the safety of the clinical relationship and the therapeutic holding environment, the patient revealed she felt understood and disclosed the extent of her depression and the energy she expended to deny it and present a false face to the world. I prescribed antidepressant medication and she experienced significant benefit.

© Shutterstock.com

Compare the clinical picture of a patient to an iceberg and notice what's under the surface. Rational psychopharmacology must address as much of the clinical picture as possible. The more the prescriber understands, the more effective the prescriber can be with intervention. The more understood the patient feels, the more likely the patient is to trust the prescriber.

## Medications

Medications have approved indications and "off-label" uses. The FDA ensures that "American consumers benefit from having access to the safest and most advanced pharmaceutical system in the world. The main consumer watchdog in this system is FDA's Center for Drug Evaluation and Research (CDER)" (FDA, 2018, para. 1). Furthermore, "FDA approval of a drug means that data on the drug's effects have been reviewed by CDER, and the drug is determined to provide benefits that outweigh its known and potential risks for the intended population" (FDA, 2018, para. 6).

FDA approval determines the indications (conditions) that a company may include on the "label" for a medication. However, the FDA leaves it up to prescribers to determine the individual needs of a patient in the selection of treatment including prescription of medications. The prescriber may prescribe a specific medication for a condition "on-label" (FDA approved) or "off-label" (a condition not reviewed for approval by the FDA).

For example, providers may prescribe fluoxetine for conditions including anxiety disorders, post-traumatic stress disorder, prophylaxis (prevention) of migraine headaches, premature ejaculation, fibromyalgia, and neurocardiogenic syncope (fainting).

When it comes to medications, it is unlikely that any prescriber is familiar with all possible medications. Prescribers tend to have a selection of preferred medications for each condition they treat. A formulary is a list of medications selected by prescribers, pharmacists, and committees who determine which medications they deem most valuable in cost and effectiveness. Hospitals and insurances carriers will have their own formularies. Prescribers vary from their own favorite selections when a patient has insurance coverage under a plan that has a specific formulary that requires prescription of certain medications first. If the patients fail to respond to formulary selections, the prescriber may obtain prior authorization from the insurance carrier for a medication that is not on the insurance formulary.

Medications may have drug–drug interactions, drug–food interactions, and drug–condition interactions. Prescribers must review all other medications taken by a patient to ensure they do not prescribe an additional medication with serious interaction potential. They must educate patients regarding potential interactions with food, beverages, and conditions before obtaining informed consent for the prescription of many medications. Under the best of circumstances, it is likely that the prescriber does not cover all possibilities, and the patient may not recall what the prescriber says Often the prescriber may provide the patient with printed materials, which the patient may or may not read or understand for various reasons.

Counselors may wish to assist patients in seeking resources to understand their medications and precautions. If the counselor suspects a patient is experiencing an interaction, the best choice is to refer the patient to discuss the concern with the prescriber or to have the patient authorize the counselor to contact the prescriber. Another option is to review with a pharmacist.

## Most Prescribed Psychiatric Drugs for 2016

1. Zoloft (sertaline)—Depression
2. Xanax (alprazolam)—Anxiety
3. Lexapro (escitalopram)—Depression
4. Celexa (citalopram)—Depression
5. Wellbutrin (bupropion)—Depression
6. Desyrel (trazodone)—Anxiety and depression
7. Prozac (fluoxetine)—Depression
8. Adderall (dextroamphetamine and amphetamine)—ADHD
9. Ativan (lorazepam)—Anxiety
10. Cymbalta (duloxetine)—Depression
11. Effexor (venlafaxine)—Depression
12. Seroquel (quetiapine)—Bipolar disorder and depression
13. Concerta (methylphenidate)—ADHD
14. Kapvay (clonidine)—ADHD
15. Lamictal (lamotrigine)—Bipolar disorder
16. Paxil (paroxetine) —Depression
17. Elavil (amitriptyline)—Depression
18. Remeron (mirtazapine)—Depression
19. Vyvanse (lisdexamfetamine)—ADHD

20. Depakote (divalproex)—Bipolar disorder

21. Risperdal (risperidone)—Bipolar disorder and schizophrenia

22. Abilify (aripiprazole)—Bipolar disorder, depression, and schizophrenia

23. Zyprexa (olanzapine)—Bipolar disorder and schizophrenia

24. Intuniv (guanfacine)—ADHD

25. Lithium (lithium carbonate)—Bipolar disorder

Grohol (2017)

## Four Major Domains of Diagnosis and Relevant Medications

Diagnosis refers to the characteristics of a disease, condition, problem, situation, or phenomenon. For mental health, the American Psychiatric Association publishes the *Diagnostic and Statistical Manual of Mental Disorders* (DSM), which is in its 5th edition (*DSM-5*). It provides criteria to guide diagnosis of mental disorders based on contributions from international experts.

There are many domains of diagnosis with significant variety and complexity within each domain. For this text, four major domains of diagnosis include the following:

1. Mood disorders (depression and bipolar disorder)

2. Anxiety disorders (generalized anxiety disorder and panic disorder)

3. Psychotic conditions (such as schizophrenia)

4. Attention-deficit hyperactivity disorder (ADHD)

This text provides a brief overview of diagnoses within these four major domains and the names and common side effects of medications that providers may prescribe for those diagnoses. It is advisable for counselors to develop an ongoing up-to-date understanding of diagnoses and medications to better understand the treatment their patients receive from prescribers. With this understanding, the counselor may assist the patient in understanding treatment and engaging in active participation not only with the counselor but also with other providers including prescribers.

Mental disorders are patterns of behavioral, psychological, and physiological (bodily function) symptoms. A disorder exists if these symptoms cause distress for the person and produce impact and impairment in one or more areas of life. For example, anxiety is a normal symptom but may produce a disorder if it causes distress and impaired function for the person (Knight & West, 2010).

# Mood Disorders

Mood is a feeling experienced by a person at any given time. The mood will vary based on the circumstances of an individual. The mood tends to be a temporary state of mind and feelings. Mood may be sustained. Mood disorder occurs when a person experiences distress as a result of a lowering or elevation of mood. There are many factors that impact mood.

## Depression

Depression is a lowering of the mood, and a depressive disorder is a sustained lowering of the mood with subsequent impairment. Common symptoms of depression include the following:

- Constant feeling of sadness, anxiety, and emptiness

- Feelings of hopelessness

- Irritability

- Loss of interest in activities or hobbies once enjoyed

- Restlessness

- Low energy, fatigue, and diminished interest in sex

- Complaints of aches and pains

- General feelings of pessimism

- Difficulty concentrating, remembering details, or making decisions

- Sleep disturbance—sleeps too much or too little

- Change in eating habits—eats too much or may have no appetite

- Suicidal ideations

**Interventions for Mood Disorders Including Depression and Bipolar Disorder:**
Interventions must strive to "tune" or improve regulation of the brain and body circuits. Types of intervention include:

- Social support (relationships, spirituality)
- Lifestyle measures (sleep, nutrition, exercise, skills for self-regulation
- Psychoeducation
- Psychotherapy or counseling
- Medical evaluation to determine contributing problems
- Medication

NIMH (2017) reports that in 2016, "an estimated 16.2 million adults in the United States had at least one major depressive episode. This number represented 6.7% of all U.S. adults. The prevalence of major depressive episode was higher among adult females (8.5%) compared to males (4.8%)" ("Adults", para. 1).

## Antidepressant Medication

The role of an antidepressant is to stabilize and normalize the function of neurotransmitters in our brain. There are many neurotransmitters, including serotonin, dopamine, and norepinephrine, that play a role in regulating moods and emotions. The mechanism of action is very complex and includes impacting neurotransmission in the synapse. Some effects occur quickly, and others may take weeks to months to produce benefit for the person. The patient must be patient and allow the medication time to exert its effect. Antidepressants may take one to four weeks to take effect. Antidepressants are not addictive.

Antidepressant medicines may help improve mood, sleep, appetite, and concentration. They may help reduce anxiety, fear, and social withdrawal. Antidepressants may be of benefit for many conditions including the following:

- Major depression and dysthymia
- Obsessive-compulsive disorder
- Post-traumatic stress disorder (PTSD)
- Anxiety disorders
- Disruptive mood dysregulation disorder
- Bipolar disorder type II (with mood stabilizer)
- Menopausal symptoms, fibromyalgia, and chronic neuropathic pain
- ADHD and other conditions

Potential side effects of antidepressant medications include the following:

- Nausea
- Insomnia
- Dry mouth
- Blurred vision
- Constipation
- Dizziness
- Agitation
- Irritability
- Anxiety
- Fatigue and drowsiness
- Increased appetite and weight gain
- Loss of sexual desire and other sexual problems

Counselors will find it useful to be able to recognize the names of medications that patients may take. There are several classes of antidepressant medications. The understood mechanism of action determines the name of the class. For example, SSRIs are thought to exert action by inhibiting or limiting the reabsorption of serotonin by the presynaptic neuron. The result is more serotonin available in the synaptic cleft between neurons to permit better transmission of signals from the presynaptic neuron to the postsynaptic neuron.

Medications have a brand name applied by the manufacturer of origin and a generic name (chemical name). The following list may be useful for recognition of the chemical names and the brand names (in parentheses) of common antidepressants under their class of antidepressant:

Selective serotonin reuptake inhibitors (SSRIs)

- Citalopram (Celexa)
- Escitalopram (Lexapro)
- Fluoxetine (Prozac)
- Fluvoxamine (Luvox)
- Paroxetine (Paxil)
- Sertraline (Zoloft)

Norepinephrine dopamine reuptake inhibitors

- Bupropion and budeprion (Wellbutrin, Zyban)

Serotonin norepinephrine reuptake inhibitors (SNRIs)

- Venlafaxine (Effexor)
- Desvenlafaxine (Pristiq, Khedezla)
- Duloxetine (Cymbalta)
- Levomilnacipran (Fetzima)

Tricyclic antidepressants

- Amitriptyline (Elavil)
- Clomipramine (Anafranil)
- Desipramine (Norpramin)
- Doxepin (Silenor)
- Imipramine (Tofranil)
- Nortriptyline (Pamelor)
- Protriptyline (Vivactil)
- Trimipramine (Surmontil)

Tetracyclic antidepressants:

- Amoxapine (Asendin)
- Maprotiline (Ludiomil)
- Mirtazapine (Remeron)

Serotonin antagonist and reuptake inhibitors

- Trazodone (Desyrel)

- Long-acting trazodone (Oleptro)

Norepinephrine antagonist serotonin antagonist

- Mirtazapine (Remeron)

Monoamine oxidase inhibitors (MAOIs)

- Isocarboxazid (Marplan)

- Phenelzine (Nardil)

- Selegiline (Emsam)

- Tranylcypromine (Parnate)

Newer antidepressants:

- Vilazodone (Viibryd) (5-HT1A receptor antagonist)

- Desvenlafaxine (Pristiq)

- Vortioxetine (Brintellix)

MAOIs are older antidepressants. They have more side effects than SSRIs and SNRIs. When SSRIs and SNRIs have an undesirable side effect, MAOIs and tricyclics are used. Patients taking MAOIs have to be careful with their diet and other medications, as potentially serious interactions with cheeses, wines, pickles, and decongestants can occur. These items are high in tyramine, which interacts with MAOIs. Patients may experience significant rise in blood pressure, thus increasing the risk of stroke. Patients must receive a comprehensive list of foods, medicines, and substances to avoid.

Examples of foods high in tyramine include:

- **Strong or aged cheeses,** such as aged cheddar, Swiss and parmesan; blue cheeses such as Stilton and Gorgonzola; and Camembert. Cheeses made from pasteurized milk—such as American cheese, cottage cheese, ricotta, farmer cheese, and cream cheese—are less likely to contain high levels of tyramine.

- **Cured meats,** which are meats treated with salt and nitrate or nitrite, such as dry-type summer sausages, pepperoni, and salami.

- **Smoked or processed meats,** such as hot dogs, bologna, bacon, corned beef, or smoked fish.

- **Pickled or fermented foods,** such as sauerkraut, kimchi, caviar, tofu, or pickles.

- **Sauces,** such as soy sauce, shrimp sauce, fish sauce, miso, and teriyaki sauce.

- **Soybeans** and soybean products.

- **Snow peas, broad beans (fava beans),** and their pods.

- **Dried or overripe fruits,** such as raisins or prunes, or overripe bananas or avocados.

- **Meat tenderizers** or meat prepared with tenderizers.

- **Yeast-extract spreads,** such as Marmite, brewer's yeast, or sour dough bread.

- **Alcoholic beverages,** such as beer—especially tap or homebrewed beer—red wine, sherry, and liqueurs.

- **Combination foods** that contain any of the above ingredients.

- **Improperly stored foods or spoiled foods.** Doctors often recommend eating only fresh foods, not leftovers or foods past their freshness dates, for patients taking an MAOI.

## Bipolar Disorder

Bipolar disorder is a mood disorder involving extreme mood shifts or mood swings. One "pole" includes episodes of elevated or emotionally high moods known as mania (intense) or hypomania (less intense). The other "pole" includes emotional lows known as depression. Manic depressive disorder was the former name for this condition.

Depression is the most common feature of this condition. To qualify for the diagnosis of bipolar disorder, a person must have experienced at least one manic episode (bipolar disorder type 1) or hypomanic episode (bipolar disorder type 2). Features of a manic episode include euphoria, excitement, high energy, decreased need for sleep, inflated self-esteem or grandiosity, a pressure to keep speaking, and racing thoughts. This condition causes impaired thinking, judgment (decision making), and reality testing. Without treatment, this condition may have a devastating biopsychosocial impact on the life of a person.

The *DSM-5* provides the following criteria for a diagnosis of bipolar disorder:

> During the period of mood disturbance and increased energy or activity, three (or more) of the following symptoms (four if the mood is only irritable) are present to a significant degree and represent a noticeable change from usual behavior: (a) Inflated self-esteem or grandiosity. (b) Decreased need for sleep (e.g., feels rested after only 3 hr of sleep). (c) More talkative than usual or pressure to keep talking. (d) Flight of ideas or subjective experience that thoughts are racing. (e) Distractibility (i.e., attention too easily drawn to unimportant or irrelevant external stimuli), as reported or observed. (f) Increase in goal-directed activity (either socially, at work or school, or sexually) or psychomotor agitation (i.e., purposeless nongoal-directed activity). (g) Excessive involvement in activities that have a high potential for painful consequences (e.g., engaging in unrestrained buying sprees, sexual indiscretions, or foolish business investments). (p.124)

Most often, medications are necessary in the treatment of bipolar disorder. Medications may include the following:

Mood stabilizers:

- Lithium (Lithobid)

- Valproic acid (Depakene)

- Divalproex sodium (Depakote)

- Carbamazepine (Tegretol, Equetro, others)

- Lamotrigine (Lamictal)

Antipsychotics may be used alone or in combination with a mood stabilizer:

- Olanzapine (Zyprexa)

- Risperidone (Risperdal)

- Quetiapine (Seroquel)

- Aripiprazole (Abilify)

- Ziprasidone (Geodon)

- Lurasidone (Latuda)

- Asenapine (Saphris)

- Olanzapine-fluoxetine combination (Symbyax)

Antidepressants may be necessary to manage depression but may trigger a manic episode. Prescribing a mood stabilizer or antipsychotic first and then adding an antidepressant may alleviate depression without triggering mania.

## Anxiety Disorders

Fear is a response to an actual threat. Anxiety is an anticipatory response to perceived threat, either internal or external. Both elicit the distressing fight-or-flight response, an instinctive physiologic reaction to a threat that prepares the body and brain for resisting or escaping a danger.

## Physiology of fear

When the senses perceive a threat of danger or an unexpected event, the senses dispatch signals to the cerebral cortex (the thinking part of the brain) and the amygdala (the emotional center of the brain). The amygdala sets off a very rapid automatic response that mobilizes the brain and body to deal with the danger at hand before the cortex is aware of what is happening. The amygdala's rapid response system causes release of stress hormones into the blood—accelerating the heart, diverting blood from internal organs to muscles, and pouring sugar into the bloodstream in preparation for action for fighting or fleeing. The cerebral cortex receives the sensory information and determines what to do. The amygdala stores the event data for future reference. This response may be lifesaving in dangerous situations. The brain learns and prepares for future situations. Unfortunately, the brain may react to harmless situations with the fight–flight response.

The apprehensive anticipation of future danger or misfortune involves anxiety and worry. Anxiety suggests feelings of fear and apprehension. Worry implies persistent doubt or fear or to torment oneself with or suffer from disturbing thoughts or to fret. Anxiety is normal. Anxiety disorder occurs when excessive fear and worry that is recurrent and long-lasting causes symptoms of distress and interferes with day-to-day activities. It may lead to inflexibility in thinking and behavior.

Symptoms and signs of anxiety disorders include the following

- Excessive worry or preoccupation with stressful thoughts or situations

- Nervousness, muscle tension, restlessness

- A sense of impending danger or doom

- Increased heart rate, rapid breathing, sweating, trembling

- Feelings of weakness, tiredness, and fatigue

- Difficulty concentrating

- Difficulty falling asleep or staying asleep

- Gastrointestinal problems

- Difficulty controlling worry

- An urge to avoid things that trigger anxiety

**The Anxiety and Depression Association of America ([ADAA], n.d.) the following statistics about anxiety disorders:**

- Anxiety disorders are the most common mental illness in the United States, affecting 40 million adults in the United States aged 18 and older or 18.1% of the population every year.

- Anxiety disorders are highly treatable, yet only 36.9% of those suffering receive treatment.

- People with an anxiety disorder are three to five times more likely to go to the doctor and six times more likely to be hospitalized for psychiatric disorders than those who do not suffer from anxiety disorders.

- Anxiety disorders develop from a complex set of risk factors, including genetics, brain chemistry, personality, and life events.

(para. 1)

## Intervention for Anxiety Disorders

### Nonpharmacologic

- Listening, education, and reassurance

- Lifestyle changes (exercise, sleep, nutrition, etc.)

- Social support (relationships, spirituality)

- Psychoeducation

- Counseling

- Medical evaluation to determine contributing problems

- Goal setting and problem solving

- Anxiety and stress reduction and management

- Relaxation, rhythmic or controlled breathing, visual imagery

- Meditation, hypnosis, self-hypnosis

- Cognitive behavior therapy, graded exposure therapy

> "The **goal of CBT** is to improve the accuracy of such appraisals. Ultimately, the aim is to increase cognitive control over the person's fear response." —Edna Foa (Foa & Andrews, 2006, p. 29).

### Pharmacologic (medications)

Many antidepressants may reduce anxiety. The older tricyclic antidepressants (such as imipramine and clomipramine) work well but have significant side effects such as dry mouth, blurred vision, constipation, drowsiness, dizziness, and weight gain. SSRIs (such as fluoxetine and sertraline) are the mainstay of medication management of anxiety disorders and have fewer side effects including nausea, sexual dysfunction, and jitteriness. MAOIs may be helpful, but they require caution regarding food and beverages high in tyramine. MAOIs may produce side effects including dry mouth, headache, drowsiness, insomnia, and dizziness. Some antidepressants (such as bupropion) are not useful for anxiety disorders but may help patients who have anxiety associated with depression.

Benzodiazepines (BDZs) are very good at reducing anxiety but may be addictive. Prescribers and patients must exercise caution in the use of these medications. The Drug Enforcement Administration classifies BDZs as schedule IV depressants. The most common side effects include sedation, dizziness, weakness, and unsteadiness. They may also produce depression and memory impairment.

### BDZs include the following:

- Alprazolam (Xanax)

- Chlordiazepoxide (Librium)

- Clonazepam (Klonopin)

- Diazepam (Valium)

- Flurazepam (Dalmane)

- Lorazepam (Ativan)

- Oxazepam (Serax)

- Temazepam (Restoril)

- Triazolam (Halcion)

Buspirone is a medication to treat anxiety disorder, primarily generalized anxiety disorder. It may augment or improve the effect of antidepressants in the treatment of depression. It does not have the risk of physical dependence or withdrawal symptoms. Side effects include nausea, dizziness, and headaches.

Propranolol is a beta-blocker that may be helpful in the treatment of anxiety disorders accompanied by physiological symptoms, such as rapid heart rate, sweating, shaky hands, and tension. It may be helpful for reducing fear of public speaking or stage fright. Side effects may include drowsiness, headache, weakness, dry mouth, diarrhea, constipation, and upset stomach.

Antihistamines, specifically hydroxyzine (Atarax, Vistaril), are useful in the short-term treatment of anxiety disorders. Hydroxyzine has a calming effect. It is often used on an as-needed basis to reduce anxiety sufficiently that the patient may employ other coping strategies successfully. Side effects may include drowsiness, dizziness, blurred vision, headache, dry mouth, and upset stomach.

Antiseizure medications are helpful as mood stabilizers, and they may be helpful in managing anxiety. They include gabapentin (Neurontin), pregabalin (Lyrica), lamotrigine (Lamictal), topiramate (Topamax), and valproate (Depacon). The most common side effects include headache, nausea, dizziness, fatigue, and tremor. Lamotrigine requires close monitoring and slow dosing due to risk of a serious skin rash that may herald a severe, potentially life-threatening medical condition.

## Schizophrenia and Other Psychotic Conditions

Psychosis is a severe mental condition in which a person has severe impairment of thinking, emotions, and behavior associated with loss of contact with reality. Psychosis (or psychotic symptoms) may include delusions, hallucinations, and disorganization of thinking. A delusion is a false belief that a person maintains despite evidence to the contrary. A hallucination is the apparent perception of something not present and may involve one or more of the senses. Many medical and psychiatric conditions may have psychotic symptoms. Medications, substance abuse, environmental factors, and life circumstances may cause psychotic symptoms. Treatment depends on the identifiable cause and the manifestations in an individual.

Schizophrenia is a severe mental disorder affecting a person's thinking, feeling, and behaviors. The symptoms of schizophrenia fall into three domains: positive, negative, and cognitive.

Positive symptoms refer to symptoms that generally are not seen in the general population. They include hallucinations, delusions, agitated body movements, and disturbances of thinking (unusual or dysfunctional thinking).

Negative symptoms refer to the absence of thinking and behavior that would normally be present. They represent a degree of loss of normal function. These symptoms may include a reduction of motion (initiation and continuation) and emotional response (affective flattening). Anhedonia is an inability to experience pleasure. Avolition is a lack of motivation. Alogia is an inability or poverty of speech due to a mental condition. Apathy is a loss of caring. Negative symptoms are the major cause of low functional levels and the major contributor to ultimate outcome.

Cognitive symptoms may range from subtle to severe and include difficulty focusing and paying attention, difficulty with working memory, and difficulty understanding information to make decisions.

Psychosocial treatments have been found to be effective in the management of patients with schizophrenia (Bellack, 2001). The goal is to prevent relapses, improve functional ability, and improve quality of life.

# Medications for schizophrenia (and other psychotic conditions):

First-generation antipsychotics are effective but have risk for side effects affecting muscle movements, including extrapyramidal (nerves involved in motor activity) side effects. Tardive dyskinesia produces repetitive jerking movements primarily of the face, neck, and tongue. Tardive dyskinesia may or may not be reversible. First-generation antipsychotics include:

- Chlorpromazine (Thorazine)

- Fluphenazine (Prolixin)

- Haloperidol (Haldol)

- Perphenazine (Trilafon)

Second-generation antipsychotics are referred to as *atypical antipsychotics* because they do not typically cause muscle movement issues to the extent of the first-generation antipsychotics. They are different in what side effects predominate with each individual medication. Metabolic syndrome (prediabetes) is a concern for individuals with schizophrenia, and many of the second-generation antipsychotics may add to the risk. Second-generation antipsychotics include the following:

- Aripiprazole (Abilify)

- Asenapine (Saphris)

- Brexpiprazole (Rexulti)

- Cariprazine (Vraylar)

- Clozapine (Clozaril)

- Iloperidone (Fanapt)

- Lurasidone (Latuda)

- Olanzapine (Zyprexa)

- Paliperidone (Invega)

- Quetiapine (Seroquel)

- Risperidone (Risperdal)

- Ziprasidone (Geodon)

## Attention-Deficit / Hyperactivity Disorder (ADHD)

ADHD is a disorder of brain function causing ongoing symptoms of inattention and/or hyperactivity or impulsivity. Many conditions may cause symptoms that look like ADHD, and many conditions occur with ADHD. To make a diagnosis of ADHD, the symptoms must be present at baseline when a person is just being who he is. The symptoms must be present in more than one environment. The symptoms of ADHD include inattention, hyperactivity, and impulsivity. Refer to the *DSM-5* (2013) for full details. Examples of inattentive symptoms include but are not limited to: being easily distracted; having difficulty following instructions; having difficulty sustaining focus of attention on a task or topic; being forgetful; and having trouble organizing tasks. Symptoms of hyperactivity and impulsivity include but are not limited to: having difficulty sitting still; being fidgety; squirming; interrupting; blurting out comments; being impatient; and talking excessively. The CDC (2018) reported that "approximately 9.4% of children 2-17 years of age (6.1 million) had ever been diagnosed with ADHD, according to parent report in 2016" (para. 4). It is reported that 4.4% of adults have ADHD (Kessler et al., 2006).

The *DSM-5* provides criteria for ADHD as follows:

© Photographee.eu/Shutterstock.com

Interventions for ADHD include the following:

- Education and training of patients and their families

- Environmental restructuring including making changes that help the patient achieve better function at home, in the classroom, at work, and in leisure activities.

- Individual counseling to address self-awareness, skill development, self-regulation, and self-esteem.

- Behavior therapy

- Educational support

- Medication

The Children and Adults with Attention-Deficit Hyperactivity Disorder (CHADD) organization is a national resource on ADHD.

## Medications for the Treatment of ADHD

Stimulant medications are the mainstay treatment for ADHD. Owing to the potential for abuse, dependence, and diversion, they are controlled substances under Schedule II with the Drug Enforcement Administration. They work by increasing dopamine and norepinephrine in the prefrontal cortex or executive center of the brain and other parts of the brain to improve attention span, impulse control, and activity regulation. The stimulant medications that help ADHD include various amphetamine and methylphenidate preparations. Side effects include decreased appetite, insomnia, sedation, headaches, stomachaches, moodiness, and motor tics.
Amphetamine preparations (brand names in parentheses):

- Dextroamphetamine (Dexedrine)

- Mixed amphetamine salts (Adderall)

- Mixed amphetamine salts extended release (Adderall XR)

- Amphetamine extended-release oral suspension (Dyanavel XR)

- Amphetamine (Evekeo)

- Dextroamphetamine liquid formulation (ProCentra)

- Lisdexamfetamine (Vyvanse)

**Methylphenidate preparation brand names**

- Aptensio XR

- Concerta;

- Cotempla XR-ODT

- Daytrana

- Metadate CD; Metadate ER

- Methylin; Methylin ER

- Quillichew ER

- Quillivant XR

- Ritalin; Ritalin LA; Ritalin SR

- Dexmethylphenidate: Focalin (short-acting) and Focalin XR (long-acting)

**nonstimulant medications useful for treatment of ADHD**

- Atomoxetine (Strattera)

- Clonidine short-acting (Catapres)

- Clonidine long-acting (Kapvay)

- Guanfacine short acting (previously Tenex)

- Guanfacine long-acting (Intuniv)

- Bupropion (Wellbutrin an antidepressant that may be useful)

Side effects of atomoxetine include insomnia, sedation, decreased appetite, headache, abdominal pain, vomiting, and irritability. Clonidine and guanfacine may cause sedation, drowsiness, dizziness, headache, sore throat, cough, runny nose, and ear pain. Because clonidine causes sedation, prescribers will provide it at bedtime to assist with initiation of sleep. This brief overview will assist counselors in having a basic knowledge and understanding of diagnoses and medication. For further information on diagnoses and medications, counselors may consult the recommended reading.

## Recommended Reading

If you would like to enhance your expertise on this topic, consider reading the following:

- American Psychiatric Association. (2013). *Diagnostic and statistical manual of mental disorders* (5th ed.). Arlington, VA: Author.

© Shutterstock.com

- Preston, J., O'Neal, J. H., & Talaga, M. C. (2013). *Handbook of clinical psychopharmacology for therapists* (7th ed.). Oakland, CA: New Harbinger.

- Stahl, S. M., Teton Data Systems (Firm), & STAT!Ref (Online service). (2013). *Stahl's essential psychopharmacology: Neuroscientific basis and practical application* (4th ed.). Cambridge, England: Cambridge University Press.

- U.S. Food and Drug Administration (FDA) website: (http://www.fda.gov/)

## Chapter Summary

As stated in a previous chapter by Drs. Sibcy and Kuhnley, purposeful counseling involves working together with clients to form collaborative goals that both client and counselor agree on. Part of the therapists's skill is being able to listen, be empathic, understand, help the patient translate their global problems into smaller problems, and then formulate those agreed-upon goals.

Many patients will have medication from one or more prescribers for psychiatric and medical conditions. Counselors can form a strong counselor–patient relationship or secure base within which to facilitate the patient's active engagement in their treatment with all providers, including the counselor and prescribers of medication. With a basic understanding of diagnoses and medications useful for those diagnoses, the counselor can help the patient achieve understanding of his or her conditions and medication management and enlighten the patient as to information to provide to their prescribers relevant to their medication experiences. With authorization by the patient, the counselor can communicate and collaborate with providers to help the patient achieve improved health and well-being.

# Closing Thoughts

We would like to close with an expression of care, something that Mr. Fred Rogers used to close his program (called *"Mr. Rogers' Neighborhood"*), we would like to add our own twist to make it relevant here: "You have made this day a special day, by just your being you. [And you have made this book a special book, just by your reading it.] There is no one else in the whole world like you, and we like you, just the way you are."

With Much Appreciation, The Authors

# References

Adams, J., Piercy, F. and Jurich, J. (1991) Effects of solution-focused therapy's "formula first session task" on compliance and outcome in family therapy. *Journal of Marital and Family Therapy, 17*(3), 277–290.

Aesop. (1919). *The Aesop for children with pictures by Milo Winter*. Chicago, IL: Rand McNally & Co.

Allen, J. G., & Fonagy, P. (2006). *The handbook of mentalization-based treatment*. Hoboken, NJ: Wiley and Sons.

Allen, J. G., Fonagy, P., & Bateman, A. (2008). *Mentalizing in clinical practice*. Washington, DC: American Psychiatric Publishing.

Alperin, M., & Daubney, K. (2015). *Goldilocks and the three bears*. Wilton, CT: Tiger Tales.

Amen, D. G. (2010). *Change your brain, change your body: Use your brain to get and keep the body you have always wanted* (1st ed.). New York, NY: Harmony Books.

American Association of Christian Counselors (2014a). Retrieved from https://www.aacc.net/.

American Association of Christian Counselors. (2014b). *American Association of Christian Counselors code of ethics*. Retrieved from https://www.aacc.net/wp-content/uploads/2017/10/AACC-Code-of-Ethics-Master-Document.pdf

American Counseling Association. (2014). *ACA code of ethics*. Washington, DC: Author.

American Psychiatric Association. (2013). *Diagnostic and statistical manual of mental disorders* (5th ed.). Arlington, VA: American Psychiatric Publishing.

Anderson, T., Ogles, B. M., Patterson, C. L., Lambert, M. J., & Vermeersch, D. A. (2009). Therapist effects: Facilitative interpersonal skills as a predictor of therapist success. *Journal of Clinical Psychology, 65*(7), 755–768. doi:10.1002/jclp.20583

Anxiety and Depression Association of America. (n.d.). Facts & statistics. Retrieved from https://adaa.org/about-adaa/press-room/facts-statistics

Applewhite, A., Evans, W. R., III., & Frothingam, A. (2003). *And I quote: The definitive collection of quotes, sayings, and jokes for the contemporary speechmaker*. New York, NY: St. Martin's Press.

Augsburger, D. W. (1982). *Caring enough to hear and be heard*. Ventura, CA: Regal Books.

Axelson, J. A. (1999). *Counseling and development in a multicultural society* (3rd ed.). Pacific Grove, CA: Brooks/Cole.

Baker, A. & Peluso, P. (2018). *Researching therapeutic relationship behaviors among expert therapists*. Atlanta GA: Paper presented at the American Counseling Association 2018 Conference & Expo.

Baldwin, S. A., Wampold, B. E., & Imel, Z. E. (2007). Untangling the alliance-outcome correlation: Exploring the relative importance of therapist and patient variability in the alliance. *Journal of Consulting and Clinical Psychology, 75*(6), 842–852. doi:10.1037/0022-006X.75.6.842

Bandura, A. (1997). *Self-efficacy. The exercise of control*. New York, NY: W. H. Freeman and Company.

Bandura, A. (1986). *Self-efficacy. The exercise of control*. New York, NY: W. H. Freeman and Company.

Barlow, D., & Craske, M. (2006). *Mastery of your anxiety and panic: Therapists guide* (4th ed.). New York, NY: Oxford University Press.

Barlow, D. H., Farchione, T. J., Sauer-Zavala, S., Murray Latin, H., Ellard, K. K., Bullis, J. R., . . . Cassiello-Robbins, C. (2017). *Unified protocol for transdiagnostic treatment of emotional disorders: Therapist guide* (2nd ed.). New York, NY: Oxford University Press.

Barrett-Lennard, G. T. (2003). *Steps on a mindful journey: Person-centered expressions*. Ross-on-Wye, United Kingdom: PCCS Books.

Bateson, G., Jackson, D. D., Haley, J., & Weakland, J. (1956). Toward a theory of schizophrenia. *Behavioral Science, 1*(4), 251–264. doi:10.1002/bs.3830010402

Bellack, A. S. (2001). Psychosocial treatment in schizophrenia. *Dialogues in Clinical Neuroscience, 3*(2), 136–137.

Bennet, E., Bennett, W., Sylvester, A., Roth, B., & Cataldi, J. (2014). Concordance and the counselor's role in supporting medical compliance. *American Counseling Center Knowledge Center, 12*, 1–15. Retrieved from https://www.counseling.org/docs/default-source/vistas/article_12.pdf?sfvrsn=99ff6c6a_12

Bennett-Levy, J. (2006). Therapist skills: A cognitive model of their acquisition and refinement. *Behavioral and Cognitive Psychotherapy, 34*(1), 57–78. doi:10.1017/S1352465805002420

Berkhout & Malouff (2016). The efficacy of empathy training: A meta-analysis of randomized controlled trials. *Journal of Counseling Psychology, 63*(1), 32.

Bertolote, J. M., & Fleischmann, A. (2002). Suicide and psychiatric diagnosis: A worldwide perspective. *World Psychiatry, 1*(3), 181–185.

Blair, R. J. R. (2005). Responding to the emotions of others: Dissociating forms of empathy through the study of typical and psychiatric populations. *Consciousness and Cognition, 14*(4), 698–718.

Blatt, S. J., Sanislow, C. A., III., Zuroff, D. C., & Pilkonis, P. A. (1996). Characteristics of effective therapists: Further analyses of data from the National Institute of Mental Health Treatment of Depression Collaborative Research Program. *Journal of Consulting and Clinical Psychology, 64*(6), 1276–1284. doi:10.1037/0022-006X.64.6.1276

Bohart, A. C., Elliot, R., Greenberg, L. S., & Watson, J. C. (2002). Empathy. In J. Norcross (Ed.), *Psychotherapy relationships that work: Therapist contributions and responsiveness to patients* (pp. 89–108). New York, NY: Oxford University Press.

Bohecker, L., Schellenberg, R., & Silvey, J. (2017). Spirituality and religion: The ninth CACREP common core curricula area. *Counseling and Values, 62*(2), 128–143.

Bordin, E. S. (1979). The generalizability of the psychoanalytic concept of the working alliance. *Psychotherapy: Theory, Research & Practice, 16*(3), 252–260. doi:10.1037/h0085885

Bounds, P. S., Washington, A. R., & Henfield, M. S. (2018). Individuals and families of African descent. In D. G. Hays & B. T. Erford (Eds.) *Developing multicultural counseling competence: A systems approach* (3rd ed., pp. 256–285). Upper Saddle River, NJ: Pearson.

Bowlby, J. (1980). *Loss: Sadness and depression*. New York, NY: Basic Books.

Bowlby, J. (1988). A secure base. New York, NY: Routledge.

Bowlby, Ainsworth, & Main.

Boyd-Franklin, N. (2003). *Black families in therapy: Understanding the African American experience* (2nd ed.). New York, NY: Guilford Press.

Bray, J. H., Shepherd, J. N., & Hays, J. R. (1985). Legal and ethical issues in informed consent to psychotherapy. *The American Journal of Family Therapy, 13*(2), 50–60.

Breunlin, D. C., Schwartz, R. C., & Kune-Karrer, B. M. (2001). *Metaframeworks: Transcending the models of family therapy*. San Francisco, CA: Jossey-Bass.

Brown, B. (2010). *The power of vulnerability* [Video file]. Retrieved from https://kickingthepants.com/2012/05/31/lean-into-the-discomfort

Brown, B. [The RSA]. (2013, December). *Breneé Brown on empathy* [Video file]. Retrieved from https://www.youtube.com/watch?v=1Evwgu369Jw

Brown, H., Guskin, E., & Mitchell, A. (2012). *Arab-American population growth*. Retrieved from http://www.journalism.org/2012/11/28/arabamerican-population-growth/

Brown, M. T., & Bussell, J. K. (2011). Medication adherence: WHO cares? *Mayo Clinic Proceedings, 86*(4), 304–314. doi:10.4065/mcp.2010.0575

Bureau of Indian Affairs. (2017). Indian entities recognized and eligible to receive services from the United States Bureau of Indian Affairs. Federal Register: The Daily Journal of the United States Government. Retrieved from https://www.federalregister.gov/documents/2017/01/17/2017-00912/indian-entities-recognized-and-eligible-to-receive-services-from-the-united-states-bureau-of-indian

Burns, D. D. (2008). *Feeling good together: The secret of making troubled relationships work* (1st ed.). New York, NY: Broadway Books.

Burns, D. D., & Nolen-Hoeksema, S. (1992). Therapeutic empathy and recovery from depression in cognitive-behavioral therapy: A structural equation model. *Journal of Consulting and Clinical Psychology, 60*(3), 441–449. doi:10.1037/0022-006X.60.3.441

CACREP. (2016). *2016 CACREP standards*. Retrieved from http://www.cacrep.org/wp-content/uploads/2017/08/2016-Standards-with-citations.pdf

Carkhuff, R. R. (1969). *Helping and human relations* (Vol. 1). New York, NY: Holt, Rinehart & Winston.

Carlson, N. R. (2013). *Foundations of behavioral neuroscience* (9th ed.). New York, NY: Pearson Education.

Casa, J. M., Suzuki, L. A., Alexander, C. M., & Jackson, M. A. (2017). *Handbook of multicultural counseling* (4th ed.). Los Angeles, CA: Sage.

Cassidy, J. (1994). Emotion regulation: Influences of attachment relationships. *Monographs of the Society for Research in Child Development, 59*(2/3), 228–249. doi:10.1111/j.1540-5834.1994.tb01287.x

Cassidy, J., & Shaver, P. R. (2002). *Handbook of attachment: Theory, research, and clinical applications*. New York, NY: Guilford Press.

Centers for Disease Control and Prevention. (2017). *Attention-deficit / hyperactivity disorder* (ADHD). Retrieved from https://www.cdc.gov/ncbddd/adhd/data.html

Centers for Disease Control and Prevention. (2018). *Attention-deficit / hyperactivity disorder* (ADHD). Retrieved from https://www.cdc.gov/ncbddd/adhd/data.html

Chaplin, T. M. (2015). Gender and emotion expression: A developmental contextual perspective. *Emotion review, 7*(1), 14–21. doi:10.1177/1754073914544408

Chapman, G. (2004). *The 5 love languages: The secret to love that lasts.* Chicago, IL: Northfield Publishing.

Chou, R. S., & Feagin, J. R. (2014). *Myth of the model minority: Asian Americans facing racism* (2nd ed.). New York, NY: Routledge.

Clinton, T., & Sibcy, G. (2002). *Attachments: Why you love, feel, and act the way you do.* Nashville, TN: Integrity Publishing.

Clinton, T., & Sibcy, G. (2006). *Why do you do the things you do: The secret to healthy relationships.* Nashville, TN: Thomas Nelson.

Clinton, T., & Sibcy, G. (2012). Christian counseling, interpersonal neurobiology, and the future. *Journal of Psychology and Theology, 40*(2), 141–145.

Coan, J. (2008). Toward a neuroscience of attachment. In *Handbook of attachment: Theory, research, and clinical applications* (5th ed., pp. 241–258). New York, NY: Guilford Press.

Coan, J. A., & Gottman, J. M. (2007). *The specific affect coding system.* In J. A. Coan & J. N. Allen (Eds.), *Handbook of emotion elicitation and assessment* (pp. 106–123). New York, NY: Oxford University Press.

Coan, J. A., Kasle, S., Jackson, A., Schaefer, H. S., & Davidson, R. J. (2013). Mutuality and the social regulation of neural threat responding. *Attachment & Human Development, 15*(3), 303–315. doi:10.1080/14616734.2013.782656

Conzemius, A., & O'Neill, J. (2005). *The power of SMART goals: Using goals to improve student learning.* Bloomington, IN: Solution Tree Press.

Corey, M. S., & Corey, G. (2015). *Becoming a helper.* Boston, MA: Cengage Learning.

Costa, B. (2017). Team effort – Training therapists to work with interpreters as a collaborative team. *International Journal for the Advancement of Counselling, 39*, 56–69. doi: 10.1007/s10447-016-9282-7

Covey, S. R. (2004). *The 7 habits of highly effective people: Restoring the character ethic* (Rev. ed.). New York, NY: Free Press.

Cuff, B. M., Brown, S. J., Taylor, L., & Howat, D. J. (2014). Empathy: A review of the concept. *Emotion Review, 8*(2), 144–153.

Damgarrd, M., & Gravart, C. (2017). Now or never! The effect of deadlines on charitable giving: Evidence from two natural field experiments. *Journal of Behavioral and Experimental Economics, 66*, 78–87.

Decety, J., & Moriguchi, Y. (2007). The empathic brain and its dysfunction in psychiatric populations: Implications for intervention across different clinical conditions. *Biopsychosocial Medicine, 1*, 22. doi:10.1186/1751-0759-1-22

Department of Health and Human Services, Substance Abuse and Mental Health Services Administration. (2009). *SAFE-T* (HHS Publication No. [SMA] 09-4432). Retrieved from http://store.samhsa.gov/shin/content//SMA09-4432/SMA09-4432.pdf

De Shazer, S., Dolan, Y. M., & Korman, H. (2007). *More than miracles: The state of the art of solution-focused brief therapy*. New York, NY: Routledge.

Devoir, L. (2014). *Smart goal setting: Proven tips & tricks to better, deeper sleep for your health, happiness & success* [Audiobook]. Retrieved from https://www.amazon.com/Smart-Goal-Setting-Happiness-Success/dp/B00NMPJFQU/ref=sr_1_fkmr0_1?ie=UTF8&qid=1532634237&sr=1-1-fkmr0&keywords=SMART+Goal+Setting%3A+Proven+tips+and+tricks+to+better%2C+deepr+sleep+for+your+health%2C+happiness+and+success

Diller, J. V. (2015). *Cultural diversity: A primer for the human services* (5th ed.). Stamford, CT: Cengage Learning.

Dozier, M., & Kobak, R. R. (1992). Psychophysiology in attachment interviews: Converging evidence for deactivating strategies. *Child Development, 63*(6), 1473–1480. doi:10.1111/j.1467-8624.1992.tb01708.x

Dreyfus, H., & Dreyfus, S. (1986). *Mind over machine*. New York, NY: The Free Press.

Duke Integrative Medicine. (n.d.) *What is integrative medicine?* Retrieved from https://www.dukeintgegrativemedicine.org/about/what-is-integrative-medicine

Duncan, B. L., Miller, S., Wampold, B., & Hubble, M. (2010). *The heart and soul of change: Delivering what works in therapy* (2nd ed.). Washington, DC: American Psychological Association. doi:10.1037/12075-000

Duncan, S., Rice, L. N., & Butler, J. M. (1968). Therapists' paralanguage in peak and poor psychotherapy hours. *Journal of Abnormal Psychology, 73*(6), 566–570. doi:10.1037/h0026597

Dweck, C. (2007). *Mindset: The new psychology of success*. New York, NY: Ballentine Books.

Education Development Center & Screening for Mental Health. (2009). *SAFE-T*. Retrieved from https://www.integration.samhsa.gov/images/res/SAFE_T.pdf

Egan, G. (1975). *The skilled helper: A model for systematic helping and interpersonal relating*. Pacific Grove, CA: Brooks Cole.

Egan, G. (1976). *Interpersonal living: A skills/contract approach to human relations training in groups add to references*. Belmont, CA: Brooks Cole.

Egan, G. (1994). *The skilled helper: A problem-management approach to helping*. Pacific Grove, CA: Brooks Cole.

Egan, G. (2010). *The skilled helper: A problem-management and opportunity-development approach to helping* (9th ed.). Belmont, CA: Brooks/Cole, Cengage Learning.

Egan, G. & Reese, R. (2019). *The skilled helper: A problem-management and opportunity-development approach to helping*. Boston, MA: Cengage.

Elles, T., Sperry, F. L., & Sperry, J. (2002). *Case conceptualization: Mastering the competency with ease and confidence*. New York, NY: Routledge.

Emerson. (1875).

Entwistle, D. N. (2015). *Integrative approaches to psychology and Christianity: An introduction to worldview issues, philosophical foundations, and models of integration* (3rd ed.). Eugene, OR: Cascade Books.

Erdman, P., & Lampe, R. (1996). Adapting basic skills to counsel children. *Journal of Counseling and Development, 74*(4), 374–377.

Falicov, C. J. (1998). *Latino families in therapy: A guide to multicultural practice.* New York, NY: Guilford Press.

Fasano, L. (2015). *Engineer your own success.* Hoboken, NJ: John Wiley & Sons.

Feller, C. P., & Cottone, R. R. (2003). The importance of empathy in the therapeutic alliance. *Journal of Humanistic Counseling, Education and Development, 42*, 53–61.

Fischer, P., Frey, D., Peus, C., & Kastenmueller, A. (2008). The theory of cognitive dissonance: State of the science and directions for future research. In P. Meusburger, M. Welker, & E. Wunder (Eds.), *Clah of knowledge: Orthodoxies and heterodoxies in science and religion* (pp. 189–198). New York, NY: Springer.

Foa, E. B., Andrews, L. W., & Annenberg Public Policy Center. (2006). *If your adolescent has an anxiety disorder: An essential resource for parents.* New York, NY: Oxford University Press.

Foa, E. B., Chrestman, K. R., & Gilboa-Schechtman, E. (2008). *Prolonged exposure therapy for adolescents with PTSD: Emotional processing of traumatic experiences.* Cary, NC: Oxford University Press,

Foster, R. J. (1988). *Celebration of discipline: The path to spiritual growth* (Rev. ed.). San Francisco, CA: Harper.

Foster, R. J. (1992). *Prayer: Finding the heart's true home.* San Francisco, CA: Harper.

Frankl, V. (2000). *Man's search for meaning.* Boston, MA: Beacon Press.

Fretz, B. R. (1966). Postural movements in a counseling dyad. *Journal of Counseling Psychology, 13*(3), 335–343. doi:10.1037/h0023716

Fripp, J. A., & Carlson, R. G. (2017). Exploring the influence of attitude and stigma on participation of African American and Latino populations in mental health services. *Journal of Multicultural Counseling & Development, 45*, 80–94. doi:10.1002/jmcd.12066

Fritz, G. K. (2004). Children and adults need family traditions. *Brown University Child & Adolescent Behavior Letter, 20*(1), 8.

Garrett, J. L., Jr. (1990). *Systematic theology: Biblical, historical, and evangelical* (Vol. 1). Grand Rapids, MI: William B. Eerdmans.

Garrett, M. T., Garrett, J. T., Portman, T. A. A., Grayshield, L., Rivera, E. T., Williams, C., & Parrish, M. (2018). Counseling individuals and families of Native American descent. In D. G. Hays & B. T. Erford (Eds.) *Developing multicultural counseling competence: A systems approach* (3rd ed., pp. 394–430). Upper Saddle River, NJ: Pearson.

Gaume, J., Magill, M., Longabaugh, R., Bertholet, N., Gmel, G., & Daeppen, J.-B. (2014). Influence of counselor characteristics and behaviors on the efficacy of a brief motivational intervention for heavy drinking in young men—A randomized controlled trial. *Alcoholism Clinical and Experimental Research, 38*(7), 2138–2147.

Geller, S. M., & Greenberg, L. S. (2012). *Therapeutic presence: A mindful approach to effective therapy.* Washington, DC: American Psychological Association.

George, C., Kaplan, N., & Main, M. (1985). *The Adult Attachment Interview.* Unpublished manuscript, University of California at Berkeley.

Gladding, S. T. (2009). *Becoming a counselor: The light, the bright, and the serious* (2nd ed.). Alexandria, VA: American Counseling Association.

Gladding, S. T. (2016). *Groups: A counseling specialty* (7th ed.). Englewood Cliffs, NJ: Prentice-Hall.

Gladding, S. T. (2018). *Samuel T. Gladding's site: Background.* Retrieved from http://college.wfu.edu/sites/sam-gladding/my-background

Gladding Website, (2018). *Samuel T. Gladding's site: Background.* Retrieved from http://college.wfu.edu/sites/sam-gladding/my-background

Goleman, D. (2004, January). What makes a great leader. *Harvard Business Review.* Retrieved from https://hbr.org/2004/01/what-makes-a-leader

Goleman, D. (2006). *Emotional intelligence* (Bantam tenth anniversary hardcover ed.). New York, NY: Bantam Books.

Gottman, J. (1979). *Marital interaction: Experimental investigations.* New York, NY: Academic Press.

Gottman, J. (1994). *What predicts divorce: The relationship between marital process and marital outcomes.* New York, NY: Psychology Press, Taylor and Francis Group.

Gottman, J. (2007). *Why marriages succeed or fail and how to make yours last.* London, England: Bloomsburry.

Gottman, J. M., & Krokoff, L. J. (1989). Marital interaction and satisfaction: A longitudinal view. *Journal of Consulting and Clinical Psychology, 57*(1), 47–52. doi:10.1037/0022-006X.57.1.47

Gottman, J. M., & Levenson, R. W. (1986). Assessing the role of emotion in marriage. *Behavioral Assessment, 8*(1), 31–48. Retrieved from http://psycnet.apa.org.ezproxy.liberty.edu/search/display?id=38aae778-5f10-41bd-c7c7-5e2dd9ae4b73&recordId=9&tab=all&page=1&display=25&sort=PublicationYearMSSort%20desc,AuthorSort%20asc&sr=1

Gottman, J. M., & Levenson, R. W. (1999). What predicts change in marital interaction over time? A study of alternative models. *Family Process, 38*(2), 143–158. doi:10.1111/j.1545-5300.1999.00143.x

Gottman, J. M., & Silver, N. (2012). *What makes love last? How to build trust and avoid betrayal.* New York, NY: Simon and Schuster.

Gottman, J. M., & Silver, N. (2015). *The seven principles for making marriage work: A practical guide from the country's foremost relationship expert.* New York, NY: Harmony Books.

Greenspan, S. I. (1997). *The development of the ego: implications for personality theory, psychopathology, and the psychotherapeutic process.* Madison, CT: International Universities Press.

Greenspan, S. I. (1999). *Developmentally based psychotherapy.* Madison, CT: International Universities Press.

Greggo, S. P., & Becker, S. P. (2010). The attachment paradigm: A secure base for counselor education? *Journal of Psychology and Christianity, 29*(1), 46–56. Retrieved from http://ezproxy.liberty.edu/login?url=https://search-proquest-com.ezproxy.liberty.edu/docview/237251818?accountid=12085

Grice, H. P. (1975). Logic and conversation. In P. Cole & J. L. Morgan (Eds.), *Syntax and semantics* (Vol. 3, pp. 41–58). New York, NY: Academic Press.

Grice, H. P. (1991). *Studies in the way of words: Paul Grice*. Cambridge, MA: Harvard University Press.

Grohol, J. (2017). *Top 25 psychiatric medications for 2016*. Retrieved from https://psychcentral.com/blog/top-25-psychiatric-medications-for-2016/

Grudem, W. A. (1995). *Systematic theology: An introduction to biblical doctrine*. Grand Rapids, MI: Zondervan.

Haase, R. F., & Tepper, D. T. (1972). Nonverbal components of empathic communication. *Journal of Counseling Psychology, 19*(5), 417–424. doi:10.1037/h0033188

Haas, L. J., Malouf, J. L., & Mayerson, N. H. (1986). Ethical dilemmas in psychological practice: results of a national survey. *Professional Psychology, Research, and Practice, 17*(4), 316–321.

Hadziabdic, E., Albin, B., Heikkilä, K., Hjelm, K., Linnéuniversitetet, Institutionen för hälso- och vårdvetenskap (HV), & Fakulteten för Hälso- och livsvetenskap (FHL). (2014). Family members' experiences of the use of interpreters in healthcare. *Primary Health Care Research & Development, 15*(2), 156–169. doi:10.1017/S1463423612000680

Hamilton, M. (1960). A rating scale for depression. *Journal of Neurology, Neurosurgery, and Psychiatry, 23*, 56–62.

Harley, W. F. (2011). *His needs, her needs: Building an affair-proof marriage* (Rev. and expand ed.). Grand Rapids, MI: Revell.

Hatchett, G. T. (2004). Reducing premature termination in university counseling centers. *Journal of College Student Psychotherapy, 19*(2), 13–27. doi:10.1300/J035v19n02_03

Hays, D. G., & Erford, B. T. (2018). *Developing multicultural counseling competence: A systems approach* (3rd ed.). Upper Saddle River, NJ: Pearson.

Hays, D. G., & McLeod, A. L. (2018). The culturally competent counselor. In D. G. Hays & B. T. Erford (Eds.) *Developing multicultural counseling competence: A systems approach* (3rd ed., pp. 2–36). Upper Saddle River, NJ: Pearson.

Health Insurance Portability and Accountability Act of 1996, Pub. L. No. 104–191 § 110 Stat 1936 (1996).

Hermansson, G. L., Webster, A. C., & McFarland, K. (1988). Counselor deliberate postural lean and communication of facilitative conditions. *Journal of Counseling Psychology, 35*(2), 149–153. doi:10.1037/0022-0167.35.2.149

Herne, M. A., Bartholomew, M. L., & Weahkee, R. L. (2014). Suicide mortality among American Indians and Alaska Natives, 1999–2009. *American Journal of Public Health, 104*(Suppl. 3), S336–S342. doi:10.2105/AJPH.2014.301929

Hiebert, P. G. (1985). *Anthropological insights for missionaries*. Grand Rapids, MI: Baker Books.

Health and Human Services. (1996). *SAFE-T* (HHS Publication No. [SMA] 09-4432). Retrieved from http://store.samhsa.gov/shin/content//SMA09-4432/SMA09-4432.pdf

Highlen, P. S., & Hill, C. E. (1984). Factors affecting client change in individual counseling: Current status and theoretical speculations. In S. D. Brown & R. W. Lent (Eds.), *Handbook of counseling psychology* (pp. 334–396). New York, NY: Wiley.

Holmes, J. (1993). *John Bowlby and attachment theory* (2nd ed.). New York, NY: Routledge.

Holms, J. P., & Baji, K. (1998). *Bite-size Twain: Wit and wisdom from the literary legend.* New York, NY: St. Martin's Press.

Hook, J. N., Farrell, J. E., Davis, D. E., DeBlaere, C., Van Tongeren, D. R., & Utsey, S. O., (2016). Cultural humility and racial microaggressions in counseling. *Journal of Counseling Psychology, 63*(3), 269–277. doi:10.1037/cou0000114

Howard, K. I., Kopta, S. M., Krause, M. S., & Orlinsky, D. E. (1986). The dose-effect relationship in psychotherapy. *American Psychologist, 41*(2), 159–164. doi:10.1037/0003-066X.41.2.159

Howard & Steele, (2008).

Hughes, J. N., & Baker, D. B. (1990). *The clinical child interview.* New York, NY: Guilford Press.

Huppert, J. D., Bufka, L. F., Barlow, D. H., Gorman, J. M., Shear, M. K., & Woods, S. W. (2001). Therapists, therapist variables, and cognitive-behavioral therapy outcome in a multicenter trial for panic disorder. *Journal of Consulting and Clinical Psychology, 69*(5), 747–755. doi:10.1037/0022-006X.69.5.747

Isaacson, R. (2001). The limbic system. In N. Smelser & P. Bates (Eds.), *International encyclopedia of the social & behavioral sciences* (pp. 8858–8862). Amsterdam, Netherlands: Elseveir.

Ivey, A. E., Ivey, M. B., & Zalaquett, C. P. (2013). *Intentional interviewing and counseling: Facilitating client development in a multicultural society.* Belmont, CA: Brooks/Cole.

Ivey, A. E., Ivey, M. B., & Zalaquett, C. P. (2018). *Intentional interviewing and counseling: Facilitating client development in a multicultural society* (9th ed.). Boston, MA: Cengage Learning.

James, I. A., Morse, R., & Howarth, A. (2010). The science and art of asking questions in cognitive therapy. *Behavioral and Cognitive Psychotherapy, 38*(1), 83–93. doi:10.1017/S135246580999049X

Jones, S. & Butman, R. (2013). *Modern psychotherapies: A comprehensive Christian appraisal.* Christian Association of Psychological Studies: Batavia, IL.

Kawaii-Bogue, B., Williams, N. J., & MacNear, K. (2017). Mental health care access and treatment utilization in African American communities: An integrative care framework. *Best Practices in Mental Health, 13*(2), 11–29.

Kelly, E. W., Jr., & True, J. H. (1980). Eye contact and communication of facilitative conditions. *Perceptual and Motor Skills, 51*(3), 815–820. doi:10.2466/pms.1980.51.3.815

Kennedy, K., Abrams, J. J., Kasdan, L., Bergman, R., & Kinberg, S. (Producers) & Johnson, R. (2017). *Star wars: The last Jedi* [Motion picture]. USA: Lucasfilm Ltd.

Kessler, R. C., Adler, L., Barkley, R., Biederman, J., Conners, C. K., Demler, O., . . . Zaslavsky A. M. (2006). The prevalence and correlates of adult ADHD in the United States: Results from the National Comorbidity Survey Replication. *American Journal of Psychiatry, 163*(4), 716-723.

Khanna, S., Penberthy, J. K., & Gioia, C. (2018). Integrated treatment for persistent depression and alcohol use disorder: An innovative pilot study. *American Journal on Addictions, 27*(4), 310–311.

Kim, B. S. K., Liang, C. T. H., & Li, L. C. (2003). Counselor ethnicity, counselor nonverbal behavior, and session outcome with Asian American clients: Initial findings. *Journal of Counseling & Development, 81*(2), 202–207. doi:10.1002/j.1556-6678.2003.tb00243.x

Kim, N., & Lee, K. (2018). The effect of internal locus of control on career adaptability: The mediating role of career decision-making self-efficacy and occupational engagement. *The Journal of Employment Counseling*, 55(1), 2–15. doi:10.1002/joec.12069

Kirkpatrick, L. A., & Shaver, P. R. (1990). Attachment theory and religion: Childhood attachments, religious beliefs, and conversion. *Journal for the Scientific Study of Religion, 29*(3), 315–334. doi:10.2307/1386461

Kitchener, K. S. (1984). Educational goals and reflective thinking. *The Educational Forum, 48*(1), 74–95. doi:10.1080/0013172830933588

Knight, A. M. (2009). *The effectiveness of counselor skills training and its relationship with emotional intelligence.* Retrieved from ProQuest Digital Dissertations (AAT 3353962) https://search.proquest.com/openview/94f03963062d56baa2027910f2b852a6/1?pq-origsite=gscholar&cbl=18750&diss=y

Knight, A. M. & West, L. (2010). *Mastering test anxiety.* Alexandria, VA: ASCA.

Knight, A. M. (2011a). Carl Rogers. In T. Clinton & R. Hawkins (Eds.), *Popular encyclopedia of Christian counseling.* Eugene, OR: Harvest House.

Knight, A. M. (2011b). Grief, crisis, and trauma intervention. T. Clinton & R. Hawkins (Eds.), *Popular encyclopedia of Christian counseling.* Eugene, OR: Harvest House.

Knight, A. M. (2011c). Measurement and evaluation. T. Clinton & R. Hawkins (Eds.), *Popular encyclopedia of Christian counseling.* Eugene, OR: Harvest House.

Knight, A., & Sibcy, G. (2018). *Redeeming attachment: A counselor's guide to facilitating attachment to God and earned security.* Dubuque, IA: Kendall Hunt.

Knight, A., Sibcy, G., Gantt, A., Carapezza, K., & Macon, K. (2018). The impact of brief god attachment workshop attendance on god attachment. *Virginia Counselors Journal, 36,* 48–55.

Knight, A., & Tetrault, D. (2018). *Research methods and program evaluation key concepts: A study guide.* Matthews, NC: Kona.

Kochnar, R., & Cilluffo, A. (2018). *Key findings on the rise in income inequality within America's racial and ethnic groups.* Retrieved from http://www.pewresearch.org/fact-tank/2018/07/12/key-findings-on-the-rise-in-income-inequality-within-americas-racial-and-ethnic-groups/

Kruger, J., & Dunning, D. (1999). Unskilled and unaware of it: How difficulties in recognizing one's own incompetence lead to inflated self-assessments. *Journal of Personality and Social Psychology, 77*(6), 1121–1134. doi:10.1037/0022-3514.77.6.1121

Kruijshaar, M. E., Barendregt, J., de Graaf, R., Spijker, J., & Andrews, G. (2005). Lifetime prevalence estimates of major depression: An indirect estimation method and a quantification of recall bias. *European Journal of Epidemiology, 20*(1), 103–111.

Kuhlmann, D. O., & Ardichvili, O. (2015). Becoming an expert: Developing expertise in an applied discipline. *European Journal of Training and Development, 39*(4), 262–276. doi:10.1108/EJTD-08-2014-0060

Kuhnley, J. (2013). *When to refer: Collaborating with a psychiatrist for medication evaluations* [Blog post]. Retrieved from https://www.aacc.net/2013/11/14/when-to-refer-collaborating-with-a-psychiatrist-for-medication-evaluations/

Kuntze, J., van der Molen, H.T., & Born, M. P. (2009). Increase in counselling communication skills after basic and advanced microskills training. *The British Journal of Educational Psychology, 79*(Pt 1), 175–188. doi:10.1348/000709908X313758

Lambert, M. J., & Cattani-Thompson, K. (1996). Current findings regarding the effectiveness of counseling: Implications for practice. *Journal of Counseling and Development, 74*(6), 601–608.

Lambert, M. J., Harmon, C., Slade, K., Whipple, J. L., & Hawkins, E. J. (2005). Providing feedback to psychotherapists on their patients' progress: Clinical results and practice suggestions. *Journal of Clinical Psychology, 61*(2), 165–174. doi:10.1002/jclp.20113

Lambert, M. J., & Okiishi, J. C. (1997). The effects of the individual psychotherapist and implications for future research. *Clinical Psychology: Science and Practice, 4*(1), 66–75. doi:10.1111/j.1468-2850.1997.tb00100.x

Lang, G., Molen, H., Van der Molen, H., Trowere, P., & Look, R. (1990). *Personal conversations: Roles and skills for counselors.* London, England: Routledge.

Lapertosa, L. (2009). Counseling—Based on science, but an art form, too. *The Advocate, 32*(9), 15. Retrieved from http://link.galegroup.com.ezproxy.liberty.edu/apps/doc/A374334930?AONE?u=viceliberty&sid=AONE&xid+542d02b4

Lash, L. (1980).

Lawrence, B., Delaney, Nouwan, H. (1977). *Practicing the presence of God.* New York, NY: Double Day, Random House.

Lazarus, A. (1981). *The practice of multimodal therapy: Systematic, comprehensive, and effective psychotherapy.* New York, NY: McGraw-Hill.

Lazarus, A. (1989). *The practice of multimodal therapy: Systematic, comprehensive, and effective psychotherapy.* Baltimore, MD: Johns Hopkins University Press.

Lee, A. (2015, January 3). Sheryl Sandberg offers grieving guidance, calls for support systems after husband's death. *The Hollywood Reporter.* Retrieved from https://www.hollywoodreporter.com/news/sheryl-sandberg-offers-grieving-guidance-799865

Lee, E., & Mock, M. R. (2005). Asian families: An overview. In M. McGoldrick, J. Giordano, & N. Garcia-Preto (Eds.), *Ethnicity & family therapy* (3rd ed., pp. 269–289). New York, NY: Guilford Press.

Lewin, K. (1952). *Field theory in social science: Selected theoretical papers.* London, England: Tavistock.

Lifespan Learning LA. (2009, January 8). *John Bowlby attachment and loss.* [Video file]. Retrieved from https://www.youtube.com/watch?v=VAAmSqv2GV8

Lipsitt, D. R. (2010). Helping primary care physicians make psychiatric referrals. *Psychiatric Times, 27*(12), 28.

Livingston, G., & Brown, A. (2017). Intermarriage in the U.S. 50 years after Loving v. Virginia. Retrieved from http://www.pewsocialtrends.org/2017/05/18/intermarriage-in-the-u-s-50-years-after-loving-virginia/

López, G., Ruiz, N. G., & Patten, E. (2017). *Key facts about Asian Americans, a diverse and growing population.* Retrieved from http://www.pewresearch.org/fact-tank/2017/09/08/key-facts-about-asian-americans/

Luborsky, L., Crits-Christoph, P., McLellan, A. T., Woody, G., Piper, W., Liberman, B., . . . Pilkonis, P. (1986). Do therapists vary much in their success? Findings from four outcome studies. *The American Journal of Orthopsychiatry, 56*(4), 501–512. doi:10.1111/j.1939-0025.1986.tb03483.x

Luedke, A. J., Peluso, P. R., Diaz, P., Freund, R., & Baker, A. (2017). Predicting dropout in counseling using affect coding of the therapeutic relationship: An empirical analysis. *Journal of Counseling & Development, 95*(2), 125–134. doi:10.1002/jcad.12125

Luft, J., & Ingham, H. (1955). *The Johari window: A graphic model of interpersonal awareness.* San Diego, CA: University of California Western Training Lab.

Lusko, L. (2017). *Swipe right: The life-and-death power of sex and romance.* Nashville, TN: W Publishing,

Luu, L. P., Inman, A. G., & Alvarez, A. N. (2018). Individuals and families of Asian descent. In D. G. Hays & B. T. Erford (Eds.) *Developing multicultural counseling competence: A systems approach* (3rd ed., pp. 2–36). Upper Saddle River, NJ: Pearson.

Luxton, D. D., Nelson, E., & Maheu, M. M. (2016). *A practitioner's guide to telemental health: How to conduct legal, ethical, and evidence-based telepractice.* Washington, DC: American Psychological Association.

Main, M., Goldwyn, R., & Hesse, E. (2002). *Adult attachment classification system.* Berkeley, CA: Regents of the University of California.

Malott, K. M., & Paone, T. R. (2008). Using interpreters in mental health counseling: A literature review and recommendations. *Journal of Multicultural Counseling and Development, 36*(3), 130–142. doi:10.1002/j.2161-1912.2008.tb00077.x

Marvin, R., & Seagroves, W. (2017). *Attachment, trauma, and the circle of security.* Continuing Education Presentation at Liberty University.

Masci, D. (2018). *5 facts about the religious lives of African Americans.* Retrieved from http://www.pewresearch.org/fact-tank/2018/02/07/5-facts-about-the-religious-lives-of-african-americans/

Masson, P. C., & Sheeshka, J. D. (2009). Clinicians' perspectives on the premature termination of treatment in patients with eating disorders. *Eating Disorders, 17*(2), 109–125.

Matthews, T. J., & Johnson, G. S. (2015). Skin complexion in the twenty-first century: The impact of colorism on African American women. *Race, Gender, & Class, 22*(1/2), 248–274.

Mayer, J. D., Salovey, P., & Caruso, D. R. (2002). *Mayer– Salovey–Caruso emotional Intelligence Test (MSCEIT) item booklet.* Toronto, Canada: MHS Publishers.

Mayer, J. D., Salovey, P., & Caruso, D. R. (2008). Emotional intelligence: New ability or eclectic traits? *American Psychologist, 63*(6), 503–517. doi:10.1037/0003-066X.63.6.503

Mayo Clinic. (2013, June 19). Nearly 7 in 10 Americans are on prescription drugs. Retrieved from www.sciencedaily.com/releases/2013/06/130619132352.htm

McCullough, J. P. (2000). *Treatment for chronic depression: Cognitive behavioral analysis system of psychotherapy (CBASP).* New York, NY: Guilford Press.

McCullough, J. P., Schramm, E., & Penberthy, J. K. (2015). *CBASP: A distinctive treatment for persistent depressive disorder.* New York, NY: Routledge.

McCullough, J., Lord, B., Martin, A., Conley, K., Schramm, E. & Klein, D. (2018). The significant other history: an interpersonal-emotional history procedure used with the early-onset chronically depressed patient. *The American Journal of Psychotherapy, 65*(3), 225–248.

McGee, D., Del Vento, A., & Bavelas, J. B. (2005). An interactional model of questions as therapeutic interventions. *Journal of Marital and Family Therapy, 31*(4), 371–384.

McGoldrick, M., Giordano, J., & Garcia-Preto, N. (2005). *Ethnicity and family therapy* (3rd ed.). New York, NY: Guilford Press.

McLean, C. P., & Foa, E. B. (2011). Prolonged exposure therapy for post-traumatic stress disorder: A review of evidence and dissemination. *Expert Review of Neurotherapeutics, 11*(8), 1151–1163. doi:10.1586/ern.11.94

Gretzinger, S., & Riddle, J. (2017). King of my heart. On *Starlight* [CD]. Redding, CA: Bethel Music.

McMinn, M. R. (2011). *Psychology, theology, and spirituality in Christian counseling.* (2nd ed.) Wheaton, IL: Tyndale.

Meichenbaum, D. (2017). *The evolution of cognitive therapy: A personal and professional journey with Don Meichenbaum.* New York, NY: Routledge, Taylor and Francis Group.

Melton, G. D. (2016). *Love warrior: A memoir.* New York, NY: Flatiron Books.

Meyer, J. (2010). *Power thoughts: 12 strategies to win the battle of the mind.* New York, NY: FaithWords.

Moitinho, E., Moitinho, D., Freyre, F. & Freyre, S. (Fall 2018). Encouraging a more perfect union: Strategies for counseling clients in interracial/interethnic marriages. *The Advocate Magazine.* American Mental Health Counselors Association. 34–37.

Montgomery, M. L. (2004). *Conversations with Gloria Naylor.* Jackson, MS: University Press of Mississippi.

Moore-Thomas, C. (2018). Cultural identity development. In D. G. Hays & B. T. Erford (Eds.) *Developing multicultural counseling competence: A systems approach* (3rd ed., pp. 37–64). Upper Saddle River, NJ: Pearson.

Morrow, M. T., Lee, H., Bartoli, E., & Gillem, A. R. (2017). Advancing counselor education in evidence-based practice. *International Journal for the Advancement of Counselling, 39*(2), 149–163. doi:10.1007/s10447-017-9288-9

Moyers, T. B., & Miller, W. R. (2013). Is low therapist empathy toxic? *Psychology of Addictive Behaviors, 27,* 878–884. doi:10.1037/a0030274

Murphy, B. C., & Dillon, C. (2008). *Interviewing in action in a multicultural world* (3rd ed.). Belmont, CA: Thomson Brooks/Cole.

National Behavioral Intervention Team Association (n.d.) *Duty to warn.* Retrieved from https://nabita.org/documents/DUTYTOWARN.pdf

National Behavioral Intervention Team Association (NaBITA). (n.d.). *Duty to warn breakdown per state.* Retrieved from https://nabita.org/documents/DUTYTOWARN.pdf

National Center for Biotechnology Information. (2015). *Using technology-based therapeutic tools in behavioral health services.* Retrieved from https://www.ncbi.nlm.nih.gov/books/NBK344038

National Center for Injury Prevention and Control. (2018). *Suicide: Risk and protective factors.* Retrieved from https://www.cdc.gov/violenceprevention/suicide/riskprotectivefactors.html

National Institute of Mental Health. (2017). *Major depression.* Retrieved from https://www.nimh.nih.gov/health/statistics/major-depression.shtml

Neborsky, R. J. (2006). Brain, mind, and dyadic change processes. *Journal of Clinical Psychology, 62*(5), 523–538. doi:10.1002/jclp.20246

Norcross, J. C., & Wampold, B. E. (2011). Evidence-based therapy relationships: Research conclusions and clinical practices. *Psychotherapy, 48*(1), 98–102. doi:10.1037/a0022161

Orlinsky, D. E., & Howard, K. I. (1986). Process and outcome in psychotherapy. In S. L. Garfield & A. E. Bergin (Eds.), *Handbook of psychotherapy and behavior change* (3rd ed., pp. 311–381). New York, NY: Wiley.

Paone, T. R., & Malott, K. M. (2008). Using interpreters in mental health counseling: A literature review and recommendations. *Journal of Multicultural Counseling Development, 36*, 130–142.

Parker, S., & Moriarty, G. (2007). Working with God images in therapy. In P. Hegy (Ed.), *What do we imagine God to be? The function of "God images" in our lives* (pp. 255–269). Lewingston, NY: Edwin Mellen Press.

*Paul Grice.* (2017). Retrieved from Stanford Encyclopedia of Philosophy's website: https://plato.stanford.edu/entries/grice/

Payrato, L. (2009). Nonverbal communication. In J. Verschueren, J. Östman (Eds.), *Key notions for pragmatics* (pp. 163–195). Philadelphia, PA: John Benjamins Publishing.

Penberthy, (2019)

Pitte, F. P. (1971). *Kant as philosophical anthropologist.* The Netherlands: The Hague.

Pope, V. T., & Kline, W. B. (1999). The personal characteristics of effective counselors: What 10 experts think. *Psychological Reports, 84*(3, Pt 2), 1339–1344. doi:10.2466/pr0.1999.84.3c.1339

Premack, D., & Woodruff, G. (1978). Does the chimpanzee have a *theory of mind? Behavioural and Brain Sciences, 1*, 515–526

Preston, J., O'Neal, J. H., & Talaga, M. C. (2013). *Handbook of clinical psychopharmacology for therapists* (7th ed.). Oakland, CA: New Harbinger Publications.

Prochaska, J. O. (1979). *Systems of psychotherapy: A transtheoretical analysis.* Homewood, IL: Dorsey Press.

Prochaska, J. O., & DiClemente, C. C. (1982). Transtheoretical therapy: Toward a more integrative model of change. *Psychotherapy: Theory, Research & Practice, 19*(3), 276–288. doi:10.1037/h0088437

Prochaska, J. O., & Prochaska, J. M. (2016). *Changing to thrive: Using the stages of change to overcome the top threats to your health and happiness.* Center City, MN: Hazelden Publishing.

Remley, T. & Herlihy, B. (2016). *Ethical, legal, and professional issues in counseling.* New York, NY: Pearson.

Remley, T. P., Jr, & Herlihy, B. (2007). *Ethical, legal, and professional issues in counseling* (Updated 2nd ed.). Upper Saddle River, NJ: Pearson Merrill Prentice Hall.

Richards, P. S., & Bergin, A. E. (1997). *A spiritual strategy for counseling and psychotherapy.* Washington, DC: American Psychological Association.

Rochlen, A. B., & O'Brien, K. M. (2002). Men's reasons for and against seeking help for career-related concerns. *The Journal of Men's Studies, 11*(1), 55–63. doi:10.3149/jms.1101.55

Rodolfa, R., Bent, R., Eisman, E., Nelson, P., Rehm, L., & Ritchie, P. (2005). A cube model for competency development: Implications for psychology educators and regulators. *Professional Psychology: Research and Practice, 36*(4), 347–354. doi:10.1037/0735-7028.36.4.347

Rogers, C. (1965). *Carl Rogers and Gloria: Full Session.* Retrieved from: https://www.youtube.com/watch?v=24d-FEptYj8

Rogers, C. R. (1957). The necessary and sufficient conditions of therapeutic personality change. *Journal of Consulting Psychology, 21*(2), 95–103. doi:10.1037/h0045357

Rogers, C. R. (1961). *On becoming a person: A therapist's view of psychotherapy.* Boston, MA: Houghton Mifflin.

Rohn, J. (2006). *The treasury of quotes.* Dallas, TX: Success Books.

Rolston, A., & Lloyd-Richardson, E. (2017). *What is emotion regulation and how we do it?* Retrieved from: http://www.selfinjury.bctr.cornell.edu/perch/resources/what-is-emotion-regulationsinfo-brief.pdf

Rosenthal, R., & Jacobson, L. (1992*). Pygmalion in the classroom: Teacher expectation and pupils' intellectual development* (newly expanded). New York, NY: Irvington.

Rubino, G., Barker, C., Roth, T., & Fearon, P. (2000). Therapist empathy and depth of interpretation in response to potential alliance ruptures: The role of therapist and patient attachment styles. *Psychotherapy Research, 10*(4), 408–420.

Salter Ainsworth, M. D., & Bell, S. M. (1970). Attachment, exploration, and separation: Illustrated by the behavior of one-year-olds in a strange situation. *Child Development, 41*(1), 49–67. doi:10.2307/1127388

Sapir, E. (1949). *Culture, language and personality: Selected essays.* Berkeley, CA: University of California Press.

Savickas, M. L. (1998). Career style assessment and counseling. In T. Sweeney (Ed.), *Adlerian counseling: A practitioner's approach* (4th ed., pp. 329–360). Philadelphia, PA: Accelerated Development Press.

Savickas, M. L. (2011). *Career counseling: Theories of psychotherapy.* Washington, DC: American Psychological Association.

Schore, A. N. (1994). *Affect regulation and the origin of the self: The neurobiology of emotional development.* Hillsdale, NJ: Lawrence Erlbaum Associates.

Shallcross, L. (2012). Client, counselor, prescriber. *Counseling Today, 55*(1), 38-42.

Shapiro, F. R. (2006). *The Yale book of quotations.* New Haven, CT: Yale University Press.

Sharma, R. (2008). *The greatness guide: 101 Lessons for making what's good at work and in life even better.* New York, NY: Harper Collins.

Shea, S. C. (1998). *Psychiatric interviewing the art of understanding: A practical guide for psychiatrists, psychologists, counselors, social workers, nurses and other mental health professionals* (2nd ed). Philadelphia, PA: Saunders Company.

Showers, A. (2013). *The feelings wheel developed by Dr. Gloria Willcox.* Retrieved from http://msaprilshowers.com/emotions/the-feelings-wheel-developed-by-dr-gloria-willcox

Sibcy, G. (2007). Attachment therapy for complex trauma. *Christian Counseling Today, 15*(3), 24–27.

Sibcy, G., & Knight, A. (2017a, August). *Treating chronic depression and attachment wounds with research based practices.* PowerPoint presented at the meeting of the American Association of Clinical Chemistry, San Diego, CA.

Sibcy, G., & Knight, A. (2017b). *Emotional intelligence, attachment theory, and neuroscience: implications for counselors.* Presented at AACC 2017 World Conference, Nashville, TN.

Siegel, D. (2010a). *Mindsight: Transform your brain with the new science of kindness.* Oxford, England: OneWorld.

Siegel, D. (2010b). *Mindsight: Transform your brain with the new science of kindness.* Oxford, England: OneWorld.

Siegel, D. J. (2010). *About interpersonal neurobiology: An introduction to interpersonal neurobiology.* Retrieved from http://www.drdansiegel.com/about/interpersonal_neurobiology/

Silvera, A. (2015). *More happy than not.* New York, NY: Soho Press.

Sinek, S. (2009a). Start with why: How great leaders inspire everyone to take action. New York, NY: Penguin.

Sinek, S. (2009b). Start with why: How great leaders inspire everyone to take action. New York, NY: Penguin.

Sinek, S. (2009). *Simon Sinek: How great leaders inspire action* [Video file]. Retrieved from https://www.ted.com/talks/simon_sinek_how_great_leaders_inspire_action

Singer, T., & Lamm, C. (2009). The social neuroscience of empathy. *Annals of the New York Academy of Sciences 1156,* 81–96.

Sinsky, C., Colligan, L., Li, L., Prgomet, M., Reynolds, S., Goeders, L., . . . Blike, G. (2016). Allocation of physician time in ambulatory practice: A time and motion study in 4 specialties. *Annals of Internal Medicine, 165*(11), 753. doi:10.7326/M16-0961

Sire, J. (2009). *The universe next door: A worldview catalogue.* Downers Grove, IL: InterVarsity Press.

Smaby, M., & Maddux, C. (2010). *Basic and advanced counseling skills: The skilled counselor training model.* Belmont, CA: Brooks/Cole.

Smalley, G., & Trent, J. (1986). *The blessing.* Nashville, TN: Thomas Nelson/HarperCollins.

Smith, D. (1982). Trends in counseling and psychotherapy. *American Psychologist, 37*(7), 802–809. doi:10.1037/0003-066X.37.7.802

Smith, R. (1995). Logic. In J. Barnes (Ed.), *The Cambridge companion to Aristotle* (pp. 27–65). New York, NY: Cambridge University Press.

Smith-Hanen, S. S. (1977). Effects of nonverbal behaviors on judged levels of counselor warmth and empathy. *Journal of Counseling Psychology, 24*(2), 87–91. doi:10.1037/0022-0167.24.2.87

Sobel, D. (1990, August 20). B. F. Skinner, the champion of Behaviorism, is dead at 86, *New York Times.* Retrieved from http://www.nytimes.com

Sommers-Flanagan, J. (2015). Evidence-based relationship practice: Enhancing counselor competence. *Journal of Mental Health Counseling, 37*(2), 95–108. doi:10.17744/mehc.37.2.g13472044600588r.

Speechley, G. (2016, July 29). *Who is watching you.* Retrieved from http://leadershipquote.org/who-is-watching-you/

Sperry, L. (2010). *Core competencies in counseling and psychotherapy: Becoming a highly competent and effective therapist.* New York, NY: Routledge.

Sperry, L., & Sperry, J. (2012). *Case conceptualization: Mastering this competency with ease and confidence.* New York, NY: Routledge.

Spring, B. (2007). Evidence-based practice in clinical psychology: What it is, why it matters; what you need to know. *Journal of Clinical Psychology. Wiley Periodicals. 63*(7), 611–632. doi:10.1002/jclp.20373.

Stahl, S. M., (2013). *Stahl's essential psychopharmacology: Neuroscientific basis and practical application* (4th ed.). Cambridge, England: Cambridge University Press.

Steele, H., & Steele, M. (2008). *Clinical applications of the adult attachment interview.* New York, NY: Guilford Press.

Stein, G. L., Rivas-Drake, D., & Camacho, T. C. (2017). Ethnic identity and familism among Latino college students: A test of prospective associations. *Emerging Adulthood, 5*(2), 106–115. doi:10.1177/2167696816657234

Stockton, R. (2010). The art and science of group counseling. *The Journal for Specialists in Group Work, 35*(4), 324–330. doi:10.1080/01933922.2010.515904

Stoker, J. (2013). *Overcoming fake talk: How to hold real conversations that create respect, build relationships, and get results.* New York, NY: McGraw Hill.

Ström, F. (1981) [1926]. Svenska Ordspråk. Gütersloh: Mohn Scandinavia. ISBN 91-518-1367-X.

Studtmann, P. (2017). *Aristotle's categories.* In A. Editor (Ed.), *The Stanford encyclopedia of philosophy* (Foll 2007 ed.). Retrieved from: https://plato.stanford.edu/entries/aristotle-categories/

Sue, D. W., Capodilupo, C. M., Torino, G. C., Bucceri, J. M., Holder, A. M. B., Nadal, K. L., & Esquilin, M. (2007). Racial microaggressions in everyday life: Implications for clinical practice. *American Psychologist, 62*, 271–286. doi:10.1037/0003-066X.62.4.271

Sue, D. W., & Sue, D. (2016). *Counseling the culturally diverse: Theory and practice* (7th ed.). Hoboken, NJ: John Wiley & Sons.

Summers, R. F., & Barber, J. P. (2009). *Psychodynamic therapy: A guide to evidence-based practice.* New York, NY: Guilford Press.

Szapkiw, A. & Silvey, R. (2010). The use of wikis to aid in communication and collaboration within the helping profession: A pilot study. *Journal for Human Service Education, 30*(1), 71–75.

Teding van Berkhout, E., & Malouff, J. M. (2015). The efficacy of empathy training: A meta-analysis of randomized controlled trials. *Journal of Counseling Psychology, 63*(1), 32.

Teich, N. (1992). Backgrounds: Origins, locations, and multiple definitions of empathy. In N. Teich (Ed.), *Rogerian perspectives: Collaborative rhetoric for oral and written communication* (pp. 241–247). Norwood, NJ: Ablex, Guilford Press.

Teufel-Prida, L. A., Raglin, M., Long, S. C., & Wirick, D. M. (2018). Technology-assisted counseling for couples and families. *The Family Journal: Counseling and Therapy for Couples and Families, 26*(2), 134–142.

Thomas, A. J., & Schwarzbaum, S. E. (2017). *Culture and identity: Life stories for counselors and therapists* (3rd ed.). Thousand Oaks, CA: Sage

Thomson, P. (2010). Loss and disorganization from an attachment perspective. *Death Studies, 34*(10), 893–914.

Tollison, S. J., Lee, C. M., Neighbors, C., Neil, T. A., Olson, N. D., & Larimer, M. E. (2008). Questions and reflections: The use of motivational interviewing microskills in a peer-led brief alcohol intervention for college students. *Behavior Therapy, 39*(2), 183–194. doi:10.1016/j.beth.2007.07.001

Trager, G., L. (1958). Paralanguage: A first approximation. *Studies in Linguistics, 13*, 1–12. Reprinted from *Language in culture and society,* pp. 274–288, by D. Hymes, Ed., 1964, New York, NY: Harper and Row.

Truax, C. B. (1962). *Intensity and intimacy of interpersonal contact: Relationships between the level of intensity and intimacy of inter- personal contact offered by the therapist throughout the course of psychotherapy and the degree of positive personality change occur-ring in the patients.* (Brief Research Report No. 55.) Madison, WI: Wisconsin University Psychiatric Institute.

Tzu, L. (2010). *Tao Te Ching: A new translation.* (W.S. Wilson, Trans.). Boston, MA. Shambhala Publishing. (Originally published 4th century B.C.).

Umbarger, C. C. (1983). *Structural family therapy.* New York, NY: Grune and Stratton.

U.S. Census. (2015a). *Facts for features: Black (African-American) history month: February 2015.* Retrieved from https://www.census.gov/newsroom/facts-for-features/2015/cb15-ff01.html

U.S. Census. (2015b). *Facts for features: Hispanic heritage month 2015.* Retrieved from https://www.census.gov/newsroom/facts-for-features/2015/cb15-ff18.html

U.S. Department of Health and Human Services. (n.d.) *Fact sheet: A health care provider's guide to the hipaa privacy rule: Communicating with a patient's family, friends, or others involved in the patient's care.* Retrieved from: https://www.hhs.gov/sites/default/files/ocr/privacy/hipaa/understanding/coveredentities/provider_ffg.pdf

U.S. Public Health Service. (1999). *Risk and protective factors.* Retrieved from https://www.cdc.gov/violenceprevention/suicide/riskprotectivefactors.html

Van Dijke, A., Hopman, J. A. B., & Ford, J. D. (2018). Affect dysregulation, adult attachment problems, and dissociation mediate the relationship between childhood trauma and borderline personality disorder symptoms in adulthood. *European Journal of Trauma & Dissociation, 2*(2), 91–99. doi:10.1016/j.ejtd.2017.11.002

Vocisano, C., Klein, D. N., Arnow, B., Rivera, C., Blalock, J. A., Rothbaum, B., . . . Thase, M. E. (2004). Therapist variables that predict symptom change in psychotherapy with chronically depressed outpatients. *Psychotherapy: Theory, Research, Practice, Training, 41*(3), 255–265. doi:10.1037/0033-3204.41.3.255

Wampold, B. E. (2007). Psychotherapy: The humanistic (and effective) treatment. *American Psychologist, 62*(8), 857–873. doi:10.1037/0003-066X.62.8.857

Wampold, B. E. (2015). How important are the common factors in psychotherapy? An update. *World Psychiatry, 14(*3), 270–277. doi:10.1002/wps.20238

Weiss, R. L., & Summers, K. J. (1983). Marital interaction coding system-111. In E. Filsinger (Ed.), *Marriage and family assessment* (pp. 85–115). Beverly Hills, CA: Sage.

Welfel, E. R., & O'Donnell, D. (2013). Legal and ethical issues: Promoting responsible practice and commitment to ethical ideals. In D. M. Perera-Diltz & K. C. MacCluskie (Eds.), *The counselor educator's survival guide: Designing and teaching outstanding courses in community mental health counseling and school counseling* (pp. 115–134). New York, NY: Routledge.

Whitman, W. (1855). *Leaves of grass.* Boston, MA: Thayer and Eldridge.

Wilcox, G. (1982). The Feeling Wheel: A tool for expanding awareness of emotions and increasing spontaneity and intimacy. *Transactional Analysis Journal*, 12(4), 274–276.

Willis, J., & Todorov, A. (2006). First impressions: Making up your mind after a 100-ms exposure to a face. *Psychological Science, 17*(7), 592–598. doi:10.1111/j.1467-9280.2006.01750.x

Winnicott, D. W. (1953). Transitional objects and transitional phenomena; A study of the first not-me possession. *The International Journal of Psycho-Analysis, 34*(2), 89. Retrieved from https://pdfs.semanticscholar.org/a56f/ba056a21039574e5b2371f4ad01728b54366.pdf

Winnicott, D. W. (1988). *Human nature.* Philadelphia, PA: Taylor Francis Group.

Wintle, W. (1927). Thinking. In J. G. Lawson (Ed.), *The world's best-loved poems.* New York, NY: Harper & Brothers.

Wood, L. (2014). *The trouble with paradise: A humorous enquiry into the puzzling human condition in the 21st century.* Bloomington, IN, Author House.

Yalom, I. D. (1975). *The theory and practice of group psychotherapy* (2nd ed.). New York, NY: Basic Books.

Yalom, I. D. (1980). *Existential psychotherapy.* New York, NY: Basic Books.

Yalom, I. D. (1999). *Momma and the meaning of life: Tales of psychotherapy.* New York, NY: Basic Books.

Yalom, I. D. (2017). *Becoming myself: A psychiatrist's memoir.* New York, NY: Basic Books.

Yalom, I. D., & Leszcz, M. (Collaborator). (2005). *The theory and practice of group psychotherapy* (5th ed.). New York, NY: Basic Books.

Young, M. (2016). *Learning the art of helping: Building blocks and techniques.* 5th ed. New York, NY: Pearson.

Young, M. E. (2017). *Learning the Art of Helping: Building blocks and techniques.* 6th ed. New York: Pearson.

Zahavi, D. (2008). Simulation, projection and empathy. *Consciousness and Cognition, 17*, 514–522. doi:10.1016/j.concog.2008.03.010

Zimmerman, E. R. (2018). Preoccupied attachment as predictor of enabling behavior: Clinical implications and treatment for partners of substance abusers. *Clinical Social Work Journal, 46*(1), 48–56. doi:10.1007/s10615-018-0645-x

# Glossary

**Advanced empathy:** The expression of attunement to another person's emotional state by articulating another person's emotion or state of mind before the other individual is even aware of his or her own emotion.

**Affective empathy:** The ability to go beyond understanding or identifying the emotions of others by actually experiencing what those emotions are like for, in this case, the client.

**Affective neuroscience:** Neuroscience that addresses the limbic system and the brain structures associated with emotion regulation.

**Approach goal:** A goal that involves moving toward an outcome in a positive direction, such as increasing one's felt level of peace on a scale of 1 to 10, with one representing no stress and 10 representing peace.

**Attachment theory:** The theory that human beings are born without the capacity to care for themselves and must rely on a caregiver to take care of all of their needs for survival. The attachment relationship between child and caregiver sets the stage for future relationships, self-confidence and exploration, and emotion regulation.

**Before-During-After (BDA):** It is an acronym that represents an idea developed by psychiatrist John Kuhnley that suggests where possible it is helpful to facilitate client's adjustment to important life events by discussing the event or transition before, during, and after.

**Behavioral system:** an organized set of behaviors designed to accomplish an important survival goal.

**Bicultural:** The ability to function in two cultures and, usually, speak two languages.

**Brief Motivational Interviewing (BMI):** A brief approach to motivational interviewing which involves facilitating a client's movement away from indecision toward the sweet spot of decision and motivation for change.

**Case conceptualization:** A tool in the counselor's tool kit that helps with the process of treatment planning and identifying the best interventions to facilitate client movement toward treatment goals.

**Catastrophizing:** a type of automatic negative thought (ANT) has also been referred to as "awfulizing" and involves predicting the worst.

**Challenging while supporting:** Reflecting two aspects of the self that are not congruent and inviting the client to consider these parts.

**Clinical empathy:** includes exhibiting the capacity to care for clients via the effort to seek to understand their experience and feelings about their experience and implementation of helpfulness via the facilitation of the development of agreed-upon goals and agreed-upon means of accomplishing those goals.

**Closed-ended questions:** Questions or prompts that stop the flow of dialogue and elicit very brief or even one-word answers.

**Closing skills:** Skills used toward the end of a counseling session often used to bring closure to the session. These skills include summarizing, scaling, assigning collaborative homework. and consolidating gains or identifying a "takeaway" from the session.

**Cognitive dissonance:** The experience of having two conflicting thoughts, feelings, or attitudes.

**Cognitive empathy:** The ability of an individual to understand the mental state or emotions of another.

**Cognitive empathy:** The capacity to understand the emotions of others, which may also involve the capacity to understand one's own emotions.

**Cognitive room:** refers to the mental space that is allocated to another person. For example, a husband or wife may say, to their spouse, "Honey, I hope your meeting with your colleagues about the project goes well today and that you enjoy lunch with your friend Sally!" This illustrates that this husband has cognitive *room* devoted to his wife and what she may be doing throughout the day.

**Collaborative goal setting:** The skill of establishing mutually agreed-upon goals for the direction of counseling.

**Collectivism:** A strong core value of What culture? culture that emphasizes the group rather than the individual.

**Confluence:** A merging of different streams of thoughts or ideas.

**Congruence:** Consistency between internal self-talk and external communication between internal nonverbal messages (such as feelings) and external nonverbal messages such as SOLER & minimal encouragers.

**Consultation:** When one licensed professional clinician meets with another licensed professional clinician to discuss a case and receive feedback and input.

**Counseling Context:** the different settings in which a professional counselor practices.

**Contingency-based knowledge:** A knowledge base that emerges out of both factual and procedural knowledge and allows the counselor to make contingency-based decisions or if–then decisions.

**Countertransference:** The phenomenon whereby a therapist projects feelings about a previous relationship onto a client.

**developmental neuroscience:** How the nervous system develops from conception and beyond on a cellular basis; what underlying mechanisms exist in neural development. (https://neuro.georgetown.edu/about-neuroscience).

**Double bind communication:** Communication in which the receiver of a message receives two conflicting messages.

**Emotionally corrective experience:** An emotionally healing experience that may be described as a relational healing balm applied through experiential learning of what a safe and intimate relationship feels like with God and/or other people. (Clinton & Sibcy, 2002).

**Empathy:** the expression or acknowledgment of another person's feelings and why he or she feels that way.

**Enrichment/enriching:** Interjecting during a client's narrative in order to create dialogue and use another reflecting skill such as paraphrasing or reflecting feeling.

**Epistemic humility:** A sense of humility about how we know what we know and an openness to an openness to incorporating new information and insight.

**Evidence-based practice:** An integrative approach to counseling in which the clinical utilizes interventions by appropriately taking into consideration client preferences, therapist expertise, cultural implications, ethical guidelines, and research evidence.

**Expert counselor:** A counselor who is highly competent and effective due to thousands of hours of intentional, focused learning and practice.

**External locus of control:** Behaviors or processes that are out of the direct control of the self, such as powerful others. If a client has an external locus of control, then this may manifest in more passive behaviors. (Kim & Lee, 2018).

**Factual/declarative knowledge:** It represents the conceptual and factual foundation needed to practice as a counselor.

**Flooding:** A physical state of being physiologically overwhelmed that is associated with a heart rate of over 100 bpm and oxygen concertation that falls below 95.

**Four Horsemen of the Apocalypse:** four prophetic beings ushering in the end.

**Four major domains of diagnosis:**
1. Mood disorders (depression and bipolar disorder)
2. Anxiety disorders (generalized anxiety disorder and panic disorder)
3. Psychotic conditions (e.g. schizophrenia)
4. Attention-deficit hyperactivity disorder (ADHD)

**Good guiding theory:** A framework that assists a counselor in understanding a client's intended meaning and in constructing reasonable questions.

**God image:** A person's emotional experience of God, which can impact God attachment.

**Here and now immediacy:** A technique that involves discussing what is going on in the present moment within the interpersonal interaction.

**High acculturated:** A description of an individual who lives by the norms and values of American culture and often speaks English as the first language.

**Homeostasis:** The "normal" state of a system of state of being. As goals are met, changes in the system disrupt the current homeostasis, just as when a ripple effect occurs when a rock is tossed into a pond.

**Imago Dei:** The *image of God.*

**Immediacy:** Being present with the person in this present moment, and exploring what is going on in the moment.

**Inquiry:** The process of seeking clarification via asking questions, probing with statements, or otherwise seeking additional information.

**Insanity:** As commonly attributed to Albert Einstein, doing the same thing over and over again and expecting different results.

**Internal locus of control:** It relates to a person's effort and abilities. Internal locus of control can be defined as one's sense of responsibility over behaviors under his or her jurisdiction (Kim & Lee, 2018).

**Internal working model (IWM):** the formulation of a set of beliefs one has about oneself (Am I worthy of love and capable of experiencing intimacy?) and others (can I trust others to be there for me in times of trouble and can they help me?).

**Interviewing skills:** Interviewing is another term that is sometimes interchanged with counseling, the first session often considered the intake interview, and the primary skills used are the listening skills such as the door opener, minimal encouragers, paraphrasing, summarizing, reflection of content, and reflection of meaning.

**Ironic law of timing:** *We get there faster by going slower.*

**Johari window:** A tool created by psychologists Luft and Ingham to illustrate relationships in terms of awareness between people (1955).

**Leading questions:** Questions that are guided by an agenda.

**Lighthouse:** "A structure (such as a tower) with a powerful light that gives a continuous or intermittent signal to navigators" that is especially helpful to sailors during times of low visibility or other unfavorable conditions at sea (adapted from Merriam-Webster, 1828).

**Limbic brain:** A collective term for a group of nuclei, tracts, and cortical areas lying beneath the neocortical surface that covers the brain and that surrounds the thalamus at the core of the forebrain. (Isaacson, 2001, p. 8858)

**Locus of control:** the degree to which an individual expects that he or she is responsible for an outcome or a behavior, thought to be a somewhat stable trait that does not change considerably over time (Kim & Lee, 2018).

**Low acculturated:** A description of one who has high affiliations with his or her country of origin and may need the services of interpreters.

**Mentalization:** The interaction between the ability to be aware of one's own thoughts, feelings, and behaviors while maintaining empathy for and awareness of the thoughts, feelings, and behaviors of others (such as clients).

**Mindful empathy:** mindful empathy is exhibited when an individual is fully present with another in a state of empathic connection.

**Minimal encouragers:** nonverbal or verbal counseling skills that can be used to encourage clients to continue on sharing their story but indicate to the speaker that the listener is present and engaged, which may include a nod or gesture encouraging the client to continue or a sound such as "mm hmm," "uh huh," "hmm," "huh," and "mmm."

**Neocortex:** The phylogenetically newest cortex, including the primary sensory cortex, primary motor cortex, and association cortex. (Carlson, 2014, p. 58)

**Nonverbal counseling skills:** Therapeutic communication that involves vocal tone and quality, body posture and movement, and facial expressions.

**Open-ended questions:** Questions designed to open up the dialogue and to help the client expand on important content.

**Paralanguage:** word-like utterances that communicate to the client that the counselor is listening. These may be sounds such as "mm, uh huh, mm hmm, hmm, huh, hm, ah," among others.

**Paraphrasing:** A relatively brief enriching of the session by restating in your own words the essence of what the client has communicated.

**Personalism:** Another essential value that denotes personal dignity of each individual.

**Pharmacokinetic:** The processes that includes absorption, distribution, metabolism, and excretion of the medication by the body.

**Positive relationship rules:** Rules about the self and others that indicate whether or not one deems oneself worthy of love and able to explore the world and whether others are competent and able to love and be depended upon.

**Positive sense of others:** The belief that one can rely on attachment figures to be reliable, accessible, and trustworthy, capable of meeting my needs and helping me in times of distress.

**Positive sense of self:** A belief that the self is worthy of love and that the self can explore the world and make a contribution to society in a meaningful way.

**Proximity seeking:** Behavior used by a child to get closer to an attachment figure (such as crying, walking or running, lifting arms). Often involves a goal-directed partnership with the attachment figure which helps the child experience safe haven (for young children, melting into a parent's arms.)

**Procedural knowledge:** the "how-to" knowledge that is needed to function as a professional counselor.

**Prolonged exposure:** a specific exposure therapy program that is considered a first-line evidence-based treatment for PTSD (McLean & Foa, 2011, p. 1151).

**Psychiatrist:** A physician who specializes in the prevention, diagnosis, and treatment of mental illness. A psychiatrist must receive additional training and serve a supervised residency in his or her specialty.

**Psychodynamic therapy:** Exploration of current conflicts and relationships in order to understand how they relate to the past, the search for recurring patterns, and a focus on the therapeutic relationship to see how conflicts are repeated (Summers & Barber, 2009, p. 10).

**Psychopharmacology:** the study of drugs (medications) to treat psychiatric or mental conditions.

**Purposeful counseling:** Counseling that is in alignment with the agreed-upon goals of therapy.

**Reflecting content:** Restating the themes of a client's thoughts or experience in your own words.

**Reflecting meaning:** A skill involving identifying values and/or purposes that underlie client experiences and provide a sense of purpose and restating or reflecting it back to the client in a concise statement.

**Reflexive knowledge:** Sometimes referred to as "gut"-based knowledge, when procedural knowledge and practices associated with a skill set are so practiced and embedded that carrying out the skill set becomes automatic and reference to a user's manual is not required. also considered the highest level of learning and signifies the beginning of expertise.

**reframing:** Looking at a situation or an experience from a different, often more adaptive perspective and paraphrasing it back to the client in the counselor's words.

**Relational mutuality:** the extent to which each partner in a couple relationship shows mutual interest in the disclosure of emotions, cognitions, dreams, and joys.

**Relationship immediacy:** Having the capacity to have a dialogue with a relationship partner about where you stand within the relationship.

**Relationship rules:** How one perceives the self and others, whether one is worthy to receive love and in terms of whether others are competent and capable of giving love (Clinton & Sibcy, 2006).

**Safe haven:** In attachment theory, an attachment figure who is available and responsive during times of distress.

**Schadenfreude:** The derivation of pleasure from another person's experience of pain.

**Schoolism:** The practice of identifying primarily with one theoretical school of thought and identifying oneself with the therapist who developed that school of thought.

**Secure base system:** A behavioral system governed by three different, but dynamically interactive, behavioral systems: the caregiving system, the exploration system, and the attachment system.

**secure and secure base system:** In attachment theory, a launchpad or home base from which a child moves to explore the environment. In counseling, a springboard the clinician provides for the client from which to engage in a discourse on emotion that is free flowing.

**Self-awareness:** An awareness of multiple perspectives and a broad perspective of how to cope with such circumstances developed when counselors take time to "sit in the other chair," the client chair, and do their own clinical work, journal about feelings, or participate in group therapy.

**SOLER: S**—Squarely face client
**O**—Open posture
**L**—Leaning in
**E**—Eye contact
**R**—Relaxed

**Summarizing:** a counseling skill that involves an articulation of the central themes related to content, feeling, and/or meaning from a client's narrative. It is longer than a paraphrase and is often used to begin and/or end a session.

**Emergent Model of Clinical Expertise in Counseling and Psychotherapy:** A developmental model of skill acquisition with an implied aim of expertise development. The acquisition of knowledge, skills, tactics, strategies, and techniques are seen as an emerging model, where more complex skill sets and capacities emerge out of more basic skill sets.

**Theory of mind:** The ability to express the mental constructs of another, such as thoughts, desires, and beliefs, leading also to the prediction of behavior.

**The Love Lab:** The affectionate name given to the family research institute where Drs. John and Julie Gottman conduct rigorous research on predictors of relationship success.

**The Prefrontal Cortex (PFC):** PFC is the executive command center of the brain; this is the region of the brain associated with planning and goal-directed behavior.

**therapeutic bank account:** A metaphor that represents the rapport built through an intentional series of deposits made by the counselor's effective use of counseling skills and empathy.

**Therapeutic bond:** Essentially refers to the affective quality of the relationships; the sense of mutual trust and respect, liking, and caring between the patient and the client.

**Therapeutic factors:** human interactions or experiences that are complex and intricate and associated with therapeutic change; 11 primary therapeutic factors were identified by Irvin Yalom. These therapeutic factors include "(a) instillation of hope, (b) universality, (c) imparting information, (d) altruism, (e) the corrective recapitulation of the primary family group, (f) the development of socializing techniques, (g) imitative behavior, (h) interpersonal learning, (i) group cohesiveness, (j) catharsis, and (k) existential factors" (Yalom & Leszcz, 2005, p. 1–2).

**Thought-feeling fusion:** When a person struggles to distinguish thoughts from and the two become entangled.

**Transference:** The phenomenon whereby a client projects perceptions of earlier relationships onto the relationship with the therapist.

**Transtheoretical model (TTM) of change (also behavior change model):** Developed out of four tenets: there are preconditions for therapy, there are processes of change, there is content to be changed, and the therapeutic relationship.

**The Specific Affect Coding System (SPAFF):** The Specific Affect Coding System (SPAFF) was Developed by Gottman and a colleague, Krokoff, to be used in research for the systematic coding of affective behavior in the context of marital conflict.

**Umbrella skill:** a skill that should be used with all other skills.

**Universality:** A therapeutic factor that represents the idea that there are certain problems common to human beings that although they may be taboo and there may be shame associated with the mention of them, can be normalized as common struggles. One example may be feeling a sense of inadequacy (Yalom & Leszcz, 2005).